A DESCRIPTION
OF
INDIAN AND ORIENTAL ARMOUR

A DESCRIPTION
OF
INDIAN AND ORIENTAL ARMOUR

ILLUSTRATED FROM THE COLLECTION FORMERLY IN THE INDIA OFFICE NOW EXHIBITED AT SOUTH KENSINGTON

AND

THE AUTHOR'S PRIVATE COLLECTION
With a Map, Twenty-three Full-page Plates (Two Coloured), and Numerous Woodcuts

WITH

AN INTRODUCTORY SKETCH OF THE
MILITARY HISTORY OF INDIA

HON. LORD EGERTON OF TATTON

NEW EDITION

(With Considerable Additions to Illustrations and Text).

GYAN

Published by

GYAN

Gyan Publishing House
5, Ansari Road
Daryaganj, New Delhi-110002
Phone: 011-47034999, 9811692060
E-mail: books@gyanbooks.com

Distribution Network
gyanbooks.com
India, USA, Canada, UK, Australia, France

ISBN : 978-81-212-3303-3 (PB)
First Published, London, 1896

2nd Impression 2020

Printed at: Gyan Press, Delhi.

A Description of Indian and Oriental Armour
Author: Egerton of Tatton

(apter on Decoration)

Plate III.

SWORDS FROM THE ZARKOE SELO COLLECTION

1—2, Persian.

3—7, Indian.

W. GRIGGS PHOTO LITH. LONDON, S. E.

CONTENTS.

GROUP V.

GROUP VI.

GROUP VII.

GROUP VIII.

GROUP IX.

GROUP X.

GROUP XI.

GROUP XII.

LIST OF ILLUSTRATIONS.

PLATES.

FIGURES.

PLATES TO ILLUSTRATE THE EGERTON COLLECTION.

ABBREVIATIONS.

Z. S. Coll. Zarkoe Selo Collection.
E. Coll. Egerton Collection.
B. M. British Museum.
T. Tower Collection.
L. Length.
W. Width.
Bl. Blade.

PREFACE TO NEW EDITION.

As the catalogue originally drawn up for the illustration of the arms at the India Museum has been to a certain extent rendered useless by the transfer of the collection to South Kensington, yet, as neither South Kensington nor the British Museum have published a separate catalogue, and as the Handbook of Oriental Arms alludes to both those collections, it has been thought desirable to bring out a new edition, and to add a chapter on the Arab Arms, with which our campaigns in the Soudan have recently made us more fully acquainted, so as to complete the sketch of Oriental Arms, which it was the purpose of the author to illustrate. He also desires to place on record the catalogue of his own collection, which contains some examples not found in either of our national collections, and which also exemplifies the great variety and richness of design to be found in Oriental Arms. He trusts that it may lead others who have in their private collections any rare or richly-decorated Oriental Arms to take a greater interest in them, and to communicate to the author an account of any exceptional specimens in their possession.

NOTE ON THE TRANSLITERATION AND SPELLING OF INDIAN WORDS. BY COLONEL YULE, C.B.

WHEN the completed sheets of this work were in type Mr. Egerton was good enough to ask me to look over them. I found that the spelling of Oriental words was in much need of revision, all the more that the names of weapons, and the places whence they came, had been derived from the entries in the records of the India Museum, and these naturally enough had been inscribed without system or consistency. It did not seem well that a work of the kind, and one too so creditable in all other respects, should issue under the authority of the Secretary of State for India, without some endeavour to reduce the orthography to order, and I took this task (by no means a light one) upon me. This was not done because of any claim to either learning or leisure, but because there was no prospect of its being done by anybody else; and it had to be done without delay. As the work now stands I have endeavoured to reduce the spelling to consistency with the system of Shakepear's Hindustani Dictionary, which is essentially that of Sir William Jones, and is the basis (subject to some simplification) of the systematic orthography of vernacular proper names, which Dr. W. W. Hunter has been striving, for some years past, to get rooted in official use. After all the labour expended on my task it has been, I fear, very imperfectly accomplished. Such a catalogue naturally contains words that are hard to identify, owing not only to loose, sometimes merely phonetic, transcription, but also to the use of local terms which do not enter dictionaries, or of dialects (*e.g.*, Nepalese) of which no dictionaries have been accessible. I will note the following as examples which have puzzled, not me only,—that would be a small matter,—but also Sir Henry Rawlinson and Dr. Rost, whom I have consulted:—

Tschehouta, maktah, banch, bhelheta (p. 23; these words are taken, as Mr. Egerton tells me, from a French version in Langlès' Monuments; they are not in Blochmann's *Áín*); *pulouar* (p. 51 and *passim*); *Bedouh* (for the figures in a magic square, p. 53); *Khora or Kora* (pp. 55, 68, 101, and elsewhere, apparently Nepalese); *Cha cutty, cumber jung* (p. 78); *Venmuroo* (p. 82, probably Telugu); *Ayda Kathi* (p. 83, probably Telugu); *Chilanum, Chellanum* (pp. 102, 116); *gargaz* (pp. 108, 115); *Haladie* (p. 109); *Hoolurge* (pp. 115, 118); *dhara, buckie* (p. 115); *junghcerdha* (p. 125); other anomalous words at p. 123, such as *Kassidgode, Lall-i-wall, Mahmúd-Bandar*, are apparently names of places in Hyder's dominions. The last was (see p. 33) the official Mysore name of Porto Novo. *Pultah* and *Oostuck* (p. 125) *Garsoee* (p. 138).

H. YULE.

INTRODUCTION.

When in 1855 I began to form a collection of arms in India I found the want of a book to assist me; there was none available, nor any information about Indian weapons and their manufacture, except that which was to be found in books of travel, or in the notices scattered through Oriental magazines. I therefore noted all references to arms in any books bearing on the subject; and having accumulated a certain mass of information, I now venture to submit it in the present shape to collectors and to the public, in the hope of arousing a more general interest in the history and manners of our fellow-subjects in India. At a time when the weapons of even the earliest and rudest races of mankind are engaging the attention of science as illustrative of the life of prehistoric man, a greater share of attention than they have hitherto received, may well be devoted to the arms of so large and important a portion of the globe as India.

Since the publication of the Ain-i-Akbari in the time of Akbar, no detailed descriptions of Indian arms have appeared. The arms of Europe have been fully illustrated by Meyrick, Hewitt, and a few writers on the Continent; but their references to Oriental weapons are usually brief and occasionally inaccurate, and often serve only to illustrate the European arms worn in the middle ages, such as chain mail armour or steel flails.[1] The present time is favourable for the examination of the national and private collections of Indian arms in this country, as they are not likely to receive many new additions. The use of many of the weapons has become obsolete within the present generation; the great military despotisms of India have crumbled to pieces; those that remain are gradually adopting European arms, and with the pacification of the country, the necessity for carrying weapons is gradually disappearing or has altogether passed away. After the Sikh wars, and again after the mutiny of 1857, a general disarmament took place, many of the old armouries were broken up, and many curious old weapons destroyed and sold as old metal.

There are in this country collections of Oriental arms, such as no other country can show, which have been either brought back by successful commanders or governors-general as trophies of our victories, collected by private hands, or presented to our sovereigns or to the East India Company.[2] I need

---

[1] Ancient Armour, Vol. 1, p. 58.

[2] By Her Majesty's gracious permission I have been enabled to describe the principal arms at Windsor Castle, and by photographs to reproduce some of them in this work.

only mention the national collections at the India Office and at the Tower, Her Majesty's collection at Windsor, and that presented to H.R.H. the Prince of Wales, so liberally sent for exhibition at Paris and elsewhere. The British Museum has lately been enriched by the Henderson and a portion of the Meyrick collection, the rest of which has been unfortunately dispersed. The Christy collection is shortly to be added to it. The South Kensington Museum has acquired the Tayler collection, and some fine Persian arms from the Basilewsky Collection.

The Museums of Paris, Copenhagen, Stockholm, Vienna, and Turin contain a few choice specimens. The only collection which can vic with ours is that belonging to the Emperor of Russia at Zarkoe-Selo, to which the Soltikoff collection, made in India about 1841, has been lately added. It is very rich in Circassian, Persian, and Turkish arms; the Indian arms comprise some unique specimens of artistic work. They have been splendidly illustrated in three large folio volumes, to which, as well as the catalogue *raisonné* in French, I shall frequently allude.

These collections, however, are not arranged on any definite plan, but merely for the purpose of artistic display, and are subordinate to the general decoration of a room. In Copenhagen alone are the arms arranged as part of an ethnological series.

I had the option of arranging the arms on an ethnological, a historical, or an artistic basis. I think identity of arms to a greater extent than identity of language or religion denotes identity of ethnical origin, and shows the influence of race in their ornament and character long after the traces of language have disappeared.[1] I have, therefore, tried to arrange this collection as far as possible from an ethnological point of view, as it is on the whole the classification most instructive to the general visitor, and one which moreover gives some idea of the number of different races of which our Indian Empire is composed. It is interesting, too, to note these distinctions ere they fade away before the progress of European civilization and manners.

If I had tried to arrange the collection on an historical basis, as is usually done in the case of European arms, I should have had great difficulty in determining the date of the specimens. For not only do we find in India the rudest and the most civilized races living side by side, but from the stationary character of Indian art, the changes produced during a period of several centuries may be less strongly marked than those effected during a few generations in Europe. Whilst, therefore, in arranging and describing the collection, the ethnological method has been adhered to, it appeared

[1] The ethnical and linguistic strata of the population are not parallel. The weight of evidence seems to be in favour of the fact that the Bhils and Bhars, presumably Kolarians, have lost their language and adopted Hindi.—Robert Cust, "Languages of the East Indies," p. 10.

desirable to introduce the Catalogue by a brief sketch of the military history of India, with the view of showing how the English have been successively brought in contact with the various races whose arms are represented in our national collections.

I might also have arranged the arms as a history of art, but then I should have had to account for the difference between Turanian and Aryan civilization, and for the way in which each runs into and overlaps the other in some places, and in others is entirely distinct. Even in the present ethnological treatment of the subject it was necessary to make some reference to this question. The development of art and civilization, as exhibited in the transition from the rudest type of weapon to the most artistic, is shown in the series of Turanian arms passing to those of the Aryan races. I have dealt in a separate chapter with the peculiar characteristics to be found in the arms of each race. No other manufactured article calls into play the use of such varied materials for its decoration, and hence the art displayed in warlike accoutrements deserves special consideration. It will be found to have been influenced by the early civilization of Egypt, Assyria, Persia, and Greece, and to contain within itself some of the germs of Chinese and Japanese ornament, if, as is probable, the art of China and Japan was affected by the Buddhist religion, which was introduced in the first case directly, and in the second indirectly, from India.

I may say in conclusion that it is a matter of regret that the two national collections belonging to the India Museum and the Tower are not united to illustrate the history of our relations with India, and to complete the series of arms. The fact that the India Museum is the property of the Government of India, inherited from the East India Company, while the Indian arms at the Tower—mainly presented by the East India Company—are the property of the Crown, should not prevent a partial amalgamation of the two collections. The courtesy of the War Department has permitted the temporary exhibition of a few of the arms from the Tower in the India Museum. That is a step in the right direction which I hope may be followed by at least such a re-arrangement of the Tower collection as may permit an interchange between the two collections of duplicates, and of the arms necessary to fill up the gaps in both. Neither collection is rich in Southern Indian arms, and it is a matter of regret that the Government in India, while professing to watch over the preservation of archæological remains, has neglected to take advantage of the opportunity of acquiring old weapons from the armouries at Tanjore and Madras, and allowed them to be broken up and the contents sold as old metal.

I am fully sensible of the many inaccuracies and omissions which will be found in the wide field which I have attempted to traverse in these pages, and trust that those who take an interest in the subject, both in India and at home, will communicate to me any information bearing on it. It is with this hope that I have undertaken this work, and I must rely on the generosity of my readers not to make it a "target for the arrows of censure."[1]

I take this opportunity of expressing my thanks for the assistance which has been afforded me by Dr. Forbes Watson in these inquiries, and for the readiness with which Mr. Aston and Mr. Little have provided me with any information which lay in the records of the India Office during the preparation of the catalogue and the arrangement of the arms.

In passing this work through the press I have also to thank for giving me much valuable information Mr. A. W. Franks of the British Museum, and Mr. W. Seabrook of Windsor Castle; Major-General Sir H. Rawlinson, K.C.B., Mr. Clements Markham, C.B., who have read through the proofs; and Colonel Yule, C.B., who has kindly undertaken to correct the spelling of the Indian names and quotations, and has furnished me with several notes which will be included in this work.

W. EGERTON.

Since this work was written, the Secretary of State for India has come to the determination to part with the India Museum. I have expressed my opinion on this matter in another place, and will not therefore question its policy on this occasion.

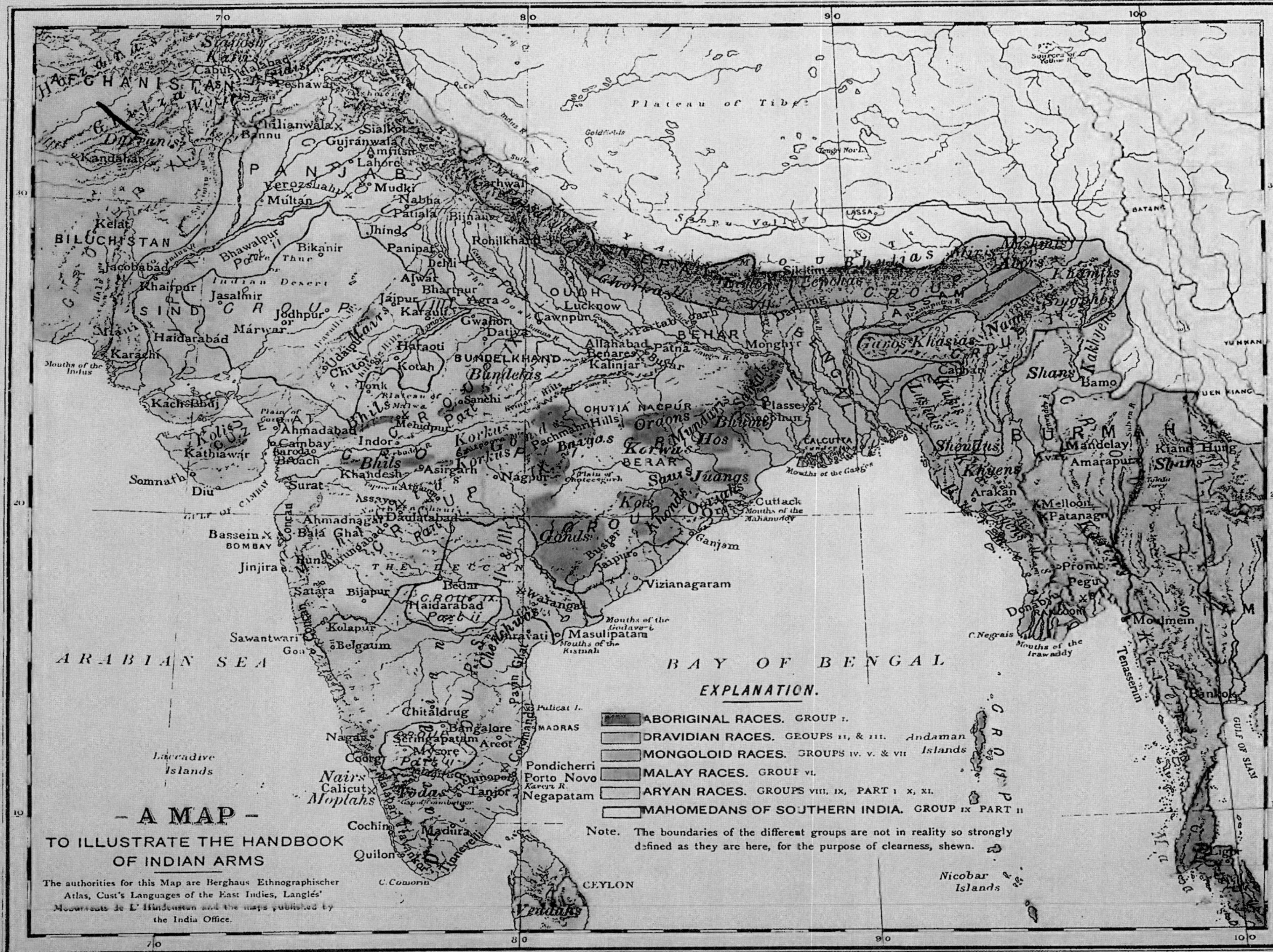
- A MAP -
TO ILLUSTRATE THE HANDBOOK
OF INDIAN ARMS
The authorities for this Map are Berghaus Ethnographischer Atlas, Cust's Languages of the East Indies, Langlés' Monuments de L' Hindoustan and the maps published by the India Office.
EXPLANATION.
ABORIGINAL RACES. GROUP I.
DRAVIDIAN RACES. GROUPS II, & III.
MONGOLOID RACES. GROUPS IV. V. & VII
MALAY RACES. GROUP VI.
ARYAN RACES. GROUPS VIII, IX, PART I X, XI.
MAHOMEDANS OF SOUTHERN INDIA. GROUP IX PART II
Note. The boundaries of the different groups are not in reality so strongly defined as they are here, for the purpose of clearness, shewn.
ARABIAN SEA
BAY OF BENGAL
Plateau of Tibet
AFGHANISTAN
BILUCHISTAN
PANJAB
SIND
BUNDELKHAND
OUDH
BEHAR
BERAR
CHUTIA NAGPUR
THE DECCAN
BURMAH
SIAM
CEYLON
Andaman Islands
Nicobar Islands
Laccadive Islands
GULF OF SIAM
Tenasserim
W. GRIGGS, PHOTO-LITH LONDON S.E.

A SKETCH

OF THE

MILITARY HISTORY OF INDIA.

CHAPTER I.

FROM THE EARLIEST INVASIONS TO THE CONQUEST OF BABER.

In giving a sketch of the arms and military tactics in India as far as it can be gathered from the testimony of history and public monuments, I do not propose to treat of the arms of the prehistoric period, though that field of inquiry is still open.[1]

The rich and fertile plains of India have always proved a tempting prize to an invader from the west, and the classic tradition is therefore not altogether unworthy of belief that about 2,000 B.C. there was an invasion by the Assyrian Queen Semiramis. Her opponent Stabrobates may be identified with Sthabarpati, "Lord of hills, trees, and plains," who appears in the Indian legends as the antagonist of Shama, the wife of Mahadeva.

Another legendary invasion of India appears to have proceeded from Egypt under the leader who figures under the different names of Bacchus, Sesostris, or Parusram, so called from the Parusa or battle-axe with which he fought.[2]

The oldest extant traditions of purely Indian origin give an account of a great contest between Rama, King of Ayodhya or Oude, and Ravana, King of Lanka or Ceylon, which has been usually referred to a period of remote antiquity, but which a recent writer has attempted to identify with the struggle between Brahminism and Buddhism.[3]

It is in the poetic histories—the Ramáyana and the Mahábhárata—that we find the earliest references to Indian arms. The Ramáyana celebrates the deeds of the above-mentioned Ráma, the conqueror of the Deccan and Ceylon. The Mahábhárata describes the wars of the two branches of the reigning family of Hastinapura, the Pandavas, and the Kauravas. The triumphant Pándavas transferred the seat of government to Indraprashtha, the site of the modern Delhi.

---

[1] Stone implements of three distinct classes, similar in character to those found in other countries, have been found over nearly the whole of India from Burma to Biluchistan, and from Assam to Bombay and Madras. Copper axe-heads found at Gangra near Mhow, 1873, are exhibited in the British Museum. Even iron was known before the separation of the Aryan races, if we may believe the testimony of language as interpreted by Max Müller, who has shown that the Sanscrit and Gothic terms for iron are respectively "ayas" and "ais." Science of Language, p. 239.

[2] See Dowson, Classical Dict. of Hindu Mythology, "Parasu Rama." Prof. Dowson thinks that the war of Parasu Rama indicates the struggle between the Kshatriyas and the Brahmins.

[3] Historical Studies, Shoshee Chunder Dutt, pp. 151–184. 1879.

"Hastinapura, in which the first scenes of the 'great war of Bharat' are laid, is an ancient and vanished city, formerly situated about 60 miles north-east of the modern Delhi. The Ganges has washed away even the ruins of the metropolis of King Bharat's dominions. The poem opens with a 'sacrifice of snakes,' but this is merely a prelude connected by a curious legend with the real beginning. That beginning is reached when the five sons of 'King Pandu the Pale' and the five sons of 'King Dhritarashtra the Blind,' both of them descendants of Bharat, are being brought up together in the palace. The first were called Pandavas, the last Kauravas, and their life-long feud is the main subject of the epic. Yudisthira, Bhima, Arjuna, Nakula, and Sahadeva are the Pandava princes; Duryodhana is chief of the Kauravas. They are instructed by one master, Drona, a Brahmin, in the arts of war and peace, and learn to manage and brand cattle, hunt wild animals, and tame horses. There is a striking picture in the earlier portion of an Aryan tournament, wherein the young cousins display their skill, 'highly arrayed, amid vast crowds,' and Arjuna especially distinguishes himself. Clad in golden mail, he shows amazing feat with sword and bow. He shoots 21 arrows into the hollow of a buffalo horn while his chariot whirls along; he throws the 'chakra,' or quoit, without once missing his victim; and, after winning the prizes, kneels respectfully at the feet of his instructor to receive his crown. Part of the story refers obviously to the advances gradually made by the Aryan[1] conquerors of India into the jungles still peopled by aborigines. Forced to quit their new city, the Pandavas hear of the marvellous beauty of Draupadi, whose *Swayamvara*, or 'choice of a suitor,' is about to be celebrated at Kampilya. This again furnishes a strange and glittering picture of the old times; vast masses of holiday people, with rajahs, elephants, troops, jugglers, dancing women, and showmen, are gathered in a gay encampment round the pavilion of the King Drupada, whose lovely daughter is to take for her husband (on the well-understood condition that she approves of him) the fortunate archer who can strike the eye of a golden fish, through a 'chakra' whirling round upon the top of a tall pole, with an arrow shot from an enormously strong bow. The Princess, adorned with radiant gems, holds a garland of flowers in her hand for the victorious suitor, but none of the rajahs can bend the bow. Arjuna, disguised as a Brahmin, performs the feat with ease, and his youth and grace win the heart of Draupadi more completely than his skill. The Princess henceforth follows the fortunes of the brothers, and, by a strange ancient custom, lives with them in common.[2]"

The honourable position accorded to the profession of arms at an early period is shown by the fact that the Kshatriyas, or Rajputs, in the Vedic period were the dominant race, and subsequently stood next in the scale of caste to the Brahmins or priests; they originally enjoyed the exclusive privilege of carrying arms.

In the Institutes of Menu (Chap. VII. sec. 185) we learn that the constitution of the army was sixfold, viz., elephants, cavalry, cars, infantry, officers, and attendants. The division was, however, practically into the four

---

[1] Aryan, the name by which the people of the Rig-Veda called men of their own stock, as opposed to the Dasyus or aborigines.—Dowson, Dictionary.

[2] Review of "The Vedic Period of the Mahábhárat" (Vol. I., History of India), by J. Talboys Wheeler, in the *Daily Telegraph*, May 19th, 1875.

first parts only.[1] The chariots were large, and hung round with bells, and, together with the elephants, carried the chief men of the army. The infantry were probably armed with a spear or short broad sword, and with bows and arrows. They wore a turban and girdle, short breeches, and a piece of leather about the loins, from which were suspended a number of small bells. The cavalry were not then so numerous as in later times. The plan of a campaign is simple, as might be expected, being drawn up by Brahmins. The king is to march when the vernal or autumnal crop is on the ground, and is to advance straight to the capital. When marching he is to "form his troops "either like a staff or in an even column, or in a wedge with the apex fore-"most, like a boar, or in a rhomb, with the van and rear narrow and the "centre broad, like a macara, or sea monster, that is, in a double triangle "with the apices joined; like a needle, or in a long line; or like the bud of "Vishnu, that is, in a rhomboid, with wings far extended. Let him at his "pleasure order a few men to engage in a close phalanx, or a larger number "in loose ranks, and having formed them in a long line like a needle, or in "three divisions like a thunderbolt, let him give orders for battle. On a "plain let him fight with his armed cars and horses, on watery places with "manned boats and elephants, on ground full of trees and shrubs with bows, "on cleared ground with swords and targets and other weapons."

One hundred bowmen in a fort are said to be a match for 10,000 enemies, so far was the art of attack behind that of defence.

Their castles were built on precipitous rocks, and were impregnable to an enemy who possessed no warlike engines.

The laws of war are honourable and humane. Poisoned and mischievously barbed arrows, and fire arrows, are prohibited. Among those who must always be spared are unarmed or wounded men, and those who have broken their weapon, or who surrender themselves and beg for their lives.

The different "puranas" contain allusions to works on the art of war, called *Dhanur Veda*, or the science of bows, none of which unfortunately have been preserved, but from the Agni[2] Purana we learn that the bow was the principal weapon of war.

"The Hindus," says the Abbé Dubois, "have 32 different kinds of weapons, "and each of the 32 gods has his own peculiar weapon.[3] Krishna and Ram "are armed with a battle-axe and a bow and arrow. Vishnu holds the "'chakra" (steel quoit). Kartikeya, the god of war, and Ravan, the giant, bear in their hundred arms a display of every species of military offensive weapon. Indra, the god of the Kshatriyas, is represented as riding on an elephant, and armed with the sword and 'chakra,' the battle-axe and the thunder-bolt. (Wheeler, Vol. III., p. 21.)

---

[1] To this fourfold division of armies into elephants, chariots, cavalry, and infantry our game of chess, said by Firdusi to have been introduced by an ambassador from the King of Kanauj to the Court of Naushirvan, or by Sassa, son of Dahir, in the reign of Bahram, King of Persia, bears interesting witness. The "castles" represent the howdahs carried by the elephants, which the Greeks in the expedition of Alexander magnified into castles. The "bishops" take the place of cars, and where we have a "queen" they have a "mantri" or minister of state—a leader who mingles everywhere in the fight. The "knights" and "pawns" represent the two other classes. —Cf. Translation of the "Siyaru-l Muta-akhkhirin," "Review of Modern Times," Calcutta, 1789. Tom. I., p. 72, note 6.

[2] Agni = Ignis.

[3] Moor's Hindu Pantheon.

There has been considerable controversy as to the extent to which firearms were known at this period. Sir H. Elliot comes to the conclusion, after examining all the best authorities, that they were used (see Vol. VI., p. 481, History of India, Appendix). Rockets, or weapons of fire, "Agny astra," were certainly known at a very early period. They were a kind of fire-tipped dart, discharged horizontally from a bamboo, and were used against cavalry. The invention is ascribed by the "puranas" to Visvacarma, their Vulcan, who for 100 years forged all the weapons for the wars between the good and bad spirits. The knowledge, however, of the manufacture of gunpowder or some material composed of sulphur and saltpetre, and the use of projectiles, probably died out before the historic times, and only an inflammable projectile or naphtha ball was used till the revival of firearms from the West.

The period just described may be characterised as the legendary and heroic age of India. Already, in that remote age, there appears to have existed an intercourse for purposes of trade, dating probably from the earliest times, between India and the countries on the seaboard of the Mediterranean, and especially Phœnicia. It is probable that Southern India is the land of Ophir from which Solomon obtained "gold and silver, ivory and apes, and peacocks"[1] (I Kings, x. 22). Of Indian manufactured products, probably iron and steel were the most important, as even at so early a date as that of the Institutes of Menu, iron is mentioned as an article of great consumption. In later times they are mentioned in the "Periplus" as imports into the Abyssinian ports.

But it is only with the appearance of the Greeks that the historic age of India may be said to commence. Already in Herodotus[2] and Ctesias we find allusions to the Indians who followed Xerxes to Greece, and who came probably from the Punjab. They wore cotton dresses, and carried bows of cane with iron-tipped arrows.

The Eastern Ethiopians, who came from Bilúchistán, and were probably of a Cushite race, were marshalled with the Indians, and their equipment in most points resembled that of the Indians, but they wore on their heads scalps of horses with the ears and mane attached; the ears were made to stand upright, and the mane served as a crest. For shields they made use of the skins of cranes. The cavalry were dressed in like manner; they rode in chariots drawn by horses and wild asses.

Herodotus[4] tells us that the Indians (probably those in Sind) clothe themselves with garments made of rushes, and formed into a "thorax" by being interlaced into mats. He further states that the swords taken by the Greeks were golden, *i.e.*, *inlaid* with gold.[5]

In the Greek writers we also find references to two Persian invasions of India. The first of these is said to have been led by Cyrus, who according to Xenophon made the Indus the eastern boundary of his empire, and whose

---

[1] Renan has shown the connexion of India with Phœnicia, by proving that the words in the Semitic languages for monkey, peacock, and elephant have been borrowed from the Aryan languages of India.—Histoire Générale des Langues Semitiques, Ernest Renan, 1855. See also Handbook to Indian Court, 1878, p. 16. Dr. Birdwood.

[2] Book VII. c. 65-70.

[3] Rawlinson's Herodotus, Vol. IV.

[4] Book III. c. 98.

[5] Book IX. c. 80.

general Rustum, according to the Persian writers, penetrated into the heart of India. At a later time Darius sent an expedition under Scylax to the mouth of the Indus, and probably conquered a few provinces on the banks of the Indus, which were made into a satrapy, and paid tribute to himself and his successors.

But it is only since the invasion of India by Alexander in the year 327 B.C. that India is brought into a direct contact with the classic world. The relations then established lasted for several centuries, and we owe to them the full descriptions of India found in the contemporary classic authors. From the accounts of Quintus Curtius [1] we learn something of the character and condition of Indian armies at that period, how gallant was their defence, but how little able they were to oppose the superior tactics of the Greeks. Alexander crossed the Jhelum by a stratagem, taking advantage of the cover afforded by a wooded island. The opposing force of Porus consisted of 85 elephants, 300 chariots, each of which carried six men, two bearing shields, two archers, and two driving the horses and throwing darts ; 30,000 foot, among whom were archers who shot barbed arrows difficult to extract, and 4,000 horse. Alexander's first onset was with the chariots, which got into confusion from the slippery nature of the ground, and lost their drivers, after inflicting some damage on the Macedonian infantry by the vigour of their charge. The elephants formed the second line, and behind them were the infantry, and the archers who beat drums during the fight.

The Macedonian phalanx pressed them in front, and the cavalry took them in flank. The elephants, on which they most relied, were maimed by the axes and swords of the Greeks, and at last gave way, and the capture of Porus put an end to the fight.

The next object of Alexander's ambition was to attack the great Gangetic kingdom of Magadha beyond the Sutlej. Its king could bring 30,000 cavalry, 600,000 foot, and 9,000 elephants [2] into the field. Alexander's troops, however, refused to cross the Sutlej, and after his death we have no further accounts from India, till one of his successors, Seleucus, crossed the Indus, and defeated Sandracottus (Chandragupta), and the whole strength of the Magadha empire. The result of that expedition was that he sent as his ambassador to that monarch Megasthenes, from whom we derive some knowledge of Indian arms at that time. [3]

After the period just mentioned the connexion between India and the classic world was maintained by the Greek kingdom of Bactria. The rule of the Bactrians and their successors, the Indo-Scythian kings, extended at times over a considerable part of Upper India, where the influence of the Greeks was long felt, and may be traced even as far as Orissa. On the defeat of the Scythians by Vikramaditya several Hindoo dynasties shared Hindostan between them, but our knowledge of the military events of this period is extremely imperfect, and continues so until the time of the conquest of India by the Mahomedans.

---

1 I. 27. Quintus Curtius speaks of armour made of iron laminæ connected in rows within each other.

2 For these numbers Quintus Curtius substitutes 20,000, 200,000, and 3,000 respectively.

3 He describes the army as consisting of 400,000 men, including 20,000 cavalry and 2,000 chariots. The chief city was defended by 574 towers, and a ditch 30 cubits deep, and entered by 60 gates.

The accounts of the Greek historians and geographers refer only to the earlier part of the period just mentioned, but they may be supplemented by a mass of invaluable contemporary evidence in support of history in the shape of coins and sculptured bas-reliefs, extending from the 3rd century B.C. to the 15th A.D.

The art of coinage seems to have been introduced into India by the Bactrian Greeks, and the numerous coins extant of the Bactrian and other dynasties of Northern India frequently afford most interesting illustrations of the arms of the period.

The Indo-Scythian kings, the successors of the Bactrian dynasty, are represented on their coins as wearing coats of chain mail, with a short straight sword sheathed by their side, and a lance. Kanerki holds a short curved sword, others hold a club and a short sword or dagger. (*See* Fig. 1.)

Fig. 1.—Coin of Vasu Deva, Indo-Scythic King, King of N.W. India in the 2d or 3rd century A.D.[1] (E. Coll.)

The most accurate description, however, of the early Indian arms may be obtained from the sculptures of the Sánchi (*see* Fig. 2), and other topes described by Cunningham and Fergusson. "In one of them," says Cunningham, "there is the representation of a siege, probably undertaken "to recover possession of some holy relic. The soldiers wear a tight fitting "dress and kilt; the arms are a sword and "bows and arrows.[2] The swords are short "and broad, and tally exactly with the de-"scription of Megasthenes."[3] "All wear "swords of a vast breadth, though not ex-"ceeding 3 cubits in length; when they "engage in close fight they grasp these with "both hands to fetch down a lustier blow." At the same time "the infantry usually car-"ried a bow of the same length with the "bearer." This agrees with the bas-reliefs, which represent nearly all the foot soldiers as archers; but the less ancient bows are much shorter than the bearers, and do not appear to have been more than 4 feet in length. Most of the bows appear to be straight pieces of bamboo, but a few have the double curve, with a straight handpiece in the middle. "Their arrows," says Arrian, "are little less than 3 cubits long, and fly with such force

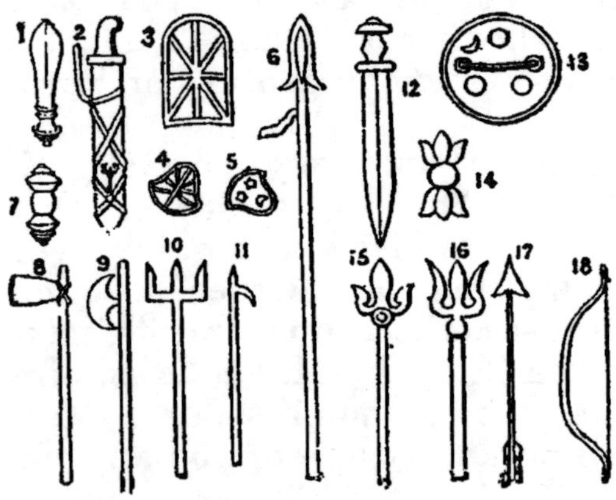

Fig. 2.—Arms from Sanchi and Udayagiri.

[1] For the following description of this coin the author is indebted to Mr. Percy Gardner, of the British Museum:—

Obv., PAO NANO PAO BAZΔHO KOPANO (in barbarised Greek letters). The King, nimbate, sacrificing at altar. He wears conical helmet, coat of mail, and suit of chain (?) armour reaching to his feet, and holds a spear, sword slung round his waist. Behind altar, a trident-standard fixed in the ground and bound with fillet. *Rev.*, OKPO (retrograde), Siva (or Ugra the fierce one), naked from waist upwards holding wreath and trident; behind him the bull Nandi; above a symbol of uncertain meaning.

[2] The arms represented on the Bhilsa Topes are bows and arrows, dagger, sword, spear with triangular head, axe, battle-axe, trident, infantry and cavalry shield. At Udayagiri, bow and arrows, trident, sword, and circular shield.—Bhilsa Topes, p. 216.

[3] *Arian*, Indica XVI.

" that neither shield nor breastplate nor any armour is strong enough to " withstand them." The arrows in the bas-reliefs appear to be from 3 to 5 feet in length. " Some of them," he adds, " use darts instead of arrows, and " the horsemen are equipped with two lances, like the lances called *saunia*." In one of the bas-reliefs a soldier covered by a shield is represented holding a dart horizontally, ready to launch it forward. " Upon their left arms they " wear something resembling " peltæ " made of raw hides, rather narrower " than their bodies, but nearly as long." So the most usual shield represented in the bas-reliefs is long and narrow and rounded at the top. It covers the bearer from the head to the knee, and must therefore have been about 3½ feet in length and 1½ feet in breadth. In the time of Megasthenes, however, it was fully 5 feet in length. The shields of the cavalry were smaller than those of the infantry. Throughout the bas-reliefs the horseman's shield is always about 2 feet in length, bell-shaped, and much rounded at the bottom. The usual ornament, both for horse and foot, was a double cross, the St. George and the St. Andrew; but a cavalry shield in the Western Gate bears only a crescent and two stars. These sculptures are fixed by Cunningham to be of the date A.D. 17-39; by Fergusson between A.D. 64 and 120, and those at Udayagiri, A.D. 401.

On one of the bas-reliefs at Sánchi is represented the legend of Prince Siddhártha, thus described by Fergusson: " When the prince had reached " his 16th year, his father sought a wife for him among the daughters of the " neighbouring rajahs. All refused, however, because the prince, though hand- " some, had not been taught any martial accomplishments, and was therefore " incapable of controlling women. To prove, however, his power in this respect, " he strung a bow that no one else could string, pierced with his arrows iron " targets thicker than those of the 'Warrior' or 'Minotaur,' and at distances " which neither Armstrong nor Whitworth could attain; and lastly shot an " arrow an inconceivable distance, and where it lighted a spring of water " gushed forth, which afterwards, Fa-Hian tells us, was formed into a fountain " for travellers." In the foreground of the picture are three warriors armed with Parthian bow and short straight sword of Roman shape, carried over the right shoulder; they also wear cross straps for carrying their quivers. Drums and fifes accompany them.

On a pillar of the Amravati Tope, 300 years later than that at Sánchi, is portrayed the scene thus described.[2] A king is seated on his throne, to whom a messenger with clasped hands brings intelligence or solicits orders. In front of him a part of the army is seen defending the walls of the citadel, and armed with straight and scythe-shaped swords, long spears, and long bows. In front the infantry is advancing, and the rear is brought up by horsemen and elephants.[3] There are no chariots as at Sánchi, but this is probably owing to some local peculiarity. In Pl. LXIX. of the same work are represented men bearing narrow oblong shields apparently of wicker-work.

Of almost equal interest are the hill caves in Orissa, which date from 200 B.C to 474 A.D.[4] In one of the later ones there are representations of a battle, in which the combatants are using the sword and oblong shield, and

---

[1] Tree and Serpent Worship, Pl. xxxvi.

[2] Fergusson, op. cit, Pl. lxi.

[3] See Fergusson, Hist. of Architecture, p. 101.

[4] Hunter's Orissa.

a bow, in height about two-thirds that of a man, drawn in the perpendicular fashion of English archers; the swords are nearly straight and of a medium size.

In the paintings of Cave No. 16 at Ajanta (copies of which are to be seen at the South Kensington and India Museums), about 400 A.D., the warriors are armed with a short sword, like a kukri, and ornamental shield (*see* Catalogue of Indian Art, by Lieut. Cole, p. 51).

In the temple of Bhuvaneswar, about 650 A.D., swordsmen and archers, infantry, cavalry, and elephants are represented.[1]

In the Jain sculptures (circa 1100 A.D.) at Saitron in Rajputana, casts of which are possessed by the South Kensington Museum, we find represented combatants using swords either short and straight, or curved forward at the point, and short straight daggers, both weapons furnished with square pommels, but without guards to hilts.

The Sun temple at Kanarak[2] erected about A.D. 1237 is full of sculptures. Two colossal horses guard the southern façade; one of them is covered with heavy chain armour, and adorned with tasselled necklaces, jewelled bracelets on all four legs, and a tasselled breast-band which keeps the saddle in position; a scabbard for a short Roman sword hangs down on the left, and a quiver filled with feathered arrows on the right. The war horse has trampled down two rakshasas, or aborigines, who wear short curved swords similar to the Goorkha *kukri*, half billhook, half falchion, and heavy armlets, but no armour; they carry a round shield made of several plies of metal richly carved, with a boss in the centre, and tassels or tufts of hair hanging down from it. The shields appear to have borne some heraldic device, one of them representing two lizards climbing up on either side of the boss.

At Mandór, the ancient capital of Márwár, there are sculptures cut out of the rock before the 15th century, which represent nine chieftains, mounted, in attendance on Ravana, who came from Ceylon to marry the daughter of the King of Mandór; they are armed with lance, sword and buckler, with bow, arrows, and quiver, and the peshkabz in the girdle, and each is followed by his "paudú" or squire.

The sculptures last described already belong to what may be called the early Mahomedan period of Indian history, extending from the first invasions by the Arabs in the eighth century, to the final establishment of the Mogul dynasty under Baber.

The first Mahomedan invasion was under Khalif Wálid, A.D. 711. His youthful general, Muhammad Kásim, with an army of only 6,000 men, attacked Dewal, a seaport in Sind. He was provided with catapults and other engines for a siege, and having soon captured that town, defeated the Raja Dahir in the field, and took possession of Sind. The Arabs did not hold their conquest for more than 36 years.

The next attack was from Afghanistan. Alptigín had made himself ruler of Ghazni, and his successor Sabaktigín was attacked, A.D. 980, by Jaipál, Rajah

---

[1] Journ. Asiat. Soc. VI., VII.

[2] Hunter's Orissa, p. 290. Fergusson fixes the date about 850 A.D.

of Lahore. After an unsuccessful attempt to come to terms, Sabaktigín marched towards the Indus. The Hindu Rajas of Delhi, Ajmír, Kalinjar, and Kanauj advanced to Lamghán near Jellalabad with an army of 100,000 horse and a prodigious number of foot soldiers. Sabaktigín came down from his heights and attacked his enemy in the plains with successive charges of cavalry, and when they wavered he advanced along the whole line and pursued them with great slaughter to the Indus.

It was not, however, till three centuries and a half after the Mahomedan conquest of Persia that Sabaktigín's son Mahmúd of Ghazni first seriously undertook the invasion of India. About 1001 A.D. Mahmud defeated Jaipál near Peshawur, took him prisoner and returned with the spoils of his capital. Jáipál on returning from his captivity burnt himself on the funeral pyre, in accordance, it is said, with the custom that a prince twice defeated by Mahomedan arms was unworthy to reign.[1]

In his fifth expedition to India, A.D. 1008, Mahmúd met the combined forces of the Rajahs of Northern India under the command of Anandpal, son of Jeipal, in a great plain near Peshawur. The Sultan, having entrenched himself, sent 6,000 archers to the front, who were met by 30,000 Gakkhars with their heads and feet bare, and armed with spears and other weapons, who forced their way into the Mahomedan cavalry and nearly defeated them, when the elephant of the king took fright at the flights of arrows and the effects of the naphtha balls, and caused the Hindoos to fly in a panic.

After the conquest of Multan he penetrated as far as Kanauj, and took Gwalior and Kalinjar. In 1022 he is said to have mustered 54,000 horse, besides those employed in different parts of his kingdom, and 1,300 elephants. In his sixteenth expedition he took the idol called Somnáth, believing that when the Hindoos saw their prayers to be in vain, they would more readily embrace the Mahomedan faith. In his last expedition, in order to punish the Jats who had molested him on his return from Somnath, he attacked them on the Indus near Multan. He built for the occasion 1,400 boats, each of which was armed with six iron spikes to prevent the enemy from boarding, and in each were 20 archers and five naphtha men. The Jats opposed him in 4,000 boats, but were completely defeated, many of their vessels being set on fire by the naphtha. He died A.D. 1030.[2] Of his son Masa'úd it is related that "no man "could lift his mace from the ground and no iron target stay his arrow."[3]

The whole of this period of history is obscure from the conflicting accounts of the Mahomedan writers, many of which are mere historical romances founded on but slender bases of facts.

The house of Ghazni[4] fell, and Kutbuddín Aibak, the Turkish slave of Mu'izzuddín Muhammad of Ghazni, was raised to power and invaded India. Prithvi Rai, King of Ajmír, and Chand Rai, his brother, and Viceroy in Delhi, advancing to meet him, he was after a desperate hand to hand fight completely routed (A.D. 1191) at Narain, between Thaneswar and Karnál.[5] The following year, with a large force of 120,000 men, he met the combined Rajahs of Hindostan, amounting, it is said, to no fewer than 150

[1] Elphinstone's India, Vol. I., 508-36; Elliot, History of India, Vol. I.

[2] Elliott, Vol. VI., p. 456. [3] The Tabaqát i Násiri, translated by Major Raverty, pp. 91-507.

[4] Mill, Vol. II., p. 260. [5] Historical Studies, Shoshee Chunder Dutt. 1879.

kings. Their armies, according to the most moderate account, amounted to 300,000 horse, 3,000 elephants, and a great body of infantry. While the Hindus spent the night in revels and joy, the Pathans crossed the river and fell upon them suddenly, yet not before part of their army had time to form itself, and oppose the invaders. The Sultan drew up his battle array, leaving his main body in the rear, with the banners, canopies, and elephants. Having divided his light unarmoured horsemen into four parts of 10,000 each, he wearied the enemy with successive attacks and flights of arrows till sunset, when he charged with 1,200 of his best horse, whose riders were covered with steel, and utterly routed them. Chand Rai left his elephant and fell a victim to the foe. The victor, Kutbuddín Aibak, took Delhi and founded the "Slave" dynasty, which extended the Mahomedan power over a great part of Hindostan.[1] The Kutb Minar near Delhi, 242 ft. high, was built to commemorate his victories.

His successors reduced many of the Rajput tribes, and repelled successive invasions of the Moguls. In the time of Násir-ud-dín, Ulugh Khan defeated the numerous Hindu Ranas, and carried off great spoil from them. By his advice the embassy from Hulagu, the grandson of Genghis, was received with great magnificence (A.D. 1259). Determined to impress the Mogul with the military resources of his master, he met the ambassador with an escort of 50,000 horse, with banners and accoutrements; 200,000 infantry were drawn up shoulder to shoulder in 20 lines along the road, with 3,000 artillery chariots, and 2,000 war elephants in the intervals.

Passing now to the history of the Deccan we find that the Mahomedan arms were first carried across the Nerbudda by Alá-ud-dín Khilji in A.D. 1294. In 1323 Ghiyás-ud-dín Tughlik-Sháh took Warangal from the Hindus after plying it for a few days with arrows from the "nawaks" and stones from the "maghribis" or western mangonels.[2] He changed its name to Sultanpur. In the reign of his son Muhammad, who had transferred the seat of government from Delhi to Deogiri, which he called Daulatábád, the Deccan threw off its allegiance, and several Mahomedan dynasties were formed.

The Sultan of the Deccan, founder of the Bahmani dynasty (1347), conferred lands on some of the chiefs with military rank, and appropriated lands in Jágír for the maintenance of small bodies of horse.[3] Most of the Polygars, or independent chieftains of Southern India, submitted to the new Mahomedan rulers, and took service with them. This dynasty lasted about 150 years, and broke up into five independent States.

Nikitin,[4] in the 15th century, describes the Mahomedan Sultan of the Deccan as a powerful monarch who, in addition to his own army, had four great Hindu Viziers, each with an army of 40,000 mounted men and 100,000 foot.

"The Sultan of Beder goes out with 300,000 of his own troops, and many are the Khans that keep 10,000 armed men. In the Bairam he wears a suit of gold armour inlaid with sapphires, and three swords, mounted in gold.

[1] This dynasty is called the Ghorian dynasty by most writers. Cf. Tabaqát i Násiri, p. 509, note by translator. Its founder was a freedman of the Ghori Kings of Ghazni.

[2] See Chapter on Artillery

[3] Elliot, History of India, Vol. III., p. 233.

[4] P. 14.

When he goes out hunting he has a train of 10,000 men on horseback, 50,000 on foot, and 200 elephants in gilded armour."

Reverting to the north once more, in 1397 India was again invaded by the Tartars. Timur crossed the Indus, and with 10,000 of his chosen troops marched against the fortress of Bhatnír.[1] Ráo Dúl Chain, with his fighting Rajputs, drew up at the gate of the fort and gave battle, but the Mogul horse fell upon them, routed and pursued them into the city, of which they soon made themselves masters. By the execution of 500 of his captives, he drove the Hindus to desperation. They shut up their wives and children in their houses, set fire to the place, and, rushing out, sold their lives as dearly as they could. Sultan Mahmud drew up his forces in defence of Delhi. Timur having massacred 100,000 captives, left his entrenched camp to meet him. Mahmud's army was composed of 40,000 foot and 10,000 horse, and 125 elephants covered with armour, carrying howdas, in which were throwers of grenades (r'ad-andáz), fireworks (átash báz), and rockets (takhsh-andáz).[2] The right wing of Timur's army fell upon the enemy and poured down on it a shower of arrows, while the left by an ambuscade of part of their forces fell sword in hand on the rear of the Sultan's right wing. After a short struggle, the Tartar force drove back the main body of the Hindus, and put them to flight, and having taken the city, gave it up to pillage and indiscriminate slaughter (1398). Timur, after a brief raid into the country near the upper part of the Ganges, did not pursue his conquests further, and during the century which followed his departure from India, a succession of weak rulers enabled the Hindus to some extent to regain their independence under the nominal rule of the Emperors of Delhi.

As may be gathered from the following notes gleaned from the accounts of the early Arabic and other travellers to India the general character of the arms, and the art of warfare during this early Mahomedan period, exhibits no important changes from that of the previous period, and no marked distinction appears to have existed in this respect between the remaining Hindu powers and the newly established Mahomedan Kingdoms.

Al Idrisi, the Arab geographer, born about the end of the 11th century,[3] describes one of the princes of India in the following terms:—

"Nahrwára is governed by a great prince, who bears the title of Balhará, or king of kings. He has troops and elephants; he worships the idol Buddha, wears a crown of gold upon his head, and dresses in rich stuffs. He rides a good deal on horseback, but especially once a week when he goes out attended only by women, 100 in number, richly clad, wearing rings of gold and silver on their feet and hands, and their hair in curls. They engage in various games and in sham fights while their king marches at their head. The ministers and the commanders of the troops never accompany the king, except when he marches against rebels, or to repulse encroachments made upon his territories by neighbouring kings. He has numerous elephants which constitute the chief strength of his army."[4]

---

1 Murray, p. 226.

2 Elliot, History, Vol. III., p. 439.

3 His authorities were probably of a much earlier date.

4 Hist: of India, Elliott, Vol: I., p. 88, by Prof. Dowson.

Marco Polo, the earliest European traveller to India, thus describes a war between the king of Burma and the troops of the Emperor Kublai :—

" The King of Mien and Bangala (or Burma and Bengal) is said to have had 2,000 great elephants, on each of which was set a tower of timber, well framed and strong, and carrying from 12 to 16 well-armed fighting men. And besides these he had of horsemen and of footmen good 60,000 men. The Tartars were not so numerous, and were mounted on horses, who took fright at the elephants, but they immediately dismounted, and tying their horses to the trees of the forest plied their bows so stoutly that the advancing elephants were in a short space either killed or wounded, or turned tail and fled. When the Tartars saw that the elephants could not be brought to face the fight again, they got to horse at once, and charged the enemy, and then the battle began to rage furiously with sword and mace, ' but the Tartars had the best of it.' "[1]

Ibn Batuta, in his travels, circa A.D. 1333, mentions the Emir of Multán. He had always before him a number of bows of various sizes, and when any one who wished to enlist as a bowman presented himself, the Emir threw one of these bows to him which he drew with all his might, then as his strength proved to be so was his situation appointed, but when anyone wished to enlist as a horseman a drum was fixed, and the man ran with his horse at full speed and struck the drum with his spear, then according to the effect of the stroke was his place determined.

At that time, therefore, it is evident that though the knowledge of fire-rockets was so ancient, matchlocks or firearms were not common, perhaps not even known, as they would certainly have been mentioned by that writer in his travels.

The Institutes of Timur (who died A.D. 1405) likewise make no allusion to matchlocks in the equipment of his soldiers, who were thus armed.[2] The common soldiers used a bow and arrows with a sword. The select guards the same, with the addition of a skull-cap and breastplate, the " Ounbashee," or petty officer, a coat of mail, the " Euzbashee, " a mace or club, the " Mingbashee," a helmet and club in addition.[3]

The travellers Nicolo Conti and Nikitin, in the 15th century, do not mention matchlocks.[4] After describing the arms of the Hindus the latter says :—

" Elephants are greatly used in battle. The men on foot are sent first. The Khorossamans or rulers of the country are mounted in full armour for man as well as horse. Large scythes are attached to the trunks and tusks of the elephants. They carry a citadel, and in the citadel 12 men in armour with bows and arrows. The smaller elephants carry six men."

Shaháb-ud-dín, in his account of Muhammad Tughlik, describes the constitution of his army :—

" The army consists of 900,000 horsemen, some of whom are stationed near the prince, and the rest are distributed in the various provinces of the empire. They consist of Turks, inhabitants of Khatá (Cathay), Persians and Indians.

---

[1] Col. Yule, Marco Polo, Vol. II., p. 63.

[2] Timur may have acquired the secret of gunpowder in his first expedition into Asia Minor. The manufacture of gunpowder, matchlocks, and cannon was prevalent in Asia Minor (1402), and it is probably that he carried back artificers with him to Bokhara, who introduced the art into Asia.—History of Gunpowder. By Colonel W. Anderson, p. 11, 1862.

[3] Unbáshí, leader of ten ; Yúzbáshi, of a hundred ; Mingbáshí, of a thousand.

[4] See Chapter on Artillery for the use of firearms in the East.

Among them are to be found athletes (pahlwán), runners (shattár), &c. There are 20,000 Turk Mamluks, they have excellent horses, magnificent armour, and a fine costume. The Sultan has 3,000 elephants, which when accoutred for battle, wear a covering of iron gilded. The soldiers are summoned by the Sultan, and paid from the public treasury. The pay of the officer varies from 10,000 to 1,000 tankas.[1]

CHAPTER II.

FROM BABER TO THE DEATH OF AURUNGZEBE.

We now come to a period when the European powers were brought more directly into contact with India through the discovery by the Portuguese of the passage round the Cape of Good Hope. Under Cabral and Vasco di Gama they gradually established themselves in Southern India, and by their use of cannon, musquets, and swords, for which Spain was already celebrated, introduced gradually weapons of an European character, which soon had a marked influence on the arms of India. One of their first pretexts of attack was to assist the Rajah of Cochin against the Samorin of Malabar.[2] The latter, supported by a fleet of 160 vessels, proceeded to Cochin, and assaulted the position held by the Portuguese, under Pacheco, and the troops of Cochin. The fleet attacked the four Portuguese barks, which kept up so well sustained a fire that the vessels were either sunk or dispersed; some which were bound together by an iron chain held out the longest, but were at length driven back by a well-aimed shot, which cut the chain in two. The infantry in vain attempted by their numbers to force the 400 Portuguese to retire; in spite of the javelins discharged from a huge turret, the Europeans kept up so well directed a fire of musketry, that more than a thousand fell without mortally wounding any of their opponents, and eventually the Samorin was, after repeated attacks, compelled to return to Calicut.

Albuquerque (1510) followed up the successes of the Portuguese by the assault of Calicut. The Indians were surprised, but the chief Nair "uttered a cry, "which, repeated from mouth to mouth to the distance of several miles, drew "quickly around him 30,000 men well armed." The Portuguese were attacked from the roofs of the houses by a shower of darts, and being threatened in the narrow lanes by a host of men, both in front and rear, they set fire to the city, under cover of which they retreated to their ships. Coutinho and others, who in their fancied security had advanced as far as the fortified palace of the Samorin, were surrounded, and many lost their lives in fighting their way out. Albuquerque was more fortunate in the capture of Goa (1510), which laid the foundation of the power of the Portuguese along that coast.

In 1536 Nuno da Cunha erected a fort at Diu which brought him into contact with the Kings of Cambay and Guzerat. They were both Mahomedans,

[1] Elliot, History, Vol. III., p. 577.

[2] Murray's History of India.

and maintained an alliance with the Turks in Egypt, through whom Solyman Pasha. the Governor of Cairo, was induced to give his assistance against the Portuguese; Solyman sailed from Suez with 70 galleys, with 7,000 men on board and a train of artillery, and being joined by 20,000 troops of Guzerat laid siege to the Portuguese fort. After a long and desperate defence, and prodigies of valour on both sides, they were driven back and the fleet returned to Egypt.

Barbosa, in the beginning of the 16th century, gives an account of the King of Cambay, and shows that the arms of that part of India were influenced by the importation of Turkish weapons, of which the traces remain to the present day. "The King of Guzerat is a Moor. His men-at-arms carry very thick "round shields, edged with silk, and two swords each man, a dagger, and a "Turkish bow, with very good arrows; some carry steel maces, and many of "them coats of mail, and others tunics quilted with cotton. The horses have "housings of steel head-pieces." . . . . "The Moorish governor makes much "artillery, and has had constructed in the port a very strong and fine bulwark "in which he has very good artillery."[1]

The siege of Goa (1570) by the united forces of the Samorin and the Mogul rulers of the Deccan was the most important attempt made to drive the Portuguese out of India. Adil Khán led a force of 100,000 men against it. After an obstinate defence of about five months he was compelled to withdraw with a loss of 12,000 men.

Barbosa further describes the armies of the Deccan at that time. He says of the Moorish lords, [2]"they ride a small saddle, and fight tied to their "horses. They carry in their hands very long light lances, with four-sided "iron points, very strong, and three palms in length." Of the "Gentiles," or common soldiers, "most of them fight on foot, and these foot soldiers are "very good archers. Their bows are long, after the fashion of Englishmen." He also mentions[3] the fighting men of Delhi, and the number of their weapons, among which are "steel wheels," which they call "chacarani" (chakram), and he describes the way in which they are carried, seven or eight on the left arm, and spun on the fingers of the right hand.

The Portuguese accounts of the Native princes and their armies seem to be of an exaggerated character, and must be received with caution. We are told that [4]in 1520 Krishnaráo, King of Vijayanagar, covered the hills and plains, and drank up rivers with an army of 35,000 horse and 733,000 foot, 586 elephants loaded with castles, each containing four men. He besieged the city Rachol and took it, having first defeated Hidalcan, and taken from him 4,000 horses, 100 elephants, and 400 great cannon, besides the small.

Bahádur, King of Cambaya, in 1534, when he made war against Humáyun, the son of Baber, gathered 100,000 horse, 415,000 foot, 1,000 cannon, many of great bulk, 600 armed elephants, and besieged the city Chitor. But he was driven by want of provisions to fly and to leave his camp a prey to the Moguls.[5]

[6]In 1537, after the death of Bahádur, the Portuguese took the palace and

---

[1] Barbosa, published by Hakluyt Society, pp. 59, 60. [2] *Ibid.*, p. 78. *Gentiles*, properly of course=Idolaters or Hindoos. [3] *Ibid.*, p. 100.

[4] The Portuguese Asia, Vol. I., p. 236, by De Faria y Sousa, translated by Stephens, 1695.

[5] *Ibid.*, *p.* 373. [6] *Ibid.*, *p.* 407.

town of Diu. Among the spoils were 160 vessels, some of great bulk. No less wonderful was the number of brass cannon, for those of iron were not reckoned. Among the first were found three basilisks, of such prodigious greatness that Nuno da Cunha sent one as a rarity to Portugal, which is to this day kept in the Castle of St. Julian, and called the "Gun of Diu."

The Portuguese were content to limit their conquests to the coasts of India and the neighbouring islands, over which they maintained their supremacy till the Dutch disputed their power, and drove them from their possessions on the islands of Ceylon and Sumatra.

The Dutch made Java the principal settlement, and only held a few places on the continent. When they besieged the city of Coulang (Quilon) in 1661, Philip Baldæus relates that they were met by 7,000 or 8,000 Nairs of Malabar, who were well acquainted with the use of bows and arrows, and muskets and great cannon. "They make," he remarks, "their own gun-" barrels, gunpowder, and matches. On the hilts of their sword they wear " certain pieces of metal, which, making a noise as they move, serves them for " a certain musick. They are very dexterous in defending their bodies with " their shields, and consequently are better at warding blows than at firing, " for they commonly fire too high."[1] Dr. John Fryer, in 1672, describes the Nairs as armed in part with "naked swords rampant in one hand, and a target " made of buffalo's hide, lacquered and curiously painted, in the other," and partly with "a spiked lance barbed, as long as a javelin and poised at the " butt end with lead, at darting of which they are very expert."[2]

But although the Europeans had thus managed to establish themselves on the coast of India, their political influence on the country at large remained insignificant during the whole of this period. Indeed the French and the English, who at a subsequent period struggled for the supremacy of India, appear as yet in no other light than as private traders, whilst it is during this very time that the Mahomedan power in India attained its greatest development under the Mogul dynasty founded by Timur's grandson, Báber, which for 150 years ruled with splendour over the greater part of India. The court of the great Mogul attracted the best artificers from all parts of Persia and India to fabricate and ornament their arms, which then attained the highest perfection. Few, however, if any, arms produced anterior to the 16th century are known to have been handed down to our times.

When Báber succeeded to a small portion of the inheritance of Timur in the territory of Khokan and north of the Oxus, the art of war was in a rude state. The sword and the bow were the principal weapons. In his Memoirs he mentions the "shashpar," or 6-bladed mace, the javelin, the battle-axe, and broad axe, as only to be relied on for a single blow. The matchlock was beginning to be introduced into these armies, but the people of Bajour, on the borders of Cabul and India, had never seen any matchlocks (1519). The large cannon were called Feringiha, and the smaller ones "zarbuzan," now the word used for a swivel. The Turks had not long previously taken Constantinople, and made use of large cannon against it, yet from the word Feringi or Frank,

[1] Description of Malabar, Coromandel, and Ceylon, by Philip Baldæus, Amsterdam, 1672.
[2] Fryer, p. 215. 1873, London.
[3] Leyden, Memoirs of Baber, pp. 100, 247.

it is clear that they were then regarded as an European invention. All the masters in the art of gunnery in Asia were denominated Rúmi or Osmanli Turks, and almost all the terms used by Asiatics, such as gun, cannon, magazine, &c., are of Turki derivation. Báber, at first, was not acquainted with artillery, but when he was established at Agra, he directed Ustád 'Ali Quli to cast a large cannon.

Baber seems to have introduced greater discipline and military skill in the arrangement of his forces than had hitherto been prevalent in India. His chief strength was in a disciplined body of musqueteers and a train of artillery.

At the decisive battle of Pánipat, 1526, Báber formed his line of battle in six brigades, besides his body guard in the centre, where he posted himself. Before each of the brigades he placed a squadron of light horse, and in front of the whole his artillery and rocket wagons, in three divisions. He directed "that according to the custom of Rúm (Constantinople) the gun carriages "should be connected together with twisted bull hides, as with chains; between "every two gun carriages were six or seven 'turas' or breast works." The artillery commenced the action, and in spite of being surrounded by the enemy's cavalry, caused great slaughter among them. Baber ordered his right and left wings to fall back, by which his army was thrown into a circle, and after standing the repeated assaults of the enemy he collected two brigades of chosen troops, and led them to a grand charge, before which the enemy gave way, and their most distinguished chiefs fell.

On the death of Báber, Humáyún succeeded to a troublous inheritance. When quite young he took the fortress of Champánír by surprise, having clambered up the face of the perpendicular rock on which it stood by fixing in it iron spikes. Though brave he was unfortunate in all his undertakings. During the whole of his reign the country was divided by intestine wars and usurpers. In 1540, Sher Khán after defeating Humáyún drove him from the throne; Humáyún fled to Persia, but after some years, with the help of Shah Tahmasp, defeated the Pathans under Sikandar, and again entered Delhi a short time before his death in 1556, leaving his son Akbar, at the age of 13, to regain the remainder of the empire.

One of Akbar's first feats of valour was at the siege of Chitor. With his own hand he shot the Rajput commander as he was giving orders on the ramparts. On the death of their leader, the garrison performed the sacrifice of "jauhar," and the city was then soon taken by assault. After the submission of the Rajputs, he enlisted the chiefs with their retainers in his service, and made them useful auxiliaries of his Mogul mercenaries. His life was a career of success.[1] He led his troops with the impetuosity of a Rupert, and though his

[1] The following are the dates of his principal exploits :—

Conquest of	Márwár and Málwa	1562
,,	Chitor	1567
,,	Guzerat	1572
,,	Behar and part of Bengal	1575-84
,,	Kashmir	1586
,,	Sind	1592
,,	Kandáhár	1594
,,	Ahmadnagar and Berar	1597
,,	Khandesh	1598
,,	Deccan made tributary	1599

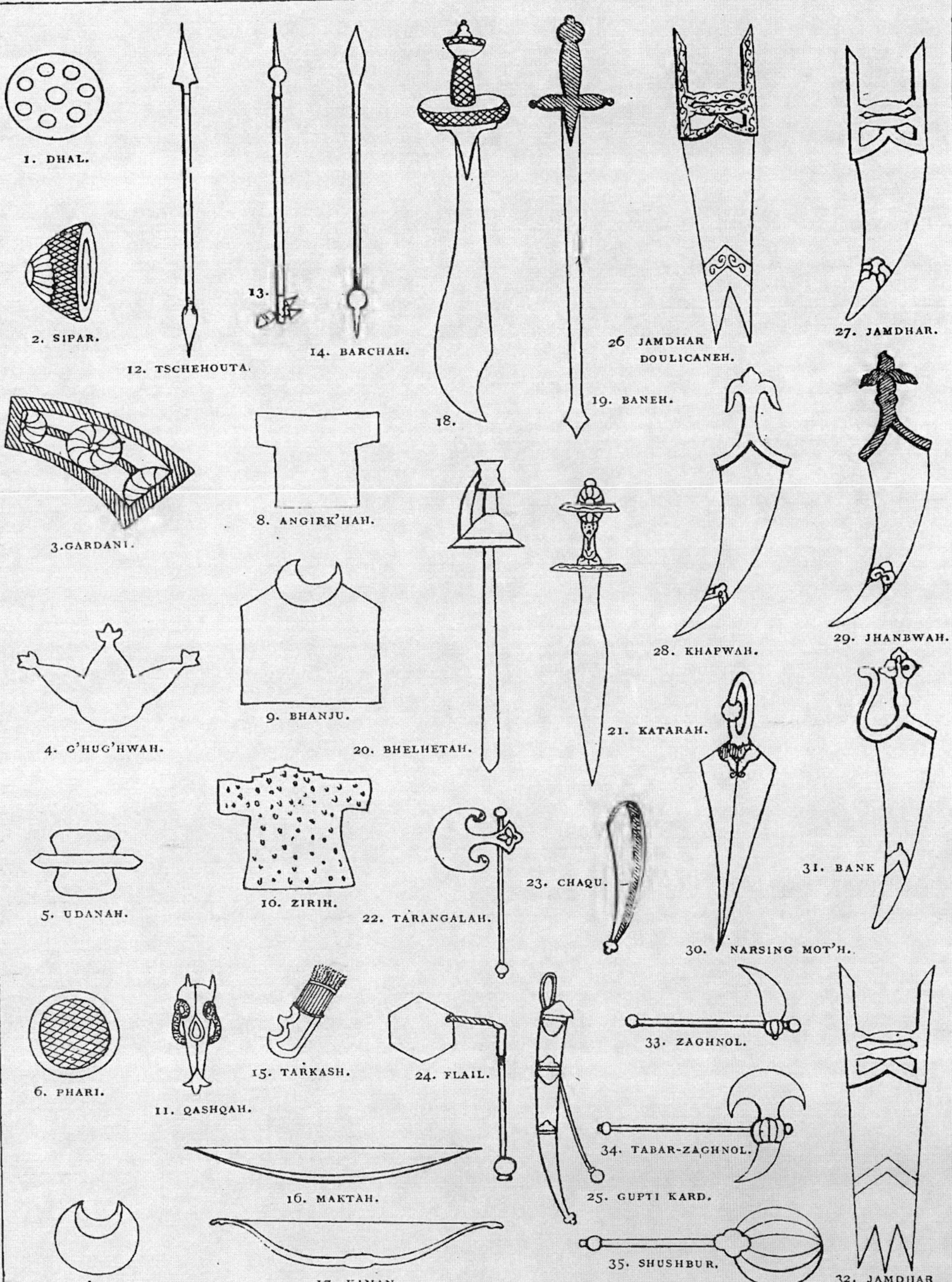

INDIAN ARMS AND ACCOUTREMENTS IN THE TIME OF AKBAR.
FROM COPY OF ORIGINAL COLOURED DRAWING, IN MANUSCRIPT
OF THE AIN-I-AKBARI. MONUMENTS DE L'HINDOUSTÀN LANGLÈS VOL. I. p. 228.

army was not in a high state of discipline, or skilled in military manœuvres, he carried everything before him.

The arms depicted in the accompanying Plate[1] are taken from the description of India at that time which we owe to Abul Fazl, and which was carried out by him under the direction of Akbar in the work called after him Ain-i-Akbari.[2] Abul Fazl describes the arsenal, to which Akbar paid the greatest attention. "There is always kept in store armour sufficient for the equipment " of an army. All weapons for the use of His Majesty have names, and a " proper rank is assigned to them. There are 30 'Kháçah' swords (applied to " His Majesty's particular use), one of which is carried to the Haram every " month, and the former one is returned. There are also in readiness 40 " other swords, which they call 'Kotal,' out of which the complement of 30 is " made up. There are also 12 sword belts (Yakbandi) kept apart, and sent into " the Haram one every week alternately. There are likewise 40 'jamdhars' " and 40 'k'hapwahs' (kinds of daggers). Their turn recurs every week, and " each has 30 'kotals,' from which deficiencies are supplied as before. " There are besides 8 knives worn in the girdle, 20 nezas or spears, and 20 " barch'has (kinds of spears); a different one of each is used every month. " 86 Mashhadí and Bhadáyan bows, with 24 others, out of which, in every " solar month of 32 days, one bow is sent to His Majesty every day; and " during every month of 31 days, two every week alternately. Every one " of these has its rank assigned to it, and when His Majesty goes abroad, " the sons of the Amirs and other Mansabdars and Ahadis carry the Qur in " their hands and on their shoulders, *i.e.*, every four of them carry 4 bows, " 4 quivers, 4 swords, and 4 shields; they take besides lances, spears, a " tabar-zághnol (kind of battle-axe), war clubs, sword sticks (gupti), pellet-" bows, pestles, and a footstool, all properly arranged.

[1] The following is the list of the native names, with their English equivalents, of the arms depicted in the plate :—

1. Dhál—shield.
2. Sipar—shield.
3. Gardani (for the protection of a horse).
4. G'hug'hwah (mail-coat for head and body in one piece).
5. Udánah.
6. Phari—cane shield.
7. Kant'hah Sobhá—neck-piece or gorget.
8. Angirk'hah—long coat worn over armour.
9. Bhanjú—coat with gorget attached.
10. Zirih—coat of mail.
11. Qashqah—head protection for horse.
12. Tschehouta—spear.
13. Javelin.
14. Barchha—lance.
15. Tarkásh—quiver.
16. Maktah—bow.
17. Kamán.
18. Scymitar.
19. Báneh—sword.
20. Bhelhetah—sword.
21. Kaṭárah—dagger.
22. Tarangálah—axe.
23. Cháqú—clasp knife.
24. Flail.
25. Gupti kárd—long dagger.
26. Jamdhar doulicaneh—two-pointed dagger.
27. Jamdhar—broad dagger.
28. K'hapwah—dagger.
29. Jambiyah—dagger.
30. Narsingmot'h—dagger. (Dagger used by Narsinga—an incarnation of Vishnu.)
31. Bánk—dagger.
32. Jamdhar sehlicaneh—three-pointed dagger.
33. Zághnol—pointed axe, *i.e.*, crowbill.
34. Tabar-zághnol—double axe.
35. Shashpar—globular mace.

Jamdhar, Sanscrit = Yama-dhára—"death-bringer (?)"

"Doulicaneh" and "sehlicaneh," appear to be hybrid words (Pers. and Hind.): "dú-likhána," two-scratcher; "seh-likhána," three-scratcher. From likhna, to write or scratch.—*Note by Col. Yule.*

[2] Ain 35, the Qur Khaneh, Gladwin, 1783; H. Blochmann, M.A., 1873.

"At Court receptions the Amirs and other people stand opposite the 'Qur' "ready for any service, and on the march they follow behind it, with the "exception of a few who are near His Majesty.

"With the Qur are caprisoned elephants, with camels, chariots, Naqqárahs, "flags, Kaukabas, and other ensigns of state. The mace-bearers close the "whole, being assisted by the Mír Bakshis in clearing the way."

The following interesting account of the Mogul army under Akbar and his immediate successors has been left us by De Mandelsloe (1638). "The "horsemen use no firearms, but the infantry use the musket tolerably well. "The pikemen have pikes 10 or 12 feet long, which they dart at the enemy. "Some use coats of mail reaching down to their knees, but are without "headpieces. They understand nothing of martial exercises. Their chief "trust lies in their elephants, on the backs of which are fixed certain wooden "towers, carrying three or four men with arquebuses, but the worst is that "these beasts being terrified by fireworks make a greater havock among their "own people than the enemy. They commonly have a great train of artillery "and some very large pieces. They also make gunpowder, but not so good "as ours." Akbar is said to have possessed 6,000 war elephants.

Akbar was succeeded in 1605 by his son Jehangir. The latter in his memoirs describes his father's prowess in the field of battle; he mentions the fact previously alluded to, that in conducting the siege of Chitor, Akbar with his own hand shot through the head the commander of the garrison, who was viewing the operations of the besiegers through one of the embrasures of the place. He called the gun which he used on this occasion 'Durust-andáz,' "straight-shooter."[1]

Sir Thomas Roe, in his embassy to Jehangir, speaks of the store of ordnance which he visited near Brampore (Burhánpúr), 223 miles east of Surat, "divers "of brasse, but generally too short and too wide bored," and he found by experience sword blades were well sold in the armies; he speaks of the gift by the Persian ambassador of a "fair quiver for bow and arrows delicately em- "broydered," and the richness of the swords and targets which were given as presents. One given by the king had the scabbard "all of gold set with "stones, valued at 100,000 rupees, and a dagger at 40,000." One of their generals asked for English cloth and swords for the supply of his soldiers, and he drily says, "In my opinion that had been a good employment of "some idle men, and a way to vent our dead commodities."

Shah Jehan, when he ascended the throne, turned his arms against the Portuguese in Bengal, but his reign was chiefly remarkable for the constant wars between his four sons, Dara, Shuja, Murad, and Aurungzebe. The last, who defeated all his opponents, developed great military qualities, and raised the power of the Great Mogul during the course of his long reign to the highest pitch, by the conquest of the Deccan and the Carnatic.

[1] It is clear from the following anecdote related by him that a flint and steel gun was very rare at that time in India:—"I had in my possession a certain fowling piece, for which I understood "Mirza Rustum had offered to the former owner the sum of 12,000 rupees and 12 horses without "success. As this appeared to me an extravagant price I wrote to inquire what were the peculiar "excellences of the piece, and I was informed in reply that if fired 100 times successively without "intermission, it never was inconveniently heated; and, secondly, that it was a firelock and not a "matchlock, being self-igniting; thirdly, that a ball discharged from it never missed the mark; "and lastly, that it carried a ball of five mathkals weight," p. 63.—Autobiographical Memoir of Jahangir, translated by Major Price, 1829.

In the struggle for empire among the sons of Shah Jehan, the Rájpút princes played an important part.[1] The Rahtór Prince Jaswant Singh, the most celebrated of the Rahtór race, was declared generalissimo of the army destined to oppose Aurungzebe, and he marched from Agra at the head of the united contingents of Rájpútáná, and the imperial guards. He advanced to the Ujjain river, and with a magnanimity amounting to imprudence allowed the junction of Murád with Aurungzebe, who, under cover of artillery served by Frenchmen, crossed the river almost unopposed. The next morning the action commenced, which continued throughout the day. The Mogul horse deserted and left him at the head of 30,000 Rájpúts. In spite of the immense superiority of the imperial princes, night alone put a stop to the contest of science, numbers, and artillery against Rájpút courage. The Maharajah retreated, and such was the spirit of his wife, the daughter of the Rana of Udaipur, that she "disdained to receive her lord, and shut the gates of the "castle till she was assured that he would raise another army to fight "Aurungzebe and repair his honour."

Bernier, in 1658, gives the following account of a battle between Dárá and Aurungzebe, on the Chambal river, which ended in the complete defeat of Dárá:—

"The former placed in the front all his cannon, causing them to be tied the one to the other with chains to shut the passage to the cavalry. Behind these pieces of cannon he placed also, front wise, a great number of light camels on the fore part of the bodies whereof they fasten a small piece of the bigness of a double musquet, a man sitting on the hind part of the camel being able to charge and discharge without lighting; behind these camels stood the greatest part of the musqueteers of the rest of the army which chiefly consisted of cavalry furnished with bows and arrows (as ordinarily are the Mogols), or with a sword and kind of half pike, as commonly are the Rájpúts. Of all these I say there were made three different bodies. . . . .

"On the other side, Aurungzebe and Murad put also their army almost into the same order, except that in the midst of the troops of some 'Omrahs' they hid some small field pieces. They hardly made use of any more art, only they placed here and there some men casting 'bannes,' (bān, 'rockets') which is a kind of grenade fastened to a stick, that may be cast very far through the cavalry, and which extremely terrifieth horses, and even hurts and kills sometimes.

"All this cavalry turns about very easily, and they draw their arrows with marvellous swiftness, one man being able to draw six of them before a musqueteer can twice discharge his musquet. . . . .

"All things being thus disposed the artillery began to play on both sides, for 'tis always the cannon that makes the prelude amongst them, and the arrows were now seen to fly through the air. But to say truth their arrows do but little execution; more of them are lost in the air or broken on the ground than hit. The first discharges of arrows being made, they fought hand to hand with their sabres, 'pesle mesle.'"

Bernier[2] seems to think that the descriptions of the large armies of the East have been greatly exaggerated. The cavalry immediately attached to the residence of the Great Mogul did not exceed 35,000 or 40,000, nor did the

[1] Tod's Rajasthan, Vol. II., p. 8. [2] Bernier's Mogul Empire, 2nd Ed.: 1676. pp. 74, 157.

whole much exceed 200,000. The infantry, including the artillery, might amount to 15,000. The foot soldiers, said to compose the mass of the army, consisted mostly of camp followers. When the imperial troops marched, all Delhi and Agra might be described as proceeding along with them; on the other hand the camps, with their streets of tents and bazaars, might be viewed as moving cities. His estimate of the quality of the soldiers was low; they fought with great bravery, but as they were destitute of all discipline they were frequently struck with panic and became incapable of command.

The heavy Mogul cavalry covered with armour, and the elephants with their towers full of armed men, were able to manœuvre with facility on the plains of India or on the table land of the Deccan; but the defects of their military organisation were clearly revealed when at the end of the seventeenth century they were brought into collision with the rising power of the Mahrattas, whose country was more hilly and required a lighter equipped and more active cavalry to march with rapidity.[1] The Mahrattas had long served as mercenaries in the armies of the contending Mahomedan kings of the Deccan. But it was the genius of Sívají that laid the foundation of their military reputation. He himself, though of good birth, could never write his name, but was a good archer and marksman and skilled in the use of the spear, and the various swords and daggers common in the Deccan. He first of all organized the infantry. They were raised in the máwal or mountain valleys in the Ghauts and the Concan. They brought their own arms, and were only furnished with ammunition by the State. Their dress, though not uniform, consisted of a turban cloth round the waist tightly girt about the loins, and a pair of short drawers coming half way down the thigh, a turban and sometimes a cotton frock; they were generally armed with sword, shield, and matchlock; some of them were armed with a species of flint firelock, which invention had early been received from the Portuguese. Every tenth man carried a bow and arrows, which were useful in night attacks and surprises, when firearms were kept in reserve or prohibited. The Heṭkarís or down-country men of the Southern Concan excelled as marksmen, while the Máwalis were celebrated for their desperate attacks with the sword. Every ten men had an officer called a "Naík," every fifty a "Havildár." The officer over a hundred was called "Jumladár," and over a thousand "Ek-hazárí."

The cavalry had a like organization: to every 25 horsemen a "Havildár," to 125 a "Jumladár," to 625 a "Súbahdár," to 6,250, who were rated as 5,000, a "Panch-házari." The chief commander for cavalry was "Sarnaubat," and the infantry had a separate one. The cavalry were composed of two classes of men, Bárgírs, who were supplied with a horse by the State or by individuals, and "Silladárs" or gentlemen providing a horse at their own expense. They generally carried shield, sword, and spear, in the use of which they were very expert. The trained spearmen ride very long, the ball of the toe touching the stirrup; the matchlock men, of which there is a proportion in each body, ride very short. They wear a pair of tight breeches covering the knee, a frock of quilted cotton, a cloth round their waists, with which they generally gird on their swords in preference to a belt, and a turban, which many of them fasten by passing a fold of it under the chin.

[1] Duff's Mahrattas, Vol. I., pp. 224–227.

SIVAJI ON THE MARCH.

TAKEN FROM A MINATURE IN THE ROYAL LIBRARY AT PARIS,

("MONUMENTS DE L'HINDOUSTAN." LANGLÈS. 1821)

W. GRIGGS, PHOTO LITH. LONDON. S. E.

The standard and national flag of the Mahrattas was called "Bhagwá Jhanḍá;" it is swallow-tailed and of a deep orange colour emblematic of the followers of Mahadeo.

Like all successful generals in the East, Sivaji gained the affections of his soldiers by liberal gifts when they were victorious. At the capture of Singharh he gave to every private soldier a silver bangle. His conquests were principally owing to the rapidity with which his light cavalry moved and surprised his enemy, nor was he wanting in those artifices with which he first lulled his foe into security, and then surprised him unawares. It was thus that he murdered the general of the army of Bíjapur, Afzal Khan, after inviting him to a conference, in which each should come with one attendant only. The latter dressed in a thin muslin garment, armed only with his sword, and attended by a single armed follower, advanced in his palanquin to an open bungalow prepared for the occasion. Sivaji made his preparations to receive him. He put on a steel chain cap and chain armour under his turban and cotton gown, concealed a crooked dagger or "bichhwá" (scorpion) in his right sleeve, and on the fingers of his left hand he fixed a "wághnak" (a steel instrument with three curved blades like the claws of a tiger). Thus accoutred he slowly descended from the fort. The Khan had already arrived at the place of meeting, when Sivaji was seen advancing apparently unarmed, and like the Khan attended only by one armed follower.

Sivaji, in view of Afzal Khan frequently stopped, which was represented as the effects of alarm, a supposition more likely to be admitted from his diminutive size. Under pretence of assuring Sivaji, the armed attendant by the contrivance of the Brahmin stood at a few paces distance. Afzul Khan made no objection to Sivaji's follower, though he carried two swords in his waistband, a not uncommon circumstance among the Mahrattas. He advanced two or three paces to meet Sivaji. They were introduced, and in the midst of the customary embrace, Sivaji struck the wagnakh into the bowels of Afzal Khan, who quickly disengaged himself, clapped his hand on his sword, exclaiming "treachery and murder;" but Sivaji instantly followed up the blow with his dagger. The Khan had drawn his sword and made a cut at Sivaji, but the concealed armour was proof against the blow. The whole was the work of a moment, and Sivaji was wresting the weapon from the hand of his victim before the attendants could run towards them. The sword of Afzal Khan is still a valued trophy in the armoury of Sivaji's descendants (Vide Group IX. No. 527, note).[1]

In order to meet the forces of Aurungzebe, Sivaji purchased a supply of artillery from the French at Surat. This, however, was of little avail. Driven to his last stronghold he was compelled at length to yield himself up to him. But having escaped from captivity he regained his kingdom, and extended its limits till his death in 1680.

The military system and discipline introduced by Sivaji soon fell into decay. His son Sambaji gallantly but ineffectually resisted the final invasion of Aurungzebe, whose army is thus described by Duff:[2] "Aurungzebe march-" ing against Sambaji presented an array of gigantic men and horses com-

[1] One of Sivaji's swords preserved by the Bhonsla family at Kolapore was presented to the Prince of Wales. Dr. Birdwood, Handbook, p. 59.

[2] History of Mahrattas, Vol. I., p. 330.

" pletely armed and accoutred, drawn from Cabul, Kandahar, Lahore, " Mooltan, and the extended provinces of his empire." His infantry was composed of musqueteers, matchlock men, and archers, besides bodies of hardy Bundelás and Mewátís, trained to predatory contests among the mountains. In addition to these many thousands were raised in the Carnatic. There were several hundred pieces of cannon, manned by natives, and directed by European gunners. The imperial camp was fitted with every luxury which a court could require. A menagerie accompanied the court, a complete armoury, and every necessary for field sport.

The capture and death of Sambaji did not, however, prevent the irregular bands of Mahrattas from making inroads upon the neighbouring countries, and from this time they appear constantly on the scene till they became the chief power in India.

CHAPTER III.

FROM THE DEATH OF AURUNGZEBE TO THE FALL OF THE MOGUL EMPIRE.

THE death of Aurungzebe was the first step in the decline of the Mogul empire, which owing to a succession of feeble emperors now gradually broke up. The Rajputs regained their independence, the Sikhs[1] commenced their ravages in the Punjab, and the Mahrattas under the able management of Balaji Viswanath, the founder of the Brahmin dynasty of the Peshwas, established their power on a secure basis, and claimed to levy by their own officers or Mahratta chiefs, the " chout," or fourth part of the revenue of the districts ceded to them as payment for immunity from their depredations. Under Muhammad Shah, the two powerful ministers who, respectively governed Oude and the Deccan, Sa'ádat Khan and A'ṣaf-Jáh, Nizám ul Mulk, established their authority in those provinces nominally as viceroys, but virtually as independent sovereigns.

This gradual decay of the Mahomedan power at Delhi invited the invasion of Nadir Shah, 1739, who, having risen against the Afghans who had conquered Persia, drove them out and followed up his successes into Afghanistan and India. After the defeat of Sa'ádat Khan at Karnál, Delhi became the spoil of the invader, who carried off to Persia the jewels and jewelled arms which had been amassed by the Mogul Emperors. Nadir contented himself with annexing all the territories west of the Indus, and did not leave any garrison in India.

The Afghans and Mahrattas now disputed the possession of the capital in several engagements, which were not decisive till the battle of Pánipat, 1761, when the Mahrattas under Bhao were attacked by the Afghans under Ahmed Shah. The latter had 24 dastas, each containing 1,200 horsemen; there were also 2,000 camels, on each of which were mounted two musqueteers armed with

---

[1] Elphinstone, History of India, Vol. II., p. 595.

pieces of large bore called "zamburaqs," or "sháhín," a swivel gun, and a great number of "shutrnáls" also mounted on camels; these, together with his allies, composed a force of 46,800 horse, 38,000 foot, and about 70 pieces of cannon.[1] The men who composed the royal army were Durránis, Kazalbáshes, and Kábulis, who used the "Sher-bachas," and in company with each Durrani were four "yatím" (pupil or apprentice) horsemen.[2] They were intended solely for harassing and pillaging the enemy; they had no pay, and lived on their depredations.[3]

The Mahrattas had 55,000 horse, 15,000 foot, 9,000 of whom were Sepoys with firelocks, disciplined after the European manner, 200 pieces of cannon, beside Pindarrees and a host of camp followers. After some preliminary engagements, which were protracted for three months, they left their entrenched camp. Their rockets marched first with their cannon, swivels or "shuturnals," musquetoons mounted on camels; their cavalry and infantry followed. The ends of their turbans were let loose, their hands and faces were anointed with a preparation of turmeric,[4] signs that they were come forth prepared to die.

The Afghans on their side brought their forces in array,[5] and a general cannonade began on each side. The Mahratta guns being very large and heavy, and their level not easily altered, their shot began to pass over their opponent's head, while the Mahomedans fired but little, except from the chief division. When the combatants had out-marched the artillery, the battle became general; a tremendous charge was made by the Mahrattas, who at first gained the advantage by their dash and the vigour of their onset. The Mahomedan "Alláh! Alláh!" and the incessant "Har! Har! Mahdeo" from the Mahrattas were mingled together in the crash of the combatants. One of the divisions of the Durráni force was composed of 800 Rohilla infantry and 6,000 horse. They advanced slowly under cover of breastworks of sand hastily thrown up in succession. They were opposed by Junkogee Sindia, and as they had a great number of rockets with them, they fired volleys of 2,000 (?) at a time, which terrified the horses of their opponents and prevented their charges. At last while the right wing of the Afghans was broken, the left was still intact, and the Afghans by their greater physical strength overpowered the endurance of the Mahrattas. This close and violent attack lasted for nearly an hour, during which they fought on both sides with spears, swords, battle-axes, and even daggers,[6] till a complete massacre of the Hindu force ensued.

A letter in these terms conveyed the news of this defeat to the Peshwa: "Two pearls have been dissolved, twenty-seven gold mohurs have been lost, "and of the silver and copper the total cannot be cast up." By this the fate of Sivadás Ráo, Viswás Ráo, the officers and the army was understood.

But while the Mahomedans and the Mahrattas were thus engaged in a final struggle for the supremacy of India, events were taking place in the South

---

1 Duff's Mahrattas, Vol. II., p. 149. Sháhín=a royal falcon. Compare the falcon-beaked hammers of the 16th century, and the old falcon and falconet pieces.

2 Sher-bacha=pistol or young tiger.

3 Elliot, Vol. VIII., p. 399.

4 Each person had taken a betel leaf in the presence of his fellows, in confirmation of the engagement to fight to the last.

5 The artillery and rockets were in front of the line; behind them were the camels mounted by musqueteers carrying "zambúraq," supported by a body of Persian musqueteers.

6 An account of the battle of Pánipat.—Asiat. Researches.

which completely changed the character of Indian history. From their first establishment in Southern India, the French and the English acquire a preponderating influence over the various native powers with whom they come into contact. The ascendancy of the European element is shown in the fact that even the native powers which remain independent gradually abandon their old methods of warfare and adopt European armament and military organisation, and engage European officers for the command of their armies; and before the close of the period described in this chapter both Mahomedan and Mahratta have to relinquish their claims to the Empire of India, and England appears as the power paramount over the whole country in a far more extended sense than can be applied to any previous ruling power.

In 1746 the French took and held the settlement of Madras for a short period, till it was restored to the English by treaty at the peace of Aix-la-Chapelle, 1748. In the struggle that followed the death of the Viceroy of the Deccan, the French and English took different sides. The English supported the claims of Názir Jang and Mahomed 'Ali, who became respectively Subahdár of the Deccan and Nawab of the Carnatic. The French took up the cause of Muzaffar Jang and Chandá Sáhib. On the murder of Názir Jang by one of his chiefs, 1750, Muzaffar Jang, by the aid of the troops under Dupleix, obtained the throne of the Deccan, and gave his allies a large territory round Pondicherry and Masulipatam. His successor Salábat Jang was installed in 1751, at Aurungábád as Subahdár of the Deccan by Bussy, and was probably the first to allow native troops to be trained in European discipline. The latter took advantage of his position to dictate to the Subahdár the concession of large territories to the French. Thus the whole Deccan was placed virtually under the French.

The success of the French discouraged the English, who suffered some reverses, till Clive, with only 200 Europeans and 300 Sepoys, took Arcot in 1752. The English then relieved Trichinopoly, closely invested by the French, and reseated their ally Mahomed 'Ali, the Nawab of the Carnatic, on the *masnad* of Arcot.[1] After the departure of Dupleix hostilities again broke out between Lally and the English, and the war was closed by the defeat of the French on the field of Wandewash, 1759, and the capture of Pondicherry by Coote in 1761. This shattered the power of the French in India, and from henceforth the English were the dominant power.

In Bengal Clive had recovered Calcutta from the Nawab of Bengal, and captured the French settlement of Chandernagar. After which he defeated Síraj-ud-Daulah at Plassey, and placed Mír Ja'far on the throne of Bengal, 1757. This victory he obtained over 35,000 foot, 15,000 horse, and 40 cannon, with a loss of only 22 killed and 50 wounded out of 750 British soldiers (the remainder of his small force was composed of natives drilled by the English).

The Great Mogul having attempted to reconquer Bengal with the aid of the Nawab of Oude and some French mercenaries under Law, he was defeated by Major Carnac, through whose offices Mír Kásim was invested Subahdár of Bengal, Behar, and Orissa. He was soon, however, deposed by the English and Mír Ja'far reinstated.

[1] Historical Studies, Shoshee Chunder Dutt, 1879, p. 301. Masnad = a throne, literally a cushion.

In 1764, Munro defeated Shah Shuja at Buxar, and with the fall of Allahabad the representative of the Great Mogul and the Nawab of Oude were forced to come to terms. Lord Clive reinstated the latter on the throne as an ally, and obtained the "dewáni" or concession of the government of Bengal from the Mogul on the payment of a fixed pension (1765).

A new power then attempted to arrest the progress of the English. Hyder Ali[1] early showed his courage in the field in the service of the Rajah of Mysore, and when he was about 25 years of age was presented with an elephant, a flag, and "naqqárahs," or kettledrums, as the insignia of command. He then enlisted about 4,000 foot or musqueteers, and disciplined them after the European mode, and 1,500 horse, and these he called his own troops. He learned the rudiments of European warfare at the siege of Trichinopoly, first against the French, and afterwards as their ally, and so highly did he appreciate their advantages over the native methods that he sent to Pondicherry to purchase stores, such as cannon, muskets, powder and shot, and to procure able gunners, and other Frenchmen whom he retained in his service. Hyder Ali from his successful attacks with his "qaẓẓáks," or light horse, and trained soldiers acquired such wealth and reputation that he was soon able to dispossess the Rajah of Mysore of his throne, and imprison or put to death his ministers. He took the name of "Chaqmaq Jang," alluding to the flint and steel of the musquet used by the Sepoys who gained his victories.

He made constant attacks on the Mahrattas, who overran the country. In 1762 the latter invaded it with 100,000 horse, 60,000 Pindáris, and 50,000 matchlock footmen. Their light horse, however, were completely outdone by the daring and villainy of his "qaẓẓáks." He took advantage of the want of watchfulness of his enemy to attack them suddenly by night; and on one occasion completely routed their advance guard, which in Persian is called the Bíní-i-'Asákir, or "nose of the army." Alluding to this, with a play upon the word, Madhoo Rao, when he heard of it, said to the leader, who had escaped by flight, "by thy folly thou hast cut off the Peshwa's nose."

His usual tactics were to post his artillery in advance, his lines of musketeers in rear of them, and the "*bándárs*" or rocketmen on the flanks. His favourite manœuvre was to place his infantry and artillery in ambush; for instance, either in the dry bed of a river or behind a wood, and then to order his light horse to attack the enemy. When the enemy came forward to meet the charge, Hyder's horse turned and fled, and upon their being pursued they led their pursuers into the ambush, where they were received with such a volley of musquetry as generally decided the fate of the battle.

Another time his "qaẓẓáks," by changing their dress and altering the cut of their beards, joined the foraging party of the Mahrattas without suspicion, and having associated with them for some time without discovery, raised a tumult among their quondam friends, and after slaying them without compunction relieved them from the charge of 5,000 horses, 19 elephants, and 90 camels."[2]

In 1768 the Mahrattas by their superiority in cavalry forced Hyder to retreat to Seringapatam.[3] He marched with his horse in the centre and his

---

[1] Life of Hyder Ali, from the Persian of Mir Husein, by Colonel Miles, p. 25.

[2] *Ibid.*, pp. 121, 314.

[3] *Ibid.*, p. 195.

advanced and rear guards, formed of his infantry and artillery, on his flanks. Near the hill of Churkuli, a shot from one of the Mahratta guns fell among a string of camels carrying rockets, and in the confusion one of the rockets took fire, and blew up one of the boxes of ammunition. The Pindárí horse took advantage of the confusion and (insinuating themselves into the mass) completely routed Hyder's force and captured all his artillery. Hyder himself having taken refuge in the fort was so rejoiced at the escape of his son Tippoo, that he gave every soldier who had survived that disastrous fight two handfuls of gold, and to every man who returned with his horse and arms five handfuls of gold and a dress of honour. By the report of his generosity he soon collected a large force and drove back the Mahrattas. No sooner had he reduced all the neighbouring states to submission than he further strengthened himself by collecting guns and firelocks from the French, Dutch, and Portuguese ports. Thirty of the guns were of French manufacture cast in the reign of Louis XIV., which had been recovered from the wrecks of the squadron of De la Haye, lost in the roads of Masulipatam. In all his battles he seems to have been most indebted to his artillery, and his regular infantry under Marceul, Lally, and other French or Portuguese officers.

The fame of his victories attracted to his standard troops of experienced soldiers with horses and arms complete, " not only from Hind and the " Deccan, but even from Iran and Turan,"[1] when they received pay according to their merits. " His dastas " or household cavalry became in appearance like a " gul dasta " or handful of roses. His matchlock men were clothed in red, yellow, green, or black broadcloth. Nearly a thousand camels taken from the Mahrattas were trained to carry swivels. Each carried two men and a firelock of great length throwing a three oz. ball. These were posted in covered places to flank the enemy. There were also 3,000 men who carried rockets of iron, which are boxes of plate iron in the form of fusees and attached to direction rods. They are of various sizes, some containing more than one pound of powder, and carry 1,000 yards. Many of these rockets are charged to burst. Others are sharpened at the end, and others are pierced at the foremost end, so that the wind acts strongly on the flame and sets fire to anything it may strike on its course. A troop of Arabs or Africans from Abyssinia and Zanzibar, who were armed with richly ornamented bows and arrows, were also employed. He had 2,000 to 3,000 select cavalry clad in complete armour. His regular infantry was recruited from every country.

In 1771 the Nizam Ali made an alliance with Hyder to attack the English. He brought a large army into the field with good artillery, all brass guns of European make; but it was so wanting in discipline and courage, that Hyder's chronicler says that the English did not estimate the Mogul's army at the value of a grain of barley, and so complete was the rout, that after very little fighting, even round the elephant of the Nizam, scarcely 2,000 horse remained. Hyder was successful in cutting off the small detachments of the English forces by his superiority in cavalry; and on one occasion, to deceive the English as to the number of his forces, which were really small, he provided

[1] Mir Husein, p. 432.

20,000 of the peasantry whom he assembled together with wooden muskets of ebony, and furnished them with standards of black, white, and yellow cloth, one flag or "beiruk" being assigned to every 1,000 men. With these he marched and countermarched his troops before the English.[1]

In 1780, Hyder raised a large army to attack the English, consisting of 12,000 household cavalry, 10,000 qazzáks, 15,000 silladar horse, 24,000 regular infantry, 60,000 irregular foot, with 70 guns. Opposed to him were the small forces of General Munro and Colonel Baillie. In an engagement with the latter near Conjeveram, Lally commanded one flank of Hyder's force. He had under him 2,000 infantry, 500 Europeans or Portuguese, and 100 Allemand horse; and they contributed materially to the defeat of Colonel Baillie, who, after a desperate resistance and the loss of his powder waggons by an explosion, was forced to surrender.[2]

It was not till General Coote assumed the command of the English forces that Hyder, shortly before his death in 1782, was thoroughly defeated in the battle of Mahmúd Bandar (Porto Novo), but though his army was beaten, his draught cattle were so good that he managed to draw off his guns, and cover his retreat with his numerous cavalry. Hyder had previously made a treaty with the Dutch at Nagapatam, from whom he purchased guns and muskets. This was followed by the capture of all the Dutch settlements on the coast, when war broke out between the English and the Dutch, in the course of which a British detachment under Colonel Braithwaite was betrayed by spies and surrounded by a large army under Tippoo, the son of Hyder, and cut to pieces.[3] Tippoo on succeeding to the throne of Mysore continued the war with various success in conjunction with his French allies, till 1783, when he concluded peace with the English. Tippoo carried on the work begun by his father, and endeavoured to extend his kingdom by raising the efficiency of his army in military skill and weapons to the highest pitch. The first change in the army that he made was the substitution of Persian and Turkish words of command for the French, in which Hyder's army had been drilled. A treatise called Fattah al Mujáhidin was written by Zein al'Abidín[4] confirming the new arrangement, which extended to the formation of the regiments of cavalry and infantry.[5]

After his conquest of Coorg he erected wooden or stockaded forts called Lakar Koti, and the prisoners who had been taken were formed into eight regiments styled Ahmadi. The uniform of these regiments was made up of tiger cloth, and the officers of the Asad Iláhi and Ahmadi regiments were presented with gorgets of gold, silver, and jewels.

---

1 Mir Husein, p. 269. 2 Mir Husein, p. 390. Mill, Vol. IV., p. 191.

3 Mir Husein, p. 446. 4 Mir Husein, History of Tippoo, translated by Colonel Miles.

5 Five thousand of the regular infantry formed a "qushún," commanded by a sipahdar. In each "qushún" were four risáladárs, or colonels of infantry, and one of cavalry; these again had under them a towkdar for every 100 men. Every "towk," or company, included two "sarkhail," 10 jemadars, and 10 duffadars. The regiments of regular horse were formed after the European model, but the names of the major and adjutant were changed from típdár and subadár to yúzdár and naqíb. The officer commanding four "típs" or regiments of cavalry was called maukibdár. The bar kutchery, or regular infantry, consisting of five or six "qushúns," or brigades, each about 2,000 men, was called the Jaish kutchery; the regular cavalry kutchery, the 'askarí kutchery; the bandah or slave kutchery; the asad illáhi kutchery (lions of God).

He also stockaded the frontier between his own dominions and the Carnatic Payin Ghát, and 12,000 foot soldiers were stationed along this line as a cordon to prevent any one from entering or quitting the Bálá Ghát..

Tippoo had nearly completed the conquest of the whole of the south-west of India, when the English, under General Meadows, came to the assistance of the Rajah of Travancore. It was not, however, till Lord Cornwallis made an attack on the Bálá Ghát of Mysore that his progress was arrested by the capture of Bangalore. The English had for allies the Mahrattas and the troops of the Nizam (about 10,000 horse), but who were not of much assistance to them, as, from the description of Wilks, they appear to have been a force without discipline or cohesion, each man following the flag of his leader as an independent warrior, and accoutred according to his own fancy. The Parthian bow and arrow, the iron club of Scythia, sabres of every age and nation, lances of every length and description, matchlocks of every form, and helmets of every pattern were to be seen in this motley crowd. These troops were left in the rear of the British army when they attacked Seringapatam. The encampment of Tippoo's army was well chosen, covered on one side by a thick bamboo hedge, and by the river Cauvery and a canal, in front by a fortified hill and plain of redoubts, and in the rear by the works of the town and island to which they could retreat. By a night attack his position was taken, and the port was so closely invested by approaches for an assault, that Tippoo was compelled to make peace on the most humiliating conditions, 1792. During the next seven years he intrigued with the Shah of Persia, the Afghans, and the French to recover and increase his power.[1] He also made some changes in the names of his forces and military weapons, partly from a childish love of verbal refinement, and partly from the superstition which in the latter years of his life had great hold on him. He named his kutcheries, divisions or brigades, after the names of the Most High, which are 99 in number, and appointed three or four thousand sipahis to each kutchery, and called them all " 'Askar" instead of "Jaish." He changed the names of "bandúq" (matchlock) to "tufang," "tópi" (cannon) to "daraksh" or "lightning" (Pers.), and a "bán" (rocket) to "shiháb" or "falling star" (Arab.). He also selected 10,000 men from his soldiers, shaikhs, and sayyids, inhabitants of Seringapatam, Kolar, Huskoti, Dewán Hully, Souba Sura, Great Balapore, and Tanjore, and called them his "Zamrah-i-Khás," or body guard, the sign or motto of their incorporation being derived from the sentence, "Dar zamrah-i-má ghamm nabáshad," "in our company sorrow shall find no entrance."

Lord Wellesley took advantage of the arrival of some French officers from the Mauritius to provoke a war with Tippoo, and on his refusal to dismiss them he marched against Seringapatam with a force of 4,381 European, and 10,695 Native infantry from Bengal and Madras, 884 European and 1,751 Native cavalry, and with 608 gunners and 104 pieces of cannon. To these were added 6,000 horse and 10,157 infantry belonging to the Nizam, which had been lately trained under Raymond and Perron, the French officers, and now re-organized by the English, were efficient troops. General Harris crossed the Cauvery, and attacked the forts from the west and the north-west, where they could be

[1] Mir Husein, p 237.

enfiladed from the opposite side of the river. They soon breached the walls and set fire to the city by throwing shells. The storming party consisted of 4,000 men divided into two columns; the right supported by a powerful enfilading fire drove before them the enemy, and forced their way to the palace. The left encountered a formidable resistance from Tippoo's body guard, who had entrenched themselves behind an inner rampart, protected by a deep ditch. Tippoo seeing the enemy approaching, and his followers retreating, rallied them and made a stand near a narrow gateway, when, having with his matchlock and sword killed several of the enemy, he was attacked by an English soldier who attempted to detach his sword belt. The Sultan made a cut at him and wounded him on the knee, upon which the soldier shot him through the head.[1] The sword found on him was presented to the Regent and is now at Windsor.[2] (*See* Fig. 3.) His death removed the most formidable opponent which the English had yet met with in India. He was a most active and enterprising commander, full of resources and cunning, and he made use of his wealth to build up his military power to the highest pitch. He was the first to trust not so much to the sword and spear, familiar to the native soldiery, as to the musquet and artillery with which the Europeans had conquered all Oriental armies.

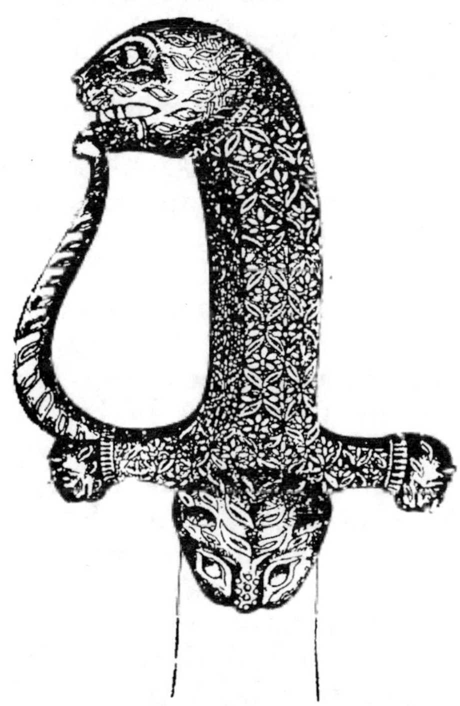

Fig. 3.—Sword of Tippoo, from H.M. Collection at Windsor.

When Seringapatam was taken, says Scurry,[3] Tippoo's repositories of curious and costly fire-arms and swords were equally astonishing, and some of the latter were most magnificently adorned with gold and jewels. The greater part of these were presents, and several of them were of English manufacture.

The cannon mounted on the works were very numerous; all his brass 6-pounders, 51 in number, were said to be English, the others in general cast in his own foundry, and curiously ornamented. One brass 42-pounder, and one brass 6-inch howitzer, and a great number of his iron ordnance, were likewise English. It was said he did not succeed in casting iron so well as brass. He employed French and English mechanics in the manufacture of his cannon.[4] One, by name White, pretended to be a skilled workman, but when he had expended a great deal of money on a foundry and the necessary tools for it, he showed his ignorance by spoiling all the metal casting. Shortly afterwards 30 artizans were sent from France, two of each trade or profession, such as founders, glass-blowers, armourers, and watch-makers. Some of his guns were lion-mouthed, and his musquets with two

[1] Mill, Vol. VI., p. 137.
[2] It was presented by Sir J. Craddock, 1811, and was in the Carlton House Collection.
[3] Scurry's Captivity, London, 1824.
[4] James Bristow, London, 1793.

or three barrels. They also made daggers, called "ṣaffdará," and a kind of shield, woven and formed so as to resist a musket ball ?[1]

The Mahrattas were the next to provoke the interference of the English. The Mahrattas, whose progress we have already seen, were under the rule of four great chieftains, the Gaikwar in Guzerat, the Rajah of Nagpore (Bhonsla), Holkar, and Sindia. These were all nominally under the hereditary Peshwa, who held his court at Poona.

While the English were engaged with these wars in the south of India, Sindia had acquired a pre-eminence over the other chiefs, and had by the assistance of a French officer, De Boigne, a native of Chambery, raised and disciplined his troops on the same system as the English, with European officers of all nations.[2] They were hardy men from Oude, Rohilcund, and the Doab. He first taught the native infantry to use the bayonet, which was added to their matchlocks. He enlisted a warlike Rajpoot sect, the Goseins, and even Mogul soldiers, among his cavalry. His train of artillery consisted of upwards of 200 pieces of different calibre. Sixty of his best guns were cast by Sangster, an Englishman.

He extended his territory to Bundelkhand on the east, and reduced the Rajput princes for some time to be his tributaries. He took under his protection the Mogul Emperor, and thus became master of Agra, Delhi, and the surrounding districts. After the fall of Seringapatam Sindia assisted the Peshwa against the troops of Holkar, who disputed with Sindia the supremacy over the Mahrattas.

In the battle of Púna Holkar, with 14 battalions under English officers, completely routed the opposing forces. The Peshwa then threw himself into the arms of the English (A.D. 1801), and by the treaty of Bassein bound himself to keep no European of a nation hostile to the English, and ceded to them some territory round Bombay. In return for this the British Government undertook to furnish 6,000 men, and to re-establish the Peishwa. They therefore seized Baroda, which was in the hands of the Arab mercenaries of the Guikwar, who had revolted against him, and put him in prison. The two main forces were sent against Rághúji Bhonsla, Rajah of Berar, and Sindia, who together brought 100,000 men into the field, of which 50,000 were horse and 30,000 regular infantry and artillery, commanded by European officers, and the rest half disciplined corps of matchlock men and rocket-men; they had also more than 100 pieces of cannon.

In Central India a decisive action was soon fought by Sir Arthur Wellesley in 1803, who with a small force of about 7,000 English infantry, 1,900 cavalry, and 5,400 natives, defeated on the plains of Assaye an immensely superior body of Sindia's force. The British infantry advanced under a very heavy fire of artillery, and, notwithstanding the charges of Mahratta cavalry, drove the enemy from their guns. Some of the Indians in their retreat threw themselves on the ground, and feigning to be dead were passed over by the advancing troops; but as soon as they had passed they sprang up, and seizing some of the captured guns turned them on the rear of the English. Wellesley, however, was not disconcerted by this manœuvre, but

[1] Mir Husein, p. 256. History of Tippoo, translated by Colonel Miles.
[2] Duff's Mahrattas, Vol. III., p. 35.

detaching a force to take the guns, steadily pursued the enemy till they were completely routed. Sindia's infantry fought well, and his ordnance was well served, and of superior quality. While the battle of Assaye completed the defeat of the Rajah of Berar, General Lake, after taking 'Aligarh, defeated Bourquin, who, after Perron's retirement, commanded the well-disciplined infantry of Sindia. The Mahrattas were strongly posted under the walls of Delhi; by a feigned retreat Lake drew them from their position, and having completely defeated them, entered Delhi.

Here the last representative of the Great Mogul Emperors, Sháh 'Alam, was taken by the English out of the hands of the Mahrattas and pensioned in his palace. His capture forms an important epoch in the history of India, as from thenceforth the English succeeded to the power which the Moguls had held over the whole of India, and which with some temporary interruption they have held to the present day. The campaign was closed by the defeat of Sindia at Laswari, where the well disciplined troops, led by native officers, made a desperate resistance to the charges of the British infantry. In these battles, and in the capture of the forts of Ahmadnagar, 'Aligarh, Baróch, Asírgarh, &c., 713 pieces of ordnance were captured by the English.[1]

CHAPTER IV.

FROM THE FALL OF THE MOGUL EMPIRE TO THE END OF THE FIRST BURMESE WAR.

After the fall of the Mogul Empire we no longer see those constant struggles for supremacy between the principal native states which had formerly kept the country in a chronic state of war. The English Government, which now extended its sway over a large part of India, was desirous of maintaining peace; and tranquillity was only broken when they were brought into collision with the different native forces which, one after the other, assailed them, but were eventually forced to submit. After the rapid defeat of the Mahrattas under Sindia, Holkar, with the assistance of the Rajah of Bhartpur, attacked the English. He brought a powerful army into the field of 60,000 cavalry, 15,000 well-disciplined infantry, and 192 pieces of artillery.[2] Though at first he gained some successes and laid siege to Delhi, he was forced to retire by General Lake, and defeated at Díg and Furruckabad. His ally, however, had fortified himself strongly in Bhartpur, the walls of which were lofty banks of earth of great thickness, with a broad and deep ditch, and six miles in circumference. They made the breach impracticable by raising stockades behind it, and when the assault was made they met the attacking party by discharges of grape, and by throwing down logs of wood, pots of combustibles, and burning cotton bales steeped in oil.[3] Four times they repulsed the English, and such was the obstinacy of the

[1] Parliamentary Report, 1803. [2] Murray. [3] Mill's India, Vol. VI.

defence that the English were glad to come to terms with the Rajah, and peace was soon after concluded on the arrival of Lord Cornwallis as Governor-General. It was reserved for Lord Combermere to direct the capture of Bhartpur, 1826, by the explosion of an enormous mine, which opened a practicable breach.

With the exception of the expeditions against the Búndelas and the Játs, the military operations of the English were now suspended for some years. The conquest of Java from the Dutch led to an expedition against the Sultan of Palembang, a state on the north-east of Sumatra.[1]

The Gorkhas in 1814[2] came in contact with the British on the frontiers, which for more than 700 miles extended along the North-west Provinces of India. In 1765, the chief of a mountain tribe, named Gorkha, had overpowered the Hindu Rajahs who reigned over the mixed population of Hindus and Thibetans inhabiting Nepal; and the Nepalese gradually encroached upon the territories which had belonged to Oude, and were subquently ceded to the British Government. The Gorkhas did not muster more than 12,000 regular troops at the beginning of the war. They held a few forts, strongly situated, commanding the principal passes on the mountains. They were supported by some raw levies without discipline and imperfectly equipped, but their main strength lay in the bravery of their troops, and in the spirit of the Government. The fort of Kalanga in the Dehra Doon was first attacked. It was a stone quadrangular building strengthened by stockades, placed on the summit of a hill 600 feet high, covered with jungle. It was garrisoned by 600 Gorkhas armed, some with matchlocks, others with spears and arrows and other missiles. The English force,[3] about 3,500 strong under General Gillespie, attempted to carry the place by escalade, but they were met by an enfilading fire, which beat down the pioneers before the ladders could be applied; and after the death of the General, the assault was given up till the battering train was brought from Delhi. It was not till the battery of 18-pounders was erected, and a practicable breach was effected, that the troops were ordered to carry the fort at the point of the bayonet. On arriving at the breach, "they found that within it there was a precipitous "descent of about 14 feet, at the foot of which stood a part of the garrison "armed with spears and sharp-pointed arrows, supported by others with "matchlocks and various missiles." Finding it impracticable to advance in the face or such a force, the English troops were recalled, after suffering a loss exceeding that of the whole Gorkha garrison. The fort which had held out against all direct attacks was quite unprepared to resist a bombardment; which speedily rendered the place untenable, 70 only of the garrison surviving. The Nepalese at the stockade at Tamta defeated the native troops brought against them with heavy loss, using their heavy semi-circular ended swords with great effect, and "like the Highlanders of old, after discharging "their matchlocks, rushed in fierce though disorderly masses upon their "opponents." General Ochterlony afterwards, having brought batteries

[1] His sword, presented by General Gillespie in 1813 to the Regent, is now in the collection of Her Majesty at Windsor.

[2] Mill and Wilson, Vol. VIII., p. 23.

[3] Mill, Vol. VIII., p. 25.

to bear upon their stockades, took possession of the forts of Nálagarh and Rámgarh.

While the main army directed against the Gorkhas met with much opposition, and made very little impression on the enemy, the force which under Colonel Gardner attacked the province of Kumaon was more successful. The people of Kumaon and Gurwhal, who had been under the Rajah of Srinagar, and were dissatisfied with the oppressive yoke of their Gorkha conquerors, invited the approach of the English. The stockaded defences of the hill of Sitanh, in front of Almora, were stormed, but the Gorkhas did not give up the fort of Almora till two battalions of Her Majesty's 14th and 5th Regiments under Colonel Nicholls were advanced to within 70 yards of the fort, and mortars were opened on the works. On condition of the surrender of the provinces of Kumaon and Garhwál, the Gorkhas were allowed honourably to retire with their arms and personal property.

They showed equal bravery in attempting to retake the British position at Deothal, advancing to the very muzzles of the guns, and endeavouring to strike down their opponents over their bayonets ; and they kept up a destructive fire upon the guns till they were repulsed by a charge with the bayonet, resulting in a loss of more than 500 dead.

Having after considerable difficulty reduced all the detached posts, General Ochterlony determined to force their main line between Surajgarh and Malaun, and occupied the two forts of Ryla and Deothal. The surrender of Malaun following on the capture of Almora put an end to the campaign, and produced proposals for peace, which, after some delays, and another appeal to arms, was concluded.

Before entering upon the next campaign against the Pindaris, I may mention that expeditions from 1816 to 1818 were made against the turbulent Rajputs in Cutch and Kattiwar, against the Mahomedans rising in Bareilly, against the fortress of Hatras in the Doab, and the insurgents of Gumsar and Cuttack, upon which I will not dwell.

The Pindaris[1] had for a long time been entertained as mercenaries by the Mahomedan princes of the Deccan to plunder their enemies, and to serve as guides to their troops which invaded the Mogul provinces. After their downfall they attached themselves to the Mahrattas, and as the power of the latter declined made war on their own account against their previous masters, and plundered their territory.[2] In 1794 Sindia assigned them lands near the banks of the Nerbudda, which they extended by conquests from their neighbours. They added to their numbers by drawing to their camps the unemployed soldiery of India at the close of the Mahratta war. A horse and a sword were sufficient claims to be enrolled in their numbers. They were organised in troops or dhara commanded by sirdars or chiefs, and formed a body of 30,000 or 40,000 horse divided into numerous small parties.[3]

The resources of a Pindárí chief were not limited by the lands he occupied, nor were the numbers of his "dhaṛá" or company restricted to any

---

1 The word Penḍhárí is Mahráti (Cf. Wilson's Glossary); its most probable etymology is from *penḍhá*, a bundle of grass, = forager.—*Note by Col. Yule, C.B.*

2 Wilson, II., p. 185.

3 Langles, Vol. I., p. 260.

particular limit.[1] The chief himself rarely headed a mere plundering foray, but when not engaged with his main body in the service of a regular state, delegated to his sirdars the plan and conduct of the excursion. The direction of an inroad was generally concerted at the Hindu military festival of the "Dussera," when the leaders met and determined on the course to be pursued during the ensuing cold season. As soon after the cessation of the rains as the roads became practicable and the rivers fordable, the leader who had been chosen moved out with his immediate adherents generally well armed and mounted. In proportion to his reputation he was joined as he proceeded by plunderers from every quarter, some of them respectably mounted and equipped, but the greater part rode ponies and horses of inferior quality, and were indifferently armed with pikes, swords, and even with clubs and sticks pointed with iron; a few only had matchlocks. When 4,000 or 5,000 horse were thus assembled, the party marched to the destined scene of spoliation. The men carried no baggage, and supported themselves and their horses on the grain and provisions which they plundered. The Pindárís moved with great secrecy and celerity to a central spot in the proposed sphere of action, where those best armed and mounted remained round the person of the leader to constitute a rallying point; while the mass, in parties of a few hundred each, were despatched to sweep the country through a circle of many miles, and to bring in whatever valuables they could collect. They moved rapidly at the rate of 30 or 40 miles a day, never halting in one spot long enough to allow the regular troops to come up with them.

The depredations of the Pindaris were during many years confined to the neighbouring frontiers of the Nizam, the Peshwá, and the Rajah of Berar, and in general they were repeated annually.[1] In 1812 they penetrated through Bundelcund; in 1814 they menaced Bengal and invaded Behar; the following year they wasted the Madras Settlements; in 1816 they spread alarm over the whole of the South of the Deccan. In 1817 Lord Hastings determined to suppress their predatory ravages. The territories of the chiefs of the free-booters, Karim and Chitu, were situated in the south of Malwa bounded by the principality of Bhopal on the east, by the Nerbudda on the south, and on the north and west by the possessions of Sindia and Holkar. The success of the Pindaris in their marauding expeditions, which they had conducted for some years with impunity, stirred up the spirit of the Mahrattas, who took advantage of the occasion to rise against the English. The English armies[2] were therefore formed in two grand divisions to operate against the four great Mahratta powers, the Peshwa, Bájí Ráo, Appá Sáhib, and Daulat Ráo, Sindia, and Tulsi-bhái, the regent of Indore, for her son Mulhar Ráo Holkar.

The Bengal army[3] consisted of 29,000 foot, 14,000 horse and 140 guns, both horse and foot artillery, to each of the divisions bodies of irregular horse and foot were added, the contingents of several petty chiefs.

The army of the Deccan under Sir Thomas Hislop amounted to 52,000 foot, 18,000 horse, and 62 guns.

In October 1817 the Peshwá made a treacherous assault on the Presidency at Púna, which the English repulsed, and, although only 3,000 strong, attacked his forces, consisting of about 10,000 horse and as many foot, at Kharki. The

[1] Wilson, p. 191. [2] *Ibid.*, p. 261. [3] Wilson, II., 229, 233.

Mahratta cavalry inflicted some loss on the Sepoys, but were driven back by the steadiness of the British infantry. The Peshwa after the loss of his capital again attacked the English at Koregaum, where the Arab mercenaries fought with desperation, and inflicted severe losses on the English, but were compelled at length to retire. In the meantime after the brilliant defence of the Residency of Nágpur by a small body under Captain Fitzgerald, when attacked by the Arab mercenaries and the Mahrattas, numbering 8,000 foot and 12,000 horse, the Rajah of Berar was forced to come to terms, and Sindia was prevented by a superior force from assisting the Pindárís. Tulsi-Bhai, though herself favourable to the English, was unable to restrain her followers, and her murder was followed by the battle of Mehidpur, where Sir Thomas Hislop defeated the joint armies of the Mahrattas and Pindárís. They were composed of 1,600 infantry, 2,000 artillery, 1,200 matchlock men, 15,000 cavalry, besides 8,000 belonging to Amír Khan, and 4,000 Pindárís.[1]

The rout was complete, though the English lost in killed and wounded near 800 in storming their position, the enemy lost near 3,000. For miles round the battle-field the Mysorean cavalry pursued the fugitives. The Pindaris had been driven from the Nerbudda, and were now dispersed in small bodies, which were so keenly pursued that their Chief Chítú at length took refuge in the jungles, where he was devoured by a tiger.

The Peshwa was the last opponent in the field. He was pursued by General Smith, and after much countermarching he was beaten, but contrived to escape. Colonel Munro in the Southern Mahratta country, and Colonel Macdowell in the hills north of the Godavery, forming the boundary of Khandesh, reduced the strong hill forts which still held out for the Peshwa. The latter, driven to desperation, at last gave himself up to Sir John Malcolm, and the extinction of the Peshwa's name and power brought the war to an end. Peace was restored, and by it a large territory in the highlands of Central India, containing several of the aboriginal tribes, was brought under English rule.

The escape of Appa Sáhib rendered necessary an expedition against the Gonds, in whose mountain fortresses he had taken refuge. They had been constantly attacked and robbed by the Mahrattas and Pindárís, and joined them in making frequent raids on the husbandmen of the plains, "who "ploughed the fields by night, with swords and matchlocks tied to the shafts "of their ploughs."[2] These wild tribes joined with some of the Arab and Beluchi mercenaries and defended their hill forts, from which Appa Sáhib at last escaping took refuge for a short time in Asírgarh. It was one of the strongest forts in India, commanding one of the great passes from the Deccan. The summit of the rock was 750 feet above the plain, crowned with lofty ramparts and only to be approached by steep steps, and five gateways of solid masonry. It carried guns of immense calibre, but the batteries were soon silenced and the garrison surrendered. They were mostly Arabs and Beluchis, and were allowed to retain their shields and daggers, and to return to their native country.

The Rajput princes now sought closer relations with the East India Government. They required the English to protect them from each other

[1] Langles, p. 264. [2] Forsyth's Highlands of Central India, p. 15.

and their turbulent neighbours, and principally from a swarm of military adventurers, Arabs, Sindhis, and Mekranis, who, originally called in to engage in their mutual quarrels, had become to a great extent masters of the country.

The princes were divided into two classes, the five leading states, Udaipur, Jaipur, Jodhpur, Jasalmír, Bikanir, and a number of smaller chiefs; under these again were the Thakurs or nobles, who, like feudal barons, held their lands by military tenure, and who in some cases attempted to usurp the authority of their liege lords. In 1820 peace was restored by British intervention in Rajputana, and the supremacy of the British Government was recognised throughout India.

I will confine myself to one more expedition which was directed beyond the boundaries of India, and which was different in character from any of those previously mentioned. It will suffice to show the composition of the Burmese forces, to which I shall allude in detail in the Catalogue of Arms. The Burmese had always gratified their love of conquest by expeditions against the Siamese, and after the capture of Arakan the King of Burma endeavoured to annex further territory in Assam, and to check the advances of the English. In interfering with the succession to the throne of Cachar in 1823 he came into conflict with them. The immediate cause of the Burmese war was the attack made in 1824 by the Burmese Governors of Arakan on the south-eastern frontier of Bengal at Shahpuri. The Indian Government, in self-defence, directed their main force of from five to six thousand men to effect the capture of Rangoon. They landed there and awaited the attack of the Burmese, who were in arms. They soon stormed and took the stockades of the Burmese in that neighbourhood. The English then entrenched themselves in the great Dagon pagoda, and repelled the attacks of Sykia Woongee and Soomba Wongee, who were successively sent against them. The brothers of the king, the princes of Tonghoo and Tharawadi, then brought the "King's Invulnerables" and besieged the English force, and were again repulsed with great slaughter. Maha Bandula, who had been at the head of the army in Arakan, was summoned to take command of a large force which left Ava in a fleet of boats with a train of artillery. Bandula's army, supported by fire-rafts directed against the British vessels, attacked the whole line of the British force entrenched at Kemmendine. Bandula, after being repulsed, retired, and with fresh reinforcements fortified himself at Kokin. This position was then stormed by the English troops under Sir A. Campbell and General Cotton, and Bandula retreated to Donabyu.

In 1825, a combined expedition by land and water advanced up the Irawadi. 1,300 European infantry, 1,000 Sepoys, two squadrons of dragoons, a troop of horse artillery and a rocket troop marched parallel to the Irawadi river. The marine column consisted of 800 European infantry, a small battalion of Sepoys, and a powerful train of artillery, conveyed in 60 boats, each carrying one or two carronades of twelve or twenty-four pounds. These were escorted by the boats of the men-of-war lying at Rangoon, containing upwards of 100 British seamen. The stockade of Donabyu was defended by more than 150 guns and swivels, and by about 15,000 men who were the veterans of the Burmese army. The first attack was made with an insufficient force and failed, and the stockades were too strong to be carried by a *coup de main*. The fire of the Burmese was silenced by a bombardment which lasted for a day and night, when the death of Bandula caused the evacuation of the fortress and the flight of his army.

The British force wintered at Prome, and after an attempt at negotiations had failed, the Kee Woongee in person directed an attack against Prome, the Burmese force being in three divisions, and comprising 50,000 to 60,000 men. The English force in the field was about 5,000 men, of whom 3,000 were British. They attacked the enemy, and after a considerable resistance completely routed all the divisions of the Burmese. The British force now advanced upon Ava. After marching 150 miles from Prome, proposals for peace were made, but after some provisions had been made, they were not ratified by the king, and the Burmese were again defeated at Melloon and Patanagoh, and not till then was the peace made which resulted in the cession of Arakan and Tenasserim to British India, 1826.

I have now briefly traced the main features of the military history of India to a period within the memory of those living, and although the remaining history of our connection with India is characterised by not a few small, and even some important wars, yet there will not be found much in their tactics and conduct that is different in character from that which I have already described. The Rajahs of the principal native states have realised the fact, that without European discipline and arms it is impossible for them to have a well-appointed army. The supremacy of the British power after many years of struggle is now fully acknowledged, and the recognition of Her Majesty as Empress of India gives hopes of the internal peace of India being maintained, and that though in the future the turbulent tribes settled on our eastern and western frontiers may be expected to prove occasionally troublesome, there will be no interruption of the peaceful relations with the native princes and people, which are gradually more and more secured by our firm and beneficent rule.

DESCRIPTIVE CATALOGUE OF INDIAN ARMS, WITH INTRODUCTORY NOTES ON STYLES OF DECORATION, PROCESSES OF MANUFACTURE, AND ETHNOLOGICAL CHARACTERISTICS.

I.—DECORATION APPLIED TO INDIAN ARMS, AND PROCESSES OF MANUFACTURE.

A.—DECORATION.

THE decorative arts have been in all ages employed on weapons used by distinguished or royal persons, and in the East the custom of giving presents at the Durbar of the Native Chiefs, and at every public reception of a guest, has contributed to a demand for ornamental arms.

Arms belonging to kings have from the remotest antiquity been of gold or inlaid with gold and jewels both in India and Persia.[1] Fashion changes slowly in India, and although it is affected from time to time by foreign influence, yet the type of decoration has probably been handed down from a remote antiquity. It is a question how far the art died out in the dark ages, and was revived again under the Mogul empire. Few, if any, of the ornamental weapons we possess are older than the time of the Mogul invasion or the beginning of the 16th century, and it is from that period to the present that my remarks will principally apply. In treating of Art as applied to arms, I must first make a few general observations.

The writers[2] on Indian Art have been few, and their remarks have been generally directed to the architecture, which has been greatly influenced by the religions, the Brahmanical, the Buddhist, the Jain, and the Mahomedan, which have successively swayed over India. Owen Jones, in his Grammar of Ornament, takes most of his examples from the architecture of the Rock Temples, textile materials or manuscripts; only a few are taken from metal and those not from arms, but from hookahs in Bidri-ware. This course has been generally followed by other writers who have edited the catalogues at the International Exhibitions and at South Kensington.[3] There is, however, as great a variety of art in Indian weapons as there is in architecture, and there is as strongly marked a line between Aryan and

---

[1] Noteably the arms of Chosroes found in his palace by the Mahomedan general of Omar.

[2] General Cunningham, Mr. Fergusson.

[3] Dr. Forbes Watson, Vienna; Dr. Birdwood, Paris; Lt. Cole, South Kensington Museum; Major Murdoch Smith on Persian Art.

Turanian art, or, speaking roughly, between the arms of the north and south of India, as between the architecture of the Taj and the temple of Chillumbrum.

I have stated elsewhere the grounds for the ethnological classification of arms. It is, however, impossible to draw a hard and fast line in the limits of art in India. There is much in Aryan and Turanian art that has a common origin; they have both borrowed from Assyria and perhaps from Egypt.[1] The cone and flower pattern originally derived from the tree worship of the Aryan race is not only used nearly all over India, but is likewise spread over all the east from Greece to Calcutta. There is unquestionably much resemblance between the art of southern India and that of Assyria, as has been pointed out in architecture by Mr. Ferguson, and Dr. Birdwood rightly attributes to a common Turanian source all that is similar between them, that is of a coarse and grotesque character, such as is seen in the temples of southern India, redeemed as it is only by the greatest richness and exuberance of detail.

I do not think we have evidence sufficient to determine whether the Art of northern India has a common origin with that of Persia, as a branch of the Aryan stock, or has been introduced into India by the Mogul Emperors, or restored under their rule; it certainly reached its culminating point when the rule of the great Akbar extended from Bengal to Kandahar. The Aryan races of northern India, are far from being of pure unmixed descent, but the Aryans seem to have left together with the heritage of language, a certain character of art in the countries in which they settled; and even in Persia, the works of art are almost exclusively confined to the parts of the country inhabited by the old Aryan stock, *i.e.*, to the centre, south, and east, in Ispahan, Shiraz and Meshed, which are famous[2] for armour and enamels. In Cashmere, the north-west of India, as well as in Khorassan the influence of Greek art from the Bactrian rule must also have been very considerable, and can be traced in the temples and sculpture of India as far as Bengal.

Fergusson remarks that the Aryans were not such builders as the Turanians. In arms, perhaps more than in architecture, Aryan art preponderates over Turanian, and, though it is not the oldest, demands the prominent place.

It may be divided into Hindi or Indian and Iranic or Persian.

Hindi or Indian.

The purest style of ornament in geometrical and floral decoration is to be found in the north-west provinces, Kashmir and the Punjab, the most ancient settlement of the Aryan race; but it is not confined to these, as there are good workmen over the whole of Hindostan using the traditional patterns, which vary in different localities slightly, but sufficiently to enable a practised eye to tell by the style from what part of India the work comes. It will be seen from the examination of the various groups that Indian art may be divided into five zones—(1.) Punjab and north-west Provinces; (2.)

[1] The barrels of the matchlocks in Bundelcund terminate in a lotus-shape muzzle, which is an exact imitation, whether intentional or not, of the Egyptian capitals figured in Owen Jones' "Grammar of Ornament."

[2] Major Murdoch Smith, "Persian Art," p. 4.

Sind; (3.) Rajputana; (4.) Central India; and (5.) the Deccan, the differences between which will be more fully alluded to in the examples hereafter quoted.

The favourite subjects are generally drawn from the familiar flowers and indigenous birds, the lily or iris, the lotus, the pink (Fig. 32), the parrot and the peacock. When figures of beasts or men are introduced, they are more accurately drawn and more lifelike than in the south, where they are frequently of a purely conventional type, and bordering on the grotesque. Sometimes figures of the gods in relief are chiselled on the flat surface of a blade; the lion and tiger, men on horseback, hunting, or a man leading a horse or running away from an elephant are frequently selected.

Exuberant fancy is also displayed wherever the form of the arm or accoutrement permits it, such as in the elephant ankus, in the crutch, and in powder flasks. In Fig. No. 4 is seen a Fakir's crutch forming also a mace, which is formed out of a solid piece of steel, representing an antelope's horn coming out of a human hand on one side, and ending in a serpent with a tiger's head. The priming horn (E. Collection) shewn in Fig. 5 represents a winged female figure, picked out in colour, proceeding out of the mouth of a monster whose body and tail are formed out of a gayal horn. In the British Museum there is a powder flask, the horn of which terminates in a primer of similar shape, in

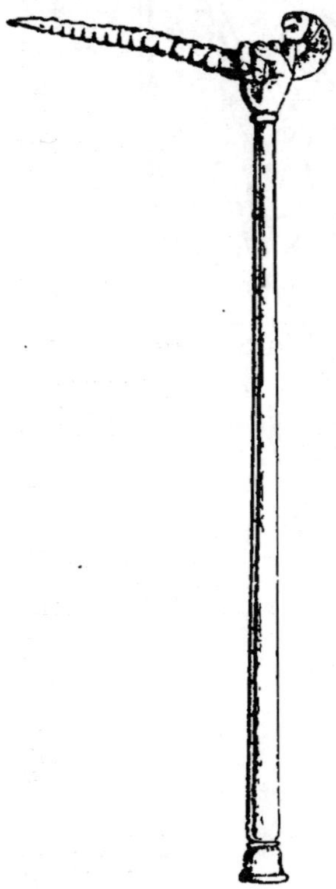

Fig. 4.—A Fakir's Crutch. (E. Collection.)

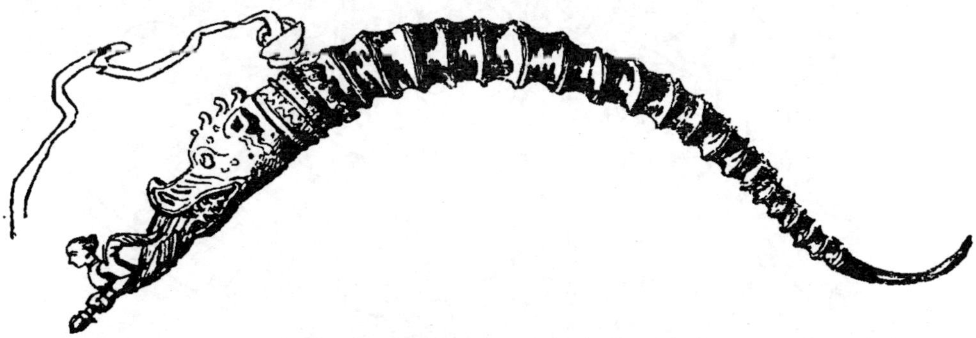

Fig. 5.—Powder Flask. (E. Collection.)

steel inlaid with gold; in another, the horn is replaced by jade, terminating in the head of an antelope with his horns thrown back. In a similar one carved in ivory there is the addition of a tiger springing on the antelope, pursued by an elephant and other wild animals. These are 16th or 17th century work.

The delicate floral patterns of Central India and the Deccan will be remarked on the plate mail and vambraces of this collection (587 T & 590).

In the Mahomedan kingdoms of the Deccan during the last century a bolder treatment of design prevailed, and raised patterns,[1] chiselled out of the solid steel, in imitation of the best period of Persian art, were common (Group IX., Part ii., *see* Plate XII.).

[1] The dynasties of Bîjapur and Golconda were connected with Persia by religious affinities, as both belonged to the Shiite sect.

The large shields of damascened steel offer a rich field for ornament in gold work; the best of them are made at Delhi and Lahore. In one in the E. Collection, inside the rich arabesque border, tigers and dragons alternate with a small palm or Soma[1] tree. In the centre, where there are usually the bosses which hold fast the handles, there are four lizards or crocodiles in high relief curled up, and in the centre of all the sun with a human face depicted on it. These are all executed with great spirit.

The following exhibit three different types of decoration. Fig. 6 represents the florid style prevalent of late years in Cashmere and the Punjab.

Fig. 6.—Section of Shield (No. 697). From Lahore.

This shield was probably made at Lahore or in Kashmír, and in its richness of detail vies with the embroidered work of a Kashmír shawl. The figures of sportsmen on foot and on elephants are usually represented pursuing the

[1] The original Haoma or Soma grows like a vine, but its leaves are those of a jessamine. The fabulous "Haoma grows in heaven, in the Vornu Kasha lake, in which ten fish keep watch on the "dragon or the lizard sent by the evil power Ahriman for the destruction of the Haoma." The Asclepias acida is now used by the Hindus for the Soma.—Kelly, "Indo-European Tradition and Folk-lore," pp. 137–8.

tiger and the antelope. A variety of birds and beasts are represented in the interstices of the Persian scroll work, which is raised and gilt. The diamond bosses in the centre are very effective, as well as the central geometrical ornament with a diaper of flowers.

The shield represented in Fig. 7 is a very fine specimen of steel work from

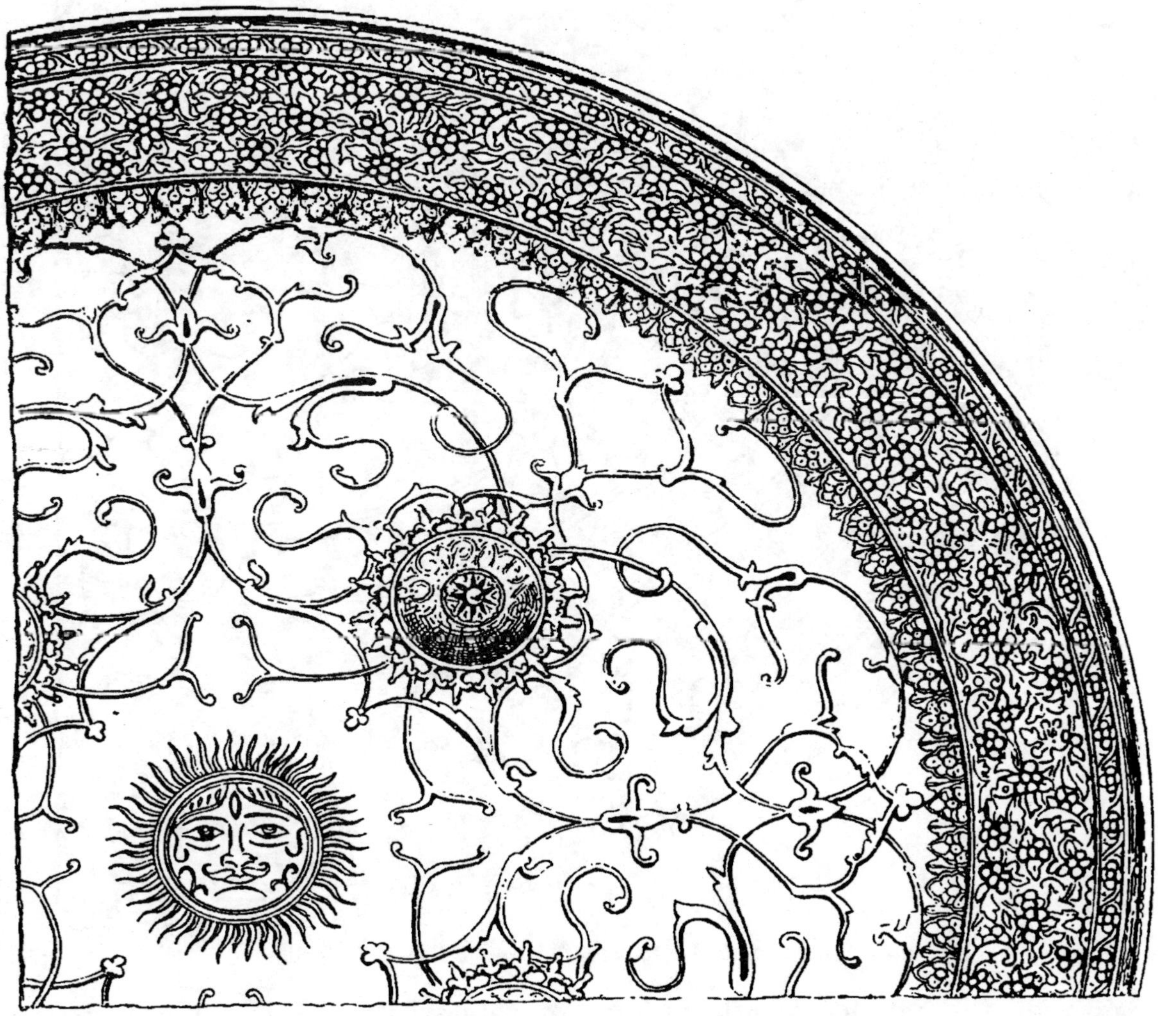

Fig. 7.—Section of Shield (No. 696). From Lahore.

the Punjab. The intertwined arabesques are somewhat Persian in character, and the border is very rich with highly raised gold-work. The shield bears the two symbols of the Crescent and the Sun, which are so often found in connexion with Indian traditions. The oldest families have always claimed descent from either a solar or a lunar race. The Persians and Rajputs are children of the Sun, the Moguls and Sunis of the Moon or Crescent.[1] This shield does not appear to belong to either family, and was probably made for ornament, or for some European exhibition, rather than for a Persian or an Indian Mahomedan.

[1] The Hindi Epic of the Ramayana refers to the Children of the Sun, the Mahabharata to those of the Moon.—Wheeler, Vol. IV., p. 277.

Fig. 8 illustrates the style of much of the "Bidri" ware—rich without being confused. The engraving, however, hardly does justice to the elabo-

Fig. 8.—Section of Shield (No. 449). From Udaipur, Rajputana.

rate design of the shield, which is not merely white upon a black ground like the finest lace, but exquisitely shaded. It offers a contrast to the treatment shown in Fig. 7, which has only sufficient pattern to show off the tints of the steel, as the background of black metal is not so highly prized as that of fine damascened steel, and is therefore more covered with ornament.

The hilts of swords in their variety of shape show how cleverly their patterns are adapted to the various surfaces which are to be covered. They are boldly drawn in outline, and are never confused or overcrowded, as are sometimes the later Persian or Turkish. The lines are free and flowing. The flowers are taken from nature, and subjected to a symmetrical arrangement, showing how far such a conventional treatment can be carried without losing its spirit.

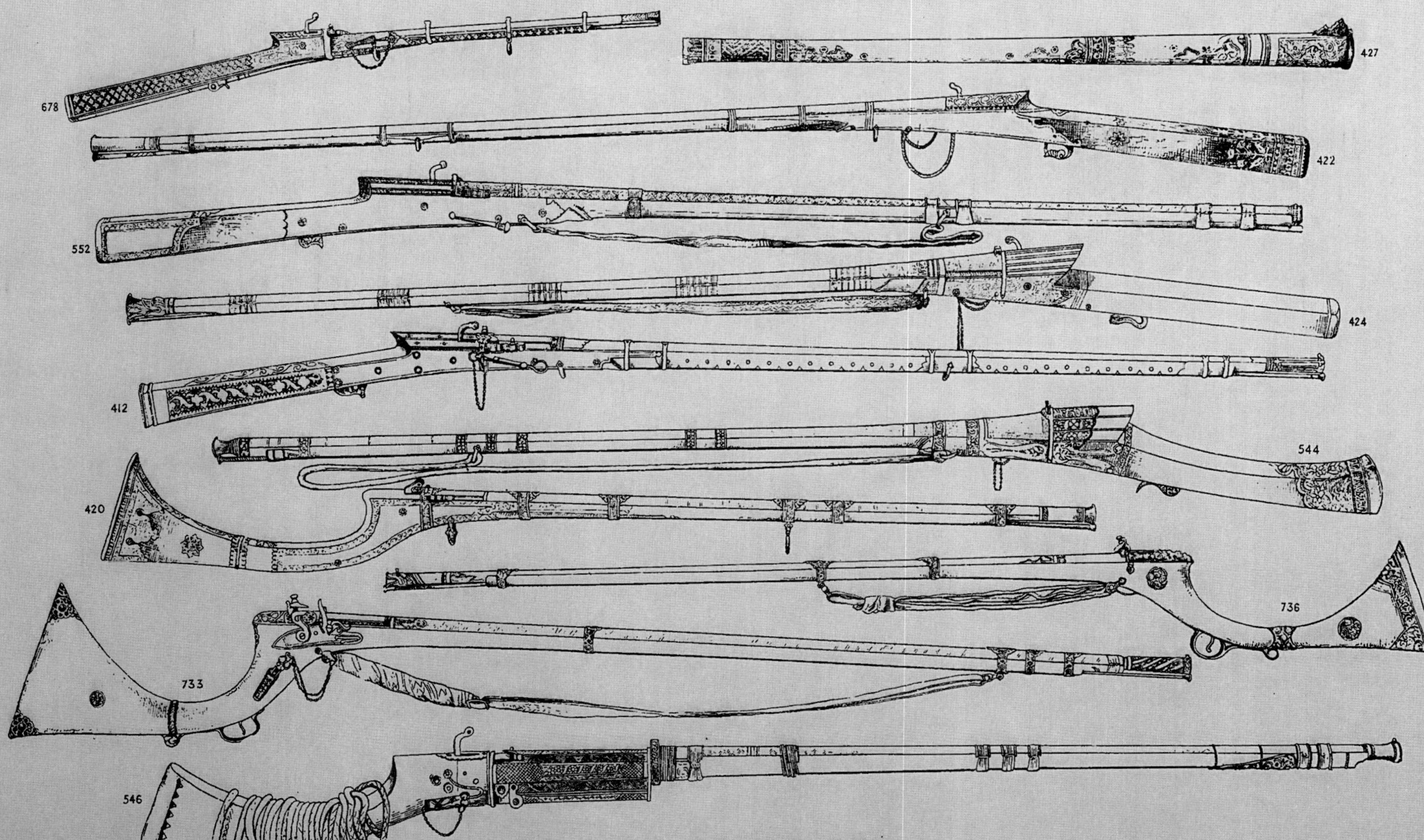

MATCHLOCKS FROM VARIOUS PARTS OF INDIA.

SEE { GROUP VIII, OF CATALOGUE FOR NOS 412, 420, 422, 424 427.
GROUP IX, PART I, FOR NOS 544, 546, 552.
GROUP X, PART I, FOR NOS 678, PART II. FOR NOS 733 736. }

W. GRIGGS, PHOTO-LITH. LONDON, S.E.

On the wide basket-hilt of a Khándá in the Egerton Collection, which probably belonged to a Rajah in Central India, are etched in gold lines, in a refined and spirited style, combats between a tiger and a buffalo with wide branching horns, antelopes and deer pursued by dogs, crocodiles rising from the water, rocks, trees of various kinds, and buildings. The swords and daggers represented in the coloured plates III. and VI. afford splendid illustrations of the various styles and modes of ornamentation used in India. No. 3 (Plate III.), represents a Khándá belonging to a Rajah, richly mounted in gold and red velvet. In the sword shown in No. 4, the whole surface of the hilt and of the blade is covered with figures in relief, traced in gold. In No. 5, the hilt is in silver, enamelled with blue and green floral decorations in relief. The hilt of the tulwar, shown in No. 6, is covered with flowers damascened in gold in relief, and No. 7 represents a "Pulouar" with a hilt of a characteristic outline, and with drooping quillons, also damascened in gold, with blade of large grained Indian damask.[1] Equally instructive are the three daggers, Nos. 5–7, shown in Plate VI., with finely worked hilts in jade and ivory.

The success with which the traditional modes of Indian decoration were applied to matchlocks, appears from the illustrations contained in Plate IV., though no mere outline drawing can reproduce the effect of the gold and silver damascening, of the inlaid ivory and other decorative material employed.

In all Indian arms, whatever material for decoration is used, it is always subsidiary to the general effect. The use of jewels in the ornamentation of arms has been pointed out by Dr. Birdwood as peculiar to the Eastern artist; chips of stones of little value according to European ideas, are made to serve as a brilliant vehicle for colour, unsurpassed in richness of effect by any of the carefully cut gems of European lapidaries.

Besides the differences of geographical position and ethnological influences, there is a distinction arising from their religion between the Hindu and Mahomedan arms, as the decoration of the Sunis in India is generally confined to inscriptions and floral ornaments,[2] but in Persia, among the Shiahs, the same objection to figures does not exist.

Iranic or Persian.

There are four periods of Persian art, into which, from the examples handed down to us, it may be divided. The *first* dates from an early period after the Arab invasion, and the effects of which we can judge by its influence on Arab art on the one side, and on Russian art on the other, of which the helmets and coats of mail in early Russian armour, as early as the 13th and 14th centuries, bear marked traces, and which the intercourse between the two countries renders most probable. The *second* dates from the beginning of the 16th century, and probably culminated in the time of Abbas the Great and his immediate successors. The character of this work will be more fully alluded to (*see* Fig. 34). The *third* period appears to date from the middle of the 17th to the middle of the 18th century, and includes the rule of Nadir

[1] Cf. Rockstühl, Vol. ii., Pl. CLXXVII.

[2] A strict Mahomedan like Sultan Firoz Shah forbade the use of sword belts, and quivers ornamented with jewels, which it had been the custom to wear, and ordered the fittings of his arms to be made of bone.—Elliot, "History," Vol. III., p. 382.

Shah. The suit of armour illustrated in Plate V. may be regarded as typical of the work of this period. (Rockstúhl, Vol. I., Pl. XXXIII.)

The helmet is divided into sixteen compartments, eight of which contain Arabic inscriptions in cartouches; in the other eight, combats between animals are represented.

The inscriptions on the cartouches are:—"Abbás, slave of 'Alí, the work of Faiz-ullah." On the porte-aigrettes, "O thou who accomplishest prayers, Sovereign and dispenser of favours. In the year 1146 of the Hegira (or 1734)." On the plaques of the cuirass, damascened in gold are verses 256, 257, 258, and 259 of the second Surah of the Koran.

The coat of mail has each link strengthened by a cross rivet.

The shield is of rhinoceros horn, lacquered in brilliant colours with outlines in gold, on a white ground, and the ornament on the outer border and centre is on a green ground. The six bosses are enamelled. It may be Persian or made in Sind.

But the degree of magnificence attained by the work of this period may be best judged by some of the presents sent from time to time by the Shahs of Persia to the Czars of Russia, and deposited at Zarkoe-Selo, which also contains the ornamental swords and horse trappings presented during the present century by the Khans of Bokhara and Khiva.

In Plates III. and VI. are shown some swords and daggers sont by the Shahs of Persia to the Russian sovereigns in the 17th and 18th centuries. The hilts of two of the daggers (Figs. 1, 2, Plate VI.), are in walrus horn, with borders of emeralds and rubies, and large turquoises set in relief on the flat top of the handle; the sheaths of one in gold, chiselled in relief with ogee medallions and floral patterns, of the other in massive gold with chevron pattern, terminating in tassel-shaped end. The third is only 8 inches long, covered, both hilt and sheath, with rich geometrical patterns in rubies, emeralds, and pearls. The fourth is 10½ inches long, the hilt and sheath alike in gold, with white, blue, green, and rose-coloured enamels representing birds, gazelles, &c., with delicate floral ornament.[1]

In Plate III.,[2] two Persian swords are represented. Fig. 1 is a Khorassan blade, the hilt and mounts ornamented with blue, green, and white enamel, and inlaid with diamonds, rubies, and emeralds. The scabbard is in leather stamped in relief (17th century). The sword represented in Fig. 2, has an ivory hilt, the pummel and quillons of which terminate in heads of horses. The belt is fastened with two clasps representing animals in white, blue, green, and red enamels. The blade of black Khorassan is the work of Asad Ullah, and contains besides the name of "Abbás."

The *fourth* and last period commences after the overthrow of the Sefavian Dynasty by the Afghans in the last century; in it the work is of a more florid character and inferior in execution. The geometrical cartouches containing quotations from the Koran are more liberally distributed over the surface, and figures of men and horses in hunting or battle scenes are carved in low relief, and less boldly than in ancient work.

Their ornaments are not usually grotesque, though a not uncommon form of the pear-shaped helmet is one which represents a man's face with two horns

[1] Plate LXX., Vol. III., Z. S.

[2] Plate XVI., Vol. III., Z. S.

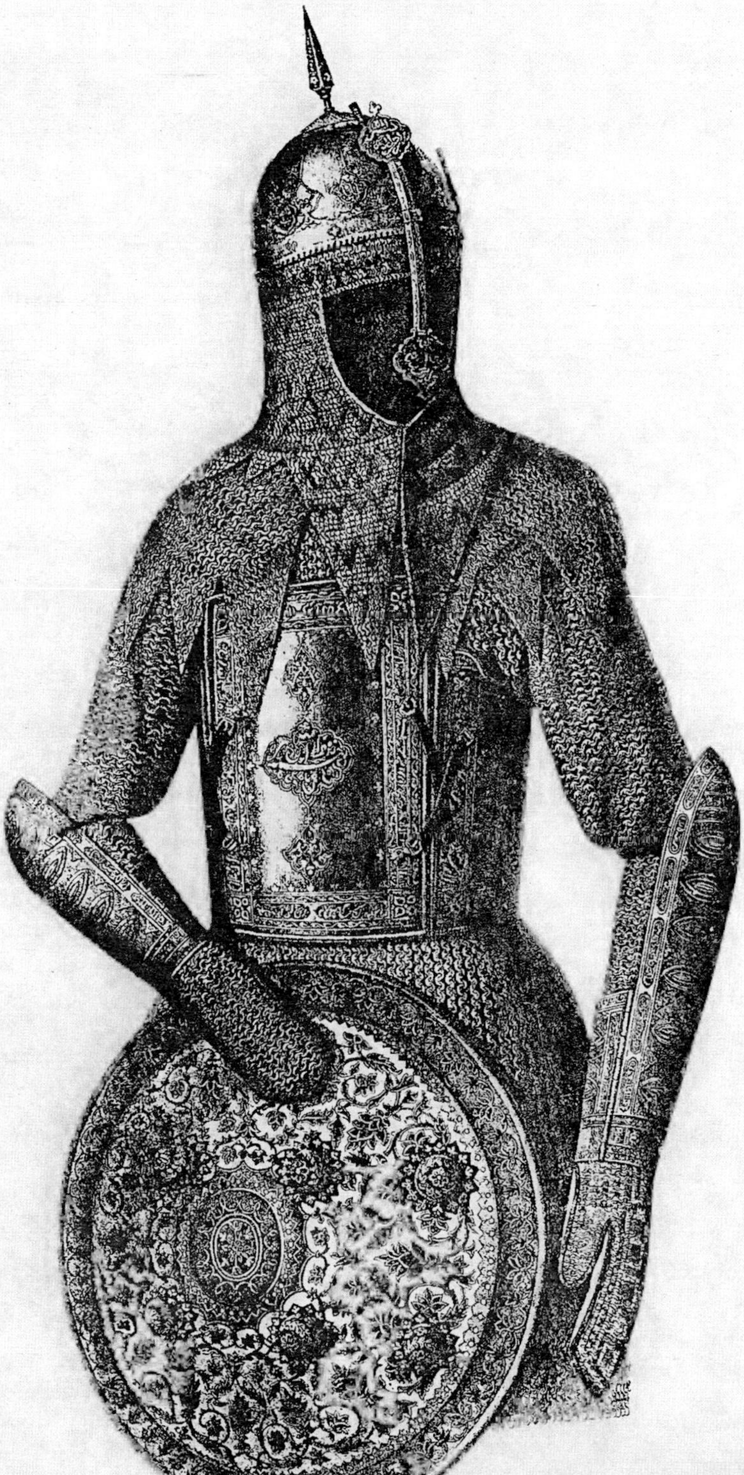

PERSIAN ARMOUR.

EARLY PART OF THE 18TH CENTURY (ZARKOE SELO COLLECTION)

W. GRIGGS, PHOTO-LITH. LONDON, S. E.

and ears in relief on the front; to match it, the shield has a raised face between the bosses; a very ancient variety of mace terminates in a cow's head and horns.

The Lion and the Sun, the tiger leaping on the gazelle or antelope are still, as they always have been, their favourite subjects. The ivory handle of their daggers are generally richly carved, and the hilts of both swords and daggers are frequently shaped like the head of a horse, or bull, or a ram, following in this the custom of the ancient Assyrians.[1]

The most valuable swords are those which have been made by celebrated armourers like Asad Ullah and his pupil, Zamán of Ispahan, and such is the esteem in which the fine varieties of watering are held, that they are frequently without any ornament except the inscription of the maker's name, or that of the owner, if he be of distinguished birth, or a verse from the Koran. The maker signed his name, and sometimes associated with it that of his sovereign, such as Abbás the Great, who is thus described, "Abbás, the Slave of the King of the Elect," *i.e.*, 'Ali.[2] There are also marks on blades which were taken by different makers, such as a flower vase, umbrella, &c. It was not, however, the best sword that was most adorned. A sword was sent by the King of Cabul to the Governor-General, which had once belonged to Tamerlane, and had been taken from Ispahan by the Afghans; it had no ornament except some gold about the hilt, and an embossed gilt sheathing about 6 or 7 inches up the scabbard.

The use of talismanic signs on arms is frequent. The square enclosing four letters, or even numbers, 2, 4, 6, 8,[3] in Arabic, thus,

4	2
8	6

which, in addition to the name of the maker is frequently found on sword blades, is called Bedouh. Some people say that the word Bedouh was the name of an ancient merchant of Arabia, who, having by his piety obtained the blessing of the Deity, was always prosperous. This figure has long been considered as a talisman in the East, engraved on seals as well as on arms; it is used especially to seal letters sent long distances across land and sea, so as to place them under the protection of the guardian angel. In the language of symbolism, the square itself was the emblem of divinity. The equality of its sides represents the immortality, and the right angles the strength of the deity.

Sometimes the whole of the blade is inscribed with large letters in relief containing quotations from the Koran, as is one in the Egerton Collection; more frequently a short inscription in gold is introduced, such as "Assistance "comes from God, and the victory is at hand; announce this good news to the "believers." Another passage frequently found on standards and arms, is

---

[1] Layard, Vol. II., p. 299.

[2] Rockstühl, Pl. 92, No. 6, represents a Persian sword with the Bedouh and inscription, "The "assistance of God and approaching victory." "The brave hero of fights, 1740;" then three Persian verses. "A spring of water arrested in its course is the sword of the Emir Kamrän," further, "The blade, even in its sheath is terrible. It is a dragon hid in its cavern." Then follows the signature of the maker, "The work of Prahim, of Meshed."

[3] The uneven numbers are unlucky. Reinaud, Monuments Musulmans, pp. 243, 307.

" Assuredly we have given you a glorious victory; God has pardoned your " sins, both past and future, so as to fulfil his favour to you, direct you in the " right way, and aid you with a mighty help." These are the words that Mahomet uttered when he entered Mecca in triumph. The attributes of God, " O sublime! O Grand!" or the words, " God be our succour," are also found engraved.

The use of these legends dates from the time of Mahomet, who was accustomed to inscribe on his swords quotations from the Koran, and recommended his followers to do the same to ensure success. Mahomedans are also in the habit of having their arms blessed. The invocations to Mahomet and to Ali, according to the prominence accorded to either, denote the sect of the owner, whether Suni or Shiite. The Sunis, after the invocations to God and Mahomet, add the ten blessed followers or companions of the prophet. The Shiites inscribe the name of Mahomet, Fatima, and the twelve Imams.[1]

I have alluded to the points of difference between Iranic and Hindi styles, but there are many points of resemblance in Aryan art, whether in India or in Persia, that may fairly be compared with Gothic; there is the same versatility and conventional treatment of floral ornaments. In those countries, at the best period, the same high standard of pure floral decoration was reached, corresponding to the style of ornament in the " decorated " period of the 14th century in France and England. Persian art for the last 150 years has more of the character of the " late decorated " or " flamboyant " style in French architecture, or that of Rosslyn chapel in Scotland, while in India, till the last 30 or 40 years, art has not declined or deteriorated in the same way, except as will be hereafter mentioned. It differs from Turanian art as much as Gothic does from Runic or Celtic art. It uses freely the quatrefoil in diaper, and the chevron,[2] as decoration for upright surfaces, such as the head of a spear or the handle of a sword hilt. It wreathes the upright handle of an axe or mace and the barrel of a gun with diagonal patterns, and carpets the ground of its surface with a floral diaper. It is an art from which inspiration for designs may be drawn suitable to the present eclectic age; and there is no floral ornament which can vie in richness with it as covering every available surface with an appropriate and graceful design. In the drawing of animal forms alone it fails, and compared with the best European art in metal it falls far short of the high standard reached by Cellini and the school of Augsburg, which, combined with their rich arabesque patterns, a knowledge of and a power of drawing the human form, never attained by the Hindoos or any Orientals since the palmy days of Greece.

At the present time there is fear that the art of India, in seeking to find

[1] In the Zarkoe-Seloe Collection (Catalogue p. 231,) there is a Persian shield of transparent rhinoceros hide, ornamented with a border of gilt flowers, and inscriptions in " naskhi " or Arabic round letters repeated four times in the bosses on the face. The inscriptions are taken from the Koran, and are used by the Mahomedans as a charm against the Evil eye, as Mahomet is said to have struck blind a magician with these words at the inspiration of the Archangel Gabriel.—Koran, Súrah 68, verses 51, 42.

[2] The chevron is also used in Egyptian, and the quatrefoil in Chinese art.

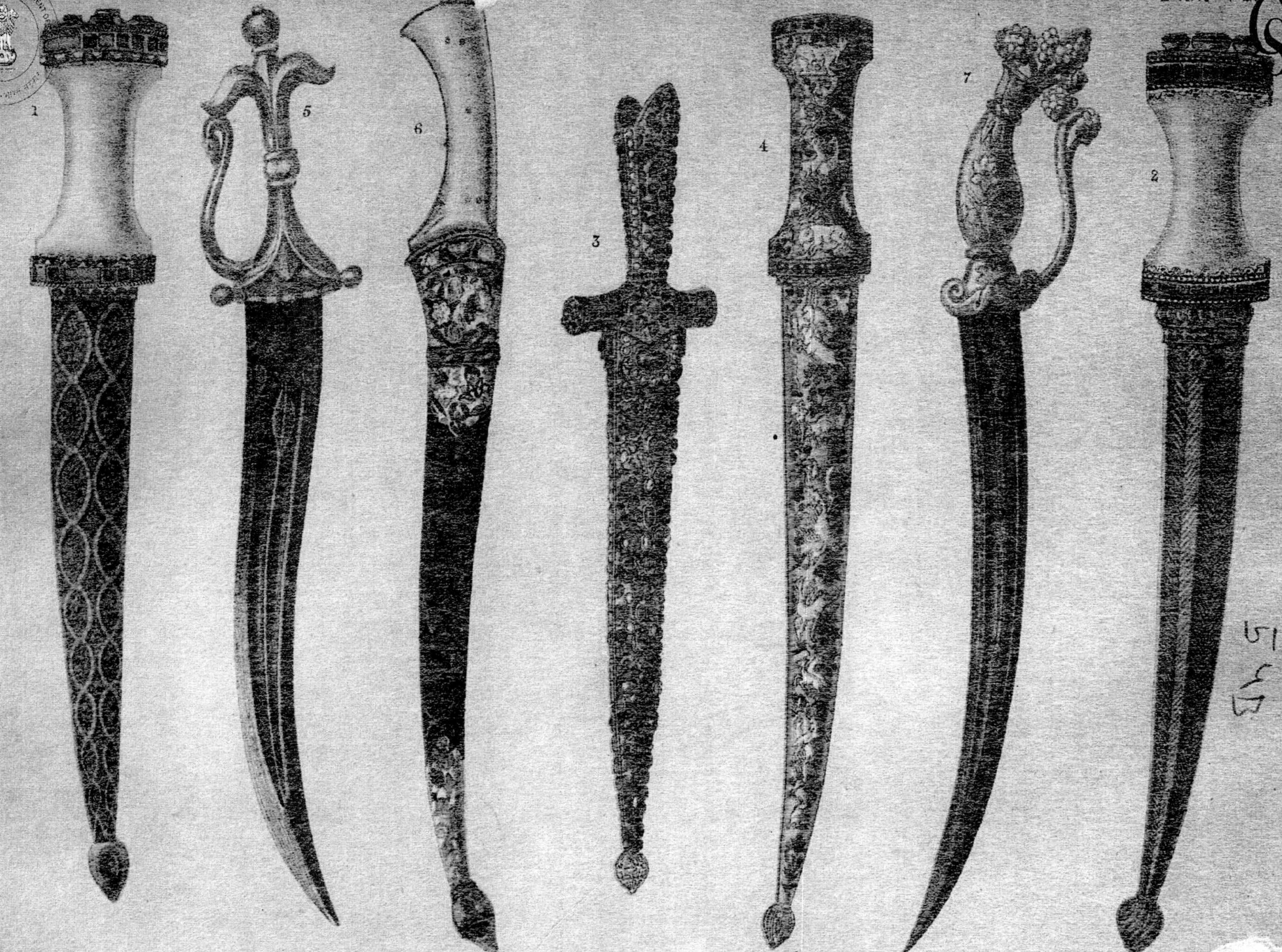

DAGGERS FROM THE ZA... SELO COLLECTION

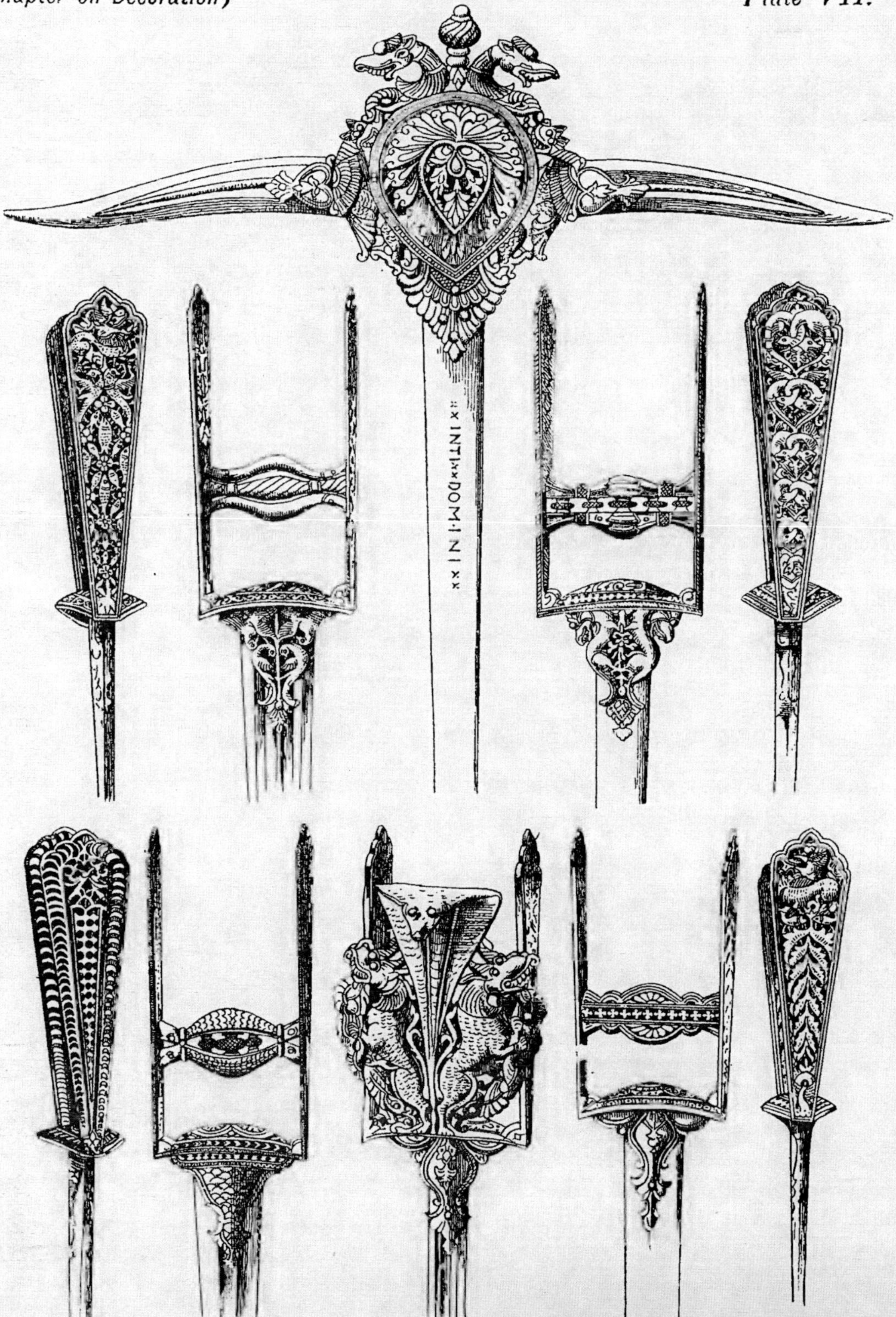

SWORDS & DAGGERS FROM THE ARMOURY AT TANJORE, SOUTHERN INDIA.

(M. J. WALHOUSE *in Indian Antiquary.*)

W. GRIGGS, PHOTO-LITH. LONDON, S. E.

favour in the eyes of Europeans, should neglect its own well-beaten track and mechanically follow European patterns and fashions. Weapons, at least, are not so dependent as textile fabrics on colour, and therefore can not be affected by the crude tints lately introduced through the aniline dyes.

Yet it is a matter of regret that the Koft-gari work now produced in India[1] should exhibit such manifest signs of deterioration both in execution and design.

Turanian Art.

Turanian art, on the other hand, shows to best advantage in its architectural sculptures, and is more at home in stone than in metal. It largely influenced the early Hindoo civilisation as is witnessed by the temples of Southern India, and the sculptures of Amravati. The religion of Southern India consisted mainly in the worship of demons or serpents, such as are represented in the open basket-work hilts of the Kaṭárs in the armoury at Tanjore, depicted in the Indian Antiquary (see Pl. VII.), and in the monsters, whether snakes, fish, lions or dragons that are frequently seen on the hilts of gauntlet swords. One in the Egerton Collection (Fig. 9), of unusual shape, attached to a Spanish blade, teems with heads of monsters.

Fig. 9.—Gauntlet Sword (E. Coll.).

The various branches of this art, Dravidian, Tibetan, and Indo-Chinese, have been exhibited in the groups and alluded to in the Catalogue. It is conspicuous in the elaborate brass and silver work of the Moplah and Coorg knives (Fig. 17, Nos. 119–128), and the silver tassels and chains which accompany them; in the tortoise-shell mounted swords and scabbards, in the silver-hilted knives bound with fine filigree wire in Ceylon and Travancore, in the gold and silver work of the sheaths of the Kora in Nepal, and the more simple swords of the Lepchas in Sikkim.

The foliage of the arabesques is stiffer, the lines are less flowing, and there is a vagueness of outline which does not draw its inspiration at once from nature, but rather attempts to copy it at second-hand.

The step from South Indian or Cingalese to Burmese art, as exhibited in Nos. 133 and 239, is not great. While the forms of weapons in Burmah show the Indo-Chinese character, the details of the carved ivory-handled Dao No. 237, have much in common with South Indian art.

Malay art is not a pure style. Its grotesque and richly carved hilts (Pl. VIII., facing p. 96), are characteristic of a rude and savage race, while its sheaths of gold, richly embossed with animals and foliage, such as those in the Tower and Windsor collections, have been modified by the influence of Aryan art.

[1] At Sialkot and Gujerat in the Panjab.

The art of the Indian Archipelago bears traces both of Indian, Polynesian, or African, and Chinese influence. This is illustrated in a long gun (Fig. 10), probably made in the island of Bali, engraved with Javanese inscriptions, of which the inlaid gold in the barrel has the Chinese key pattern, the silver-gilt mounts are of South Indian character, and the lock is formed of grotesque monsters which are of a Malay or Burmese type. The swords of the Dyaks of Borneo show a more unmistakeable Polynesian influence. The shape of the hilt No. 288 is derived from the base of a stag's horn, as may be seen in a specimen in the Christy collection.

Fig. 10.—Gun from the Indian Archipelago. (E. Coll.)

Besides these main schools of native art, and in spite of its almost unchangeable character, European influence has also left its traces. The Portuguese, the Dutch, the English have in succession left some marks, which it is difficult altogether to overlook, and the effects of which have continued down to the present day.[1]

B.—PROCESSES OF MANUFACTURE.

The East has always been famous for its blades. Damascus has obtained a reputation which it can no longer claim for the manufacture of the finest steel weapons, but in all probability the metal from which the ancient blades of Damascus were made was brought from India. Wootz or Indian steel was exported from Cutch to the ports on the Persian Gulf. Ctesias mentions two wonderful swords that he got from the King of Persia and his mother.[2] It was perhaps the "ferrum candidum" of which the Malli and Oxydracæ sent one hundred talents weight as a present to Alexander. Edrisi says, "the "Hindoos excel in the manufacture of iron, and in the preparation of those "ingredients along with which it is fused to obtain that kind of malleable "iron, usually styled Indian steel. They also have workshops wherein are "forged the most famous sabres in the world."

Colonel Yule, in his notes on Marco Polo, quotes Ramusio, who says that "Ondanique" or "Hundwániy"[3] (Indian steel) was of such surpassing value and excellence, that in the days of yore a man who possessed a mirror or sword of "ondanic" regarded it as he would some precious jewel.

The best blades at the present day are still made in Khorassan, where the manufacture has been carried on since the time of Timour, who trans-

[1] Spanish and Portuguese blades were constantly inserted in native hilts. The *repoussé* work of Cutch is said to have been borrowed from the Dutch.

[2] Colonel Yule's Marco Polo, note, Vol. I., p. 88, Arrian mentions it '*σίδηρος Ἰνδικὸς καὶ στόμωμα*' as an import into the Abyssinian ports (Periplus).

[3] The word Hundwaniy is not now used in Persia, but a writer in the Edinburgh Review says the metal may be Indian steel. (Demonstration of the use of the word Hundwaniy in Arabic for fine steel will be found in the 2nd edition of Marco Polo, I., 93. Note by Colonel Yule.)

ported thither the best artificers of Damascus. Ispahan also has been famous under Abbas the Great as the residence of Assad Ullah, whose name is found signed on the choicest specimens of his manufacture.

It is probably to the Persian blades that Paulus Jovius[1] refers in his remarks on this subject. He states that in the sixteenth century Kermán was celebrated for the fine temper of its steel in scymetars and lance points. These were eagerly bought at high prices by the Turks, and their quality was such that one blow of a Kerman sabre would cleave a European helmet without turning the edge, or cut through a silk handkerchief when drawn across it.

The imitation of the natural watering of the steel, produced by the crystallization of the metal, has been often attempted, but rarely successfully.[2] A blade taken at the capture of Seringapatam, now the property of Lord Delamere, was made in imitation of the Damascus steel by Crivelli in Italy, but the watering is in lines and not distributed throughout equally. Good watered blades have been made at the works at Zlatoust in Russia, which were carried on by Anossoff. The Indian steel, however, has never equalled the European in toughness and flexibility. It is either too brittle, like the best tempered blades, or soft and easily bent, like some of the blades used in Southern India.[3] It is said to be recognised by a peculiar musky odour given out on rubbing the blade.

Mr. Wilkinson, whose practical acquaintance with the best weapons renders him the highest authority on the subject, thus describes the general manufacture of iron in India.[4]

" The furnace is of a rude description, being composed of stones and mud or clay. The iron ore is reduced to a coarse powder. The furnace being filled with charcoal,[5] the fire is urged by two bellows, each made of a single goatskin, and furnished with a bamboo nozzle, until no moisture is given out; a small basketful of the ore is then poured in at the top, and a large basketful of charcoal, and so on alternately. The scoria begins to run in about an hour, but no flux is employed. In about six hours the process is finished."

" The crude iron thus obtained has never been really melted, but falls by its weight to the bottom of the furnace, where the grains agglutinate; in this state it is often malleable. The wall of the furnace is broken down, the red-hot mass is dragged out and divided into pieces, which are sold to the blacksmiths and forged into small bars."

The iron of Hyderabad is said to furnish the best steel exported to Persia. The Persian merchants who frequent the furnaces say that in Persia they have in vain endeavoured to imitate the steel formed from it. It is found at Konasamundrum and Dimdúrti, twenty miles east of Nirmsal, and it is made from a magnetic iron ore diffused in a sandstone-looking gneiss or micaceous schist, passing by insensible degrees into hornblende slate.

No flux is used, as the iron is obtained at once in a perfectly tough and

---

[1] History of his own Times (Book XIV.), quoted in Yule's Marco Polo, Vol. I., p. 89.

[2] By Messrs. Clouet and Breant. Cf. Dr. Ure's Dictionary of Arts and Manufactures, Vol. II., p. 5.

[3] Walhouse, Ind. Antiquary, August 1878.

[4] P. 201. Engines of War. Wilkinson.

[5] Bamboo charcoal is said to be preferred from the quantity of silica it contains, which acts as a flux.

malleable state, requiring none of the complicated processes [1] to which English iron must be subjected. But in the manufacture of the best steel, three-fifths of this iron is mixed with two-fifths of that from the Indore district, where the ore appears to be a peroxide. The use of two very different varieties of iron must have some effect on the crystallization of the steel, which probably produces the beautiful "water." Dr. Malcolmson concludes that the superior quality of the Nirmsal iron depends on the ore being a comparatively pure protoxide.

The method of preparing the steel is thus described. "The mines are "mere holes dug through the thin granite soil, and the ore is detached by "small iron crowbars; it is then collected and broken by means of a conical-"shaped fragment of compact greenstone, and when too hard it is previously "roasted. The sand thus procured is washed, and the heavier parts separated "by this process are smelted with charcoal in small furnaces four or five feet "high and five feet in diameter, sunk two feet below the surface of the "ground. The fire is kept up by a blast from four bullock skins placed at "right angles to each other, the muzzles resting on the upper edge of the "furnace so as to force the blast downwards. The bellows are plied night "and day, and during the operation the men are relieved every four hours, "each working twelve hours out of twenty-four. The iron is obtained in a "malleable state, and being cut into pieces of about one pound in weight is "converted into steel by putting it into crucibles of various sizes, according "to the purposes for which the steel is to be applied. The fire is then kept "up for twenty-four hours with the dried branches of teak, bamboo, and "green leaves of various shrubs, as the natives believe that the different "kinds of woods employed in both processes have a decided effect in pro-"ducing different qualities of iron or steel. It is then allowed to subside, "and the crucible is placed on the ground to cool gradually, so that the par-"ticles form crystals, from which the 'jauhar,' or beautiful combinations so "much prized in the sword blades, are obtained. When cold it is opened, "and a cake of great hardness is found, weighing on average about a pound "and a half. The cake is covered with clay and annealed in the furnace for "twelve or sixteen hours; it is then taken out again and cooled, and the "process is repeated three or four times till the metal is rendered sufficiently "soft to be worked. Each sword generally is made of two small cakes, "which are formed into bars and afterwards welded together. The 'jauhar' "is generally distributed evenly over the whole blade, but in some of the "most prized there is a horizontal or oblique band running across at intervals "of about one or two inches, which is called Mahomet's ladder."[2]

The great centres for the manufacture of arms were Lahore and Gujerat in the Punjab, Patiálá, Kotah, and Bundi in Rajputana for matchlocks; Nárwár and Delhi for coats of mail and damascened arms; Monghyr in Bengal for pistols; Gwalior Lushkur, and Aurungabad in Central India, besides several places in Madras. The name of Arnachellam of Salem as an armourer has been known for the last 50 years over India.

The excellent steel of Coimbatore and North Arcot is much used. At

[1] Colonel Yule, Vol. I., p. 89. The iron is converted directly into cast steel without passing through any intermediate stage analogous to that of blister steel.

[2] Cf. Journal of the Asiatic Society of Bengal, Vol. I., p. 245–253. Dr. Voysey, Journal of the R.A.S., No. X., p. 290, referred to by Wilkinson.

Elgundel there is a manufacture of swords, daggers, and spearheads from the steel obtained there. At Lingampilly, in the same district, barrels for pistols and matchlocks are prepared in the following manner: bits of old iron are formed into rods the thickness of a man's finger, which are then twisted; three or four of these are joined lengthways, another band of iron of the same breadth and one-third of an inch thick is welded to this, and both are formed into a band which is twisted and afterwards beaten into a solid cylinder, which is bored by a hard steel chisel. Pistol barrels are sold for Rs. 20, and gun barrels for Rs. 40.

Buchanan[1] thus describes the manufacture in Mysore: "In Mysore the " iron is made from the black sand found in the channels of all the rivers. " After being smelted, the iron was used by Tippoo for making into shot by " hammering. Near Seringapatam there are five forges where steel is made, " principally for exportation. It is used for stonecutters' chisels, sword blades, " and strings of musical instruments. The crucibles, made of unbaked clay, " are of a conical shape. Into each is put one third of a wedge of iron with " 531 grains of the stem of the Tangada (Cassia auriculata), and two green " leaves of the Huginay.[2] The fuel used is charcoal prepared from almost any wood. When the crucibles are opened the steel is found melted to a button, with evident marks of a tendency to crystallization, which shows clearly that it has undergone a complete fusion. The cakes of steel are annealed, previously to working them, in a charcoal fire, by keeping them for several hours nearly at the point of fusion, otherwise they would not stand the operation of drawing into bars; an excess of carbon is necessary in the first instance to ensure perfect fusion in the crucibles, the excess being driven off by the subsequent process.

The swords of Persia are so generally worn by the Indian Rajahs that the process by which they convert the Indian steel into these finely watered blades must be mentioned here:—"The most famous damascened steels," says Major Murdoch Smith,[3] "were those of Ispahan, Khorassan, Kazveen, and " Shiraz, at which last places sword blades were chiefly made. After the " object is forged, it is placed for six or eight days in the furnace of a hot bath, " where the greatest attention has to be paid to the even heating of the article. " The bath is heated with the dried dung of cows and other animals, which " gives a steady and not very intense heat, and is supposed to contain the " salts necessary for the formation of true damascene. When the article is " taken out of the furnace it is left at the temper it has therein acquired. It " is then finished and polished. To bring out the grain, a certain mineral " 'zág'[4] is then applied in the following manner. About three parts of the

[1] Journey through Mysore, Vol. II., p. 16.

[2] The leaves used to cover the iron and the wood are those of the Asclepias gigantea, or when that is not to be procured those of the Convolvulus laurifolia.

As soon as the clay used to stop the mouths of the crucibles is dry, they are built up in the form of an arch with their bottoms inwards, in a small furnace urged by two goatskin bellows. Charcoal is heaped over them, and the blast kept up without intermission for about two hours and a half, when it is stopped and the process is considered complete. The furnace contains from 20 to 24 crucibles.—Wilkinson, p. 202.

[3] Persian Art, p. 30.

[4] A mineral substance resembling salt. There are five kinds, red called Χαλκανθον in Greek, yellow zag or vitriol, green, white (Alumen iemanicum or of Yemen), black (black of shoemakers). —Z. S. Cat., p. 242. In the India Museum there is exhibited as "zág" a grey powder, which is the native sulphate of iron.

" mineral are dissolved in ten of water over a slow fire in an earthenware or " leaden vessel. The object is then slightly heated, and a little of the liquid " applied with a cotton wad, after which it is washed in cold water. If the " damascene does not appear sufficiently the operation is repeated."

It is said that the Persians distinguish by ten different names the varieties of watering. One of the most prized and rare is that which takes its name from the grains of yellow sand. There are, however, four main patterns generally recognised:—

1. "Kirk nardubán," meaning the forty steps or rungs of the ladder, in allusion to the transverse markings of fine grey or black watering. The idea is also expressed in an inscription on one of the blades, that the undulations of the steel resemble a net across running water.

2. "Qará khorásán," nearly black, with fine undulations proceeding like water either from the point to the hilt, or the reverse way.

3. Qará Tábán, 'brilliant black," with larger watering and more grey in tone.

4. Shám, or simple Damascus, including all other varieties.[1]

On the introduction of the use of firearms, the methods, long and perhaps exclusively known to the Asiatics, of manufacturing sword-blades of peculiar excellence, was transferred with some modification to that of gun-barrels, and are still in use.[2]

In Persia, Kabul, the Punjab, and Sind the same general principles prevail, but the matchlocks of the last are held deservedly in the highest estimation.

In some parts of India the workmen prefer for the material of their barrels the iron of old sugar boilers, but they use in Kashmir the iron of Bajaur (in the country of the Yusufzai) as it comes from the smelting furnace, after receiving a few blows whilst hot, which condense it into a rude kind of pig, the weight of which varies from five to eight seers (10 to 16 lbs.), and which sells as high as 4*d*. a pound. The first process consists in cutting the pig when heated into narrow strips with a cold chisel, and in this operation the iron loses one-fourth of its gross weight. Each of these strips separately is brought to welding heat, and worked smartly under the hammers of two men on a block of limestone as an anvil. When the slag is expelled, each strip is drawn out by the hammer into a strap about 2 feet long and $1\frac{1}{5}$ inch broad, and $\frac{1}{5}$th inch thick. One of these straps has its ends so brought together as to enable it to include about 20 other short straps cut up for the purpose, some being placed on their edge, and others wedged in between the lengths, so as to form a compact mass. It is then put into the fire and lightly heated, receiving a few blows upon both faces as well as upon the edges.

It is next smeared over with a paste of clay and water, and when dried it is exposed first to a light welding heat, and after a slight hammering to a stronger heat, when it is vigorously and quickly beaten into four-sided bars

[1] Çat. Mus. Zarkoe-Seloe, p. 242. In addition to these, Sir A. Burnes mentions "Akbaree," in which the pattern ran like a skein of silk the whole length of the blade, and "Begumee," where it waved like a watered silk.

[2] Moorcroft's Travels, p. 195. 1841.

about a foot long, and a finger's thickness. These are again heated, separated, and drawn out into square rods about $\frac{1}{4}$-inch broad on each face. These are then twisted from right to left, while the part which is to be twisted is heated to a red heat nearly verging upon white. This process is repeated by heating two or three inches at a time, and then cooling it with cold water, till the whole rod is converted into a fine screw, which is made as even as possible.

To make an Iran barrel six or eight rods are required. When eight are employed, four of them have the twist from right to left, and four from left to right. Every rod after having been slightly heated is lightly hammered on its two opposite sides equally, so that two sides have the threads beaten down, and the two others have the threads standing, and retaining their original roundness. Each rod is now made up of lengths of the same direction of twist, and is laid parallel to the other, so that rods of opposite twist are in alternate succession.[1]

The steel having been formed into bars is now ready for manufacture into gun-barrels.[2]

The extremities of the bars are welded together, and the band or skelp is now ready for being formed into a hollow cylinder through being twisted in a spiral line upon itself, which is begun at the breech or thicker end, and continued to the muzzle. When the twisting is so far completed that the edges of all the twists stand even, and the cylinder is nearly equal, it is coated with a thin paste of clay and water, and is then ready for being welded.

A welding heat is first taken in the middle of the cylinder, and the edges of the twists are brought together by the breech being struck down upon the stone anvil perpendicularly for the purpose of jumping up the edges. The welding is constantly repeated, so that the twist, which was jumped up, is successively hammered when the heat is well on, till the barrel has been welded up to the muzzle.

This process is then repeated, commencing from the middle to the breech, and afterwards from the middle to the muzzle, during which an iron rod is introduced at each end and used as a mandril. A third heat nearly red is now taken at the whole surface of the barrel, which is then made regular and level by smartly hammering it. The barrel is then fixed horizontally through a hole in an upright post and bored, after which its surface is filed, polished, and prepared for bringing out the damasked lines. "Jauhar" is brought out through biting the whole surface with "kasís," a sulphate of iron.

The barrel is completely freed from grease or oil by being well rubbed with dry ashes and a clean rag. About three drachms of sulphate of iron in powder is mixed with as much water as is sufficient to bring it to the consistence of thick paste which is smeared equally over the whole surface of the barrel, the muzzle and breech being at the same time carefully plugged. About two hours afterwards, when the metal has assumed a blackish colour, the coating is rubbed off, and the barrel cleaned as before.

---

[1] Barrels are called "pechdár" when plain or simply twisted, "jauhardár" when damasked. For the latter the rods are disposed according to the kind of brilliant or damasked lines to be produced, called either from the country as "Iran" or Persian, or from the figure, as "pigeon's eye," "lover's knot," "chain," &c.

[2] Cf. Journ. Asiatic Soc. 1841, p. 83.; Moorcroft, II., 195, 213.

The barrel is then smeared with a preparation composed of the same quantity of sulphate of iron and four ounces of water, and is hung up in the well.

Every gunsmith has, in the floor of his shop, a well about two yards deep, the bottom of which is covered with a layer of fresh horse-dung half a yard thick. Suspended by a string from the cross stick at the mouth of the well, the barrel which has been covered with the mixture as before is taken out every morning and cleaned with dry ashes and cloth, and hung up for 24 hours with a coating of the solution. This process is continued for 20 days or a month till prominent lines are formed on the surface of the barrel, separated from each other more or less by other depressed lines or grooves; the former will be found to have the same direction as that of the thread of the screw in the twisted rods. The prominent lines when rubbed are bright and of a colour somewhat approaching silver, while the depressed lines are dark and form the pattern.

The "zanjír" or chain damask consists in the introduction of a band of prominent and brilliant lines disposed like the links of a chain between parallel plain lines of damask. The processes are the same as before described in cutting up the "pig," and in reducing the strips into straps, but the "pie" or "ghilaf" contains only eight lengths, which when welded is drawn out into straps $\frac{1}{2}$ inch broad and $\frac{1}{8}$ inch thick. One of these straps being heated is bent backwards and forwards upon itself in eight continued loops, each an inch long, and is then worked up into straps $\frac{1}{3}$ inch broad, and $\frac{1}{10}$ inch thick. Three of this kind of strap are required in this pattern, one for the chain and two for the lines. The face of the iron anvil has a perpendicular hollow about one-quarter of an inch deep, and about one-third of an inch across. One end of the strap is laid while cold across this groove, and driven down into it by a small chisel and hammer, by which the strap receives a bend or angle. Its opposite face is then placed across the die near the acute elbow made by the chisel, and is in like manner wedged into it, after which the operation is reversed until the whole band is converted into a frill of loops. This frill is then heated, and the operator holding one end with a small pair of tongs brings two pairs of loops together leaving the ends open. This is continued till the frill is much reduced in length through the loops of the strap standing at right angles to its general direction. Different lengths of frill are welded together, so as to form a ribbon six spans long, placed in contact with two plain straps set on edge, and four rods, two on each side twisting alternately, from left to right, and the reverse. The general band of these seven straps is then treated as that for the "Irani" damask.

The chain damask is in general preferred to all other varieties, excepting the silver twist. The Kashmiris still make blades for daggers in the same way, as one which was made for the author at Srinagar to fit an Indian jade handle is damasked, and Moorcroft relates that they made sword blades for him to order, though they did not usually manufacture them. It is said that "jauhar" is imitated in Hindostan by lines being traced in a coating of wax laid over the metal, and the barrel being exposed to the action of sulphate of iron.

In the Island of Lombok, east of Java, there exists a colony of Hindus who manufacture guns nearly seven feet long, highly ornamented in silver, gold, and brass, and with very long stocks. Wallace[1] thus describes the way in which they are bored :—

" The gun is bored by a simple machine. It is simply a strong bamboo basket, through the bottom of which was stuck upright a pole about three feet long, kept in its place by a few sticks tied across the top with rattans. The bottom of the pole has an iron ring and a hole in which the four-cornered borers of hardened iron can be fitted. The barrel to be bored is buried upright in the ground, and the borer inserted with it; the top of the stick or vertical shaft is held by a cross-piece of bamboo with a hole in it, and the basket is filled with stones to get the required weight. Two boys turn the bamboo round. The barrels are made in pieces of about 18 inches long, which are first bored small and then welded together upon a straight iron rod. The whole barrel is then worked with borers of gradually increasing sizes, and in three days the boring is finished."

" The workshops where the guns were made were very remarkable. An open shed with a couple of small mud forges were the chief objects visible. The bellows consisted of two bamboo cylinders with pistons worked by hand. They move very easily, having a thick stuffing of feathers thickly set round the piston so as to act as a valve and produce a regular blast. Both cylinders communicate with the same nozzle, one piston rising while the other falls. An oblong piece of iron on the ground was the anvil, and a small vice was fixed on the projecting root of a tree outside. These, with a few files and hammers, were the only tools with which an old man makes these fine guns."

In many parts of India clever imitations of European arms are made after the latest fashion, but the process of manufacturing matchlocks has probably not much changed since the time of Akbar. The following extract from the Aín-í-Akbari is worthy of quotation here, as showing the pains taken in their manufacture and testing at that period :—

" Bandúqs or matchlocks are now made in such a manner that when filled with powder up to the muzzle there is no fear of their bursting. Formerly they could not fill them to more than a quarter. Besides they made them with the hammer and anvil, by flattening pieces of iron and joining the flattened edges of both sides.

" His Majesty has invented an excellent method of construction. After having the iron flattened, it is rolled up obliquely like a scroll of paper, so that the folds get longer at every twist. Then they join the folds, not edge to edge, but so as to allow them to lie one over the other, and heat them gradually in the fire."

There is also the following method :—Cylindrical pieces of iron are properly tempered, and then bored with an iron borer. Three or four of these are joined together to make one gun.

The smallest bandúqs that are made are two spans long, and the longest near two ells. That of one ell and a quarter is called " damáriak."

---

[1] The Malay Archipelago, Vol. I., p. 169.

The gun stocks are differently made. Some are made to fire without a match, merely by giving a little motion to the trigger. And they make some bullets that will do execution like a sword. Through the assistance of the inventive genius of His Majesty, there are now many masters to be found among gunmakers, *e.g.*, Ustád Kabír, and Husain.

In preparing the iron for banduqs half is lost in the fire. When the lengths are made, and before they are joined together, they are stamped with figures, expressing the quantity of crude iron and the quantity remaining when forged, and in this state it is called "daul." This is sent for His Majesty's inspection, and the weight of the ball being determined, the bore is made accordingly. The banduq ball is never larger than 25 tánks, nor more than 15, but, excepting His Majesty, nobody is bold enough to fire off one of the largest.

"When the bore is finished it is again carried to the Haram. From thence it is brought out again, and set in an old stock and filled with powder till within a third of the muzzle. If it stands this proof, it is carried again to His Majesty. Then the muzzle is finished, after which it is again put into an old stock as before mentioned, and tried at a mark. If it does not carry true they heat it and straighten it by means of a wooden rod introduced into the barrel. Then in the royal presence it is delivered to the filer, who fashions the outside as he is directed. When this is done the barrel is again carried to His Majesty, when the wood and form of the stock are determined. In this stage the figures marking the weight of the crude and of the manufactured iron are effaced, and in their room are engraven the maker's name, the place, the month, and the year.

"Next are made the trigger, the ramrod, and primer. After all these are finished the piece again is ordered to be proved. If it is found to carry true, it is again brought to the Haram along with five balls. In this state it is called sádah (or plain). The colour of the stock is next determined. One of the nine kinds of colours is selected for the stock. Guns differ also in the quantity of inlaid gold and enamel, the colour of the barrel being uniform. When the colouring is finished, it is called rangín (or coloured).

"It is now sent again into the Haram with five more balls. His Majesty fires it four times, and returns it back again with the fifth ball. When ten of these muskets are collected together, they are ordered to be inlaid with gold on the mouth of the barrel and butt-end, and are afterwards sent to the Haram. When ten such are completely finished they are committed to the care of the cheeyleh or slaves.

"The banduqs formerly were polished by hand, but His Majesty has invented a wheel, turned by a single bullock, which polishes 16 muskets in a very short time.

"His Majesty, out of a thousand muskets which are either bought, made in the royal workshops, or received as presents, selects 105 for his own particular use. His Majesty fires every day, and after he has discharged a piece four times, it is sent out and exchanged for another. Twelve are named after the months, so that each comes in once a year; thirty others are changed every week, and thirty-two are used alternately every day of a solar month, and the remaining thirty-one are for the kotal."[1]

The following materials are used in the decoration of weapons and their accoutrements :—

Iron.—The hilts of the oldest weapons found in Southern India (*vide* Figs. 11 and 12) as well as in Nepal, are of hammered and wrought iron, as are the rings found on the pommel of the swords worn by the Nairs (Cf. Fig. 18).

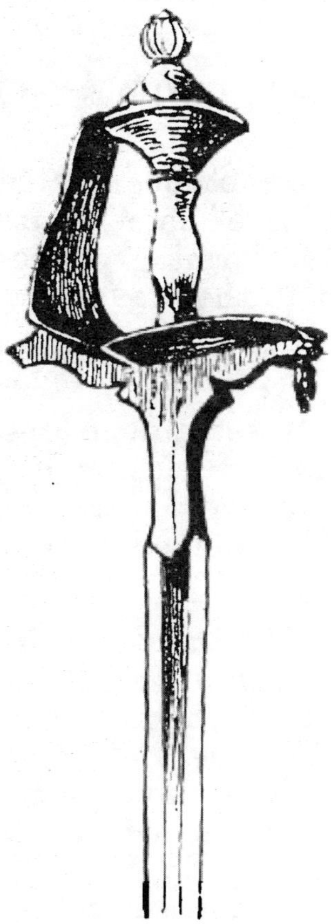

Fig. 11.—Sword with basket Hilt, and rapier blade. (E. Coll.).

Fig. 12.—Short Sword with Iron Hilt.

Steel.—The hilt and weapon in some cases are of one piece; the daggers in the Mahratta country, especially the Kaṭár, are of wrought and in South India of pierced steel like a basket (Cf Pl. VII.); their ornaments are chiselled in high relief.

Steel is inlaid with

a. Silver or gold leaf, the pattern sometimes being formed by the steel on gold ground or, as is more usual, the reverse.

b. Silver or gold wire.

Brass.—The handles of the Moplah knives, No. 119–122, are of engraved brass. This is sometimes, as in the South Indian knives, No. 100, inlaid with silver. The floral ornaments and the knobs of a two-handed sword in the E. Collection, are in brass applied in relief to the steel, and the gauntlet of another sword is in brass, with figures in relief.

Black Metal.—Inlaid with silver or white metal (Bidri ware). Sometimes, as in the case of a Mahomedan sword from Central India in the E. Collection, the flower pattern is in high relief in silver on black ground.

Silver. (*a.*) Engraved, for hilts of swords and Kaṭárs; sometimes the outline of the ornament is only pricked in, especially in Delhi work of this century.

(*b.*) As wire, bound round the hilts of weapons, as in the case of Cingalese, Burmese, Malay, and South Indian knives, and the chains and tassels hanging from the latter.

[1] Ain 37. Gladwin, and Blochmann, p. 113.

(*c.*) Chiselled in relief as in the scabbard of the Amír of Sind, and in the pierced work forming the buckles of sword belts. (E. Coll.).

(*d.*) Repoussé work, as in Kach, where the form to be decorated is filled with a kind of lacquer, and the pattern hammered on the surface.

Copper is used as a base for some enamels, and in Kach is repoussé and gilt.

Bronze.—The hilts of "paṭas" or gauntlet swords are sometimes plated with bronze, and then silvered; the handles of swords are also of fine bronze or plated with bronze; one in the E. Collection has two lions forming part of the hilt, the tails of which joining form part of the support to the blade.

Gold.—A state axe in the E. Collection is mounted with bands of pure gold on the wooden handle, and covering of the velvet sheath.

The scabbard mounts of the sword of a Rajput Rajah, with serrated edges, are of pure metal with repoussé flower patterns; the gold is soft and flexible, and would not stand much wear. The Malay and Sumatra knives are also richly plated with gold filigree work of extreme delicacy. The pierced mounts of fine gold on No. 331 are of the finest Nepalese work.

Enamel. The mounts of the finest swords, including sword belt and buckles in enamel, are manufactured at Delhi, Kotah, Jaipur, Partábgarh, in Sind, and in Persia. The hilts of Persian swords frequently terminate in the head of a dragon, a ram, or a tiger boldly incised in silver, inlaid with blue and green enamel. One[1] which belonged to Nadir Shah has green, yellow, and purple flowers and birds. The later and more florid Persian enamel is painted in gaudy colour on a white ground with copper base, and is frequently used for modern daggers. The Indian enamel most approaching the Persian is that of Sind, the ground of which is frequently blue with rich flowers. The Delhi and Jáipur enamels are generally red, with bright flowers and green leaves on a white ground. In the Windsor collection there is a sword with transparent green enamel mounts from Partábgarh.

Jewels.—Precious stones are valued for their effects in colour; hence emeralds, rubies, and diamonds are frequently inserted in enamel or jade so as to make floral patterns, the brilliancy of the enamel and the whiteness of the jade being used to set off their colours. A dagger in the British Museum which belonged to Mr. Henderson is inlaid with diamonds, rubies, and emeralds (Fig. 13, No. 1). In Her Majesty's Collection at Windsor the hilt of a sword presented by Lord Moira terminates in a parrot's head in white enamel on gold, jewelled with diamonds, holding a tassel composed of pearls and emeralds.

Jade, &c.—The handle and sheath mounts of daggers are frequently of white

[1] Now the property of Earl Amherst, whose father, the late Governor-General of India, received it as a present from the grandson of the man to whom Nadir Shah presented it, when he ordered the massacre of Delhi to cease.

or green jade inlaid with precious stones (Fig. 13, No. 1). The pommel of

No. 1. No. 2. No. 3.

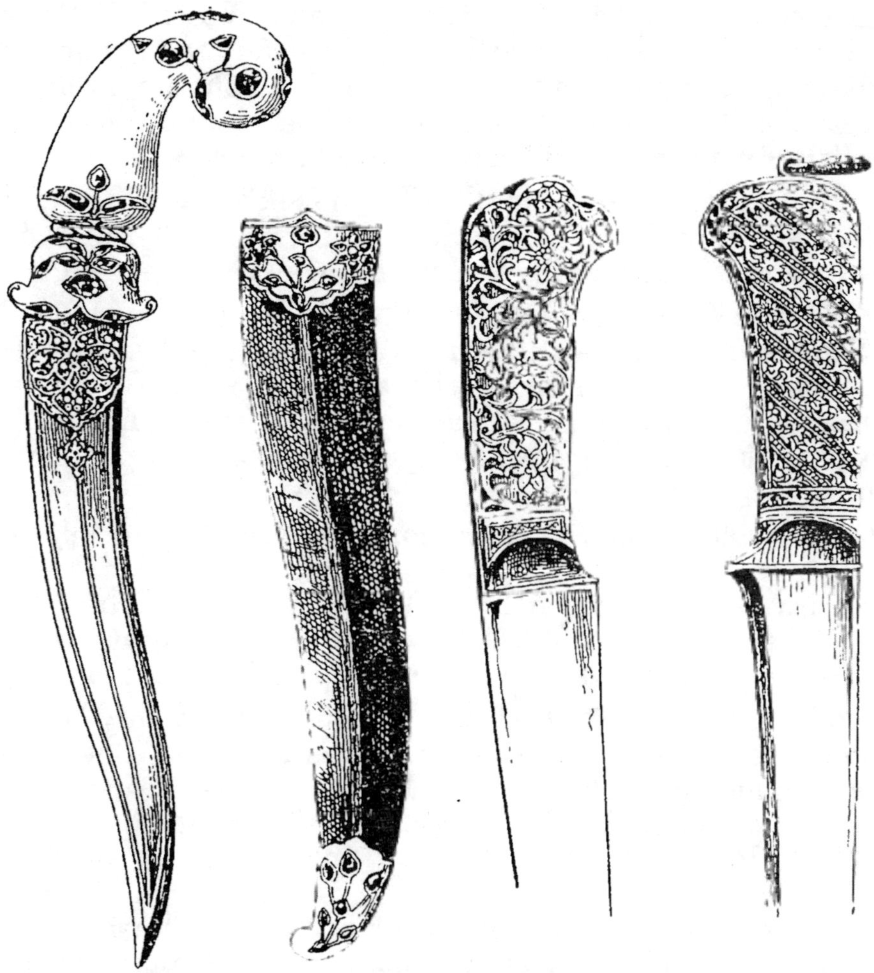

Fig. 13.—Daggers.
No. 1.—Jade Handle, Henderson Coll. (Brit. Mus.)
No. 2.—Ivory Handle, Hamilton Coll.
No. 3.—Ivory Handle, Henderson Coll. (Brit. Mus.)

the hilt is frequently either pistol-shaped, terminating in a horse's head, or is carved with the lotus flower. Jasper, walrus horn, ivory, both white and stained green, richly carved in Burmah, mother-of-pearl and horn are also used as hilts. Nos. 2 and 3 of Fig. 13, represent two carved ivory hilts from the Hamilton and Henderson Collections. Antelope horns tipped with steel are used in the hand shield (Mádú), gayal horns are used for priming flasks.

Glass.—The handles of daggers in Sind are frequently of white glass to imitate rock crystal or inlaid with green glass to replace emeralds (Nos. 719, 720). The Kach axes exhibited at Vienna were decorated with glass instead of jewels.

Wood.—The sheaths of South Indian daggers are sometimes of carved teak plated with silver and bronze. The Coorg knives are of ebony and silver. Bamboo is used for the handles and scabbards of swords in Burmah and Assam. The handles of Khond axes are of hard wood, bound with brass. The stocks of guns are lacquered and often painted with sporting scenes, nautch girls and animals coloured and gilt. In the Prince of Wales's Collection there is a gun with a stock of ebony inlaid with ivory carved in relief with rams, antelopes and goats butting at one another, tigers and elephants fighting, cranes and bustards. In the Windsor Collection there is a matchlock the stock of which is painted with gilt flowers and birds on a white ground.

Lac.—In an ancient Khánḍá in the E. Collection a pattern is chiselled in relief on the blade, and the interstices filled up with red lac, forming the background. Lac is also employed for colouring the lettering in the sacrificial axes and Koras of Nepal (Nos. 350–352).

Tortoise Shell.—The handle and scabbard of a Cingalese sword (formerly in Sir E. Tennents' possession, now in the author's) is richly carved, the handle with a grotesque dragon head overshadowing the seated figure of Buddha, and the scabbard with rich floral arabesque. A similar specimen is at South Kensington.

Papier Mâché.—This material is in common use in the Punjab, and in part of the Presidency of Bombay, for making shields, which are richly lacquered with the varnish obtained from Rhus Vernix, a shrub from which it exudes like gum.[1] The shield No. 448, from Bikanír, Rájpútáná, is an unique specimen of work with raised flowers gilt in the Japanese style.

Leather.—The leather sword straps in Sind are richly embroidered. A leather quiver from the Bhil country in the Amherst Collection is covered with coarse woollen embroidery. In Persia the scabbards are ornamented with embossed patterns on leather. That most prized is "shagreen."[2] It is made from the hide of a donkey's back, dyed green, and roughened by means a grain called "Castria," black, hard, and rather larger than mustard seed. In India rhinoceros, elephant, and sámbar hides are used for shields. In Kach the hides are boiled so as to make them transparent, and they are then gilt and painted, and in the Meyrick Collection there was a suit of armour made of rhinoceros hide, painted and covered with quotations from the Koran in gilt letters. In the Prince of Wales's Collection there is a suit of armour, presented by the Maharajah of Datiah, made entirely of the horny scales of the Indian pangolin (*Manis pentadactyla*), ornamented with gold, turquoises, and garnets encrusted on it.[3]

Velvet is used for covering the scabbard. One belonging to a Khándá in the E. Collection (Fig. 14), is red on one side and green on the other, and a rich floral pattern with border is embroidered on each in silver and gold thread respectively. The powder flasks and bullet cases are likewise embroidered in the same material. Velvet, padded and studded with brass nails called "Jazerant" work,[4] is sometimes used in combination with leather for armour, as in No. 573. Horse trappings are also frequently made of it. The umbrella taken from Bandula, now in Lord Amherst's possession, is a fine specimen of this work in geometrical patterns.

[1] See Digby Wyatt's "Industrial Arts," quoted by Lieutenant Cole.—"Cat.," South Kensington.

[2] Shagreen or Chagrin comes from the Persian "Saghrí" which means back.—"Chardin," Vol. III. p. 112. Voyages en Perse.

[3] "Hand book, Indian Court, 1878."—Dr. Birdwood.

[4] Archæo. Journal, XIV., 345.

Kincob.—The interior of hilts is lined with gold brocade. Shields also are lined with brocade or velvet embroidered with gold thread.

Herons Plumes "Kalghí."—The helmets of the Sikhs are ornamented with one or three plumes of black herons' feathers which are prized, one feather only being found in each wing. Their stems are bound with gold and silver-wire.

Peacock Feathers.—The peacock is the sacred bird of the god of war, and the Rajpoots frequently use its feathers to decorate their turbans.

The processes in decoration which are most deserving of notice are the following:—

1. *Koftgari.*—When it is proposed to ornament the blade or other part of a weapon in this manner, the blade is first "hatched" or cut across with sharp and deep lines where it is intended to place the pattern, which is then traced with a needle or wire. The pattern is engraved with a fine pointed tool called "cherma." All the tools are of the simplest kind, a punch, a nail and a hammer being all that is required. The gold is drawn into fine wire and wound on a bobbin. The native workman commences by taking one end of it, which is very soft, and fastening it to the roughened surface by a few blows with his hammer and punch; he rapidly follows out the pattern, and bends the wire backwards and forwards as often as may be required, hammering it into the surface all the time until completed. The article is then exposed to a moderate heat. When polished off with an agate rubber, "Mohari," and cleaned with lime juice, the gold stands above the surface, and is very durable.

The Koftgari work or modern imitation of the above is done more superficially with gold leaf, and does not stand in relief or last so long.

2. *Enamel.*—The art of enamelling dates from a very early period.[1] Dr. Birdwood[2] supposes it to have been an original Turanian art, but if it were it would have been preserved in Southern India, whilst it is now found in the north-west of India in the greatest perfection, into which it was probably introduced by the Mahomedans, as it was into China.[3] If the Chinese enamels recall Arabian art, the Indian may certainly claim Persia for its origin. There are different kinds of it, the ground generally being silver or gold and copper. The best enamels are found in Kashmir and in the North-west, at Delhi, Lahore, in Sind (see Pl. XIV., Nos. 721, 729), and in Jaipur. The Indian enamel is not however like the Chinese and Japanese "*cloisonné*," but "*champlevé*," and whereas the Chinese enamel is rarely pure white, the ground in that of Jaipur is generally of a dazzling white. A splendid example of this is the Ankus which was exhibited by the Maharajah of Jaipur at the Vienna Exhibition, 1873.[4] It is a matter of regret that the production of these beautiful enamels should be so restricted as it now is, all articles manufactured becoming the property of the State, which pays liberally for them. The art of enamelling in other parts of India has not attained the perfection reached at Jaipur, but occasionally beautiful specimens may be

[1] Enamelling on clay and even stone was extensively used by the Egyptians. Enamelled bricks have been found at Nimroud. "Nineveh," Layard, vol. ii, p. 312.

[2] "Handbook, Indian Section, Paris Exhibition," p. 57. Enamel on metal is probably not so ancient.

[3] "Industries Anciennes et Mòdernes de l'Empire Chinois," par Stanislas Julien, p. 250.

[4] Forbes Watson, "Cat. Vienna Exh.," p. 172.

found, as shown by the sheath of a Gorkha Kukri, enamelled with flowers in brilliant colours on a blue ground exhibited in the Windsor Collection.

The art of enamelling is, like all other handicraft work in India, handed down from father to son, and is the property of a certain caste who are traditionally supposed to be descended from some remote divine ancestor who invented the manufacture. The secret of the component parts of the Jaipur enamel is therefore confined to a few. The process of manufacture is by means of a furnace sunk into the ground about a foot and a half, with a passage below for air, and for supplying fuel, over it is placed a thin covering of clay in which are fine tubes for the draught, and under which small earthen vessels, holding the fixed glass, are placed, round which the flame issuing from the air tube plays. The colouring matter is added to the glass when fired, and when it is cool is ready for use. The best enamel is only put on pure gold. The pattern is first carved out, and the enamel previously ground into a fine powder it is made into a paste with water, and placed in the positions engraved for it. The article is then placed in the furnace until the enamel is fired, the hardest colours are first placed in the furnace and afterwards those which unite with greater facility. The work is completed when the surface is ground and polished. The colours are probably made by a combination of the various minerals. In the enamels produced at Partabghar in Bengal, delicately etched gold figures are inserted on a background of transparent green or blue enamel, while it is still in a fused state.

3. *Niello.*—This is practised principally in Persia, from which it has been introduced into Russia, where the process known as "Tula" work is borrowed from it. The handles of Persian swords and the mounts of the sheaths (Pl. XV., No. 755) are inlaid with fine arabesques of flowers and birds in black on a silver ground.

Fig. 14.—Gold embroidery on Velvet Sheath. (E. Coll.) See p. 68.

The method of working the Niello ornaments is as follows:—The object has a scroll or flower deeply engraved on it; into the design is poured a composition of silver, copper, and a small proportion of lead; the ornament is then heated in the fire, and rubbed over with borax, replaced in the fire for a short time, then withdrawn and left to cool. When cold it is burnished to a smooth and bright surface.

4. *Bidri.*—Bidri ware (so called from being made at Bider)[1] is used for the handles of weapons and shields in Central India. Its advantages are that it does not tarnish or rust. It is still more used for goblets and other utensils, and for hookahs.

Buchanan thus describes the manufacture:[2]—The grand component part of "the Bidri" is the metal called by the natives "jastá," a sort of pewter, or perhaps a tolerably pure zinc. The other ingredients are copper and lead.

In the experiment that I saw, the workman to 12,360 grains of jastá, put 460 grains of copper and 414 of lead. The greater part of the jastá was put into one earthen crucible; the lead, copper, and a small quantity of jastá were put

[1] A city about 60 miles N.W. of Hyderabad.
[2] Martin's "Eastern India, 1838."

into a smaller one, which was covered with a cap of kneaded clay, in which a small perforation was made. Both crucibles were coated inside and outside with cow-dung. A small pit was dug and filled with cakes of dry cow-dung, which were kindled, and when the fire had burned some time, the crucibles were put in and covered with fresh fuel. When the workmen judged that the metals were fused, he opened the fire, took up the small crucible and poured its contents into the layer, when the surface of the melted matter was covered with yellow scoriæ. He then, to prevent calcination, threw into the crucible a mixture of resin and beeswax, and having heated the alloy some little time, he poured it into a mould which was made of baked clay. The work is now delivered to men who complete the shape, by turning it in a lathe. It then goes to another set of workmen who are to inlay flowers or other ornaments in silver. These artists first rub the bidri with blue vitriol (sulphate of copper) and water, which gives its surface a black colour; but this is not fixed, and is removable by washing. It is intended as a means of enabling the workmen more readily to distinguish the figure that he traces; this he does with a sharp-pointed instrument of steel. Having traced the figure, he cuts it out with small chisels of various shapes, and then with a hammer and punch, fills the cavities with small plates of silver, which adhere firmly to the bidri. A final polish is given to the whole by rubbing it, first with cakes made of shell-lac and powdered corundum, and then with a piece of charcoal. When the polish has been completed, a permanent black stain is given by the following process:—

Take of		
	Sal ammoniac - - - -	1 part
	Unrefined nitre - - - -	$\frac{1}{4}$,,
	Saline earth - - -	$1\frac{1}{4}$,,

These are rubbed with a little water into a paste, with which the bidri is smeared. Then it is rubbed with a little rape-seed oil, and the latter with powdered charcoal; these are allowed to remain four days when they are washed away and the ware is found of a fine black colour not affected by water or subject to rust. It breaks with a violent blow, but is not brittle. The art has been introduced into the Deccan by Moguls from Western India.

II.—CATALOGUE OF THE ARMS IN THE INDIA MUSEUM,

WITH

NOTES ON THE DIFFERENT RACES AND TRIBES INHABITING INDIA AND THE ADJACENT COUNTRIES.

GROUP I.

ABORIGINAL AND NON-ARYAN TRIBES OF CENTRAL INDIA AND THE ANDAMAN ISLANDS.

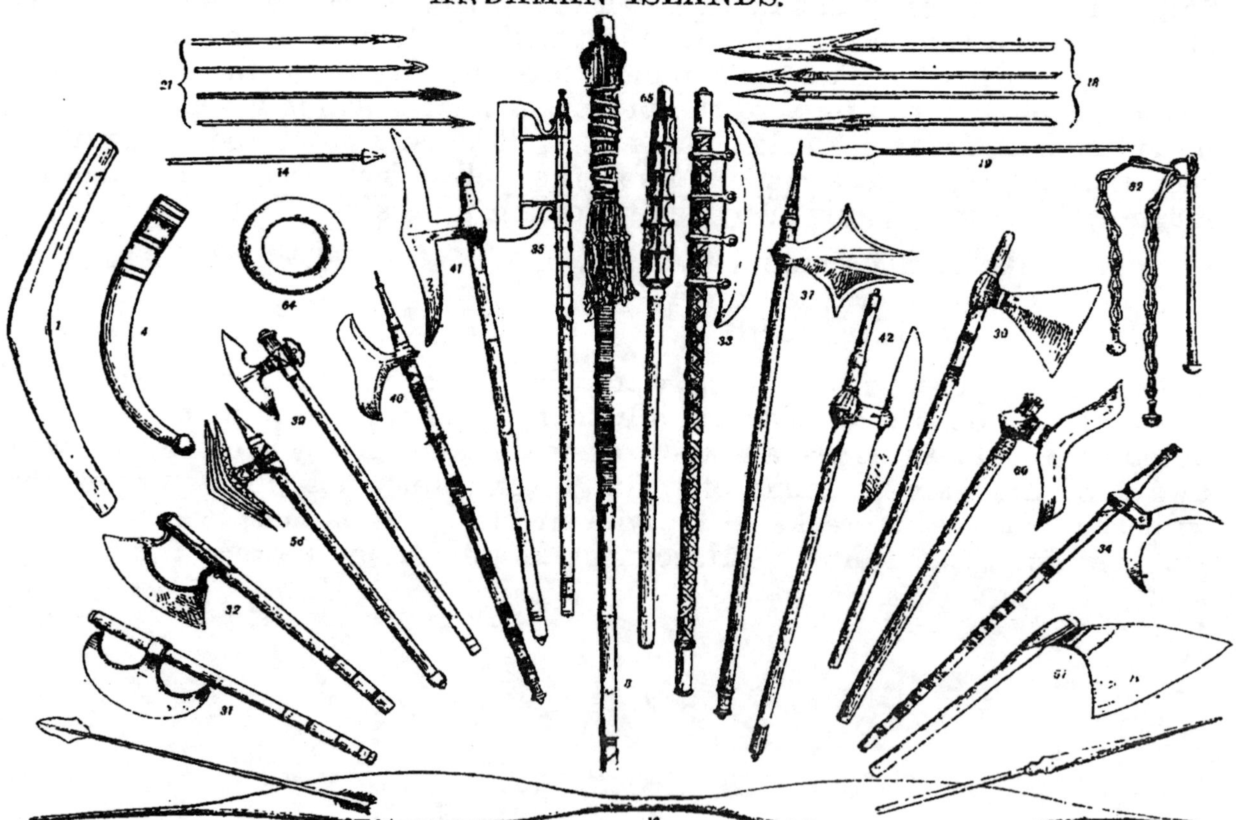

Fig. 15.—Arms of the non-Aryan and Aboriginal tribes of Central India and the Andaman Islands (Group I.).

In this group the earliest and rudest type of arms takes us back to the time when a negroid race was spread over the mainland and islands of India. Their arms can be traced on the walls of the tombs of the Kings at Thebes, and are now represented by the Bomerang, which is used by the Australian aborigines as well as by some of the hill tribes of India. But little change since that time has taken place in the habits of the natives of the Nicobar Island, whose only weapons are long sticks of a hard and knotty

wood, and a lance which they use for fishing.[1] The Bomerang is still or within the memory of man was used in Guzerat, and also in parts of Southern India, to kill hares and partridges.[2]

The only arms of the *Mincopie*, the aboriginal inhabitants of the Andaman Islands, are bows and arrows, and harpoons. The bows are of tough strong wood, about five or six feet in length. They bend them with the greatest ease, and discharge their volleys of arrows with great force, to about 40 yards distance; their arrows have formidable barbed points which inflict a very severe wound. The harpoon is used for fishing; it is provided with a moveable head with a long elastic cord attached to it, by which it may be held when fixed in its victim. Their other fishing arrows are made of smooth hard wood. Their boys at so early an age as three years have their miniature bows and arrows.[3]

Passing from the islands to the mainland, we come to the arms of the numerous aboriginal races. It is with the Non-Aryan races in Central India that we commence this series of arms, as they certainly are the descendants of that stock of Indian people which retreated before the Sanscrit-speaking people to the south, or took refuge in the fastnesses of the hills. They have been classified by different writers in various ways. Colonel Dalton divides the early races prior to the Aryan invasion into:—

1. The Kóls who entered from the N.E.;
2. The Dravidians, a Tamil-speaking people, who advanced to the far south, entering India by the Bolan pass;
3. The Scythians;

According to their legends the Aryans came from the north-west, and found dwellers in the forests and mountains, whom they called *Pulindas, Varvaras*, or *Mlech'has*,[4] *i.e.*, barbarians, "speaking a foreign language." Some of these tribes forming the low castes were doubtless even antecedent to the advent of the Dravidian races. Berghaus divides these primitive inhabitants of India into—

1. Bhils, Kóls, Korkus.
2. Todas of the Nilagiris.
3. Gonds, Khonds, Saurs.
4. Pahárís or Sontals.

I propose to divide them roughly into three groups of tribes, inhabiting respectively—

1. Central India, and Lower Bengal, and Andaman Islands. (Group I.)
2. Southern India. (Groups II. & III.)
3. Himalayan and North-East Frontier and Bootan. (Groups IV. & V.)

These aborigines are mostly found among the hills. "The Vindya and Sathpura range " of hills, which run in parallel lines north and south of the Nerbudda, appear to have " been the principal shelter and stronghold of the aboriginal inhabitants of Central " India."[5]

The most eastern of these hills were tenanted by the Kols, Khonds, and Gonds. They are scantily clothed, and armed chiefly with bows and arrows, large knives, and occasionally matchlocks.

The *Khonds* are found on the borders of Cuttack and Ganjam. The *Gonds* are more widely extended, and spread from the western and southern boundaries of Behar to those of Bandalkhand and Berar; the *Bhils* inhabit chiefly the rugged country between the Tapti and Nerbudda spreading both south of the former and north of the latter. These races, together with those about to be mentioned, form "a dense substratum among " the population of the plains, and are the sole inhabitants of mountainous or forest " regions"[6] over the whole of India.

The Bhils were one of the first of the aboriginal tribes to be brought under English rule in 1818. They had long taken advantage of the disorder consequent on the Mahratta war to plunder the neighbouring districts, and when Trimbukjee took refuge among them,

[1] Lieut. Colebrooke, Asiatic Researches.
[2] Wild Men and Wild Beasts, Colonel Gordon Cumming.
[3] Mouatt, Andaman Islands, p. 321. Flint lancets are still made by the Andamanese. V. Ball, Jungle Life, p. 211.
[4] Berghaus' Ethnological Atlas, 1852.
[5] Mill, History of India, viii. p. 373.
[6] Hunter, Annals of Rural Bengal.

Sir J. Malcolm was sent to reduce them to submission, and to train them in more peaceful habits. He accomplished this by confirming their chiefs in the possession of their lands, and by encouraging them to enlist in a militia or police for the preservation of order. The East India Company afterwards enrolled several corps of Bhils in their armies with excellent effect.

The principal weapon of the Bhils was the "kamptí" or bamboo bow of which the the bow string "challa," consisted of a thin strip of the elastic bark of the bamboo. Their quiver contains 60 barbed arrows each a yard long;[1] those intended for striking fish have the barbed head so contrived as to slip off from the shaft when the fish is struck, and to remain connected with it by a long line, so that the shaft remains as a float on the water.

The Khonds, whose arms are well represented in this group, are still one of the most numerous of the wild primitive tribes of India. "From their earliest years," writes Captain Macpherson,[2] "they are trained to the profession of arms. Their weapons "consist of the sling and the bow and arrow, in the use of which they are peculiarly "dexterous; also of an axe with a blade very curiously curved and a light long handle "strengthened by brass plate and wire. No shields are used. They adorn themselves for "battle as for a feast. They carefully trim their hair, plaiting it in a flat circle on the "right side of the head, where it is fastened with an iron pin, and adorned with peacock's "feathers or cocks' tails plumes, and bound with a thread of scarlet cloth. From the neck "to the loins the combatants are often protected by skins of bears or elks, cloth being "wound round their legs to the heel, but their arms are quite bare. Sometimes champions "from either side perform war dances till they are sufficiently excited to come to blows. "They advance with blowing of horns and beating of gongs. They often commence "with slinging showers of stones handed by the women. When they approach nearer, "arrows are thrown in flights. At length single combats spring up betwixt individuals, "and when the first man falls, all rush to dip their axes in his blood, and hack "his body to pieces. A general melée ensues which is rarely attended with great loss "of life, and at night the opposing tribes draw off only to recommence the fight next "day."

The Khond of the hills of Orissa,[3] is described by General Campbell as carrying usually a long staff, and when armed he wears a turban ornamented with a showy crest of feathers, and a strong cloth encircling his loins, and carries a bow and arrow, and a battleaxe with a broad two-edged blade. He marches to battle singing, shouting, and brandishing his battleaxe, most commonly under the influence of strong drink. They use their formidable axes against the large game in their forests, and frequently attack the bear single-handed. The matchlock and shield are the favourite weapons of the Oorya chiefs, and of those inhabiting the southern districts.

The Khonds, till the suppression of the "Meriah" rites by General Campbell, used to offer up human sacrifices to their Gods. "In Boad, the intended victim was dragged to the "place of sacrifice, and his head and neck introduced into the cleft of a strong bamboo "split in two, the ends of which were secured and held by the sacrificers. The presiding "priest then advanced, and with an axe broke the joints of the legs and arms, after "which the rest stripped the flesh off the bones with their knives, and each man having "secured a piece buried it in the fields."

At Chinna Kimedy they used to sacrifice to an elephant rudely carved in wood, fixed on the top of a stout post, which was made to revolve. The intended victim was fastened to the proboscis of the elephant, and amidst the shouts of the multitude was rapidly wheeled round, when at a given signal by the "zani," or priest, the crowd rushed in, and with their knives cut the flesh off the shrieking wretch as long as life remained.

In Jaipur "the blood-red God of Battle," "Mániksúru," was the deity whom they sought to propitiate by human victims. On the eve of a battle, or when a new fort

[1] Colonel Tod, Rajpoot Tribes.

[2] Report upon the Khonds of Ganjam and Cuttack.

[3] Campbell, Khondistan, 1864.

was to be built, or danger of any kind was to be averted, recourse was had to this sacrifice.

The early history of the *Gonds* is obscure, till the year 1564, when they were reduced by one of Akbar's lieutenants. "The Gond troops, led by the heroic Dúrgáwati, the "Rajput widow of the last chief, made a noble resistance near Jubbulpore."[1] They were not known much to us till 1818, when the Sagur and Nerbudda territories came into the possession of the English. It was, however, some time before the human sacrifices, which were prevalent among them, were put down by the influence of our rule.

In 1828, the Rajah of Bustar, a Gond, sacrificed 20 men to Devi. The hideous rite is thus described:—The unhappy victims were congregated together and kept without food for three days. On the fourth and last of their existence on earth they were shaved all over, then bathed and rubbed with oil, after which they were led out to the image of Devi, which they were made to worship. After this performance had been gone through, they were conducted to a neem tree, close by which they were sacrificed. The Gond "Pújárí" or priest, cut off their heads with the knife taken from the temple of Devi.

In Gondwana there are numerous chiefs who claim a pure or mixed descent from Rajput houses. This immigration of Rajput clans, retreating before the Mahomedan invasions, probably took place in the 14th and 15th centuries. The Gonds and Bhils have intermarried with the Rajputs, whence arose the Raj-Gonds, a mixture of Rajpút and Gond blood, and the Bhilalas, a cross between the Rajpúts and Bhils.[2]

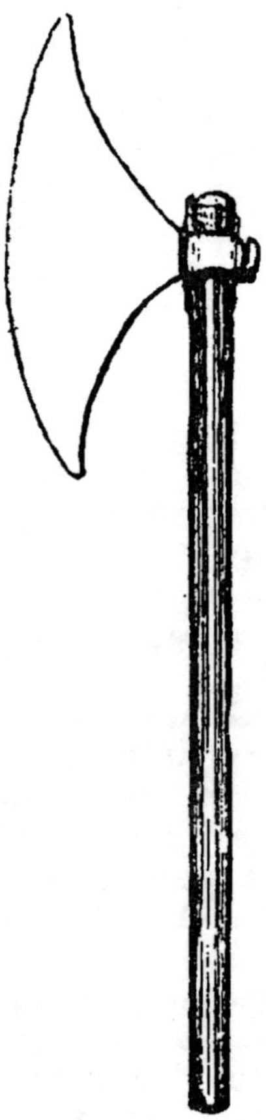

Fig. 16.—Kol Axe (E. Coll.).

The Korkus belong to the Kolarian tribes. The Thakur of Pachmarhi, a Korku with Rájpút blood, had four or five retainers, relates Forsyth,[3] "in quilted garments of many hues, and girded as to their "loins with broad embroidered belts of Sambur leather, in which were "stuck swords, daggers, and the cumbrous appointments of a match-"lock-man, the matchlock itself being borne with smoking match "over the shoulder of each."

The Korku has no implement of agriculture, but his axe.

The *Baigás* in the Pachmarhí hills use a hatchet which they throw with great skill at deer, and even at tigers. They always carry it in their hand. (Mr. C. Grant, B. C. S.)

The following races not represented in this collection are worthy of mention, as they are an important part of the aboriginal inhabitants of Bengal and Rajpootana:—Juangs, Khamas, Mundas, Kols, Bhumij, &c.

The Juangs are found in Cuttack, and claim to be autochthones in Keonghur. They live in a hill country, where prehistoric stone implements are found. They had no knowledge whatever of metals until foreigners came among them. They have no iron smiths or smelters of iron, and no word in their own language for iron or other metals. They use bows and slings of cord, and rough stones.[4]

The Kharrias in Singbhum are very similar in character and habits.

The Bhúmij occupy the Manbhum and Singbhum districts.

The Múndas and Kols in Chota Nagpore when they rose in insurrection in 1831 sent an arrow from village to village to rouse the inhabitants to arms. The Kols are not represented in this Collection. They use a short axe (Fig. 16.) and a bow.

[1] Forsyth's Highlands of Central India, p. 78.
[2] Ibid., p. 134.
[3] Highlands of Central India, p. 94.
[4] Dalton.

The Hos or Larka Kols are fair marksmen with the bow and arrow. They use a "tangi," or battle-axe, both as a weapon and an agricultural implement. They understand the smelting of iron.

The Bhuiyas,[1] found in Bágalpur and Behar, are according to Dalton of a Dravidian race. In Katak they dwell in the hills. Some of them hold their lands on conditions of military service; others merely attend on their Raja, but are not bound to fight for him, and even occasionally take up arms against him.

One of their customs is worthy of mention:—"At the installation of a Raja a very "rusty old sword is placed in the Raja's hands, and one of the Bhuiyas comes before "him, and, kneeling sideways, the Raja touches him on the neck with the weapon, as if "about to strike off his head;" and it is said that in former days this was in fact done, as their lands were held on the condition that the victim when required should be produced.

There is in the Tayler Collection (S. K. Museum) a spear used by the Ghatwáls of the Gháts (Behar). The head is bifurcated, formed of two steel points spirally twisted fixed in a brass socket. The shaft is of bamboo, and the brass shoe is square-headed. This is an ornamental weapon.

The Korwas[2] of Barwah are formidable as bowmen; their barbed arrow heads are 9 inches long and 1½ in breadth. These they make themselves of the iron smelted in their own hills. They use the battle-axe very adroitly.

The Sontals inhabit the Rajmahal hills, and were only brought into notice in 1852. Hunter, in his "Annals of Rural Bengal"[3] says;—"The Sontal never stirs without his "bow and arrows. The bow consists of a strong mountain bamboo, which no Hindoo "lowlander can bend. His arrows are of two kinds, heavy sharp ones for the "larger game, and light ones with a broad knob at the point for small birds. If he "goes after a tiger or leopard, he takes a long barrelled matchlock, loaded with a charge "of coarse slow burning powder, and rammed down with pebbles and scraps of iron."

They use a circular shield, about 12 inches in diameter, with five bosses; on one side is a rude hook on the other a spike. (*See* Tayler Collection, South Kensington Museum.)

Lieut. Shaw describes the following curious customs among the nations of the hills S.W. of Rajmahal:-

"When they wish to administer an oath, they proceed in this way. The one who administers the oath puts a little salt on the blade of a 'Tulwar,' and says: 'If you 'decide contrary to your judgment and falsely, may this sword be your death.' The person swearing applies this to himself, and the part of the blade where the salt is, is held above his mouth which he opens, and swallows the salt mixed with water. Another form is to repeat the oath, putting the hand on two arrows fixed transversely in the ground, at about a cubit's distance, with some salt between them. On some occasions, a man swearing, repeats the oath with his hand on a sword, and all these forms are considered equally binding. They barter their produce of bamboos, cotton, &c., for the products of the plain, such as iron heads for arrows, hatchets, and other iron implements."[4]

The intermixture of races, which makes it impossible to define strictly the limits of any race, is illustrated in Rajputana. In that province and in Kattywar where the ruling race is Aryan and of Rajput blood, there are still the following descendants of the non-Aryan race as noted by Tod:—

"*The Khattries,* supposed to be the ancient Cathei of Scythian race who opposed "Alexander in the Punjab, and thence migrated to their present locality.

"*The Kolis* in Guzerat, a manly, well-armed people, and great robbers."

"*The Mairs* inhabiting the Mairwarra or 'the region of hills,' occupy that portion of "the Aravalli chain lying between Comulmere and Ajmere, about 90 miles long and 6 to "20 broad. They are a branch of the Meenahs, one of the aboriginal tribes. They were "driven by the Rajpoots to the hills, and are now under the Rana of Mewar."[5]

---

[1] Dalton, pp. 190–194. [2] Ibid., pp. 228–229. [3] Hunter, p. 211.
[4] Asiatic Researches, Vol. ii. p. 639. [5] Annals of Rajasthan, Vol. i. p. 686.

1–3. Bomerangs; "Katariya." Used by the Koles of Guzerat for throwing at hares, wild boars, and other animals. *Guzerat.* L. on the outer curve from 2 ft. 6 in. to 3 ft. (Fig. 15, No. 1.) (9136.–'55.)

These bomerangs conform to the natural curvature of the wood like the Australian bomerang, which they resemble in form.—*Col. Lane Fox*, Cat. Anthropological Collection, p. 35.

4, 5. Bomerangs; wood, with engraved brass and steel mounts. *Guzerat.* L. 22 in. (Fig. 15, No. 4.) (9137.–'55.)

6, 7. Bomerangs; wood, with brass and iron mounts. Presented by Claude Russell, Esq. *Guzerat.* L. of curve, 22 in. (9137.–'55.)

8. Club; "Lohángi Káti." Bamboo shaft, iron-bound with mace head. Shaft decorated with strips of quill and a fringe of cowries. *Indore.* L. 4 ft. 4 in. (Fig. 15, No. 8.) (12687.–'71.)

9. Club; "Lobángi Káti." Bamboo shaft, iron-bound with mace head. Used by village watchmen and Ramosees. *Satara.* L. 4 ft. 6 in. (12703.–'55.)

10–13. Bows of bamboo and hard wood, the strings composed of strips of bark. *The Andaman Islands.* L. 4 ft. 4 in. to 6 ft. 2 in. (Fig. 15, No. 10.) (11546.–'57.)

The long bow is the aboriginal weapon of India. The composite or horseman's bow was introduced from Persia and Tartary.

14. Arrows; small, flat, triangular blades. *The Andaman Islands.* Presented by Sir J. Malcolm. (Fig. 15, No. 14.) (9143.)

15. Bow and Arrows; bamboo. *Ganjam.* L. of bow, 5 ft. 2 in.; L. of arrows, 2 ft. to 2 ft. 7 in. (7347.–'67.)

16, 17. Bows; bamboo; one for arrows, the other for stones or pellets of clay. *Vizianagram.* L. 4 ft. 10 in.

18. Arrows; "Tir." Broad fluted and barbed blades. *Chota Nagpur.* L. 2 ft. 6 in. to 3 ft.; Bl. 4 to 8 in. (Fig. 15, No. 18.) (7876.–'70.)

19. Bow and Arrows; bamboo. *Indore.* L. of bow, 5 ft. 3 in. Arrows, 26 to 28 in. (Fig. 15, No. 19.) (7346.–'67.)

20. Bow and Arrows; bamboo. Arrows with long flat points. *Gwalior.* L. of bow, 4 ft. 10 in. Arrows, 2 ft. 2 in. to 2 ft. 6 in. (12700.–'55.)

21. Arrows; barbed heads resembling fish-hooks. Bamboo shafts, unfeathered. Hill tribes. L. 28 to 30 in.

22. Arrows; the points of various shapes. *Khandesh.* L. 2 ft. 8 in. to 3 ft. (12670.–55.)

23, 24. Spears; Ornamented with tufts of hair. Silver mounts. *Vizianagram.* L. 7 ft. 8 in.; Bl. 24 in. (Fig. 17, No. 23.) (8854.–'55.)

25. Spear. Broad flat blade. *Vizianagram.* Fig. 17. No. 25.)

26. Spear Heads; fine steel. *Vizianagram.* L. of blade, 23 in.; W 2¼ in. (Fig. 17, No. 26.) (7350.–'55.)

27, 28. Spears; "Ballam." Barbed heads; wooden shafts. *Vizianagram.* L. 5 ft. 11 in.; L. of blade, 18 in. (Fig. 17, Nos. 27, 28.) (8837.–'55.)

29. Spear; "Pandí Ballam;" (a hog-spear), leaf-shaped blade, with a sheath of purple velvet, bamboo shaft. *Vizianagram.* L. 8 ft. 3 in.; blade, 2 ft., W. 3 in. (8830.–'55.)

30. Battle-axe; "Tabar;" triangular blade. *Chota Nagpur.* L. 2 ft. 8½ in.; Bl. 7 in. by 6. in. (Fig. 15, No. 30.) (8755.–'55.)

In Hindi, "Tonngya;" in Gond, "Pharetri."—*Forsyth*, Highlands of Central India.
Used by the Khonds; (the Kols use a somewhat similar axe for agricultural or other purposes.) Cf. Fig. 16.

31, 32. Battle-axes; "Tabar;" broad curved blade. *Chota Nagpur.* L. 20 in.; Bl. 7 in. by 9 in. (Fig. 15, Nos. 31, 32.) (8819.)

33. Battle-axe; "Tabar;" long curved blade. Iron-bound shaft. *Chota Nagpur.* L. 3 ft. 6 in.; Bl. 15 in. (Fig. 15, No. 33.) (8747.)

34. Battle-axe; "Tabar;" crescent-shaped blade. *Chota Nagpur.* (Fig. 15, No. 34.) (8789.)

35, 36. Battle-axes; "Tabar;" hoe-shaped heads. *Chota Nagpur.* L. 3 ft. L. of blade 10 in. (Fig. 15, No. 35.) (8756, 9145.–'55.)

37, 38. Battle-axes; "Tabar;" forked blades, pointed ferrules, brass mounts. *Chota Nagpur.* (Fig. 15. No. 37.) (12603.–'69.)

39–55. Battle-axes; various shaped blades. *Chota Nagpur.* L. 2 ft. 2 in. to 3 ft. (Fig. 15, Nos. 39, 42.) (7880–1, 8749, 8752–4, 8757, 8789, 9146–'55.)

56. Battle-axe; "Tabar;" grooved blade with forked ends. *Cuttack.* L. 2 ft., Bl. 9 in. (Fig. 15, No. 56.) (8758.–'55.)

57, 58. Battle-axes; broad blades. *Ganjam.* L. 16 in. and 17 in., Bl. 10 in. by 7 in. (Fig. 15, No. 57.) (9144.–'55, 12619.–'69.)

59. Axe-heads; "Chatá Katú;" plain steel, with red leather sheaths. Used both for fighting and for domestic purposes. *Vizianagram.* L. 12 in., W. 2⅓ in. (7351.–'67.)

60. Chopper; "Cha Katti (?);" undulating blade of polished steel; long wooden handle. *Vizianagram.* L. 2 ft. 2 in., L. of bl. 14 in. (Fig. 17, No. 60.) (8451.–'55.)

61. Chopper; "Congavellum;" (Kongavál), curved blade, long wooden handle, with brass mounts. *Vizianagram.* L. 24 in., L. of blade, 8 in. (Fig. 17, No. 61.) (8450.–'55.)

62. Iron Chain Flail, with balls. *Vizianagram.* L. of handle, 15 in.; chains, 19 in. (Fig. 15, No. 62.) (8453.–'55.)

One in the E. Collection was used at the siege of Delhi in the mutiny.

63T. Quoit Flail; "Cumber Jung (?)." Composed of two weighted steel quoits suspended by brass chains from the ends of a wooden shaft, about 18 inches in length. *Guzerat.* (Additional Collection, 356.)

64. Quoits; "Chakar." Steel. Diam. 6 in. (Fig. 15, No. 64.) (8765.–'55.)

GROUPS II. & III.

ABORIGINAL AND DRAVIDIAN RACES OF SOUTHERN INDIA.

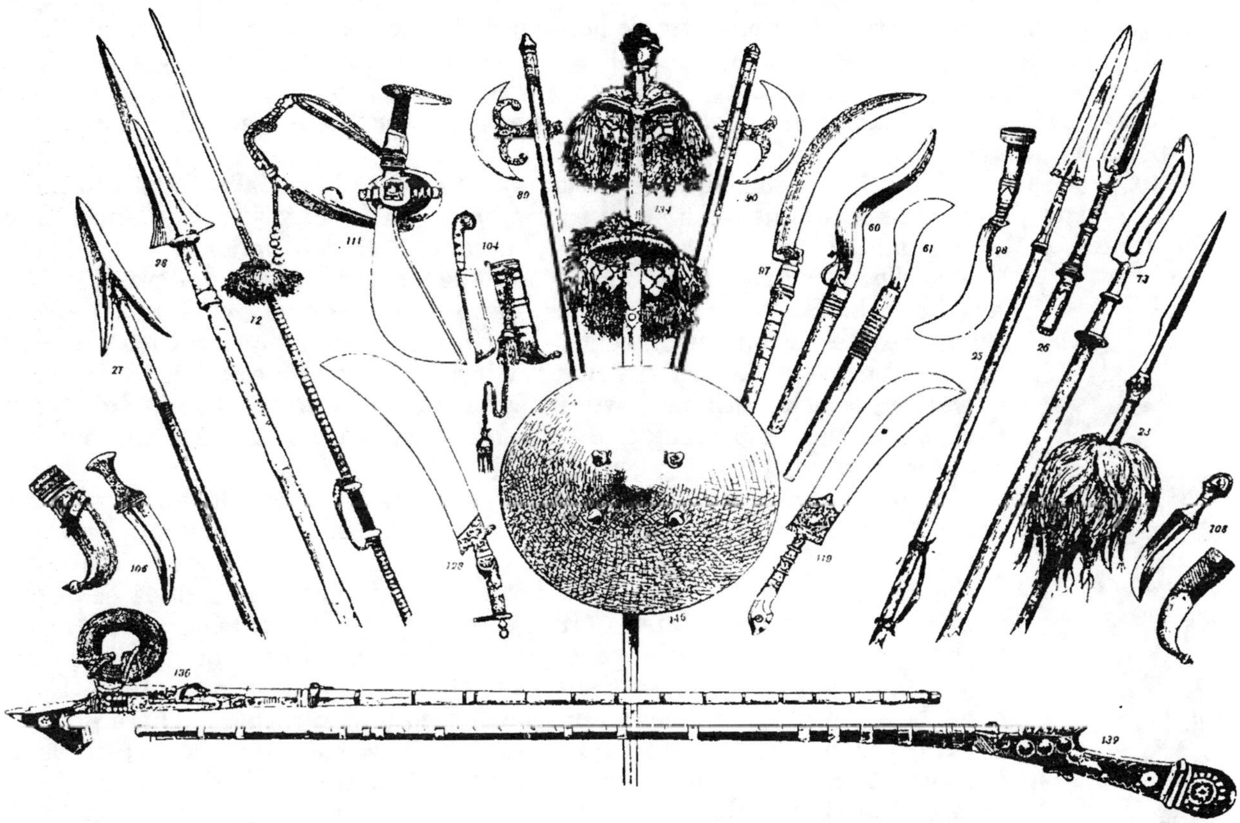

Fig. 17.—Arms of the Aboriginal and Dravidian races of Southern India (Groups II. and III.)

The second and third groups comprise the arms of those portions of the non-Aryan races which have pushed the furthest into the south of India, and whose national characteristics have been somewhat modified by contact with Brahmanical and aboriginal races; they comprise about 46 millions, of whom some have attained a superior state of civilization. They consist generally of the Dravidian races or those peoples speaking the Kanarese, Telugu, Tamil, and Malayalam languages.[1]

The most characteristic weapons in this class are the swords worn by the Nairs, the Moplah knives, and those from Coorg and Mysore.

"The *Coorgs* are active in athletic sports, capital mountaineers. They wear a blue surtout, reaching down half-way between the knee and the ankle, and midway on the arms, which is folded to the left. A handsome red scarf confines the waist, and in this is stuck a short dagger, of which the hilt and a portion of the sheath are covered with silver, a silver chain being also attached to it; on the head is a thick white turban. When passing through the woods, the Coorg carries on his back a strong wood knife, double the size of his dagger, the handle being stuck in his girdle, while the broad blade lies naked on his back. In most of the farms guns, bows, and arrows are hung up. Many proprietors can turn out 20 fighting men at least."[2]

---

[1] They probably came from Babylonia and entered India by Belochistan, where they left their traces in the Brahûi language.—Ferguson, "Hist. of Indian Architecture," p. 11. Robert Cust, "Languages of the East Indies," p. 11.

[2] Bowring, Eastern Experiences, p. 255.

Elliot[1] describes the neighbouring farmers of Munzerabad, in Mysore, as clad in a single black blanket, "so disposed as to present the appearance of a kilt at the knee, and girded "round the waist by a belt with an iron catch at the back, into which is hitched the "large hacking-knife." They also use matchlocks and spears.

The knife or bill-hook referred to in these extracts, has evidently been designed for the convenience of cutting through thick underwood, such as is found in the jungles of Mysore and Coorg whose "bamboo brakes are as intricate as the woolly curls of an Abyssinian."[2] A somewhat similar knife or sword is used by the Moplahs, who are Arabs, settled on the Malabar coast.[3] The messenger sword of Ashantee is of a similar shape, though larger.[4]

The first Samorin or ruler of the Malabar coast was converted to Mahomedanism in the ninth century, and since that time all his successors have used that title, and encouraged the spread of Mahomedanism and the settlement of Arabs in that kingdom.[5]

Fig. 18.—Southern Indian Sword (E. Coll.).

The *Nairs* or Hindoos on the Malabar coast are no longer a martial ace, but the Rajah of Travancore maintains an army of Nairs 1,400 in number with European officers.[6] A Nair of former days is thus described by Duncan:[7]—"He walks along with his naked sword held up as a "walking stick; others have it fastened to their back, the hilt being "stuck in the waistband, and the blade rising up and glittering between "their shoulders."

One of the earliest accounts of the Nairs is from Barbosa, who thus speaks of them[8]:—"The Nairs of Malabar are of noble descent, and have "to be armed as knights by the hand of the King or lord with whom "they live, and until they have been so equipped they cannot bear arms "or call themselves 'Nairs.' In general they are sent to school when "they are seven years of age to learn all manner of feats of agility and "gymnastics for the use of their weapons. They are then taught the use "of bows, clubs, or lances, and the sword and buckler. There are very "skilful men who teach this art, and they are called Panicars: these are "captains in war. They are taken as guards to the King or some other "lord, and their obligation constrains them to die at the hands of any who "should kill the King or their lord; so that if in any battle their lord "should be killed, they go and put themselves in the midst of their "enemies who killed him, but before falling he does what he can against "them, and after that one is dead another goes to take his place, and "then another, so that sometimes 10 or 12 Nairs die for their lord."

Gaspar Correa,[9] who went to India in the year 1514, gives the following account of a Nair at Calicut:—"A servant of the King, a gentleman of "birth whom they call Nair, came on board; . . . he had a very thin round "shield with slings of wood and vermilion, which glittered very much; "and a naked sword with an iron hilt; the sword was short, 27 inches "long (a Flemish ell), and broad at the point.

When Vasco di Gama had an audience of the Samorin of Calicut, "there were a great number of Moors with swords and shields after the "fashion of the Nairs. . . . Close to the King stood a boy, his page; . . . "he held a red shield with a border of gold and jewels, and a boss in the "centre of a span's breadth of the same materials, and the rings inside for "the arm were of gold; also a short drawn sword of an ell's length, round "at the point, with a hilt of gold and jewellery with pendant pearls."[10]

This description exactly corresponds with a sword which, formerly in the Meyrick is now in the Egerton Collection. (Fig. 18.) It is 27 inches

[1] Experiences of a Planter in the Jungles of Mysore.
[2] Mir Hussein, Life of Tippoo.
[3] Lassen, Indische Alterthumskunde, vol. 4, p. 225.
[4] Archæological Journal.
[5] Wilks.—Historical Sketch of S. India, vol. 1., p. 470.
[6] Rev. S. Mater, 1871.
[7] Asiatic Researches, Vol. II., p. 802.
[8] Hakluyt, Barbosa, pp. 128–129.
[9] Lendas da India, Hakluyt Society's Trans. p. 151.
[10] Id. pp. 193, 194.

in length, the blade curved with the cutting edge inwards and terminating in a double edge; attached to the pommel are two rings of twisted steel, which are mentioned by the early writers as peculiar to these swords.[1]

The *Todas*, an aboriginal race of Scythic descent, are found in the Nilagiris. They do not carry arms, except a pointed club, which they carry in their burial feasts; but lead a pastoral life.[2]

Besides these races there are others of mixed descent of whom the *Chenchwas*, a rude race of the Eastern Ghauts, are a type. They are probably a cross between the Telugu-speaking people and the aborigines of the Malay Peninsula. They are thus described:—"The elders are distinguished usually by being armed with a spear, a " hatchet, or a matchlock, while their less fortunate brethren are obliged to content " themselves with a rude bamboo bow and arrows of reeds tipped with iron. They " are not remarkably expert as archers, judging from the awkwardness they exhibit " in despatching a sheep picketed for them at 40 yards."[3]

In this class are also included the arms of Travancore and Ceylon, whose grotesque carvings, whether in gold, silver, or tortoise-shell, in their general outline recall the architecture of the temples for which Southern India is famous.

The Cingalese swords are, as becomes an effeminate and diminutive race, like children's weapons. Their tortoise-shell hilts and scabbards are finished with the greatest delicacy; the carving almost invariably represents the snake worship in the form of a dragon head overtowering the placid figure of Buddha sitting in contemplation below. The stocks of their guns are richly carved (*vide* Catalogue of Z. S. collection, Vol. III., plate 3). The daggers are small knives with carved wooden handles incrusted with silver filigree work inlaid with patterns in brass. The sheath is usually of teak covered with thin plates of silver and brass.

The *Veddahs* or aboriginal race of Ceylon are not represented in this Collection. They have a rude bow, which they use with effect against the wild elephants.

NOTE.—*A few of the more ornamental arms belonging to this Group will be found in Cases* 70 *and* 71 *(the latter fire-arms), and are distinguished in the Catalogue by an asterisk.**

65. CUDGELS OR STICKS; used by robbers. Plain and iron-bound; some terminating in iron mace-heads with projecting serrated edges. *Tinnevelli.* L. 3 ft. to 5 ft. 11 in. (Fig. 15, No. 65.) (12707.–'55.)

Cf. photographs of arms found in barrows and cairns of the Nilagiris, published in Breck's Nilagiri Tribes. They resemble many of the arms in this group.

66, 67. BOMERANGS; ivory. *Southern India.* L. of curve, 24 in. (12562.–'69.)

68. BOMERANGS; "Kaṭarí;" of wood. Roughly ornamented ends. *Madura.* L. of curve, 23 to 24 in. (9138–40.–'55.)

69. BOMERANG. "Kaṭarí;" of wood. Used by robbers. *Tinnevelli.* L. of curve, 23 in. (9139.–'55.)

70. BOMERANGS (2); "Singa;" steel. *Southern India.* L. of curve, 18 to 20 in. W. 2½ in. to 3 in. (9141.–'55.)

71. SLINGS; hempen. For hurling pellets of clay or stones. *Tinnevelli.* (12682.–'55.)

72. SPEAR; "Sangu"; ringed shaft of steel; long slender triangular head, with tuft of crimson silk. *Vizianagram.* L. 7 ft. 11 in.; L. of bl. 2 ft. 6 in. (Fig. 17, No. 72.) (8835.)

73. SPEAR; flamboyant blade. Rough wooden shaft. *Tinnevelli.* L. 7 ft. 4 in.; Bl. 16 in. (Fig. 17, No. 73.) (12750.–55.)

74–77. SPEARS; variously shaped heads, finely engraved brass mounts; shafts lacquered and painted in red, yellow, and black. *Malabar.* L. 8 ft. to 8 ft. 4 in.; Bl. 10 in. (8839.–'55.)

78, 79. SPEARS; painted wood shafts. *Malabar.* L. 10 ft., L. of blade 18 in. (12,506.–'69.)

80. BOW; wood, very broad. Painted and lacquered with representations of the incarnations of Vishnu. Presented by the Rajah of *Travancore.* L. 3 ft. 11 in., W. 5¼ in. (7335.–'55.)

In early ages the bow was the principal weapon, and was described by the poets to have had a divine origin. It bore different names, according to the material of which it was composed, either of deer's horn, or of seven joints of the bamboo, or of ivory.

The bow was 3½ or 4 cubits (5¼ to 6 feet) in length, and the two ends were of the same thickness. Some were painted at the back; others had small bells or flags or yak's tails fastened to them; others again were set with jewels.

The bow-strings were made of various materials such as nerve (tendon), the bark of trees, silk, and gold thread. Two or three strings were usually carried attached to the bow, in case one should break.

The arrows, about 2 cubits (3 feet) in length, were made of reeds pointed with iron;[1] the shafts were painted with different ornaments and mounted with the feathers of the crane, osprey, and other birds. The points of some were of a half moon shape. Others were headed with hollow brass balls perforated with three or four holes, which were to be filled with some inflammable composition, and shot burning on to roofs and into houses.[2]

[1] When tipped with iron, they are called "tir;" with hard wooden points "bitla." [2] Ward, vol., I. p. 570.

---

[1] This ancient form of sword recalls the Greek κοπὶς of which Quintus Curtius says, "Copidas vocant gladio " leviter curvatos falcibus similes," quoted by Col. Lane Fox.—Cat. Anthropological Collection, p. 174.

[2] Harkness, 1832. Breek's Aboriginal Tribes of Nilagiris. [3] Journal Asiatic, Soc., Vol. vii. p. 273.

81. Bow; painted and lacquered in red and yellow. *Travancore.* L. 5 ft. 6 in. (12560–'69.)

82. Bows and Arrows. *Travancore.* L. of bow, 4 ft. 6 in. to 7 ft. 6 in., L. of arrows 2 ft. 6 in. to 3 ft. (8840, 8845.)

83. Arrows; broad leaf-shaped blades; heavily feathered shafts. *Travancore.* L. 3 ft. L. of blade 1¾ in to 4½ in. (8846.–'55.)

84. Bow, Quiver, and Arrows; the bow of bamboo, the quiver of leather. *Coorg.* L. of bow, 5 ft. 6 in.; L. of arrows, 2 ft. 6 in. to 3 ft. (12684.–'55.)

85. Bow; bamboo; painted red. *Coorg.* L. 5 ft. 9 in. (8844.–'55.)

86. Arrows; various-shaped heads; shafts painted red. *Tinnevelli.* L. 2 ft 9 in. to 3 ft. 2 in. L. of barb, 3 in. to 5 in. (8773.–'55.)

87. Arrows; various-shaped heads; the shafts or reeds painted in red, yellow, green, and gold, *Aska, Madras.* L. 2 ft. 9 in. (12671.–'55.)

88. Chopper; incised blade, wooden handle. Used both as a weapon and an agricultural implement. *Kudúr, Mysore.* L. 21 in.; L. of blade, 15 in.; W. 1 to 3 in. (7358.–'67.)

89, 90. Battle-Axes; "Venmuroo."? Crescent-shaped blades; octagonal ebony shafts, enriched with delicately-chased mounts of brass and silver respectively. *Malabar.* L. 2 ft. 7 in.; L. of blade, 5 to 8 in.; W. 4 in. (Fig. 17, Nos. 89, 90.) (8814.–'55.)

91. Battle Axe; "Tabar." Small crescent blade; plain wood shaft. *Malabar coast.* L. 2 ft. 3 in.; L. of blade, 3½ in. by 4½ in. (12585.–'69.)

92. Battle Axe; "Tabar." Handle lacquered in light blue and red. L. 24 in.; L. of blade, 11 in. (8554.)

93, 94. Axes; rudely fashioned; long, rough, wooden handles; crescent-shaped blades. *Tinnevelli.* L. 4 ft. and 4 ft. 8 in.; L. of blade, 6 in. and 8 in. (7348.–'67.)

95, 96. Axes. Long axe-heads mounted on bamboo sticks. *Tinnevelli.* L. of handle, 5 ft. 10 in.; L. of axe-head, 20 and 25 in. (12750.–'55.)

97. Scythe-shaped Weapon; "Veecharooval." Blade rudely engraved; wooden handle bound with iron. *Tinnevelli.* L. 2 ft. 6 in.; B. 16 in. (Fig. 17, No. 97.) (12667.–'55.)

98. Sickle-shaped Weapons or Implements; wooden handles. *Coorg.* L. 18 to 20 in.; L. of blade, 12 to 15 in.; W. 3 in. (Fig. 17, No. 98.) (7363.–'67.)

99. *Knife or Dagger; silver hilt and sheath, finely chased. Attached by means of silver chains are a "tusi," or iron style, used for writing upon palm leaves, and several other small implements. *Malabar.*

100. *Small Dagger or Knife; blade partially covered with embossed silver enrichments; ebony hilt, finely carved, with embossed silver mounts. *Malabar.* (12567.–'69).

101. *Knife or Dagger; hilt and sheath enriched with delicately embossed and chased silver mounts. *Malabar.* (8458.–'55).

102. *Dagger; "Píchángatti." (Tam. = handknife.) Bright blade; silver hilt and sheath, exquisitely chased. To the sheath are attached by silver chains a toothpick, tweezers, and other small articles. Worn in the waist-band with the "Ayda-Kattí," but in front. *Coorg.* (8705.–'55.)

103.* Dagger; "Píchángatti." Bright blade; ebony sheath, decorated with richly chased silver mounts; silver chain suspending a silver and coral tassel attached. *Coorg.* (8706.–'55.)

104. Daggers (2); "Píchángatti." Silver covered hilts; wooden sheaths, mounted in silver and brass, with chains, tassel, and pendent *nécessaire* (tweezers, ear-pick, piercer, &c.) attached. Worn in front of the waist-belt with the "Ayda Kathy." *Coorg.* (Fig. 17, No. 104.) (7328, 7420.–'69.)

105. Dagger; "Píchángatti." Hilt of ivory, inlaid with silver; silver mounted wooden sheath, to which is attached a pendant of five small tools (tweezers, piercer, &c.). *Haidarabad, Deccan.* (12552.–'69.)

106. Daggers (2); "Jambiya." Hilts of horn and wood, mounted with silver. The sheath of one is covered with silver plate chased and embossed; that of the other is leather, silver mounted. *Haidarabad.* (Fig. 17, No. 106.) (8718, 12568.)

107. Dagger; of the Jambiya shape, but much longer. Hilt and sheath covered with silver, embossed and chased. *Malabar.* L. 23 in. (12568–'69.)

108. Knives; brass; curiously shaped blades. *Travancore.*

109.* Sword; "Ayda-Kattí." Ivory hilt, with broad counter-guard. Worn unsheathed upon the back, being passed through a flattened brass ring with a spike projecting from its centre (called "Todungah"), which is attached to a belt fastening by massive silver curb-chains in front. Presented by the Raja of Coorg. *Coorg.* L. 21 in.; Bl. 14 in. by 1½ to 4 in. (8444.–'55.)

110. Sword; "Ayda-Kattí." Attached to a gold, embroidered velvet belt, fastening in front by massive silver chains of curb pattern. Buffalo-horn hilt. Presented. *Coorg.* L. 18 in.; W. 1½ to 3¼ in. (8445.–'55.)

111. Sword; "Ayda-Kattí." Stamped leather belt, fastening by massive silver chains; carved ivory hilt. *Coorg.* L. 21 in.; L. of blade, 15 in.; W. 1½ to 4½ in. (Fig. 17, No. 111.) (12563.–'69.)

112. Sword; "Ayda-Kattí." Embossed leather belt; carved hilt of buffalo-horn, from which depend yellow silk tassels. *Coorg.* L. 19 in.; L. of blade, 13 in.; W. 1¼ to 3¾ in. (7438.–'55.)

113. Sword; "Ayda-Kattí." Embroidered silken belt; hilt of wood. Found on a battle-field. *Coorg.* L. 21½ in.; L. of blade, 15 in.; W. 1¼ to 5¼ in. (8447.–'55.)

114. Sword; "Ayda-Kattí;" carved ivory hilt. *Coorg.* L. 21½ in.; L. of blade, 15½ in.; W. 1½ to 4½ in. (12566.–'55.)

115. Sword; "Ayda-Kattí;" carved ivory hilt. *Coorg.* L. 23 in.; L. of blade, 17 in.; W. 1½ to 4 in. (8446.–'55.)

116. Sword; "Ayda-Kattí;" wooden hilt. *Coorg.* L. 24 in.; L. of blade, 17 in.; W. 1½ to 4 in. ('69.)

117. Sword; "Ayda-Kattí;" wooden hilt. *Hassar, Mysore.* L. 22 in.; L. of blade, 16 in.; W. 1½ to 3½ in. (7376.–'67.)

118. Sword; "Ayda-Kattí;" with leather belt. *Hassar, Mysore.* L. 21 in.; L. of blade, 15 in.; W. 1½ to 4 in. (7376.–'67.)

119–122. Swords; "Ayda Kattí;" broad, slightly incurved blades; ivory hilts, inlaid and mounted with pierced and chased brass work. Used by the Moplahs of *Malabar.* L. 22 to 24 in.; L. of blade, 15 to 17 in.; W. 2½ to 4 in. (Fig. 17, No. 119.) (8818.–'55.)

123. Sword; "Ayda Kattí;" ivory hilt, enriched with embossed and perforated silver mounts. *Malabar.* L. 23½ in.; L. of blade, 15½ in.; W. 2½ to 3¾ in. (8817.–'55.)

124. Sword; "Ayda Kattí;" broad blade, inlaid with brass; buffalo-horn hilt, brass mounts. *Malabar.* L. 2 ft. 1½ in.; L. of blade, 18½ in.; W. 2 in. to 4 in. (8815.–'55.)

125. Sword; "Ayda Kattí;" ivory hilt, inlaid and mounted with brass. *Malabar.* L. 20½ in.; L. of blade, 15 in.; W. 2½ to 4 in. (8449.–'55.)

126. Sword, "Ayda Kattí." Hilt of wood, painted red. *Malabar.* L. 21 in.; L. of blade, 16 in.; W. 2¼ to 3½ in.

127. Sword; "Ayda Kattí;" ebony hilt. *Malabar.* L. 23 in.; L. of blade, 17 in.; W. 2 in. to 3¼ in. (8448.–'55.)

128. Sword; "Ayda Kattí." Buffalo-horn hilt; chased silver mounts. *Malabar.* L. 24 in.; L. of blade, 19 in.; W. 2 in. to 3½ in. (Fig. 17, No. 128.) (8816.–'55.)

129. Sword; flexible fluted blade, probably Spanish; protected hilt; lacquered wooded scabbard. *Malabar.* L. 2 ft. 11 in. (12612.–'69.)

130–132. Swords; straight, flexible, grooved blades with rounded points, probably of Spanish manufacture; hilts mounted in silver and brass; lacquered wooden scabbards. *Malabar.* (8794.–'55.)

133.[1] Sabre. The hilt and part of the blade covered with richly embossed gold work; dragon-head pommel, profusely jewelled with diamonds and rubies; scabbard covered with gold, chased and embossed with conventional foliage. Presented by the Rajah of *Travancore.* L. 2 ft. 11 in. ('55.)

This type of sword is likewise used by the Cingalese, and is frequently, as in the S. K. Museum, carved out of tortoise shell.

134. Sword; "Mel puttah bemoh(?)." Two-handed weapon; long rapier blade; hilt deeply fringed with crimson silk tassels; scabbard, velvet-covered, with silver mounts. Presented by the Rajah of *Vizianagram.* L. 5 ft. 6 in.; L. of blade, 3 ft. 11 in. (Fig. 17, No. 134.) ('55.)

In the Windsor Collection there is a somewhat similar weapon with a dagger, and a small sword blade springing from the hilt at an acute angle, so as to be more formidable at close quarters.

135. Matchlock; "Toradár." The barrel once profusely ornamented with silver; plain stock; slightly curved butt. Presented by the Rajah of *Vizianagram.* L. 6 ft. (8662.–'55.)

136, 137. Matchlocks; "Toradár." Crook-shaped butts, with inlaid brass mounts, engraved. Barrels attached to their stocks by numerous broad bands of brass; a supply of matchcord wound round a basket-work reel is attached to each gun. Used by the Arabs. Presented by the Rajah of *Coorg.* L. 4 ft. 10 in. and 5 ft. 3 in. (Fig. 17, No. 136.) (8667–8.–'55.)

138.* Matchlock; octagonal Damascus barrel, encircled by numerous silver bands; plain wood stock; silver mounts. *Coorg.* L. ft. 1 in. (7495.–'67.)

139.* Matchlocks (2); ebony stock, with engraved brass mounts, attached to the barrel by numerous bands of brass. *Coorg.* L. 5 ft. 3 in. (Fig. 17, No. 139.) (7495.–'73.)

140.* Flint-lock Gun; ebony stock, attached to the barrel by numerous broad bands of brass. *Coorg.* L. 5 ft. 5 in. ('73.)

141. Flint Gun; stock inlaid with engraved brass mounts. *Malabar.* L. 5 ft. 2 in. (8890.–'55.)

142.* Matchlock; "Toradár." Black wood stock, ornamented with chased silver mounts, and attached to the barrel by broad bands of silver plate. *Madras.* L. 5 ft. 4 in. (12538.–'69.)

143.* Matchlock Accoutrements; "Kamr." Leather belt, suspending two pouches of black leather embroidered with silver wire, and a silver-mounted powder horn of the same material, covered with a network of silver wire. *Madras.* (6552.–'67.)

144, 145. Shields; "Ḍhál;" circular; with strongly projecting umbo, covered with lacquered ornamentation in gold and colours. *Malabar.* Diam. 18 in. (12504.)

146, 147. Shields (2); "Ḍhál;" circular and convex, with strongly projecting umbo. Made of cloth lacquered red, and ornamented with four silver bosses. *Malabar Coast* Diam. 19 in. (Fig. 17, No. 146.) (8782.–'55.)

GROUP IV.

HILL TRIBES OF ASSAM AND THE NORTH-EAST FRONTIER.

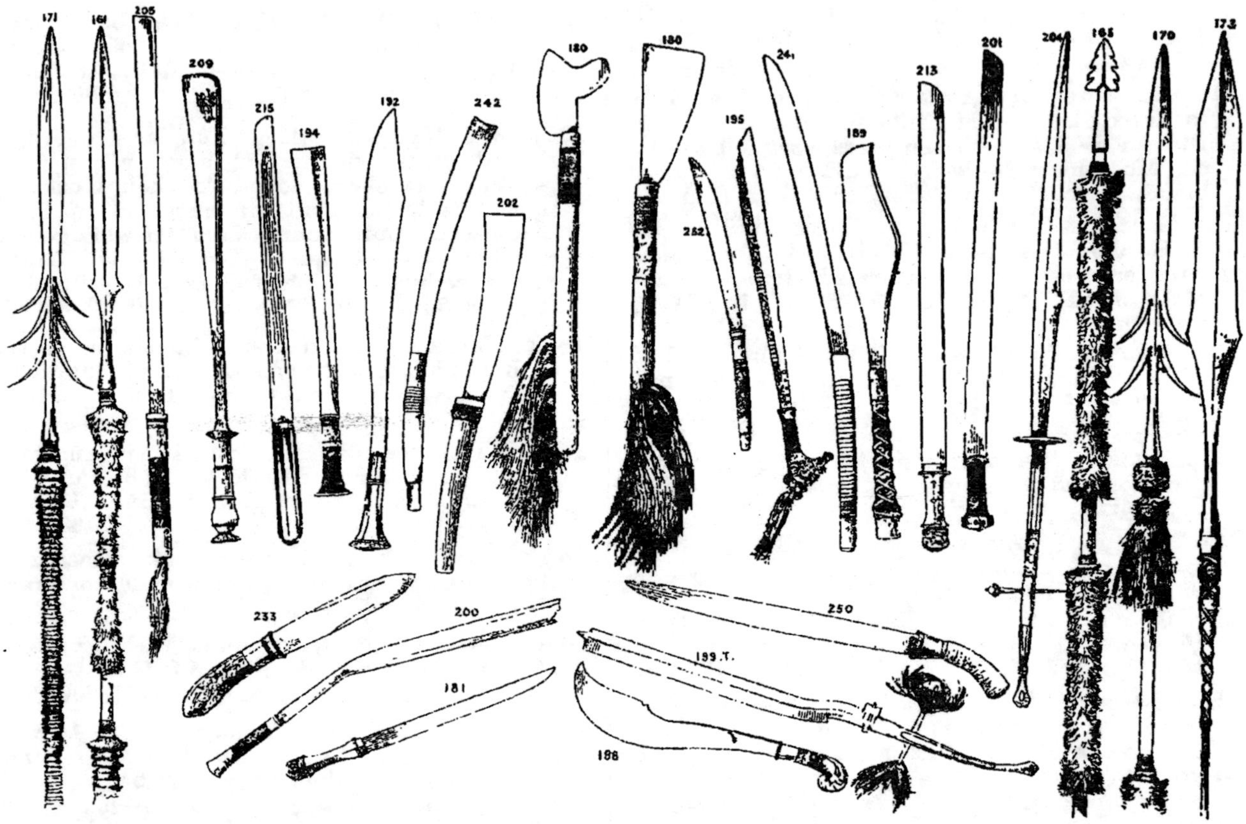

Fig. 19.—Arms of the Hill Tribes of Assam and the N.E. frontier, British and Native Burma and Siam (Groups IV. and V.)

The Indo-Chinese races occupy the north and north-east corner of Bengal, and from thence extend along the whole frontier of India from Thibet to Burmah. They are composed of a mixture of the Mongolian races with the native races of Bengal. Some of them Garos, Lushais, and Kukis, have lately been troublesome neighbours to English tea-planters and have been either brought under control or receive black mail.

The hill tribes of the northern frontier are thus classified by Colonel Dalton[1] :—

1. Khamtis.
2. Singphos.
3. Mishmis.
4. Chalikata Mishmis.
5. Abor Group.
   - α Padam and other Abors.
   - β. γ. Miris and Hill Miris.
   - δ. Doplas.
   - ε. Akas or Hrusso.
6. Nagas, Upper Assam.
7. Lower Nagas.
   - α. Nagas, west of the Doyang river.
   - β. Kukis.
   - γ. Manipuris.
   - δ. Koupouis.
8. Mikirs (unwarlike).
9. Jyntias and Kasias.
10. Garos.

[1] Ethnology of Bengal, Calcutta, 1872.

I will take the leading races in illustration of the rest.

The Khamtis[1] are a branch of the great Shan race to which the people of Laos and Siam belong, and have emigrated to Assam within the last hundred years, from the country known to us as Bor-Khamti, near the sources of the Irawadi. In religion they are Buddhists; in knowledge, arts, and civilization they are far in advance of the other tribes of the north-eastern frontier. They are very expert in carving in wood and ivory. In their weapon-handles they evince great skill, taste, and fecundity of invention, carving in high relief twisted snakes, dragons, and other monsters with a creditable unity and gracefulness of design. They work in gold, silver and iron, forge their own weapons, and make their wives' jewels. They manufacture also shields of buffalo and rhinoceros hide, gilding and lacquering them with skill and taste. Their women take part in the outdoor farm work, in cutting wood, &c., carrying for the latter purpose an axe, that borne by the chief's wife being a tiny little ornamented implement, emblematic rather than useful. The men are seldom seem without the "dao" hanging in its sheath (plain or ornamented according to the condition of the wearer) by a sling made of split rattan. It is worn somewhat in front so that the hilt is readily grasped in the right hand; with this, and a round shield of buffalo hide, the Khamti is ready to take the field, but many of them now carry muskets or fowling pieces.

The Singphos, like the Khamtis, have entered Assam within the memory of man Originally settled on the great eastern branches of the Irawadi river, they are said to have first appeared in the Assam Valley, about A.D. 1793. Their physiognomy is of the Mongolian type.

Besides the Dao they use a spear with a short shaft for thrusting, and a strong crossbow with bamboo arrows, muskets and Chinese matchlocks whenever they can get them. Their shields are of buffalo hide, four feet long; their helmets sometimes of the same material, sometimes of thick plaited rattan work, varnished black, decorated with boars tusks, &c.

In warfare their attacks are confined to night surprises. They are skilled in fortifying naturally difficult positions, using freely the "panji,"[3] a bamboo stake of different lengths sharpened at both ends and stuck in the ground. If they use muskets on these occasions the weapons are generally fixed ready loaded in loop holes of breast works, and the trigger is pulled when the enemy reaches the point of the road (previously ascertained) covered by them.

The Singphos understand the smelting of iron, and their blacksmiths with no implements but a lump of stone as an anvil, and a rude hammer, forge weapons, especially daos, which are highly prized for their temper and durability.

The Mishmis[4] are traders, and rich in the possession of large herds of cattle. Their headdress is sometimes a fur cap, sometimes a wicker helmet. Besides the dao the Mishmi carries several knives and daggers, and a very neat light spear, with head of well-tempered finely wrought steel attached to a long thin polished shaft.

"The Mishmis," writes Dr. Griffith,[5] "also carry cross-bows. The arrows for the latter " are short, made of bamboo, and on serious occasions are poisoned with 'bee.'[6] On " fighting expeditions they carry leather shields covered towards the centre with the

---

[1] Ethnology of Bengal, Calcutta, 1872, pp. 6–8.
[2] Dalton, Op. Cit., pp. 9–11.
[3] These are used by most of the tribes in Assam.
[4] Ibid., p. 17.
[5] Journ. Asiatic Society, May 1837.
[6] Cf. Tower Collection, Class 15, Nos. 154–155.

"quills of the porcupine. Their lances are made use of only for thrusting; the shafts "are made from the wood of the 'lawn.' "They are tipped with an iron spike, used "in the ascent of hills. The lance heads are of their own manufacture, and of very soft "iron."

The Chalikata (crop-haired) Mishmis[1] are a hill tribe of coarse Mongolian type. Their weapons are the same as those used by the Mishmis. They have neatly-made oblong shields of buffalo hide attached to which inside is a quiver full of finely-made poisoned "pangis." They are the only tribe who always carry poisoned arrows. By an exchange of weapons warriors become sworn comrades, and if one falls, it is the duty of the other to avenge his fate and recover his skull.

The Abors[2] have decidedly Mongoloid features. Their arms comprise the cross-bow, bows and arrows, the latter used with or without poison; very long spears, daggers, and, lastly, a long straight cutting sword, on which, by their own account, they chiefly rely in warfare. They wear coloured coats without sleeves, or long Tibetan cloaks. On State occasions they appear in imposing helmets made of cane adorned with pieces of bear-skin, yak tails dyed red, boars' tusks, and the huge beak of the buceros.

The Miris and Hill Miris[3] are of the yellow Mongolian type. Their arms are the same as those of the Abors; the arrows are generally poisoned. The Miris, when travelling, wear a cap of cane or bamboo-work with a peak behind, and over this a piece of a tiger or leopard skin, including the tail, which has a droll appearance hanging down the back.

The Nagas,[4] besides the "Dao," carry a gleaming pole-axe, with a short black handle, a broad-headed barbed spear, the shaft of which is covered with coloured hair like a brush, and a shield, which, as well as the other arms, is decorated with tufts of red goats' hair or feathers.

In their war dances the Naga warriors are armed with these weapons and a shield of buffalo-hide, wicker-work, or of bamboo, covered with tiger, bear, or other skin, large enough to cover the whole person. They advance in extended order, making admirable light infantry practice, for nothing can be seen but the black shields creeping along the ground. When sufficiently near to their imaginary enemy, they spring out and fling the spear; this is supposed to take effect; a tuft of grass represents the head of the dead foe; they seize it with the left hand, cut it out with the battle-axe, and retreat with the clod hanging by the grass over their shoulder as the skull or scalp.

The Angami Nagas occupy the tract of land immediately to the east of Northern Kachar, and use nearly the same weapons as the Nagas. The hilt of their "Dao" is ornamented with tufts of hair, frequently dyed red, each tuft representing a slain enemy. A curved shield of painted wood is occasionally carried in place of the usual oblong shield of matwork covered with bear-skin. Of late years the Angami Nagas have taken to fire-arms.

The Jyntias and Kasias[5] are a very muscular race of men inhabiting the Kasia Hills in Assam. They are of an active disposition, and fond of martial exercises. They always carry arms, generally the bamboo bow and arrow, together with a long naked sword and a shield over the right shoulder; a quiver is suspended on the left shoulder.

[1] Dalton, Op. Cit., p. 20. [2] Ibid., pp. 28 to 35.

[3] In the hills which divide Burma from Arakan the Khamis and Miris as well as the Khyens use poisoned arrows. —E. India Report, 1873, Markham.

[4] Dalton, p. 41.

[5] Dalton, p. 54. Lives of the Lindsays, Vol. IV., p. 51.

The Garos,[1] inhabiting the Garo Hills, east of the Brahmaputra in Bengal, use the following arms as represented in the Tower Collection:—

1. A straight sword, the sheath of wood. The carriage is of bearskin, the jaw and teeth of the bear forming a prominent ornament.
2. A sword with curved back and straight edge, with wooden sheath attached to a hoop belt of cane.
3. A spear with iron shoe, and narrow lozenge-shaped head.
4. A cross-bow of bamboo, the arrows feathered with leaves, and the quiver covered with fox-skin.

The Garos believe themselves to be aboriginal, and claim relationship with the Buts and the English! Their weapons or agricultural implements, for they are used indiscriminately for either purpose, are a hoe, the "dao," and either a battle-axe called "lumbiri" which is carried naked in the hand, or a spear. When anything particular is to be settled, writes Eliot,[2] the Garos all assemble in their war dress, which consists of a blue cloth, (covering part of the back and tied at the breast where the four corners are made to meet,) a shield and a sword. They sit in a circle, the sword fixed in the ground before them. The shield is described as a long oblong which covers the greater part of the body. One in the Christy collection is formed of strips of wood, with a cane handle. The sword has a long handle and a narrow blade gradually increasing in width.

The Kukis[3] of North Cachar on the frontier line of Burmah, are thus described at the end of the last century by John Macrae, (1799):—

"The Kukis are armed with bows and arrows, spears, clubs, and daos used as a hand hatchet, exactly resembling the knife of the Nairs on the Malabar coast. They use shields made of the hide of the gayal, and the inside of these shields they ornament with small pendulous plates of brass, which make a jingling noise as the warriors toss about their arms either in the fight or in the dance. They also wear round their necks large strings of a particular kind of shell (cowries) found in these hills; about their loins and on their thighs, immediately above the knee, they tie large bunches of long goat's hair, of a red colour; and on their arms they have broad rings of ivory, in order to make them appear more terrific to their enemies. They always endeavour to surprise their enemy, marching in the night, and lying concealed during the day in a kind of hammock, which they fasten among the branches of the loftiest trees. When they have approached their enemy unperceived, they generally make their attack about the dawn, and commence it with a great shout, and striking of their spears against their shields. They stand so greatly in awe of fire-arms that the report of a single musket will put a whole party to flight."[4]

Their arms are thus represented in the Tower collection:—

1. A broad knife "dao," with a case of cane wicker-work, and a belt of cowries.
2. A quiver of bamboo and poisoned arrows, with wristguard of ivory.
3. A square shield of hide, in front of which is a brass cymbal, and at the corners tufts of hair.

The *Lushai*, a tribe of the Kukis, settled in the south of Cachar and Chittagong, use the skin of the gayal (*bos frontalis*) for shields, and his horns for powder flasks, which are polished, and sometimes inlaid with silver. Their weapons are the dao, the blade of which is about 12 inches long, spears of various shapes and lengths,[5] and guns. Some

---

[1] Catalogue of Tower Collection, p. 100, where they are wrongly described as Mishmi Garos.

[2] Garrow Hills, by John Eliot. Asiatic Researches, Vol. III.

[3] Ibid., p. 99.

[4] Asiatic Researches, Vol. VII., p. 186.

[5] One which belonged to Mr. W. Tayler has a shaft about 2 feet long, terminating at one end in a long-pointed socket about 21 inches long, at the other in a broad head, about 20 inches long. It is now in the S. K. Museum.

carry a long-bladed two-handed Burmese knife slung over the shoulder. They make their oaths on the dao and the tiger.

It is only within the last few years that they have learnt the use of fire-arms and discarded the bamboo bow and arrow, their muskets being flint-locks of English make, and bearing the Tower mark. They make their own powder, which is very weak, and use bits of hammered iron or lead for bullets. The priming powder is carried in a very small horn.

The Shendus, in the Arakan hills, also manufacture their own gunpowder. Their guns do not appear to be of European manufacture; the stocks are painted red, black, and yellow, and are highly varnished. Their powder flasks are made of gayal horns, polished, and beautifully inlaid with silver and ivory. Their shields are like those (256, 257) from Arakan.

With reference to the arms in use generally among these wild tribes, Mr. Lewin[1] remarks:—The "dao" is the hill knife used universally throughout the country. It is a blade about 18 inches long, narrow at the haft, square and broad at the top, pointless and sharpened on one side only. The blade is set in a handle of wood, a bamboo root being considered the best. The fighting "dao" is differently shaped. This is a long pointless sword, set in a wooden or ebony handle; it is very heavy, and a blow of almost incredible power can be given by one of these weapons.

With both the fighting and the ordinary "dao" one can make but two cuts, one from the right shoulder downwards to the left, the other from the left foot upward to the right. The reason of this is that in sharpening the blade, one side only gives the edge slanting to the other straight face of the blade. Any attempt to cut in a way contrary to those mentioned causes the "dao" to turn in the hand on the striker.

The weapon is identical with the "parang latok" of the Malays. The ordinary hill "dao" is generally stuck naked into the waist band on the right hip, but the fighting "dao" is provided with a scabbard and worn at the waist.

When used as an agricultural implement, a dig with the blunt square end of the dao makes a narrow hole, about three inches deep; into this is put a small handful of the mixed seeds, and the sowing is completed.

The Bhutias, are Lamaitic Buddhists, and of Mongoloid type, closely allied in blood and language to the Tibetans. The earliest account of Bhutan from an English source is that given by the Mission of Mr. Bogle to Tibet in 1774,[2] who thus describes their army:—"A soldier in Bhutan has not a distinct profession. Every man is girt with a " sword, and trained to the use of the bow. The hall of every public officer is hung " round with matchlocks, swords, and shields. In times of war and danger his servants " and retainers are armed with these; the inhabitants assembled from the different " villages are put under his command, and he marches in person against the enemy.

"The common weapons are a broadsword of good temper, with shagreen handle, a cane- " coiled target painted with streaks of red, a bow formed of a piece of bamboo; a quiver " of a junk of the same tree, the arrows of reeds, barbed, and often covered with a poison " said to be so subtle, that the slightest wound becomes mortal in a few hours. Some few " are armed with a pike. They put great confidence in fire-arms, but are not so cun- " ning in the use of the matchlock as of their ancient weapons the sword and the bow. " Their warlike garb is various and not uniform. Some wear a cap quilted, or of cane, " and sugar-loaf shape, with a tuft of horse hair stained; others an iron-netted hood, or " a helmet with a like ornament. Under these they often put false locks to supply the " want of their own hair, which among this tribe of Bhutanese is worn short. Some- " times a coat of mail is to be seen. In peace as well as war they are dressed in short

[1] Wild Races of South-Eastern India.
[2] Bogle, Mission to Tibet 1774, edited by C. Markham, p. 62.

"trowsers, woollen hose, soled with leather and gartered under the knee, a jacket or a "tunic, and over all two or three striped blankets.

"The leaders only are on horseback, and are covered with a cap, rough with red-dyed "cowtails. When they go to war or to an engagement, they whoop and howl to encourage "each other and intimidate the enemy. They are fond of attacking in the night time. "As to their courage in battle, those can best speak who have tried it. I saw only some "skirmishes."

A few miserable matchlocks and blunderbusses, says a later writer in 1838, Captain R. W. Pemberton, completed the equipments of a Bhutia force in 1836.[1]

In every village there is a place set apart for the practice of archery. They shoot at a mark about 18 inches in length and 7 broad, of a triangular shape, at about 120 yards distant. The arrow is made of a very small species of bamboo, found at elevations of 10,000 or 11,000 feet above the sea, and remarkable for its extreme straightness and strength.

The Bhutanese arms, observes Dr. Rennie,[2] consist of matchlocks, jinjals, bows and arrows, heavy straight swords and large knives. Catapults are also used for throwing stones of considerable size. Some wear chain armour, others heavy iron helmets of a semi-globular shape, padded inside and with quilted cotton flaps protecting the neck. Circular shields with brass knobs and bound by a rim of the same are borne by the attendants of chiefs.

The Lepchas of Sikkim and Darjiling are not a warlike race. They carry bows and arrows, and use a short sword, the hilt and sheath of which are ornamented with pierced silver or brass work. One, in the British Museum (Henderson Collection), is ornamented with turquoises; another, presented by Dr. Hooker, is in the Christy Collection.

NOTE.—*A few of the more ornamental arms, distinguished in the Catalogue by an asterisk, will be found in Case* 70.

148, 149. BOWS, ARROWS, AND QUIVER; of bamboo; with a case of plaited cane for holding an extra bowstring. *The Abors of Assam.* (12697.–'55.)

150. QUIVER AND ARROWS; bamboo; the arrows feathered with strips of palm leaves; with a wicker-work case for holding an extra bowstring. *The Abors of Assam.* (12697.–'55.)

151, 152. BOW AND QUIVERS; of bamboo, the latter containing poisoned arrows; with a plaited case for holding an extra bowstring. *The Mishmis of Assam.* (12696.–'55.)

153, 154. BOWS; of bamboo, the strings made of strips of the same. *Assam.* L. 5 ft. (8881.–'55.)

155. QUIVER AND ARROWS; painted black. L. 20 in. *Silhet.* (8880.–'55.)

156. ARROWS; in open basket quiver. *Assam.* (12545.–'69.)

157–159. BOWS; bamboo, the strings formed of a strip of bamboo; and arrows (2), with broad barbed points. *Sikhim.* L. of bows, 4 ft. 4 in. to 5 ft. 8 in.; L. of arrows, 2 ft. 6 in. (12698.–'55.)

160. ARROWS; bamboo, with steel points. *Hill tribes of Sikhim.* L. 2 ft. 6 in. (12543.–'69.)

161–163. SPEARS; long broad points; shafts decorated with coloured hair. *The Nagas of Assam.* L. 6 ft. to 6 ft. 8 in.; L. of blade, 23 in. (Fig. 19, No. 161.) (8829.–'55.)

164. SPEAR; six-barbed blade; black palm wood shaft. *Upper Assam.* L. 7 ft. 8 in.; L. of blade, 2 ft. 6 in. (12709.–'55.)

165–167. SPEARS; very small blades; shafts covered with dyed hair. *Upper Assam.* L. 6 ft. 3 in. to 6 ft. 10 in. L. of blade, 9 in. (Fig. 19, No. 165.) (12514.–'69.)

168. SPEAR; shaft decorated with coloured hair. *Assam.* L. 6 ft. 6 in.; L. of blade, 12 in. (12715.–'55.)

169. SPEAR; of a chief; decorated with red dyed hair. L. 5 ft. 8½ in.; L. of blade, 11 in.

170. SPEAR; long four-barbed blade; shafts decorated with tufts of red and black hair. *Assam.* L. 7 ft. 6 in.; L. of blade, 2 ft. 5 in. (Fig. 19, No. 170.) (8829.–'55.)

171, 172. SPEARS; six-barbed blades; long pointed iron butts. The shaft of one ornamented with hair. *Assam.* L. 6 ft. 9½ in.; L. of blade, 2 ft. 5 in. (Fig. 19, No. 171.) (8829.)

---

[1] Report on Bootan, 1838, Captain Pemberton.

[2] Bootan, p 25, 1866.

173, 174. SPEARS; tapering iron shafts, one bound with cane; the grip near the blade. *Cachar.* L. 7 ft. 6 in to 7 ft. 8 in. L. of blade, 2 ft. 6 in. to 3 ft. (Fig. 19, No. 173.) (8852.–'55.)

175–177. SPEARS; long broad points of various shapes. *Cachar.* L. 4 ft. 10 in. to 5 ft. 10 in. L. of blade, 17 in. to 23 in. (8851.–'51.)

178. SPEAR; long blade; short ebony shaft. *Cachar.* L. 3 ft. 3 in.; L. of blade, 14 in. (8827.–'55.)

179. SPEARS (3); small blades, ebony shafts. *Cachar.* (12714.)

180. BATTLE-AXES (2); decorated with tufts of red and black hair. *The Nagas of Assam.* L. 2 ft. 6 in.; L. of blade, 7 in. (Fig. 19, No. 180.) (7878, 7877.–'70.)

181. *DAGGER OR KNIFE; hilt and sheath covered with perforated silver work, partially gilt. *Bhotan.* (Fig. 19, No. 181.) (7422.–'67.)

182. SHORT SWORD; "Dhá;" hilt covered with shark skin, with ornamental brass mounts; sheath richly ornamented with pierced silver-gilt work. *Bhotan.* L. 19 in.; L. of blade, 14 in. (116.)

183. SHORT SWORD; "Dhá;" hilt covered with shark skin; sheath richly ornamented with pierced silver-gilt work. *Bhotan.* L. 18¾ in.; L. of blade, 14 in. (8741.–'55.)

184. DAGGER; long thin blade; wooden half-sheath; belt studded with brass knobs, and circular brass plate, attached. *Cachar.* L. 17 in.; L. of blade, 12 in. (8878.–'55.)

185. KNIFE; rudely fashioned blade; buffalo-horn hilt, capped with iron. *Assam.* L. 16 in.; L. of blade, 12 in. (237.–'55.)

186. SWORD; "Kapee Dhá (?);" short broad blade; leather sheath, with a bundle of "pánjís" attached. *Sibsagar, Assam.* L. 19 in.; L. of blade, 12½ in.; W. ¾ in. to 3 in. (12677.–'55.)

187. SWORD; short broad blade; brass-mounted hilt, from which hangs a long tuft of coloured hair. *Cachar, Assam.* L. 20 in.; L. of blade, 13 in.; W. 1¼ to 4 in. (307.–'55.)

188. SWORD OR CLEAVER; pistol-shaped handle of wood, bound with brass wire. *Cachar, Assam.* L. 20 in.; L. of blade, 15 in.; W. 1 in. to 3¾ in. (Fig. 19, No. 188.) (12683.–'55.)

189. SWORD OR CLEAVER; used both as a weapon and for domestic purposes; broad blade. *Cachar, Assam.* L. 2 ft. 3½ in.; L. of blade, 16 in.; W. 1 in. to 4 in. (Fig. 19, No. 189.) (8875.–'55.)

190. SWORD; long straight blade, with carved ebony hilt; wooden scabbard, decorated with carved and painted geometrical designs, with small knife attached at the side. *Assam.* L. 2 ft. 9½ in.; L. of blade, 2 ft. 4½ in. (12608.–'69.)

191. SWORD; "Khámti Dhá;" carved wooden hilt. *Assam.* L. 2 ft. 1 in.; L. of blade, 19½ in. (12582.–'69.)

192. SWORD; "Khámti Dhá;" wooden hilt. *Assam.* L. 2 ft. 1½ in.; L. of blade, 19½ in. (Fig. 19, No. 192.) (9391.)

193. SWORD; "Khámti Dhá;" the cutting edge on one side only, with square end used for digging; hilt brass-mounted, and covered with fine plaited work of black cane; open wooden scabbard, attached to a hoop-shaped cane sling or belt. *Assam.* L. 2 ft. 3½ in.; L. of blade, 21 in. (8864.–'51.)

194. SWORD; "Khámti Dhá;" strong blade, with square end; the hilt of wood, with brass and ivory mounts and basket work ornamentation; wooden scabbard, attached to a cane sling. *Assam.* L. 2 ft. 1 in.; L. of blade, 19½ in. (Fig. 19, No. 194.) (12666.–'55.)

195. SWORD; "Khámti Dhá;" blade engraved and inlaid with brass; carved bone hilt, with tufts of hair attached; bamboo scabbard. *Assam.* L. 2 ft. 2 in.; L. of blade, 20 in. (Fig. 19, No. 195.) (8868.–'55.)

196 T. SWORD; "Khámti Dhá;" straight blade; wooden sheath, ornamented with the upper jaw and teeth of a bear. *The Kukis of North Cachar.* (No. 151.)

197. SWORD; "Abor Dhá;" the upper part of blade notched on the back; the hilt of wood and carved bone; carved wooden scabbard, containing a small knife. *Assam.* L. 2 ft. 5 in.; L. of blade, 2 ft. (8867.–'55.)

198. SWORD; "Mishmi Dhá;" rudely formed wooden hilt, bound with cane; bamboo sheath, to which is attached a small knife and a belt of plaited cane. *Assam.* L. 2 ft.; L. of blade, 18 in. (8868.–'55.)

A fine kris, with gold hilt and elaborately engraved gold work, presented by the Rajah of Assam to Her Majesty, is in the Windsor collection.

199 T. SWORD; straight blade, widening towards the point; the crosspiece guarding the hilt decorated with tufts of hair. *The Angami Nagas of Assam.* (Fig. 19, No. 199 T.) (No. 156.)

200. SWORD; abruptly incurved blade. (A similar weapon will be found in the Tower collection.) Wooden hilt, bound with brass wire. *Assam.* L. 2 ft. 2 in.; L. of blade, 21 in. (Fig. 19, No. 200.) (12584.)

201. SWORDS (2); "Dhá;" straight blades, cutting on one side only; hilts covered with brass wire. *Assam.* L. 2 ft. 2 in. to 2 ft. 5 in.; L. of blade, 20 in. to 23 in. (Fig. 19, No. 201.) (8870.)

202. SWORD; "Dhá;" square blunt end; long wooden handle. *Assam.* L. 2 ft. 2 in.; L. of blade, 13½ in. (Fig. 19, No. 202.) (9392.–'58.)

203. SWORD; long blade; hilt of buffalo-horn. *Assam.* L. 2 ft. 7 in.; L. of blade, 2 ft. (237.–'55.)

204. SWORDS (2); two-handed spear-shaped weapons of soft steel, with cross-barred hilts. *Kasia Hills. Assam.* L. 3 ft. 8 in.; L. of blade, 2 ft. 1 in. (Fig. 19, No. 204.) (12549, 12678.–'69.)

These arms of the Khasi-Jyntia tribes are as peculiar as their language. "The tiny family of Khasi is like an island in the midst of the Tibeto-Burman Sea."—(*Robt. Cust, Languages of the E. Indies*, p. 4.)

205. LONG SWORD; wooden hilt, ornamented with white metal mounts and a tuft of coloured hair; open wood scabbard. *Upper Assam.* L. 3 ft. 3½ in.; L. of blade, 2 ft. 4½ in. (Fig. 19, No. 205.) (4785.)

206. SWORD; pistol-shaped horn hilt. *Darjiling.* L. 2 ft.; L. of blade, 18½ in. (12583.–'55.)

207. SWORD; "Dhá;" short-pointed blade; ebony hilt; open wooden scabbard, to which the blade is secured by brass bands set with turquoises. *Darjiling.* L. 2 ft.; L. of blade, 16 in. (6204.–'55.)

208. SWORD; widening gradually from hilt to point; wooden hilt, brass mounted. *Darjiling.* L. 3 ft.; L. of blade, 2 ft. 4 in.; W. 2¼ in. to ¾ in. (12600.–'69.)

209. SWORD; "Dhá;" blade similar in shape to preceding example, with conventional dragon inlaid in brass; wooden hilt, brass mounts. *Darjiling.* L. 2 ft. 10 in.; L. of blade, 2 ft. 2 in. (Fig. 19, No. 209.) (12558.–'69.)

210. DOUBLE SWORD, or two swords fitting into one wooden sheath. *Darjiling.* L. 2 ft. 4 in.; L. of blade, 22 in. (12588.–'69.)

211. SWORD; sharkskin-covered hilt, enriched with perforated silver-gilt mounts; sheath of sharkskin, mounted with fine brass alloyed with silver. *Darjiling.* L. 2 ft. 5 in.; L. of blade, 2 ft. (258.)

212.* SWORD; "Bhotan dhá;" straight blade; hilt unguarded, covered with shark skin, and enriched with perforated silver mounts; sheath similarly ornamented. *Darjiling.* L. 19 in. (7421.–'67.)

213. SWORD; "Dhá;" straight one-edged blade; hilt covered with shark skin; pommel of pierced brass work. *Bhotan.* L. 2 ft. 9 in.; L. of blade, 2 ft. 4 in. (Fig. 19, No. 213.) (7372.–'67.)

214. SWORD; straight blade; buffalo-horn hilt; carved tiger's head pommel; steel knuckle guard. *Bhotan.* L. 2 ft. 3 in.; L. of blade, 23 in. (12569.–'69.)

215. SWORD OR LONG KNIFE; wooden hilt; circular sheath with brass mounts. L. 2 ft.; L. of blade, 17½ in. (Fig. 19, No. 215.) (8742.–'69.)

216. SHIELD; rudely fashioned of wood, ornamented with four iron bosses surrounding a central one of wood; iron mounts; spear point at the top, with a hook at the bottom. *Garo Hills, Assam.* Diam. 14 in.; Spear point, 11 in. (9148.–'73.)

217. SHIELD, circular, composed of narrow strips of cane interwoven concentrically in a kind of basket-work. *Assam.* Diam. 17 in. ('51.)

218, 219. SHIELDS; light, oblong, with incurved sides. Made of pieces of wood bound together by thin strips of cane. Used by the Garos. *Assam.* L. 2 ft. 3½ in. to 2 ft. 6 in.; W. 17 in. and 13 in. (9149.–'73.)

220. SHIELD; buffalo-hide, ornamented with gold leaf and red paint. Used by the Khamtis of Assam. *Assam.* Diam. 22 in. (7874.–'70.)

221 T. SHIELD; oblong; of wood, with rude incised ornaments. *The Angami Nagas of Assam.* Cl. 15. (No. 161.)

Cf. In the United Service Museum, the oblong buffalo hide shield of the Kantala Nagas, designed to protect the body from the knees upwards. In the Christy Collection, shields of the Nagas; the one of blackened buffalo hide and rattan handle, the other oblong, of plaited rattan, a war shield.

222 T. SHIELD; oblong; of buffalo hide, ornamented with tufts of hair at the upper corners, and a large circular umbo of brass. *The Kukis of North Cachar.* Cl. 15. (No. 148.)

223. SHIELD; oblong, of stiff buffalo hide; wooden handle. *Assam.* L. 2 ft.; W. 10 in. (Fig. 20.) ('55.)

Fig. 20.—Khamti Helmet from Assam (No. 226).

224. SHIELD; "Dhál;" circular and convex, with recurved edge; of black buffalo hide, the surface polished and stamped with transverse bands of floriated scroll pattern. *Silhet.* Diam. 16 in. (8618.–'55.)

225. SHIELD; "Dhál;" rhinoceros hide, studded with four circular brass bosses. *Bhotan.* Diam. 18½ in. (7359.–'69.)

226. HELMET; bell shaped, of black hide, ornamented with gold leaf and red paint, surmounted by a plume of hair. *The Khámtis of Assam. Assam.* Diam. 13 in. (Fig. 20.) (7873.–'70.)

227. HELMET; "Tōp;" hemispherical, of rough steel with brass mounts. *Bhotan.* H. 8 in. (Fig. 21.) (7319.–'67.)

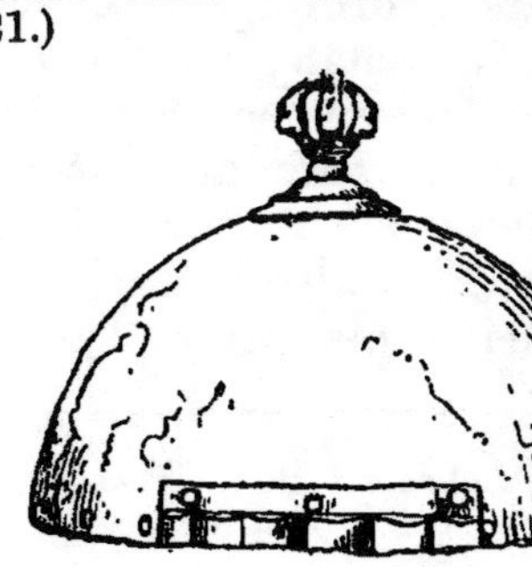

Fig. 21.—Steel Helmet from Bhotan No. (227.)

GROUP V.

BRITISH AND NATIVE BURMAH AND SIAM.

The Burmese.

In close connexion with the Indo-Chinese arms are those of the Burmese. They bear a peculiar character and seem to be the type from which the Japanese derived their arms, as did the Chinese from the Thibetans. Besides the "dao" or short sword, the common weapon is a cutlass, the blade of which is curved in continuation of the curve of the handle. It is used as a dagger or knife when small,[1] and as in Ligore, is sometimes double with a handle at either end. Their spears are 7 or 8 feet long,[2] and their swords are desperate weapons in close combat. The metal can hardly be called steel as it is easily bent. The jinjal is the only fire-arm they have perfect command of. Their muskets without bayonets are old and generally unserviceable. They are well supplied with ammunition as they have lead mines, and manufacture gunpowder.

The system of the army is a decimal one. The army is divided into lacs, or 10,000, lú tatawa, or 1,000, and lú taya, or 100 men each. Besides the superior *Bó* over the larger divisions, each company is commanded by an inferior *Bó*, or captain, and he has under him two inferior *Chekli*, and also a *Nakhan* and his assistant.[3]

Burmah is divided into provinces governed by a military chief or *Myo-woon*, aided by subordinate chiefs called Raywoon (Yé-woon). They form a provincial lotoo, or council. When the king makes war, or the kingdom is invaded, the Myowoon's duty is to raise the quota of men required, and to levy such extraordinary taxes for their equipment and support as the occasion may require. They generally take care to raise double the number of men required, allowing one half to buy their discharge, and pocketing at least half the amount collected for the equipment of the other.

"The Burmese is a born soldier, and is a fierce and daring enemy. He is possessed of "great strength and activity, and capable of enduring great fatigue," says the historian of the Burmese War (Snodgrass).

The Burmese in their usual mode of warfare rarely meet their enemy in the open field. Instructed and trained in the formation of stockades, they had been for many years successful in their warfare with all who opposed them. They had subdued and incorporated with the empire all the petty states surrounding them, and when they engaged with the English did not anticipate defeat.

In the Burmese war already described in the historical sketch, they followed their usual tactics. When the English troops forced their way over their stockades, about 8 ft. high, a fierce conflict arose; rendered desperate by the discharges of musketry poured in on them, the Burmese charged blindly on our soldiers' bayonets with spear or musket in hand, and continued fighting till all hope of success was lost.

Prominent among the native troops opposed to us in this war were "The King's Invulnerables" forming part of a corps from Ava, consisting of several thousand men, and divided into many classes, of whom a select band only are specially entitled to that appellation. They were distinguished by the short cut of their hair and the peculiar manner in which they are tatooed, having the figures of elephants, tigers, and a great variety of ferocious animals indelibly and even beautifully marked on their arms and legs. They were also remarkable for having bits of gold, silver, and sometimes precious stones in their arms, probably introduced under the skin at an early age.[4]

---

[1] In the E. Collection there is a knife or miniature cutlass, $7\frac{1}{2}$ inches long in the blade, and 5 inches in the handle; the latter is of silver, coarsely made, with bamboo sheath covered with silver, and bound with filigree wire.

[2] Captain Low, History of Tenasserim, Journ. Asiat. Soc., Vol. IV., p. 81.

[3] Snodgrass, Narrative of the Burmese War.

[4] Wilson mentions that a boar's tusk was worn as a charm against bullets

These men were considered by their countrymen as invulnerable, and exposed their persons to the fire of the enemy in support of their pretensions. In all the stockades one or two of these heroes were generally found who exhibited their war dance of defiance upon the most exposed part of the defences, frequently under the excitement of opium or stimulants. They were armed with swords and musquets, but were before long obliged to retreat before the showers of grape and vollies of musquetry with which they had to contend.

The army of Bandûla was estimated at 35,000 musqueteers, of whom many were armed with "jinjals," a small piece carrying a ball from 6 to 12 ounces, and mounted on a carriage managed by two men. Their only cavalry were 700 Manipúri horse, and the guns were carried on elephant backs. The rest of the force were armed with long spears and short swords; they were men of great physical strength, and formidable at close quarters.

On one occasion, when the stockade was 12 to 14 feet high, protected in front by abatis railing and palisadoes driven into the ground diagonally, two 18-pounders were brought to make a breach, which was soon effected, and an assault was made. When the fort was carried on the rear, the gilt *chuttah*,[1] sword, and spear of the Burmese commander Bandula was found, and his body a few yards further on. In making their trenches or earthwork approaches they formed a number of holes large enough to hold two men, and containing a sufficient supply of rice, water, and even fuel for them, and under the excavated bank one man slept while his comrade watched.

Their war boats were much used in their military operations. Symes[2] describes them as 500 in number, the largest 80 to 100 feet long, carrying 50 to 60 rowers. On the prow a 6 or 12-pounder gun was lashed, and swivels were frequently fixed on the stern. Besides the boatmen, there were 30 soldiers on board armed with musquets.

In their operations on the river Irawadi their fire rafts were made wholly of bamboo canes firmly bound together, between every two or three rows of which a line of earthen jars filled with petroleum and cotton was secured. Many of them were upwards of 100 feet in length, and divided into many pieces, so arranged that when they were directed against a ship the force of the current would carry the ends of the raft round her.

The Karens, an Indo-Chinese race, use the same arms as the Burmese, namely musket, cross-bow, spears. The Tsankoo Karens use the cross-bow with poisoned arrows, probably from the juice of the Pegu Upas tree (*Antiaris ovalifolia* of Mason).

A curious custom is related of the Karens. They are said to perform agreements by filling a bowl with "Khoung," a spirit like whisky, the contracting parties sitting round the bowl. A gun or sword and a spear are then produced, and portions of the steel therefrom carefully scraped into the spirit. These weapons are then inserted into the bowl, and simultaneously held by all the contracting parties, who drink off the spirit in witness of their agreement to the terms of the contract.[3]

The Khyens, in 1824, in the hill country of Arracan, were unacquainted with fire-arms, and used a cross-bow with poisoned arrows, spear, and dao.[4]

Siam.

The Arms of Siam are not directly represented in this collection, but they are related to those of British Burmah which includes part of the Kingdom of Siam.

The British possessions come in contact with Siam in Ligore and the Malacca peninsula, to which the Siamese have laid claim from having on several occasions overrun the

---

[1] The "Ch'hátá" or umbrella in red velvet with Jazerant work taken from Bandula is in the possession of Earl Amherst. The suit of armour worn by him is in the Tower Collection (see No. 259T.).

[2] Embassy to Ava, 1800.

[3] McMahon the Karens of the Golden Chersonese, p. 826.

[4] Two Years in Ava, 1824. They have long since used guns. Col. Yule, note.

country. The Siamese in the first Burmese War offered their aid to exterminate the Burmans.

The Siamese national arms are the sword, the spear, and the bow. They have adopted the following :—[1]

Pun yai, or cannon.
Charong, field pieces.
Pun láng cháang, a swivel gun on an elephant.
Pun khá nok yang, short wall piece.
Do. do., smaller.
Pun khass sinla, infantry muskets. The powder is kept in joints of bamboo or horns, and the balls in bags tied round the waist. The bags have a stop of iron.
Khass chút, matchlock.
Pun langmaa, pistol.
Khang prai, a blunderbuss, manufactured by Chinese in Siam and the Straits of Malacca; the outside of the barrel looks well, the inside is rough.
Thamí, cross-bow, is about five feet long; it is passed through a stock 3 or 4 feet long, tipped with hard wood or iron. The leaf of a palm supplies the place of a feather to the arrow. The bow string is drawn to the notch by the united exertion of feet and arms, and the arrows shot off by a trigger.
Hák sat is a spear about 7 feet long and is cast by the foot.
Hák, plain spear.
Khoum, a sort of lance or javelin, 7 or 8 feet long, sometimes longer. It is seized at the upper end, the forefinger resting on the top and the light missile flies for 30 or 40 yards with deadly aim. The Burmans used the same weapon in the first war.
Trí is a trident-shaped missile.
Dass is the long curved sword, 18 to 40 inches long.
Kassi, a long sabre from foreigners.
Ngao, a sort of curved knife or sword, 18 inches long, with handle about 6 feet long.
Kasún, common single bow.
Lok fai, "child of fire," a combustible ball thrown from a tower to fire a town.
Phlo, a small fire-ball.
Tront, a rocket. The Siamese use fire rafts when attacked.
Lo, a round shield.
Dang, an oblong shield formed of wood or buffalo hide.

They have also knives and daggers, but they are not often used. They use also "Panjis" bamboo "crows-feet" for the same object as the Indo-Chinese tribes.

NOTE.—*The ornamental arms belonging to this division, distinguished in the Catalogue by an asterisk, will be found in Case 70.*

228. BOWS (3); bamboo. *Arakan.* L. 4 ft. 9 in. to 5 ft. (5178.)

229. QUIVERS WITH ARROWS (2); one of black varnished bamboo, the other of red leather. *Akyab.* L. 21 in. to 3 ft. (8880.–'55.)

230. QUIVER WITH POISONED ARROWS; of bamboo, painted black and red; the arrows feathered with strips of palm leaves. Used by the Gyeikos. *Burmah.* L. 21 in. (7353.–'67.)

231. CROSSBOW; used for discharging bullets. Used by the Karens of Burmah, and in Siam.

---

[1] Captain Low, Tenasserim, Journ. R.A.S., Vol. IV., p. 317. Cf. the following weapons lent by Mr. Newman, H.B.M. Consul at Siam, and exhibited at South Kensington Museum.
1. Oblong shield with scrolls, black and gold.
2. Circular shield, black, with seven gilt bosses, and gilt scrolls.
3. Curved sword, with cutlass handle, in carved ivory and embossed silver or brass raised work.
4. A trident spear.
5. Kris terminating in a duck's head carved in wood, brass mounts.
6. Long halbert shaped spear with wooden shaft lacquered red.
7. Long spear or javelin with leaf-shaped head.
8. Long cutlass, blade 40 inches.
9. Curved knife or sword.

232. Daggers, a pair; the blades contained in one sheath. *Tounghoo, Burmah.* L. 11 in.; L. of blade 7 in. (7320.–'69.)

233. Sword or Knife; short broad blade; teak-wood hilt and scabbard, the former mounted and inlaid witb brass. *Burmah.* L. 18½ in.; L. of blade 10½ in. (Fig. 19, No. 233.) (12001.–'72.)

234. *Sword or Knife; "Dhá;" long ivory handle ornamented with conventional dragon forms carved in high relief; sheath enriched with chased and embossed silver mounts. *Rangoon.* L. 18 in. (8701.–'55.)

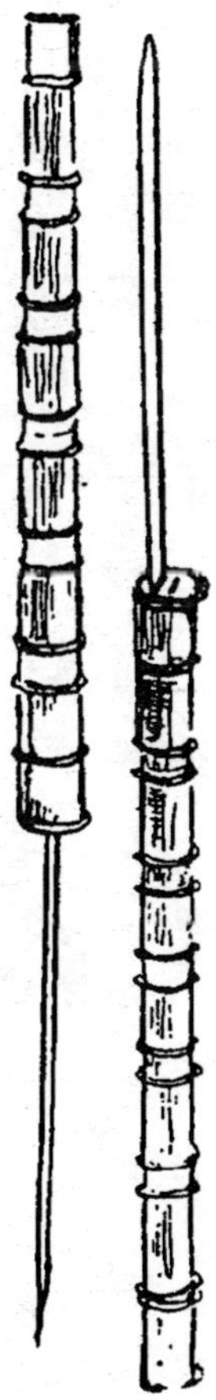

Fig. 22.—Burmese Sword (Amherst Coll.)

235, 236. *Swords or Knives; hilts of ivory and ebony, carved in high relief; wooden sheaths, silver mounted. *Rangoon.* L. 14 to 18 in.; W. 2¼ in. (7424.–'55.)

237. *Sword or Knife; "Dhá;" slightly incurved blade; ivory hilt, curved in continuation of the blade, and covered with figures carved in high relief; wooden sheath, silver mounted. *Burmah.* L. 17½ in. (1426.–'67.)

238. *Sword; "Dhá;" broad blade of soft steel; long handle of ivory, carved in high relief with figures and foliage; sheath plated with gold. Presented to Lord Dalhousie by the King of Ava. *Burmah.* L. 2 ft. 6 in.; W. of blade 2 in. (8704.–'55.)

239.* Sword; "Dhá;" narrow blade of soft steel; long hilt curved in continuation of the blade, thickly encrusted with uncut rubies mounted in pure gold; gold tassel attached; sheath plated with gold, encircled by ten bands of uncut rubies. Presented to Lord Dalhousie by the King of Ava. *Burmah.* L. 3 ft. 2 in. (8678.–'55.)

Note.—The Burmese sword is of a cutlass shape, and varies in size; when small, it is used as a dagger; in Ligore, the blade is double, the long handle of each forming the sheath of the other. (Fig 22.)—(*Amherst Collection.*)

240. Sword; "Dhá;" slightly curved blade; brass mounted wooden handle equal in length to the blade, and curved in continuation of its curve; wooden scabbard. *Burmah.* L. 3 ft. to 3 ft. 4 in.; L. of blade, 20½ in. (8824.–'55.)

241. Sword; "Dhá;" similar to No. 240; hilt bound with cane. *Burmah.* L. 3 ft.; L. of blade 22 in. (Fig. 19, No. 241.) (12555.–'69.)

242. Sword; "Dhá;" curved blade, square blunt end; cutlass handle; brass mounts. *Burmah.* L. 3 ft.; L. of blade, 19 in. (Fig. 19, No. 242.) (7370.–'69.)

243. Sword; "Dhá;" hilt mounted with brass. *Burmah.* L. 2 ft. 6¾ in.; L. of blade, 19 in. ('69)

244-246. Swords; "Dhá;" slightly curved blades with blunt ends; long hilts continuing the curve of blades. Used both for fighting and domestic purposes. *Burmah.* L. 2 ft. 3 in. to 2 ft. 6 in.; L. of blade, 19 in. (7370.–'67.)

247. Sword; "Dhá;" slightly curved blade of soft steel; long handle and black wood sheath, plated with silver. *Burmah.* L. 3 ft. in. (7423.–'67.)

248. Sword; "Dhá;" soft steel blade; hilt of wood bound with cane. *Burmah.* L. 2 ft. 7 in.; L. of blade, 18½ in. (12586.–'69.)

249. *Sword; "Dhá;" slightly incurved blade; ivory handle, carved in high relief; wooden sheath, silver mounted. *Rangoon, Burmah.* L. 2 ft. 2 in.

250. Sword; "Dhá;" straight blade; pistol-shaped hilt covered with sharkskin; wooden sheath, mounted with silver. *Burmah.* L. 2 ft. 3 in.; Bl. 20 in. (Fig. 19, No. 250.) (7425.)

251. Sword; "Dhá;" long straight blade; handle of ebony; sheath covered with sharkskin and plated with silver. *Burmah.*

252. Sword or Knife; "Dhá;" slightly curved blade; long ivory handle, covered with geometrical ornament in black and white. *Siam.* L. 21 in.; L. of blade, 13 in. (Fig. 19, No. 252.) ('69.)

253. Matchlocks (2); iron barrels with brass mounts; rudely constructed. Made by the Karens. *Burmah.* L. 4 ft. 10 in.

254. Ammunition Pouch and Priming Horn; painted red and black. Made by the Gyeikos. *Burmah.* (7355.–'67.)

255. Quick Match; in a case, the latter painted red and black. Used by the Gyeikos. *Burmah.* (6748.–'67.)

256, 257. Shields; of buffalo-hide, oblong in shape; the upper halves thickly studded with conical brass bosses, the lower covered with tufts of long black hair. The bosses or discs are attached by means of cords knotted at the back. *Arakan.* L. 2 ft.; W. 18 in. (8760.–'55.)

Cf. in the Christy Collection two shields of the Shendus in North Arakan, the one with a dozen brass disks belonged to the Chief, the other with one large brass disk to the second chief; their followers had plain shields.

258. Small Shield; of rhinoceros-hide; strongly projecting umbo; ornamented with concentric circles. *Burmah.* Diam. 11 in. (12551.–'69.)

259 T. Suit of Armour; mixed plate and quilted, resembling central Indian work. Worn by the Burmese General Maha Bandula at the battle of Donabyu (1825), at which he was slain.

See Z. S. Cat., Pl. xiii., for a very similar suit, described there as having been worn by Sikh chiefs at the court of the Great Mogul at the end of the 17th century.

GROUP VI.

MALAYAN PENINSULA AND INDIAN ARCHIPELAGO.

Fig 23.—Arms of the Malayan Peninsula and the Indian Archipelago (Group VI.)

The *Malays* seem to have come originally from Sumatra, and to have colonised Singapore, where the Buddhist religion was prevalent, at the end of the 12th or beginning of the 13th century. Malacca was founded at the end of the 14th century,[1] at which time, if not earlier, the King became Mahomedan, and spread Mahomedanism among the Malays who, with some exceptions, had previously been worshippers of Brahma. In 1511 Malacca was taken by the Portuguese, who carried off as booty 3,000 of the 5,000 musquets which had been furnished from Java.[2]

[1] Cf. Colonel Yule, Marco Polo, II., 263, (2nd edition).

[2] Lassen, Vol. iv., p. 541.

The *Javanese* belong partly to the Polynesian race, which extends from Borneo to Madagascar, and are descended partly from Aryan colonists who came from India at an early period, as Ptolemy gives Java a Sanskrit name.[1] Mahomedanism became the State religion about 1478. These various influences of race and religion may be traced in the character of their weapons (see p. 55), and the Arab spears which are brought back by their "Hajjis" from Mecca.

The naval force of the Javanese was certainly one of the most formidable and the bravest in the Indian seas, yet they were hardly a match for the inhabitants of Celebes, by whom they have been constantly defeated. The Dutch have on various occasions found them brave opponents.

The native armies of Java[2] consist chiefly of infantry. Each village has its provision of spears, and sometimes of fire-arms. In their tactics and conduct they endeavour to emulate the examples given in their ancient romances, and in their plans for their pitched battles, the march of their armies, &c., they strive to imitate the romantic descriptions contained in their ancient poems. In the great Mataram war, to expel the Dutch (1628–29), the disposition of the army is said to have been in the form of a shrimp; this form is termed "Mangkara boyewa," or "the shrimp which hides its soul," in allusion to the sovereign who is in the centre and not to be approached. Indian names are applied to the superior officers. The commander-in-chief is called "Senopati," and the leaders of divisions "Wadono," both Sanskrit words.[3] They are accustomed to tilts and tournaments, striking with long blunted spears, and at the conclusion of the exhibition on horseback, they sometimes dismount and practice the attack on foot.

The natives of *Celebes* are a more warlike race. At Macassar, in 1814, when the native allies of the Europeans took an oath to prosecute the war against Boni, war was determined by the Council of Chiefs with the following ceremony. The banner of State was unfurled, and dipped in blood. Each chief dipping his "kris" in a vessel of water drank of the consecrated liquid; then rising from his seat he danced round the bloody banner, brandishing his weapons, and repeating the oath.

The Malays use a straight sword, a chopper, a modification of the "dao," and several kinds of knives, as well as the "kris," which is more suitable for use in "running a muck" than in war.

The Javan kris is plainer in the handle and sheath, and differs also from that of Bali and Madura (Cf. Pl. viii.). As iron is very scarce, and consequently much prized in Java, its use is almost confined to the kris, which varies in shape with every tribe. Its varieties are said to exceed one hundred. The language furnishes us with 54 distinct names, of which 21 are with straight and 33 with waving blades.[4] They are well represented in the Christy Collection. There is one, a double dagger with the grip in the middle, and blades to the right and left.

In the sculptures of their ancient temples of Buddha, the straight sword and buckler may be observed, but it is not till the temples of the 4th class, and later date, at the beginning of the 15th century, that the "kris" is found delineated. The Javanese ascribe the invention of the "Kris" to Inakáto Pali, King of Janggolo in the 14th century, their era of fable and romance.

In the late war with the Dutch the Atchinese used bullets containing some foreign substance such as porcelain, with the view of nullifying the charms which they supposed were possessed by some against bullets of pure lead.—("Times," August 28, 1874.)

In *Sumatra*, a long thin stiletto-like blade is used, such as was taken from a chief killed by the Dutch in 1837.[5]

The tube or blowpipe with poisoned arrows is still in use among the inhabitants of Bali. But in the year 1639, in the war with Bali, the Javanese historian mentions as an extraordinary circumstance their use by them, so long had they been discontinued in

[1] He calls it IABA DIOU, *i.e.* Java-dvipa; he probably wrote from information of the first century, A.D. Note by Col. Yule. [2] Sir S. Raffles, Java, 1817. [3] Crawfurd, Hist. of Indian Archipelago, Vol. i., p. 233.

[4] Raffles, pp. 204, 296. A rare metal pamur, brought from Celebes, is used in damasking the blades.

[5] Raffles, p. 345.

the more civilized islands. In 1812, the Javanese employed stones and slings in an attack upon the palace of the Sultan, but without inflicting serious damage. The Javanese bow, 4 ft. 9 in. long, and arrow "gendewa, pana" is now seldom used except on state occasions. A horn bow and ornamental arrows are in the Christy Collection.

The *Malays* and the natives of *Celebes* use a short spear, or javelin. The Javanese use a spear 12 to 14 feet long with great dexterity.[1]

The spear and kris are used alternately, the fight commencing with the first. A mock action with sheathed spear and wooden dagger is sometimes carried on in the presence of the Court.

Coats of mail are still used by the natives of Celebes. There is a shield from this island in the Christy Collection.

The use of small arms the Indian islanders undoubtedly acquired from Europeans. The matchlock is called by its Portuguese name, the firelock by a Dutch, and the pistol by a Dutch or English one. In the use of either artillery or small arms the Indian islanders are extremely unskilful.[2]

The inhabitants of *Bali* and *Lombok*, situated at the east end of Java, are the only islanders who still practise the Hindoo religion. They are famous for the manufacture of matchlocks. Wallace saw two guns, 6 and 7 feet long respectively, and of a proportionately large bore, the barrels of which were twisted and well finished, though not so finely worked as ours. The stocks were well made, and extended to the end of the barrel. Silver and gold ornaments were inlaid on most of the surface, but the locks were taken from English muskets. (Cf. Fig. 10.)

The inhabitants of the *Nassau Islands*, off the coast of Sumatra, appear to be armed with the bow and arrow solely. "The bow" says Crisp[3] "is made from a species of palm, "called Neebong, which, when of a proper age, is very strong and elastic, the strings are "formed of the entrails of some animal. The arrow is made of a small bamboo, headed "with brass or with another piece of wood fixed to the end of the shaft and cut to a "point. Though strangers to the use of feathers to steady the flight of the arrow, they "discharge it with much strength and skill. A few are in possession of krises."

NOTE.—*A few of the most ornamental arms belonging to this group will be found in Case 70.*

260. SPEAR; watered blade; black bamboo shaft with deep (8 in.) gold ferrule of repoussé and filigree work. *Singapore.* L. of blade, 9 in. (Fig. 23, No. 260.) (12510–'69.)

Rockstühl engraves (Pl. 177, Nos. 3, 4, 5, 6) four lances of Malay Sultans. One has a flaming point, another the outline of a hideous monster, a third three flamboyant points connected by a floriated disk, and the fourth a very broad, short blade.

261. SPEAR; figured steel blade; shaft of mottled ebony, with ornamented gold ferule. *Singapore.* L. 6 ft. 4 in.; L. of blade, 12 in. (7335–'67.)

In the Windsor collection there is a lance with three flamboyant points inlaid with raised floral design in pure gold.

262. SPEAR; fine damascened blade, malacca cane shaft with embossed and gilt metal mounts. *Johore, Singapore.* L. 6 ft. 5 in.; L. of blade, 13 in. (Fig. 23, No. 262.) 7365–'67.)

263. BLOW-PIPE; 'Sampitan;" for shooting with poisoned darts. *Singapore.* L. 7 ft. 2 in. (12711–'55.)

264. BLOW-PIPE; "Sampitan;" spear point at the end of shaft. *Singapore.* L. 7 ft. 6 in.; L. of blade, 12 in. (Fig. 23, No. 264.) (12712.–'55.)

265. BLOW-PIPE; "Sampitan;" spear point at the end of shaft; copper, brass, and iron mounts. *Singapore.*

266. DOUBLE BLOW-PIPE; "Sampitan;" one tube within another. *Singapore.* L. 6 ft 6 in. (12710.–'55.)

267. QUIVER AND ARROWS; for the blow-pipe. L. of arrows, 12 in. *Singapore.* (6376.–'62.)

268. QUIVER AND ARROWS; for the blow-pipe. The arrows are made of bamboo and pith, and are poisoned. *Singapore.* L. 7 in. ('62.)

269 T. *DAGGER; "Kris;" watered blade, inlaid in the upper part with gold. Carved ivory hilt. Sheath covered with gold exquisitely embossed; the sling of delicately-wrought filigree work, with a brooch-like ornament of ruddy gold set with an emerald. Presented by the Rajah of *Keddah.* (163.)

[1] Wallace, Malay Archipelago, p. 15. [2] Crawford, p. 225. [3] Asiatic Researches, Vol. VI., p. 48.

(Group VI.)

Plate. VIII.

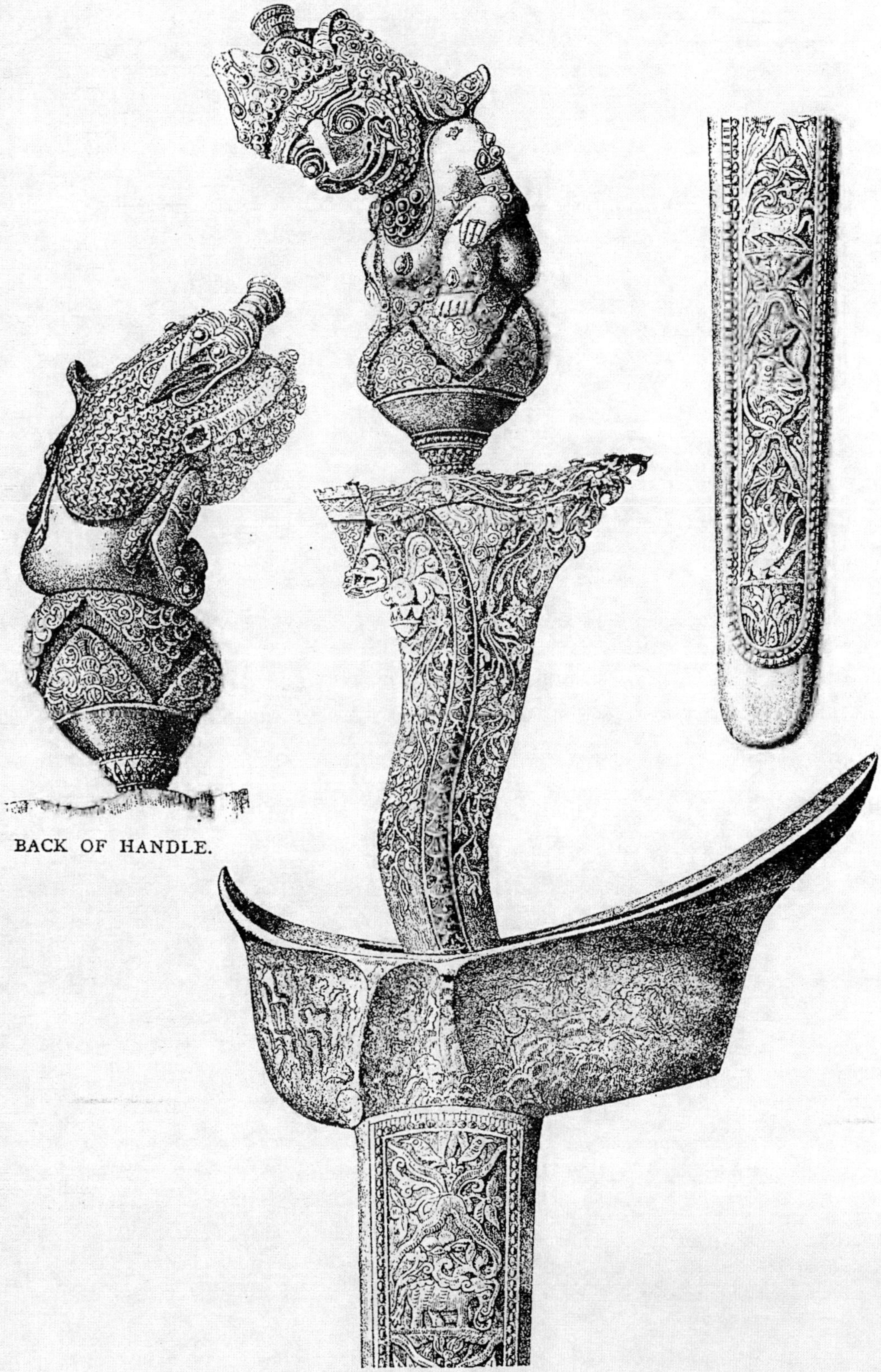

BACK OF HANDLE.

MALAY KRIS FROM Z. S. COLLECTION.

W. GRIGGS, PHOTO LITH, LONDON, S. E.

270. Dagger; "Kris;" undulating blade; carved hilt bound with silver wire; polished wood sheath. *Singapore.* L. 22 in. L. of blade, 18 in. (Fig. 23, No. 270.) ('69.)

271–273. Daggers; "Kris;" undulating watered blades; pistol-shaped wooden hilts curved at right angles to blade. *Singapore.* L. 17 in.; L. of blade, 14 in. (Fig. 23, Nos. 271–3.) (12591.–'69.)

274. Daggers (2); "Kris;" carved wood and ivory hilts. *Singapore.* L. 15 in. to 18 in; L. of blade, 12½ in. to 15 in. (Fig. 23, No. 274.) (12590.–'69.)

275–278. Daggers; "Kris;" straight and undulating, plain and watered blades; pistol-shaped carved wooden hilts; wooden crutch-shaped sheaths. *Singapore.* L. 17 in.; L. of blade, 13 in. (Fig. 23, No. 275–6.) (8876.–'55.)

279, 280. Daggers; "Kris;" ivory hilts; wooden sheaths. *Singapore.* L. 12½ in.; L. of blade, 9½ in. (Fig. 23, No. 279–80.) (12707.–'69.)

281. Dagger; "Kris;" small stiletto blade; pistol-shaped hilt; wooden sheath with ivory mounts. *Singapore.* L. 10 in. (12596.–'69.)

282. Dagger; "Kris;" long, thin, straight blade; wooden sheath. *Singapore.* L. 2 ft. 4 in.; L. of blade, 24 in. (Fig. 23, No. 282.) ('69.)

283. Dagger; "Kris;" slightly curved, grooved blade; hilt of dark wood. *Singapore.* L. 15 in.; L. of blade, 13 in. (Fig. 23, No. 283.) ('67.)

284 T. *Dagger; "Bali Kris;" painted sheath. (Fig. 23, No. 284 T.) (164.)

285 T. *Broad Knife; "Badek Palembang; blade of rough dark steel; hilt and sheath carved and lacquered in brown and gold. *Palembang.* (Fig. 23, No. 285 T.) (185.)

Cf. Windsor Collection, an ancient sword of the Sultans of Palembang, the hilt richly ornamented with gold filigree work, the border near the blade set with rubies and rose diamonds, the sheath mounted in embossed gold. L. 2 ft. 9 in.

286. Knife; "Wedung;" broad blade cutting on one edge only; wooden sheath with horn protector. *Java.* L. 12 in.; W. 2 in. (Fig. 23, No. 286.) (8883.–'51.)

Rockstühl (Pl. 120, Z. S. Cat., p. 267) mentions the following daggers from Java:—

"*Badè Badè.*" Secret dagger; slightly curved.

"*Mentok.*" Dagger, with ivory handle engraved, broad point, and back of blade round. Silver sheath.

"*Wedoeng*" (pron. Wedoung). Short powerful blade used by Hindoo races in Tinger mountains. Belonged to a chief, Wedeno.

Klevang; from Java. Sheath of wood bound with bamboo.

"*Tjoendrick.*" Long, straight poignard or short sword, with silver mounted hilt.

From Sumatra, a long, thin stiletto-like blade taken from a chief killed by Dutch in 1837.

287. Sword; "Kris;" undulating blade; hilt and sheath of carved wood. Used in Borneo, *Singapore.* L. 2 ft. 1 in.; L. of blade, 21 in. (Fig. 23, No. 287.) (12676.–'55.)

288, 289. Swords; long, straight blades; large carved wooden hilts; decorated with tufts of hair. Used by the Dyaks of *Borneo.* L. 3 ft. 1 in. to 3 ft. 3 in.; L. of blade, 2 ft. 4 in. (Fig. 23, No. 288–9.) (12607.–'69.)

The hilt and scabbard of a sword of this character in the Windsor collection are covered with plates of gold.

290. Sword; long, straight blade of bright steel; carved wooden hilt, decorated with tufts of hair. Used by the Dyaks of *Borneo.* L. 3 ft. 4 in; L. of blade, 2 ft. 6 in. (12607.–'69.)

291. Sword; straight blade, wooden hilt covered with leather, with tufts of hair attached. Used in *Borneo.* L. 2 ft. 5 in.; L. of blade, 2 ft. (Fig. 23, No. 291.) ('67.)

292 T. Sword; carved hilt of bone with tufts of human hair. Used by the Dyaks of *Borneo.* (Fig. 23, No. 292 T.) (168.)

Rockstühl (Pl. 177) figures two swords used by the Dyaks of Borneo. They are long, gradually getting broader to the point, and the hilt terminates in a thick tuft of hair.

The same author (Pl. 120-9) figures a "Kampak," a straight sword or pike from Java.

293. Shield; large, circular, convex, with pointed umbo; of painted wood. Diam. 2 ft. 6 in. Used by the Dyaks of *Borneo.* (12550.–'69.)

294. Shield; wood; oblong in shape, with incurved sides. Large, circular umbo, which, with the rest of the shield, is carved in low relief with foliated scroll ornaments and painted in red and green on a yellow background. *Borneo.* L. 3 ft. 10 in.

295, 296. Shields; oblong, of wood; the one bound with strips of cane; the other painted with grotesque dragon head and decorated with tufts of hair. Used by the Dyaks of *Borneo.* L. 3 ft. 6 in. and 4 ft.; W. 18 in. ('55.)

297 T. Coat. Composed of brass mail and small plates of buffalo horn. From *Keddah.* (Group on the left of screen.)

Cf. in the Christy Collection, a coat of brass mail with horn plates, from the Philippines.

GROUP VII.

NEPAL.

This group forms a link between the Turanian and Aryan type of arms. The *Nepalese, Gorkhas, and Parbatiyas* are a mixed race, containing more or less Turanian blood, qualified by the introduction of Rajput immigrants in the 14th century. Some of the former, like the Newars, are Buddhists, others are largely composed of the dcseendants of the Aryan settlers, and have adopted the Hindu religion. The character of their origin is well shown in their weapons, some of which are of a purely Aryan, others of a more barbarous, type.

It is worthy of remark that Nepal is the only part of Northern India which has never fallen under Mahomedan rule. It is therefore, as Ferguson well remarks of its architecture, a complete microcosm of India as it was in the seventh century, when Buddhists and Brahmins flourished side by side.

The *Gorkhas* claim to belong to the Kshatri or warrior class, and therefore to the ancient military division of Hinduism. They are a warlike race, and, as already remarked, made a determined resistance to our arms, but now form some of the best of our native infantry. Their national weapon is the *Kukri,* originally a kind of bill-hook, for cutting through small wood in the dense low jungles of the Teraí and the Himalayas. The Gorkha Kukri is generally ornamented with Aryan designs and sometimes even bears the figure of a Hindu deity inlaid in gold on the blade.

The Nepalese use a larger knife, or sword "Kora," with an inner cutting edge, with which those who use it skilfully are enabled to cut a sheep in two at a single blow. They also use broad-bladed swords, three or four inches in breadth. Their swords and sacrificial axes are generally inscribed at the end of the blade,[1] with Buddhist symbols the use of which seems to extend to Bengal.

In addition to the aboriginal tribes of *Chepang, Kusanda* and others, the chief tribes in Nepal are the *Gurungs,* a military tribe of Rajput extraction, who use the Kukri and Kora with a small shield; the *Magars,* excellent soldiers, who formed one of the first native regiments enlisted by Sir Charles Napier in 1850. They use the bow and other Gorkha weapons. The *Nepalese Brahmins,* of purer Aryan stock than the preceding tribes.

In the Himalayas there are thirty-one hill States whose rule the English Government has reinstated after their conquest by the Gorkhas. The inhabitants are a simple and unwarlike race. Many of the hill chiefs are Rajputs of good lineage.

The *Parbatiyas,* of Garhwál, generally carry in their belts a light broad-bladed hatchet, "dangra." Some substitute for it a Gorkha knife, wearing it in front, while the Gorkhas wear it behind.

NOTE.—*The ornamental arms belonging to this group will be found in Case 70. They are distinguished in the Catalogue by an asterisk.*

298. QUIVER AND ARROWS; the quiver of leather ornamented with hemi-spherical metal bosses, and *appliqué* embroidery of coloured leather. *Nepal.* L. of arrows, 2 ft. 6 in. (8763.–'55.)

299. QUIVER; similar to the preceding specimen. *Nepal.* (Pl. IX., No. 299.) (8777.–'55.)

300. QUIVER; similar to Nos. 298, 299, together with a leather case with waist strap for carrying the bow. *Nepal.* (Pl. IX., No. 300.) (8778.–'55.)

301. QUIVER AND ARROWS; the quiver of leather, green on one side, red on the other, stamped with a diaper pattern of small concentric rings. *Nepal.* L. of arrows, 2 ft. 6 in. to 2 ft. 9 in. (8764.–'55.)

(Group VII.)

Plate IX.

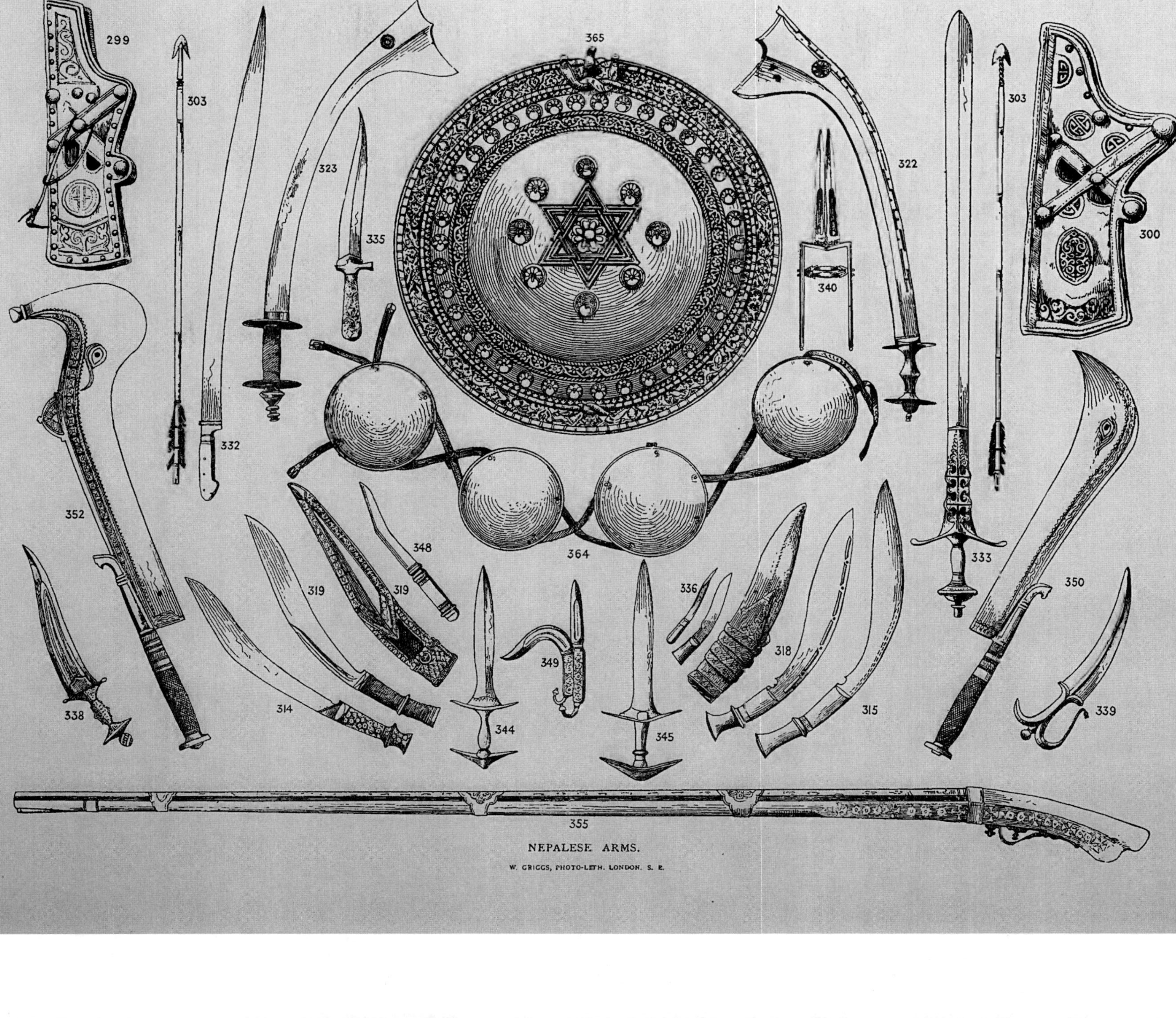

NEPALESE ARMS.

W. GRIGGS, PHOTO-LITH. LONDON, S. E.

302. Quiver; "Thakroo;" (?) bamboo, bound with light green leather. *Nepal.* L. 2 ft. 7 in. (8767.–'55.)

303. Quiver and Arrows; bamboo. *Nepal.* L. of arrows, 2ft. 8 in. (Pl. IX., No. 303.) (8762.–'51.)

304, 305. Pellet Bows; "Gulail or Ghulel;" bamboo; the strings made of thin strips of the same. For hurling pellets of clay or stone. *Nepal.* Used by the Karens of *Burmah*, as well as in *India.* L. 3 ft. 11 in. and 5 ft. 11 in. (8848.–'55.)

It is this kind of bow which appears to be alluded to in the passage "Hailstones shall be cast as out of a stone bow." (Wisdom v. 22.)

306. Sword; "Kukri;" incurved blade, widening towards the point; handle of black wood. *Nepal.* L. 19 in.; W. of blade, 2 in.

307–310. Swords; "Kukri;" similar to the preceding example. *Nepal.* L. 19 in. to 20 in.; W. $\frac{1}{4}$ in. to 2 in. (8805, 8877.–'55.)

311. Sword; "Kukri;" grooved blade, damascened with gold at its base. Wooden hilt. *Nepal.* L. 15$\frac{1}{2}$ in.; W. 1$\frac{1}{2}$ in. (8807.–'70.)

312. Sword; "Kukri;" brass blade, with steel edge; black wooden hilt. *Nepal.* L. 15 in; W. 1$\frac{1}{2}$ in. (8810.–'55.)

313. Sword; "Kukri;" sheath of wood-covered with leather. *Nepal.* L. 23 in.; W. 1$\frac{3}{4}$ in. (7882.–'55.)

314. Sword "Kukri;" bright blade, the hilt damascened in gold with a diaper of 8-petalled conventional flowers. *Nepal.* L. 19 in.; W. 1$\frac{1}{2}$ in. (Pl. IX., No. 314.) (8808.–'55.)

315. Sword; "Kukri;" bright blade; hilt of horn ornamented with flowers carved in low relief. *Nepal.* L. 23 in.; W. 2 in. (Pl. IX., No. 315.) (8809.–'55.)

316.* Sword; "Kukri;" bright steel blade; the hilt damascened with gold. Ivory hilt, with gold-damascened steel mounts. Crimson velvet sheath, with embossed silver gilt mounts. *Nepal.* L. 18 in. (7436.–'67.)

317.* Sword; "Kukri;" bright steel blade; ivory hilt, ornamented with bands of floriated scroll-work; embroidered black leather sheath, with small side sheath attached, enclosing two miniature Kukris, with ivory hilts, stained red and green respectively, and carved into grotesque heads. *Nepal.* Presented by the late Sir Jung Bahadur. L. 19 in.; W. of blade, 1$\frac{1}{2}$ in. to 2$\frac{1}{2}$ in. (8689.–'51.)

318.* Sword; "Kukri;" bright blade, the back edge perforated at intervals; hilt of dark wood; sheath of black leather, ornamented with quill embroidery. *Nepal.* Presented by the late Sir Jung Bahadur. L. 18 in. (Pl. IX., No. 318.) (8709.–'55.)

319.* Sword; "Kukri;" burnished steel blade; hilt mounted with silver and bound with plaited silver wire; sheath enriched with massive silver mounts, chased. *Nepal.* L. 19 in.; W. 1 to 2 in. (Pl. IX., No. 319.) (8700.–'55.)

320.* Sword; "Kukri;" plain bright blade; black wooden hilt; leather sheath, embroidered with peacock quills, with two small knives attached in a receptacle at the side. *Nepal.* L. 19 in.; W. 1 in. to 2 in. (8688.–'55.)

321. Sword; "Kora;" curved blade, expanding from 1 in. in width at the hilt to 3$\frac{1}{2}$ in. at its end; hilt of steel, with two circular flat disks as guards *Nepal.* L. 2 ft. ('55.)

322. Sword; "Kora;" large, heavy, curved and grooved blade, expanding from 1$\frac{1}{2}$ in. in width at the hilt to 6 in. at the point, near which it bears an eight-petalled lotus flower incised in the steel; hilt protected by circular disks; wooden sheath, covered with leather. *Nepal.* L. 2 ft. 5 in. (Pl. IX., No. 322.) (8823.–'55.)

323. Sword; "Kora" similar in form to the preceding specimens; the blade is incised with a circular conventional flower, and a small Buddhist cross. *Nepal.* L. 2 ft. 6 in.; W. of blade, 1$\frac{1}{2}$ in. to 6 in. (Pl. IX., No. 323.) (8822.–'55.)

324. Sword, "Kora;" blade incised with a many-petalled circular flower. *Nepal.* L. 2 ft. 4 in.; W. 1$\frac{1}{4}$ in. to 2$\frac{1}{2}$ in.

325. Sword; "Kora;" similar to preceding specimens. *Nepal.* L. 2 ft. 5 in.; W. 1 in. to 3$\frac{1}{2}$ in. (8734.–'55.)

326. Sword; "Kora;" blade incised with a star *Nepal.* L. 2 ft. 2 in.; W. 1 in. to 3$\frac{1}{2}$ in. ('55.)

327. Sword; "Kora." *Nepal.* L. 2 ft. 3 in.; W. 1 in. to 3$\frac{1}{2}$ in. ('55.)

328. Sword; "Kora;" embossed leather sheath. *Nepal.* L. 2 ft. 5 in.; W. 1 in. to 3$\frac{1}{2}$ in. (8738.–'55.)

329. Sword; "Kora;" the blade grooved, half-gilt, and incised with an eight-petalled flower. *Nepal.* L. 23 in.; W. 1$\frac{1}{4}$ in. to 4 in. (8821.–'55.)

330.* Sword; "Kora;" hilt covered with plaited silver wire; circular guard disks of silver, finely chased; purple velvet sheath, with massive silver mounts engraved and pierced. *Nepal.* L. 2 ft. 5 in.; W. 1 in. to 3$\frac{1}{2}$ in. (8679.)

331.* Sword; "Kora." The back of the blade is channelled, the grooves being gilt; steel hilt, with circular guard disks; sheath of black leather, embroidered with peacock quills and enriched with perforated and embossed mounts of fine gold. *Nepal.* Presented by the Marquis of Hastings. L. 2 ft. 4 in.; W. of blade, 1 in. to 4 in. (8677.–'50.)

332. Sword; watered steel blade, very slightly curved; handle of ivory. *Nepal.* L. 2 ft. 9 in.; W. 1$\frac{1}{4}$ in. to 1$\frac{1}{2}$ in. (Pl. IX., No. 332.) (12587.–'69.)

333. Sword; long, straight, double-edged blade, strengthened with raised gilt steel supports. Presented by Sir Jung Bahadur. *Ancient Nepalese.* L. 3 ft. 3 in.; W. 1$\frac{1}{4}$ in. to 2 in. (Pl. IX., No. 333.) (8793.–'55.)

334. Sword; "Kattí Talwár;" curved blade; steel hilt, with a spike projecting from the pommel. *Nepal.* L. 3 ft. 2 in.; W. 1¾ in. (8795.–'55.)

335. Dagger; "Kaṭár Bánk;" slightly curved blade, grooved on both sides, the grooves once filled with seed pearls; silver-plated hilt, embossed with floral decoration. *Nepal.* L. 15½ in.; W. 1½ in. (Pl. IX., No. 335.) (8811.)

336. Dagger; small curved blade; agate hilt. *Nepal.* L. 10 in. (Pl. IX., No. 336.) ('55.)

337. *Small Dagger; generally worn with a "Kukri," of which it is a miniature copy. *Nepal.*

338. Dagger; "Chilanum;" flamboyant blade of Damascus steel, deeply channelled; the hilt covered with simple geometrical ornaments, embossed and silver-gilt. *Nepal.* L. 15 in.; W. 2 in. (Pl. IX., No. 338.) (8801.–'55.)

339. Dagger; curved blade, thickened at the point, and ribbed; steel hilt, with knuckle-guard. *Nepal.* L. 14 in. (Pl. IX., No. 339.) (8792.)

340. Dagger; "Kaṭár;" forked blade, embossed; hilt shaped like the letter H. *Nepal.* L. 14½ in. (Pl. IX., No. 340.) (8790.–'55.)

341. *Dagger; "Kaṭár;" fluted blade, with waved edges; a rib, damascened in gold, runs up the centre from the hilt; hilt and side-guards with conventional foliage in perforated and damascened work. *Nepal.* (8791.–'55.)

342.* Dagger; "Kaṭár;" short, broad, nearly triangular blade, strongly ribbed, much thickened at the point; hilt and side guards damascened with gold. *Nepal.* L. 9 in. (8802.)

343.* Dagger; curved two-edged blade, damascened with gold near the hilt; hilt of curious shape, of steel damascened with gold; velvet sheath, with gold-damascened steel mounts. *Nepal* (?). (8534.)

344. Dagger; "Jamdhar Kaṭárí;" plain steel blade; the hilt similar in shape to that of the preceding example; bears traces of gilding. *Nepal.* L. 13½ in. (Pl. IX., No. 344.) (8803.–'55.)

345. Dagger; "Jamdhar Kaṭárí." *Nepal.* L. 14½ in. (Pl. IX., No. 345.) (8806.–'55.)

346.* Dagger or Hunting Knife; "Peshkabz;" pointed one-edged blade; broad, straight back, to which the edge gradually slopes; hilt of rock crystal. *Nepal.* Presented by the late Sir Jung Bahadur. (8707.–'55.)

347. Knife; straight blade; ivory hilt, the pommel carved with conventional dragon head. *Nepal.* L. 14½ in.; W. 1¾ in. (8813.–'55.)

348. Knife; abruptly curved, grooved blade; silvered hilt. *Nepal.* L. 11 in. (Pl. IX., No. 348.)

349. Elephant Goad; "Ánkus;" embossed steel hilt. *Nepal.* (Pl. IX., No. 349.) (8800.–'55.)

350, 351. Swords or Axes; "Rám dá'o;" broad, heavy, incurved blades, ornamented along the back with scroll patterns, and each bearing a representation of the human eye incised in the steel, and coloured; chequered ebony handles, with brass mounts. *Nepal.* L. 2 ft. 3½ in. and 2 ft. 5 in.; L. of blades, 19 and 20 in.; W. of blade, 2½ in. to 4 in. (Pl. IX., No. 350.) (11908.–'72.)

352. Sacrificial Axe; "Rám dá'o" or "Kharga;" broad, heavy, massive blade, terminating in a kind of axe-like projection, and bearing scroll ornaments, inscriptions, and the Buddhist emblem of the human eye incised in the steel, and coloured; chequered ebony handle, brass mounted. Used chiefly in the sacrifice of goats and buffaloes. *Nepal.* L. 2 ft. 7 in.; L. of blade, 23 in.; W. 3 in. to 5 in. (Pl. IX., No. 352.) (9150.–'74.)

One in the E. Collection, formerly in the Meyrick Collection, has an inscription in ancient Hindi which, from the character of its writing, must be more than 200 years old.

The use of the sacrificial axe is thus described in the sanguinary chapter translated from the "Calica Purana," by W. C. Blaquiere (Asiatic Researches, Vol. II., p. 1039):—"With regard to the sacrifices to the goddess "Chandrea and other gods, the sacrificer is directed to "use a 'Chandra-hasa,' or 'Catri,' two sorts of axes, as "the best mode, a hatchet or knife, or saw or a sangcul, "as the second best, and the beheading with a hoe, "'Bhalloc,' or sort of spade, as the inferior mode.

"Exclusive of these weapons, no other of the spear or "arrow kind ought ever to be used in performing a "sacrifice, as the offering is not accepted by the god.

"The 'Kharga,' or axe, being invoked by the text called "Calatriya Mantra, Calatri (the goddess of darkness) "herself presides over the axe uplifted for the destruc-"tion of the sacrificer's enemies.

The animals to be sacrificed are birds, tortoises, fish, "buffaloes, wild bulls, he-goats, ichneumons, wild boars, "rhinoceros, antelope, guanas, reindeer, lion, and tiger."

353. Bayonet-Sword; "Sangín;" attached as a bayonet to the muzzle of a gun. *Nepal.* L. 21 in. (8719.–'55.)

In the Windsor collection there is a small State axe, with short bayonet introduced at the head.

345. Matchlock; octagonal barrel; ebony stock, with brass mounts; short butt. *Nepal.* L. 5 ft. 7 in. (12536.)

355. Matchlock; heavy octagonal Damascus barrel, inlaid with silver, attached to the stock by broad bands of embossed silver plate; stock of ebony, inlaid with brass ornaments. *Nepal.* L. 5 ft. 11 in. (Pl. IX., No. 355.) (8891.–'50.)

356. Powder-Flask; "Baṭwál túmbí;" (powder-gourd), of leather, embroidered with coloured thread and strips of porcupine quill. *Nepal.* (8726.–'55.)

357. Pouch; leather, embroidered with strips of coloured quills in pine pattern. *Nepal.* (8731.–'55.)

358. Powder-Flask; black leather. *Nepal.* (8732.–'55.)

359. Hunting Belt, with Pouches (4); black leather embroidered with silk; one of the pouches contains a shot flask. *Nepal.* ('55.)

360. Helmet; "Tóp;" hemispherical, of polished steel, surmounted by a plume-holder, and fringed with padded lappets of Chinese brocaded silk. *Nepal.* H. 6½ in. (8648.–'55.)

361. Coat of Chain Mail; "Zirah-baktar;" the rings composing it are of brass and steel, unriveted. *Nepal.*

362. Shirt of Mail; "Zirah-baktar;" large riveted links of steel. *Nepal.* (8603.–'55.)

363. Waist-Belt; steel, formed of a series of overlapping, vertical strips of steel (about 6 in. in length) riveted to strips of leather. *Nepal.* L. 4 ft.; W. 6 in. (8735.–'55.)

364. Belt; composed of four circular, slightly convex discs or plates of steel ("Char Aina," or "the four mirrors"), connected by leather straps. Worn round the waist, outside a coat of chain-mail. *Nepal.* Presented by Sir Jung Bahadur. Diam. of discs, 7 in. (Pl. IX., No. 364.) (8737.–'55.)

365. Shield; "Nág-p'haṇí ḍhál, (Snake-hood shield;") circular, of black rhinoceros hide, enriched with copper gilt mounts. The centre is occupied by interlaced triangles, enclosing an eight-petalled lotus flower, and surrounded by eight variously-chased bosses, with pendent spangles of gilt-copper. A triple border of conventional floriated scroll-work, spangled bosses, and low-relief arabesques of birds surrounds the shield. The whole is enclosed by a coil of snakes, which meet at the top of the shield, with three uplifted heads. *Nepal.* Diam. 2 ft. 2½ in. (Pl. IX., No. 365.) (8781.–'55.)

The pentagon, or three triangles, is analogous to the hexagon engraved on the seal of Solomon. It appears to have been used as a lucky sign. The Pythagoreans regarded it as a symbol of health. It is found both in China and India, and the pentagon is said by the Indians to be one of the attributes of Buddha, god of wisdom and learning.—*Reinaud,* Vol. II., p. 241, note (Cf. As. Soc. Memoirs, Vol. I., Pt. II., p. 240, &c.).

The Greeks called it τριπλοῦς τρίγωνος διάλληλος πεντάγραμμος.—Lucian.

Solomon's seal is a double triangle, or hexagon. The Orientals attributed to Solomon's ring a magic power, which made him master of the genii and the elements and ruler of the earth. It is said by Tod to be a sign of the followers of Siva.

The interlaced triangles are engraved on a crystal ring amulet, in the Tayler Collection. This symbol is also engraved on a silver Buddhist conch in the India Museum.

GROUP VIII.

THE RAJPUTS.

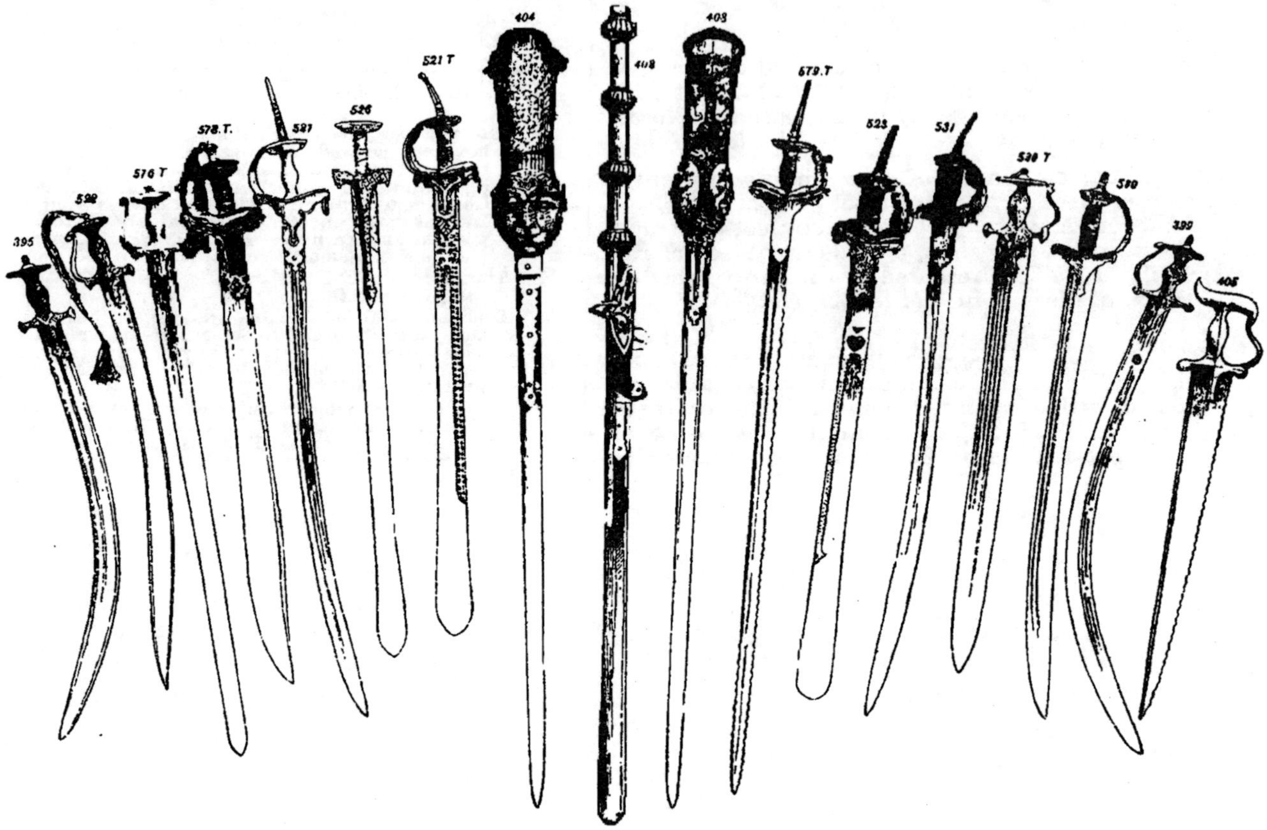

Fig. 24.—Indian Swords.

The arms of the different branches of the Aryan stock which we have next to consider, are, it must be observed, no longer confined within narrow geographical limits, as is the case with some of the non-Aryan arms, but, as one would naturally expect in the arms of the dominant race, are spread over the greater part of India.[1] They are necessarily more or less modified by the numerous descendants of the Mahomedan conquerors who have overrun India.

There are certain arms peculiar to certain localities, as the Kháṇḍá (No. 521T), the national sword of Orissa, and the gauntlet sword of the Mahratta cavalry, probably introduced by the Moguls; but even where the form of the weapons has been borrowed from other races as from Europeans, the details of the ornament exhibit a general similarity of type. It will therefore be necessary to look at the Aryan arms as a whole, and to recollect that some weapons, such as the Talwár (No. 395), or sabre, are in almost universal use; the hemispherical helmet, probably introduced by the Moguls, and chain armour, are used from Mysore to the Punjab; the Kaṭár also has a very wide range. I purpose, therefore, to point out the peculiarities of each race in the use of its arms, and in the manner of its warfare, without keeping strictly within territorial divisions.

[1] It must also be borne in mind that in a considerable part of India, especially in the wilder tracts of Central India, there is a great mixture of races living side by side. For instance, in parts of Rajputana there are, first, the pure Aborigines—the Bhils proper; next above these, the tribes of half-blood, claiming paternal descent from Aryan clans; above these again is the pure Rajput clan, and between these well-defined classes there are groups, of which it is difficult to say to which class they belong, either in the ascending or descending scale.

The Aryan arms may be most fitly introduced by an account of the Rajputs. In the different gradations of caste they hold the second place, that devoted to the military profession. They are not, as might be supposed, confined to the country between the Indus on the west, the desert on the north, Bundelkhand on the east, and the Vindhya mountains on the south, known as Rajpútáná, but are spread over a great part of Hindostan. Even after inter-marriage with the aborigines, and conversion in some cases to Mahomedanism by their conquerors, they still retain the martial characteristics of their race, and impress their fair complexions and handsome features on their descendants.[1]

The Rajputs are divided into thirty-six royal tribes. The chief clans are the *Chohán* the *Rahtore, Hara, Jharija,* and *Ratoch.* Of these, the Chohans are most numerous in Mainpuri, the Haras in Haraoti, the Jharijas in Kach and Guzerat.

The Rajputs are all brought up to the use of arms. Every village has its gymnasium where instruction is given morning and evening in the use of weapons and the practice of athletic exercises, and these must have contributed much to their martial bearing and soldierly qualities.

No prince or chief among them was without his Silleh-Khana, or armoury, in which he passed hours in viewing or arranging his arms. The chief warriors had fortified abodes, with several hundred horsemen in their train. They were styled "Sawant," and as a distinguished badge wore a waist band of small brass bells. They never went to battle but encased in armour.

Every favourite weapon, whether sword, matchlock, spear, dagger, or bow has a distinctive epithet. The broad curved sword (*teghá*) (No. 399) is in use among the Hindu Rángars and Mahomedan Rajputs. The long cut-and-thrust blade, like the Andrea Ferrara, is not uncommon, but the chief favourite of all the various swords found throughout Rajputana is the Sirohi, a slightly curved blade, shaped like that of Damascus. There is one, the "Kháṇḍá," a double-edged sword, which is the object of a special worship called "Kharga Shapna" (the imprecation of the sword). The festival in which this imposing rite occurs is the "Naurátra," sacred to the god of war, and, according to Tod, of Scythic origin. It commences on the 1st of the month Asín, and lasts for nine days. The ceremonies of the fourth day are thus described by Tod:[2]—"As on every one of the "nine days, the first visit is to the 'Chaughán,' or Champ de Mars. The day opens with "the slaughter of a buffalo. The Rana proceeds to the temple of Déví, where he worships "the sword and the standard of the Raj Jogi, to whom, as the high priest of Síva, the god "of war, he pays homage, and makes offering of sugar and a garland of roses. A buffalo "having been previously fixed to a stake near the temple, the Rana sacrifices him with "his own hand by piercing him from his travelling throne with an arrow."

On the 10th of the month Asín is held a festival, "Dasahrá," universally known and respected in India, although of an entirely military character, being commemorative of[3] the day on which the deified Rama commenced his expedition to Lanka for the redemption of Seeta. It is consequently deemed by the Rajput a fortunate day for warlike enterprise. The day commences with a visit from the prince to his spiritual guide. Tents and carpets are prepared at the *Chaughán*, where the artillery is sent, and in the afternoon the Rana, his chiefs and their retainers, repair to the "Field of Mars," worship the kaijiri tree, liberate the "niltach" ("Nílkanṭh"—*Coracias Indica*), or jay, sacred to Rama, and return amidst a discharge of guns. The following day the Rana takes the muster of his troops amidst discharges of cannon, tilting, and display of horsemanship.

The attachment of the Rajput to his arms is evidenced by the fact that, next to his sovereign's throne, his most powerful oath is by his arms; *ya sil ka án*, "by this

[1] It is related as an example of this that the "Bhálí Sultans" of Oude, a Mahomedan tribe of Rajput origin, were so called from a traditional story to the effect that an Emperor of Delhi, at a meeting of the chiefs, was so struck by the manly bearing of one who stepped to the front and stuck his spear deep into the ground, that he exclaimed, "What King (Sultan) of the Spear (Bháli) is this?" and desired that the tribe should take its name from that saying.—*Forbes Watson*, "The People of India."

[2] Tod's "Annals of Rajasthan," p. 587.

[3] Cf. Festivals, p. 147. Chaughán = Polo-ground.

weapon," as, suiting the action to the word, he puts his hand on his dagger, never absent from his girdle; *dhál talwar ka án*, " by my sword and shield."

The shield is deemed the only fit salver on which to present gifts, and accordingly, at a Rájpút court, shawls, scarves, jewels, &c. are always spread before a guest on bucklers.[1]

Tod draws a parallel between the Rajputs and the feudal races of Scandinavia and Germany. In feudal, as in Rajput communities, arms played a conspicuous part in all military pageants, as well as in all the business of life.

As in feudal times, the right of primogeniture prevailed, and when, in rare cases, it was set aside, as in the case of Amra, eldest son of Raja Gaz (1634), in favour of Jaswant, the second son, the ceremony was of a symbolic character in its connexion with arms. In a convention of all the feudality of Márú, the sentence of exclusion from the succession, accompanied by the solemn rite of Dés-vatoh, or exile, was pronounced upon him. The " Khilat " of banishment was brought forth, consisting of sable vestments, in which he was clad; a sable shield was hung upon his back, and a sword of the same hue was girded round him; a black horse was then led out, being mounted on which he was commanded to depart beyond the limits of Márú.

When in the field the Rajput warrior invokes the aid of the god of war, " Hár," and his trident (trisúla), while his battle shout is " Már! Már! " His offerings to the seven-headed god of battle, " Kumára," are blood and wine. He worships his horse, his sword, and the sun, and attends more to the martial song of the bard than to the litany of the Brahmin.

Riding in the ring in tournaments with guarded lances, defence of the sword against the lance, with every variety of noble horsemanship, are some of their chief exercises; firing at a mark with a matchlock, in which they attain remarkable accuracy of aim, and, in some parts of the country, throwing a dart or javelin from horseback are favourite amusements. The practice of the bow is likewise a main source of pastime, and, as used by the Rájpúts, requires both dexterity and strength. The Rájpút is not satisfied until he can bury his arrow to the feather in the earthen target or in the buffalo. The use of the bow is hallowed; Arjuna's bow, in the "great war," and that of the Chohan king, Prithvi Ráj, with which the former gained Draupadi, and the latter the fair Sunjogta, are immortalised like that of Ulysses. In these martial exercises the youthful Rajput is early initiated, and, that the sight of blood may be familiar, he is instructed before he has strength to wield a sword, to practise with his boy's scimitar on the heads of lambs and kids. In this manner the spirit of chivalry is continually fed, for everything around him speaks of arms and strife.[2]

The composition of the forces[3] of the Rajput sovereigns varies in each province. In Marwar the military resources of the Rahtores depended mainly on a foreign mercenary force of Rohilla and Afghan infantry, armed with musquets and matchlocks, and having cannon and sufficient discipline to act in a body.

There was also a brigade of those monastic militants, the " Bishanswámis," consisting of 700 foot, 300 horse, and an establishment of rockets (bán), a very ancient instrument of Indian warfare, and mentioned long before gunpowder was used in Europe.

In Mewar there are 16 great chiefs, in Ambér 12, and in Márwár eight. The contingents required by these princes may be estimated by the qualification of a cavalier, one for every 500 rupees of rent.

Such is the description that Tod, whose learned volumes are full of the inner life and history of the Rajputs, gives of their military spirit and innate love of arms, inherited through many generations of soldiers.

In Oude, the Rajputs are the principal land-holders. They formed the greater proportion of the Bengal sepoy army before 1857. They are thus described by Sleeman[4] before the annexation:—" The principal landholders—zemindars who are in open resistance " to the Government—have each armed and disciplined bodies of 2,000 foot and 500 " horse, and the command of as many as they like of 'Passies,' armed with bows and

[1] Cf. Festivals, p. 592. [2] Tod, p. 645. [3] *Ibid.*, II., p. 175. [4] Colonel Sleeman, Oude, 1849.

arrows. The latter are village watchmen, and at other times robbers of the lowest class. They use the bow and arrow especially, and are said to be able to send an arrow through a man at the distance of 100 yards.[1] The talookdars have each a fort mounting five or six guns, and trained bands of 500 or 600 men.

"The irregular regiments of the King of Oude are composed of men who get nominally four rupees a month, and are obliged to provide their own accoutrements, arms, and ammunition, except when on actual service. The arms they are expected to provide are a matchlock and a sword."

The arms, with the exception of some cannon and shell, and the muskets and bayonets for the few disciplined regiments, are manufactured in Oude.

In Bundelkhand the *Bundelas* are of Rajput race. They are haughty and independent, "As boorish as a Bundela," is a proverb.

Among the various tribes of the peninsula of *Guzerat*,[2] the Rájpúts are the most prominent. They were subject to a number of petty chieftains who shut themselves up in their forts, and from their battlements resisted the cavalry of the Gaikwar. The villages with their mud walls each became a fortification in turn. One of the ancient forts in this province is thus described by Forbes:[3]

"The fortress of Junjoowara forms an exact square, of which, each side measures in length about 800 yards; the walls which enclose this space are of solid masonry, about 50 feet high. In the centre of each side is a large gateway, with bracketted platform above; at each corner of the fortress is a square tower, and four rectangular bastions intervene between each corner tower and central gateway. The walls are throughout ornamented with a profusion of sculptured horizontal bands, and are completed by semicircular battlements screening the platformed way, along which the warders passed. In the centre is a tank which is approached by a ghat, and a well. This fortress was only a frontier military position, and inferior in size to the forts in the capital towns."

While treating of the Aryan races of Central India, I will briefly allude to that section of them found in Bengal and Orissa, the arms of which are scarcely represented in the Museum.[4]

The Bengalees are a feeble and unwarlike race. Although so large a proportion of them are Mohammedans, they are descendants of those who adopted the faith rather than the martial spirit of their conquerors. To the east of them are the Assamese who possess a similar religion, and speak a cognate language; on the west, a fine Aryan race inhabiting Behar, and on the south, the Ooriahs, a half Aryan people overspreading Orissa and Cuttack.

In Orissa and Cuttack a landed militia ("Paiks") is maintained by the "Khandaits" or ancient Zemindars. The "Paiks" are paid by lands which they cultivate subject to the performance of military and police duties when called upon by their chiefs. They constantly maintained the most bloody wars with the Moguls. They are divided into three classes[5]:—

1. "Pahris," who carry a large shield of wood covered with hide, and strengthened by knots and circles of iron; and the long straight national sword of Orissa, the "Khándá."
2. "Bánúa," who use the matchlock, small shield, and sword.
3. "Dhenkeyas," armed with bow and arrows, and the sword.

Their war dress consists of a cap and vest made of tiger or leopard skin, a sort of chain armour for the body and thighs, and a girdle formed of the tail of some wild animal. They further stain their faces with vermilion, and their limbs with yellow clay.

---

[1] It is made of horn, with double curve. When drawing it they support it on the ground, and bend it with their toe and right hand.

[2] Wilson's "India, Vol. I., p. 48.

[3] Ras Mala, p. 193.

[4] There is a manufactory of guns and pistols at Monghyr, which has been called the Birmingham of India. At Windsor there is a sword from Partábgarh, in N. Bengal, which is richly ornamented with enamels, and the sheath of which is covered with a floral diaper in gold.

[5] Asiatic Researches, Vol. XV., p. 201, 1825.

NOTE.—*The more ornamental arms, distinguished by an asterisk, will be found in Cases* 58 *and* 67 (*the latter firearms*).

366. *Bow; "Kamán;" curved Parthian shape. Of horn painted in various colours, and bound with gold brocade (Kincob) *Jaipur.* L. 4 ft. (6554.–'67.)

367.* QUIVER AND ARROWS; "Tír-o-tarkash." The quiver of crimson velvet embroidered with gold and coloured silk. The arrows with painted shafts and various-shaped heads, some pointed, others blunt and heavy. *Udaipur.* (8696.)

368.* PELLET BOW; "Gulel;" Bamboo, velvet grip; double string with web pellet holder. *Udaipur.* L. 4 ft. 10 in. (9686.–'55.)

369.* QUIVER; "Tarkash;" blue velvet embroidered with silver thread.

370, 371. SPEARS. The shafts lacquered in various colours, and further ornamented with gold leaf and fragments of talc, the design being a spiral scroll of roughly drawn floral ornament. *Bareli.* L. 7 ft. 10 in. L. of head 14 in. ('67.)

The Rajput lance is called "Sang." It is about 10 ft. long, and covered with plates of iron for about 4 feet.—*Tod*, Rajputana.

372. SPEAR. Long and flexible. Composed of short cylinders of ivory, connected end to end by brass bands. Small steel blade damascened with gold. Shaft ornamented with incised scrolls in red and black. *Jodhpur.*

373. MACE; "Gargaz; ?" 8-bladed head. Silver plated and partly gilt. Basket hilt with pendent gold tassel. *Myhere, Bundelkhand.* L. 2 ft. 7 in. (Pl. X., No. 373.) (7417.–'67.)

The "Garz" or mace was introduced from Persia. Made of iron, either plain or inlaid with gold, silver or brass, they are worn by men of high rank.

One in the E. Collection (Fig. 25), bought at Delhi, is like a Morgenstern, and has a dagger concealed in the handle, while the ball of the mace bristles with flamboyant spikes. It is of fine damascened steel, inlaid with gold, and is intended evidently for ornament rather than use.

374. MACE; "Gargaz;" of steel. Basket hilt. Engraved shaft. L. 2 ft. 8 in. Taken at *Lucknow.* (8745.–'69.)

375.* BATTLE AXE; "Tabar." The blade and the upper part and butt end of the shaft, ornamented with gold damascenings. The middle of the shaft is spirally twisted and covered with silver plate. *Jodhpur.* L. 2 ft. 1 in. Head 6 in. × 3 in. (8552.–'55.)

At Windsor there is a processional axe of silver, with twisted handle, 2 ft. 10½ in. long. The blade is broad, and engraved with raised pattern of grapes and vine leaves. Cf. processional battle axe in B. M., bought in 1836 from the last King of Delhi, as one of the twelve that were carried before Akbar.

376. BATTLE AXE; "Tabar;" blade, ornamented with flowers chiselled in low relief and gilt, the back ground filled in with black composition. Octagonal shaft of iron with ebony sides. *Udaipur.* L. 19 in. Head 5 in. by 4 in. (Pl. X., No. 376.) (8728.–'55.)

377. BATTLE-AXE; "Tabar;" curiously engraved shaft and blade. L. 17 in. Head 4½ in. by 3 in. (8655.–'55.)

378.* KNIFE. One-edged blade. Cornelian hilt with embossed gold mounts. Gold mounted sheath. (8459.–'55.)

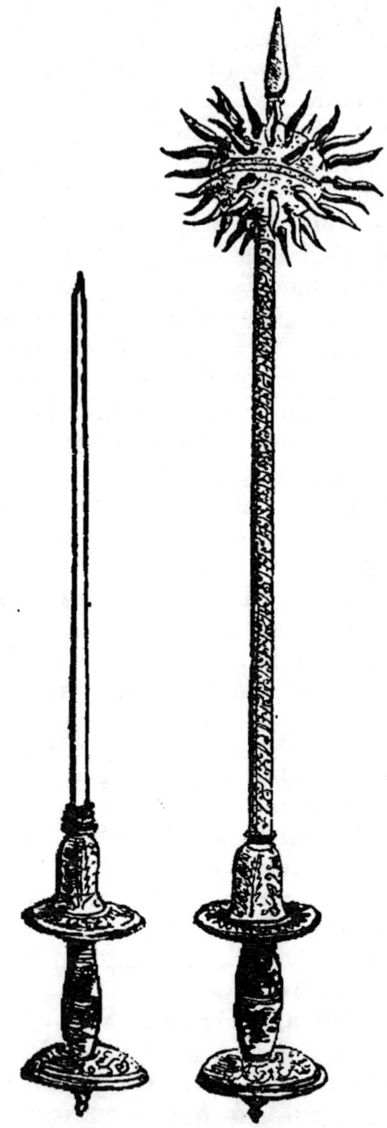

Fig. 25.—Indian Mace from Delhi, with concealed dagger. (E. Coll.)

379.* THREE KNIVES OR DAGGERS, fitting one into another. The blades and hilts of the two larger knives are hollow. The largest encloses the second, the second the smallest. Dark-veined Damascus blades, ivory hilts with damascened steel mounts. Green velvet sheath with enamelled gold mounts; gold lace belt with gold tassels attached. *Rampore.* (8541.–'55.)

380.* THREE KNIVES; "Ch'húrí;" fitting one into another. Ivory handles. Watered, dark, steel blades. *Ulwar.* (8560.–51.)

381.* DAGGER OR KNIFE; "Peshkabz;" straight one-edged blade. The hilt of steel damascened with gold, is hollow and conceals a knife, saw, chisel and file with ivory handles. *Datiah, Central India.* (7454.–'57.)

382.* DAGGER OR KNIFE; "Peshkabz." One-edged pointed blade of bright steel; broad straight back. Hilt covered with mother-of-pearl. Crimson velvet sheath, silver mounted. *Bundelkhand.* (7451.–'67.)

383.* TWO DAGGERS; "Kaṭár;" one concealed within the other. The larger blade is hollow and acts as a sheath to the smaller one, the side-guards of which are hollow, and conceal those of the outer Kaṭár. The side guards are covered with inscriptions raised and gilt. The sheath is ornamented with gilt leather, cut in delicate geometrical patterns over a background of coloured tinsel. Gold mounts. *Alwar.* L. 18 in. (Pl. X., No. 383.) (8550.–'51.)

384.* DAGGER; "Kaṭár;" fine steel blade, the centre grooved and ribbed. Hilt and side guards ornamented with gold damascenings. Green velvet sheath. *Udaipur.* L. 17 in. (8676.–'55.)

385.* DAGGER; "Kaṭár;" grooved, Damascus blade. Steel hilt, damascened with gold. Gold brocade sheath. *Bikanir.* (8546.–'55.)

386.* DAGGER; "Kaṭár;" deeply forked grooved blade. Hilt covered with floriated ornaments damascened in gold. Green velvet sheathtipped with gold. *Jhellawar.* L. 15 in. (7440.–'67.)

387.* DAGGER; "Kaṭár;" ribbed blade. Hilt damascened with gold. *Jodhpur.* (8545.)

388.* DAGGER; "Kaṭár;" blade chiselled in low relief, with representation of a tiger hunt. Hilt ornamented with perforated work. Taken at *Lucknow.* L. 19 in. Bl. 12 in. (Pl. X., No. 388.) (8787.)

Cf. Z. S. Cat. p. 354. "Kaṭár." Blade figured in relief with an elephant pursuing his mahout, and horseman pursuing a foot soldier.

The "Kaṭár," dagger, together with the straight sword are probably the national arms of India.

The figures supporting the Holy Pagoda at Ramisseram, all have the Kaṭár at the waist.

389.* DAGGER; "Kaṭár;" with five blades. By pressing together the transverse bars which form the hilt, the apparently single blade divides in a radiating fashion into five. *Chirkaree, Bundelkhand.* L. 15½ in. (7441.)

390.* DOUBLE DAGGER; "Haladie (?);" consisting of two small blades attached to one hilt, one at each end. The hilt is of steel damascened with gold. Green velvet sheath. *Chirkaree, Bundelkhand.* (7444.–'67.)

391.* ELEPHANT GOAD; "Ánkus;" steel damascened with gold. The shaft is hollow, consisting of ribs of steel, encircled by bands of the same, damascened with gold, and encloses a number of little hollow jingling bells of metal, which roll up and down when the weapon is raised or lowered. The head of the Ánkus is, together with the pommel or base by the shaft, richly ornamented with gold. L. 22½ in. (Pl. X., No. 391.) (11689.)

Cf. in the Prince of Wales' Collection a spear shaft formed in compartments each containing a hollow bell in the same way.

391A*. ELEPHANT GOAD; "Ánkus;" with dragon head inlaid with rubies, proceeding from enamelled and jewelled elephant's head; the shaft inlaid with diamonds on dark blue enamel, and the grip inlaid with enamels on gold, of the richest character, representing buildings, animals, and birds, relieved with foliage. *Jaipur.*

392.* SABRE; "Talwár;" composed of two very thin blades with half hilts, which by means of a series of catches on the inner sides, and a screw-nut pommel, are made to unite and form a single weapon. The blades, one of which bears an Arabic inscription, inlaid with gold, are of the finest black damascus steel. The hilt, of the ordinary shape, is exquisitely damascened in gold, both on the inner and outer surfaces of its halves, the outer surfaces bearing inscriptions inclosed in cartouche forms. The scabbard is covered with leather, gilt, and perforated over a back ground of coloured tinsel. *Alwar, Rajputana.* L. 2 ft. 4½ in. (8517.–51.)

Cf. from Zarkoe-Seloe Colln. "Pulouar." Remarkable for the open guard of the hilt, and the quillons with the ends drooping downwards, and terminating in dragons' heads; used probably only by rajahs or chiefs, —*Rockstühl*, p. 279.

Pulouar." The blade serrated, with an inscription on the back :—"When we hold our sword in our grasp, "we carry slaughter into the ranks of our enemies." —*Rockstühl*, pl. clxvii. 3.

393.* SABRE; small blade of black watered damascus steel, down the middle of which runs a continuous groove or channel, open at intervals and containing numerous small pearls which roll up and down when the weapon is brandished. (In the poetical language of the Persians the pearls in the blade are figurative of the "tears of the wounded.") Near the hilt will be found two similar side grooves, also filled with pearls, together with an inscription inlaid in gold. The hilt, furnished with a knuckle-guard, is damascened in gold with grapes and vine-leaves; the pommel is of crutch-shape, called Zafar Takiah. The scabbard is of leather, embossed, painted and gilt, and mounted with steel, damascened in gold. *Alwar.* L. 2 ft. (8518.–'51.)

Cf. from Zarkoe-Seloe Colln. "Zafar Takiah. Swords, one with a crescent-shaped handle, the other with a cross-piece, shaped like the crutch of a stick.

This kind of short sword is placed at the corner of the divan by the Indian rajahs as a precaution against a surprise, and when they are half lying down, the arm rests upon the handle, whence they are called "cushion of victory" (Persian Takiah-i-Zafar), to signify their use.—*Rockstühl*, Pl. clxvii. 4, 5.

One which formerly belonged to Jehangir, and was taken from the last King of Delhi, is preserved at Windsor.

These sacred crutches are generally combined with a weapon. They frequently contain a dagger concealed in the handle, and are highly ornamented. The hilt of one in the Tayler Collection is of green and white jade, set with jewels.

394. *SABRE; "Talwár;" burnished blade. Hilt with knuckle guard of steel, damascened in gold, with flowers; purple velvet scabbard. *Datiah.* L. 2 ft. 11½ in. (7453.–'67.)

395. *SABRE; "Talwár;" bright blade, notched at the back; steel hilt, covered with a small quatre-foil diaper damascened in silver; green velvet scabbard. *Kotah, Rajputana.* L. 2 ft. 10 in. (Fig. 24, No. 395.) (7343.–'67.)

396. SABRE; "Talwár;" steel hilt. *Jodhpur.* L. 3 ft. 2 in.; L. of blade, 2 ft. 8 in. (8516.–'51.)

397. SABRE; "Talwár;" steel hilt. *Rajputana.* L. 3 ft. (8796.–'55.)

398. *SABRE; "Teghá;" Damascus blade; guarded hilt, richly damascened with gold in floriated designs; purple velvet scabbard, with perforated and embossed gold mounts. *Jodhpur.* L. 3 ft. 2 in. (8513.–'55.)

Cf. from Codrington Coll. "Sooryhee" (Sirohi?") large heavy sword, of good watered steel, slightly curved, with handle slightly ornamented with gold. Much used by Mahrattas and Rajpoots in the time of Hyder Ali. Very hard and brittle.

Sooryhee; blade slightly ornamented with gold; plain handle, double guard.

399. SABRE; "Teghá;" coarse Damascus blade, with three grooves; guarded hilt, damascened silver; green leather scabbard. *Jodhpur.* L. 3 ft. 2 in.; L. of blade, 2 ft. 9 in. by 1¾ in. (Fig. 24, No. 399.) (8514.–'55.)

400. SWORD; "'Abbásí;" straight blade of Damascus steel, strengthened at the back with perforated steel supports; hilt ornamented with floriated damascenings in gold; velvet scabbard. *Udaipur.* L. 2 ft. 11 in. (8703.–'55.)

401. *SABRE; "'Abbásí;" watered Khorassan blade, bearing, inlaid in gold, numerous inscriptions inclosed in cartouche forms; hilt covered with delicate floriated arabesques damascened in gold; green velvet scabbard, with perforated gold mounts. *Udaipur.* L. 3 ft. 4 in. (8682.–'55.)

402.* GAUNTLET-SWORD; "Paṭá;" rapier blade; steel gauntlet, bearing on each side a lion rampant, chiselled in low relief. Taken at *Lucknow.* L. 4 ft. 2 in.; Bl. 3 ft. 2 in. (8856.–'70.)

Used by the Sikhs in their sword play, and by Mahomedans at the Festival of the Mohurrum. Also by Mahrattas in Southern India. Gauntlet-swords are supposed to have been used by the cavalry of the Great Mogul, and are probably of Tartar or Turcoman origin.

Cf. long two-edged blade in the Tayler collection, "Suhela," so called from a kind of steel which is always flexible and highly prized, according to the proverb "Bauddé Suhela, ruhé akela." "Put on a Suhela, and you may remain alone."

403.* GAUNTLET-SWORD; "Paṭá;" straight rapier blade of burnished steel; long gauntlet hilt, enriched with figures of animals, birds, and other ornaments, chiselled in low relief and gilt. *Oude.* L. 4 ft. 5 in. L. of blade, 3 ft 2 in. (Fig. 24, No. 403.) (7538.–'70.)

404. GAUNTLET-SWORD; "Paṭá;" straight rapier blade, probably of Spanish manufacture; long gauntlet hilt, completely protecting the fore arm, of brass ornamented in *niello;* that part immediately covering the hand is in the form of a conventional tiger head, from the mouth of which the blade issues. *Oude.* L. 4 ft. 4 in. L. of blade, 3 ft. 2 in. (Fig. 24, No. 404.) (8855.–'70.)

405. SWORD; strong blade, with serrated edge; guarded hilt, bearing traces of silvering; crutch-shaped pommel. Taken at *Lucknow.* L. 2 ft. 6 in. (Fig. 24, No. 405.) (8740.–'70.)

406.* SWORD HILTS; steel, damascened with gold. *Karauli.* (8551.–'55.)

407.* SWORD WITH PISTOLS; straight blade, of dark yellowish-tinted Damascus steel, strengthened at the back by plates of gilt steel, with escalloped edges; basket hilt, from the guard of which projects a small pistol barrel. *Jodhpur.* L. 2 ft. 11 in. ('55.)

In the Windsor collection there is an ornamental axe with pistol barrel protruding from the handle, which terminates in a pistol-shaped butt.

408, 409. TWO-HANDED SWORDS WITH CARBINES; into the pistol butts of each of which is inserted a straight double-edged sword blade, equal in length to the barrel. Each barrel is strengthened by four massive steel collars; the locks bear the mark of the Hon. East India Company, with the date 1816. Taken at *Lucknow.* L. 4 ft. 10 in.; Bl. 2 ft. 2 in. (Fig. 24, No. 408.) (8858.–'60.)

410.* MUSQUETOON; "Sher bacha" (young tiger), barrel enriched with scroll ornaments damascened in silver, the back ground filled in with some black composition. Flint-lock bearing the mark of the East India Company. *Oude.* L. 20 in. (8736.–'60.)

411.* MATCHLOCK; "Toradár;" barrel decorated throughout its entire length with floral arabesques damascened in gold; bell-shaped muzzle; stock of red wood mounted with ebony. *Bareli, N. W. P.* L. 5 ft. 2 in. (8659.–'55.)

412.* MATCHLOCK; "Toradár;" fine Damascus barrel; red wood stock, plated, and inlaid with brass and ivory. *Bijnúr, N. W. P.* L. 5 ft. 6 in. (Pl. IV., No. 412.) (7494.–'67.)

413.* MATCHLOCK; "Toradár;" Damascus barrel; red wood stock, with steel and ivory mounts. *Bijnur, N. W. P.* L. 5 ft. 3 in. (7493.–'67.)

414.* MATCHLOCK; "Toradár;" barrel of burnished steel, damascened with gold ornaments at the muzzle and breech; dark wood stock, with silver mounts. *Malwa.* L. 4 ft. 7 in. (8656.–'55.)

415.* MATCHLOCK; "Toradár;" octagonal barrel damascened with gold at the muzzle and breech; straight stock of red wood, strengthened with steel side-plates richly damascened with gold. L. 5 ft. 10 in. (8663.)

416. MATCHLOCK; wire twist barrel, attached to the stock by brass wire bands; stock mounted with steel, damascened with gold. L. 6 ft. 5 in. (12534.–'69.)

417. MATCHLOCK; "Toradár;" the barrel is covered with transverse bands of foliated scroll ornaments in low relief and gilt, the muzzle shaped as a rhinoceros head, the horn of which forms the sight of the gun; red wood and ebony stock. *Udaipur.* L. 5 ft. 11 in. (Pl. X., No. 417.) (8669.–'55.)

418.* MATCHLOCK; "Toradár;" barrel decorated throughout with floral arabesques chiselled in low relief; at the muzzle and breech these are gilt; stock of black wood, capped with ivory. *Jodhpur.* L. 5 ft. 6 in. ('55.)

419.* MATCHLOCK; "Toradár;" finely watered damascus barrel with gold damascenings at the muzzle and breech; straight rosewood stock, plated and inlaid with silver. *Jodhpur.* L. 5 ft. 1 in. ('55.)

420.* MATCHLOCK; "Toradár;" wire twist rifle barrel of damascus steel, with gold enrichments at the muzzle and breech, and inscriptions inlaid in gold; rosewood stock attached to the barrel by six bands of gold perforated and chased; broad butt with embossed and engraved gold mounts. Used for sporting purposes. Presented by the Rajah of *Jodhpur.* L. 4 ft. 8 in. (Pl. IV., No. 420.) (8571.–'51.)

421.* Matchlock; "Toradár;" fine damascus barrel attached to the stock by strips of leather; butt straight and slender, of ebony inlaid with coloured ivory. *Jaipur.* L. 5 ft. 9 in. (8626.–'55.)

422.* Matchlock; "Toradár;" fine damascus barrel attached to the stock by strips of leather; straight butt of ebony, inlaid with coloured ivory. Presented by the Rajah of *Jaipur.* L. 5 ft. 8 in. (Pl. IV., No. 422.) (8622.–'55.)

423.* Matchlock; "Toradár;" damascus barrel with inlaid gold enrichments at the breech and muzzle, the latter shaped like a tiger's head; stock slender and straight, lacquered with floral arabesques in gold on a green ground, and attached to the barrel by silver wire bands; butt capped with ivory. *Karauli, Rajputana.* L. 5 ft. (8631.–'55.)

424.* Matchlock; "Toradár;" barrel damasscened with gold at the muzzle and breech; tiger-head muzzle; stock decorated throughout with lacquered arabesques in gold, on a black ground, and strengthened by side plates of steel, richly damascened; butt straight and slender, capped with ivory. *Gwalior.* L. 5 ft. 7 in. (Pl. IV., No. 424). (8666.–'55.)

425. Matchlock; "Toradár;" wire twist barrel; brass and ivory mounts. Taken at *Lucknow.* L. 5 ft. 9 in. (8861.–'60.)

426. Matchlock-Revolver; with five chambers; plain barrel; touch-hole covered by sliding plates; trigger bird-shaped; very old. Taken at *Lucknow.* L. 5 ft. 6 in.; Barrel 3 ft. 6 in. (8860.–'60.)

Cf. from Z. S. Collection, No. 330.—Hindoo gun; 4-chambered revolver.

427. Matchlock Barrel or wall piece; large stubb-twist barrel, damascened with silver. *Oude.* L. 3 ft. 1 in. (Pl. IV., No. 427.) (8759.–'67.)

428.* Matchlock Accoutrements; "Kamr; consisting of pouches and a priming horn at tached to a belt, all covered with velvet embroidered with gold and floss silk. *Udaipur.* (8695.–'55.)

429. Matchlock Accoutrements; "Kamr;" consisting of various pouches, powder horns, &c., attached to a belt, all covered with velvet, richly embroidered with gold and floss silk. *Udaipur.* (8694.–'55.)

430.* Matchlock Accoutrements; "Kamr;" consisting of pouches, powder horn, and priming horn (Singra), attached to a belt, all covered with crimson velvet, and embroidered with gold and floss silk. *Udaipur.* (8687.–'55.)

431.* Matchlock Accoutrements; "Kamr;" consisting of four pouches and a powder horn, attached to a belt of green velvet, embroidered with gold, and studded with little silver bosses. Mahomedan. *Tonk.* ('72.)

432.* Powder Flask; buffalo horn; inlaid with ivory. *Kotah Rajputana.* (6551.–'67.)

433.* Powder Flask; inlaid with the shells of the pearly nautilus. *Bundelkhand.* (6548.–'67.)

434. Parrying Shield; "Márú," "Mádú," or "Singauṭa" (Cf. Tayler Collection, South Kensington Museum); consisting of a pair of black buck antelope horns tipped with steel, and united at their butt ends, where they are held. Used by Bhils and Hindu Fakirs. Taken at *Lucknow.* L. 2 ft. 11 in. (8748.–'70.)

Shields are generally made of steel, sambur-skin, buffalo, nylghau, elephant, and rhinoceros hide, which is most prized. The latter is sometimes painted, figured with silver leaf, and varnished, with bosses lightly ornamented with gold. Men of high rank, chiefly Brahmins, who have an objection to wearing any kind of leather, use a shield, "Ḍhal bafta," made of forty or fifty folds of silk, painted red and ornamented. (No. 52 in the Codrington Collection was made at Jeypore in Rajpootana, in the time of Tippoo.) The raw rhinoceros hides are ornamented with silver or gilt bosses, crescents, and stars.

435. Parrying Shield; "Márú;" of antelope horns tipped with steel. Similar to the preceding specimen. *Malwa.* L. 2 ft. 10 in. (7356.–'67.)

436. Shield; "Ḍhál;" circular and convex; covered with a kind of coarse embroidery in coloured cotton (blue, yellow, and white), the design being of a geometrical nature; four brass bosses. *Oude.* Diam. 10 in. (8779.)

437. Shield; "Ḍhál;" buffalo hide, with four steel bosses: circular and convex. *Agra.* (8614.–'55.)

438. Shield; "Ḍhál;" papier mâché, lacquered and gilt with floral ornaments on a light red background; bosses of white metal. *Karauli.* Diam. 17 in. (8784.)

439. Shield; "Ḍhál" with recurved edge. Of rhinoceros hide ornamented with four bosses, and a crescent of perforated copper, showing traces of gilding. *Jodhpur.* Diam. 20 in. (8607.–'55.)

440. Shield; "Ḍhál;" with recurved edge; of rhinoceros hide ornamented with four bosses of perforated steel damascened with gold. *Jodhpur.* Diam. 17 in. (8613.–'51.)

441.* Shield; "Ḍhál;" of rhinoceros hide ornamented with four massive gold bosses, and with silk and gold tassels attached. *Jodhpur.* Diam. 23 in. (8612.–'55.)

442. Shield; "Ḍhál" buffalo hide, with four perforated steel bosses. *Jodhpur.* Diam. 2 ft. (8811.–'55.)

443. Shield; "Ḍhál;" with recurved edge; of rhinoceros hide decorated with four flower-shaped bosses of gold. *Jodhpur.* Diam. 23 in. (8733.–'55.)

444. Shield; "Ḍhál;" of buffalo hide, black, with four bosses. *Jodhpur.* Diam. 2 ft.

445. Shield; "Ḍhál;" of buffalo hide, with four perforated steel bosses. *Jodhpur.* Diam. 2 ft. (8609.–'55.)

446.* Shield; "Ḍhál;" stained buffalo hide, with four floriated gilt bosses. *Jodhpur.* Diam. 23 in.

447.* Shield; "Ḍhál;" made from the prepared hide of the river porpoise (*Platanista gangetica.*) Semi-translucent, of a warm orange tint. The centre is occupied by a closely-foliated rosette painted in gold, surrounded by four curious bosses of gilt brass, each representing a recumbent tiger. A narrow foliated border of gold surrounds the shield. Diam. 21 in. Presented by the Rajah of *Haraoti, Rajputana.* (8596.–'55.)

448.* Shield; "Ḍhál;" papier-mâché lacquered and gilt. Four carved crystal bosses in perforated silver settings, round which are disposed irregular groups of flowers and grasses in raised and gilt lacquer-work. The decoration is of a strongly-marked Japanese character. *Bikanir.* Diam. 19 in. (8595.–'55.)

449. Shield; with recurved edge. Steel damascened with silver and gold on black ground (Bidri work). Four hemispherical bosses. Presented by the Rajah of Udaipur. Diam. 17 in. (8693.–'55.)

450.* Helmet and Cuirass; of steel damascened with gold. The helmet, hemispherical, surmounted by a quadrangular steel arrowhead; sliding noseguard flanked by two heron plumes; long coif of mail, the links of brass and steel.

The cuirass of four rectangular pieces ("char-aina" or "the four mirrors"); the two larger ones protect the breast and back, the remaining two are hollowed out to fit under the armpit Presented by the Rajah of *Karauli.* Plates 12 in. by 9½ in., and 10½ in. by 7½ in. (8568.)

Plate Armour is worn with a Tope or hemispherical cap of watered steel inlaid with gold and provided with a nose-guard. In the cone of the helmet is a plume of heron's feathers. Fine chain mail hangs from it on the shoulders.

The cuirass of four rectangular plates protects the body, the plates being joined together by buckles and straps. They are of fine watered steel, with sides inlaid with gold pattern in border; below there is usually a skirt of red cotton velvet embroidered with gold. Underneath is worn a "Kubcha" or jacket made of black cotton velvet, quilted and slightly ornamented. (Silken trowsers, with a pair of cashmere shawls round the waist complete the dress of an emir, or chief of high rank.)

The "Dastána" or gauntlet worn on one or both arms reaches from the elbow to the wrist, with a glove of mail, or velvet covered with gilt studs over the hand. It is made of iron for the common soldiers, and of figured steel inlaid with gold for the chiefs. It was worn by all ranks, alike in the Punjab, Rajputana, and Hyderabad.

It was occasionally made of leather in the time of Tippoo Sultan and covered with quilted red velvet, and embroidered with tiger stripes in gold.

451. Helmet; "Tóp," hemispherical, with plume-holder, sliding arrow-headed nose-guard, and two porte aigrettes. From the base, which is enriched with a border of gold damascenings, hangs a coif of fine chain-mail. Presented by the Rajah of *Karauli.* (8698.–'55.)

452. *Cuirass and Gauntlets; steel damascened with gold. Presented by the Rajah of *Jodhpur.* (8463.–'55.)

The cuirass "chár-aína," consists of four plates. To the back plate is attached a neck-guard with epaulettes of hide covered with embroidered velvet. Plates 10 to 12 in. by 7½ in. to 9 in.

The arm-guards; "Dastana," are ornamented with low relief chiselled ornaments, and gold damascening; attached at the wrist end are open gauntlets of green velvet, embroidered with gold spangles. L. with gauntlet 20 in. W. 4 in.

This *brassard* was introduced by the Arabs into Spain. Cf. Armeria Real de Madrid. Pl. xxv.

453.* Coat of Mail; "Zirah baktar;" and arm guards. The coat is composed of unriveted links of steel, brass and copper arranged in various designs. The collar and facings are covered with *appliqué* embroidery of red, green and black velvet studded with gilt-headed nails. A pointed collar of mail falls back over the shoulders.

The arm guards are of steel damascened with gold, and terminate in open gauntlets of crimson velvet studded with gilt-headed nails. *Udaipur.* (8462.)

454.* Arm-Guards; "Dastána;" steel damascened with gold. Open gauntlets of chain mail padded and lined with velvet. *Udaipur.* (8463.–'55.)

455.* Arm-Guards of bright steel with borders of gold damascened enrichments, lined with velvet and terminating in open gauntlets of crimson velvet embroidered with gold spangles. *Udaipur.* (8462.)

456.* Pieces of Chain-mail, forming part of a coat or trousers. The links are of steel, large and unriveted.

GROUP IX.

Part I.—THE MAHRATTAS.

The Mahrattas have contributed largely to the arms of Central and Southern India, represented in this group. The ranks of their armies were recruited by men of all classes in India, attracted either by love of adventure or hope of booty. According to Count Byörnstyerna,[1] they say of themselves that their prince's throne is the horse's back, their sceptre the sword, and their country every one they can conquer. All their habits and customs reflect this double character of warrior and freebooter. When the Mahratta sets out for war he cuts off a handful of ears of corn with his scymetar, and sprinkles his horse with blood, these acts being symbolic of his manner of life. A silver bangle worn on the horse's leg implies among the Mahrattas that the rider is bound to conquer or die, as related of one of their chiefs, Koneir Trimbuck Yekbootee, who obtained the title of Phakray, or heroic.

The history of the rise and fall of the Mahrattas has been detailed elsewhere. In a memorandum, dated 1795, Sir C. Malet gives the following account of the constitution of their army:—

" The general Mahratta force is composed of 'Jaghiredars' or officers holding land like " Sindia and Holcar, of 'nugdee' or corps paid by ready money, or of 'Tankardars' " holding assignments of lands resumable at pleasure, as the 'paughers' or commanders " of cavalry. The troops comprise (1) 'Bargirs' mounted by the chief or government; " (2) 'Silladars' who mount themselves, and (3) 'Yekandia' (meaning single,) generally " men of family, who, with a few attendants, go in quest of service. Of the two latter " classes many seldom encumber themselves with anything but a pair of swords; one of " a hard temper, consequently brittle and very sharp, called 'serye' (*sirohi*); the other " more tough and less sharp named 'asseel' (*aṣíl*)."

" Their food is said to consist of cakes made of *jawár* or *dál* (pulse) with a little butter and red pepper, hence it is that, owing to the irascibility of their temper, gentleness is never met with in their dispositions.[2]

Their dress is a tunic, "selá," loose mantle, and "jánghiah," short drawers.

In marching they have a large vanguard, "harole," and when they approach an enemy they divide that again by an advanced force named "fauj jarída," which signifies the unencumbered army; so that at the time of battle with the Nizam, the Mahratta army consisted of three camps, the "peshwáz," or head-quarters, being upwards of twenty miles in the rear of the "fauj jarída," whose "bahír," or baggage camp, was between both.

Their mode of taking the field is thus described by the author of "Letters from a Mahratta Camp, 1813." The camp of the Mahrattas was pitched without the smallest attention to regularity. Men, horses, camels, and bullocks are all jumbled together in a mass. The main body is called the Bara Lashkar or main army, and is generally about as many hundred yards wide from flank to flank, as it is miles in length from front to rear. The different chiefs encamp to the right and left of the principal street, which often extends from three to four miles from front to rear.

One of the bodies of irregular foot, consisting principally of Mahomedans was named "Aligol" from its custom of charging the enemy in a "gol" or mass, and invoking the aid of Ali in the onset. The Mahratta cavalry form an irregular line, three or four deep. The chief marches in front of the centre preceded by colours, kettledrums, trumpets, &c. Individuals of the corps are to be seen on all sides galloping about, and flourishing their arms to display their horsemanship. One of these Risálas attached to a brigade com-

[1] British Empire in the East, 1840.

[2] Táríkhi Ibrahim Khan. Edited by Dowson, Vol. VIII., 263.

manded by a Portuguese showed a certain degree of discipline, and was divided into three troops. It marched in files with a small gun in front.

The Indian camp, writes Forbes,[3] display a variety of standards and ensigns, in which the prevailing colour appeared to be red. The banner "Zarí-paṭṭá," which was always carried before Ragobah, was small and swallow-tailed of crimson and gold tissue with gold fringes and tassels. Among the mercenaries employed by the Mahrattas were the Gosains, a religious order of mendicants found in many parts of India, who occasionally, when they become numerous and wealthy in the service of some prince, enlisted as a military band under a leader termed "Mahant."

Another corps, the Mínás were aborigines from the Rajputana hills. They were stout, good looking men, armed with a bow and quiver of arrows, and a "Katár," in the use of which they are very expert. They wear their turbans very high, ornamented on the top with a bunch of feathers of a kind of ibis or curlew "Boza" (*Geronticus papillosus*). They have their own civil officers, and do not intermarry with other tribes. The brothers in succession marry the widow of the eldest. They live by plunder and military service.

Under the Peishwah, Arabs also took service. "They were generally armed with a " matchlock, a couple of swords, three or four small daggers stuck in front of their belt, " and a shield. On common occasions they fire but one bullet, but when pressed at the " breach they drop in two, three and four at a time from their mouths, in which they " always carry from eight to ten bullets of a small size. They attain great precision in " the use of the matchlock, bringing down not unfrequently birds with a single bullet."[2]

When not engaged in war, a Mahratta chief, surrounded by his armed escort would take part in the pleasures of the chase. Scindiah's hunting escort is described[3] as numbering about 700 horse. "First came loose, light-armed horse; then some better " clad with the quilted 'poshauk' (garment of cloth or silk, padded with cotton and " sabre-proof), and one in a complete suit of chain armour; next a few elephants with " the hunting elephant of Scindiah, then came a host of fierce chieftains on fine horses; " they were armed with lance, scimetar and shield, dagger and pistol."

The Pindárís[4] were swarms of freebooters following the Mahratta armies, and as already mentioned, subsequently began to levy war on their own account. They were a motley force. In every thousand, about four hundred were tolerably well armed and mounted; of that number about every fifteenth man carried a matchlock, but their favourite weapon was the Mahratta spear from 12 to 18 feet long. The remaining 600 were armed with every sort of weapon. Up to 1812 they overran the country in marauding expeditions.

NOTE.—*The more ornamental arms distinguished by an asterisk, will be found in Cases* 57 *and* 68 (*the latter fire-arms*).

457.* Bow; "Kamán;" bamboo, painted in green and gold. Velvet-covered grip. Gut cord, bound with silk. *Gwalior*. L. 5 ft. 9 in. (7446.–'67.)

The bows used by the chiefs and the cavalry were generally made with a double curve. In the catalogue of the Z. S. Collection (p. 318), are described two steel bows, said to have been made at Gwalior. They are of the shape usually carried by the Sikhs, and are covered on both sides with richly damascened gold ornamentation in which are traced inscriptions in Hindustani verse showing them to have belonged to the Emperor Bahadur Shah (A.D. 1707 to 1712). Translated by Mr. Garcin de Tassy, Member of the Institute of France; the verses are, "When Bahadur Shah applies " an arrow to this bow on the field of battle, the firma- " ment as a bow puts in its mouth the finger of " astonishment with the arrow of the Milky Way."

When an Oriental wishes to string his bow he places himself firmly on his centre, and grasping the upper extremity of the bow in his left hand, passes the weapon behind the left leg and over the shin-bone of the right, then bending it by forcing the upper end round towards the opposite side, he slips the string which has been already secured on the lower horn into its place with the right hand.—(*The Book of Archery*, Hansard, p. 35, 1845.)

The bowman, contrary to the English or Flemish custom, draws altogether with his thumb, the forefinger bent in its first and second joint being merely pressed on one side of the arrow 'nock,' to secure it from falling. In order to prevent the flesh from being torn by the bowstring, he wears a broad ring (called in Persian "Sefin") of agate, cornelian, crystal, green jade, ivory, horn, or iron according to his rank or means. (The writer has seen one formed out of a single emerald pierced for that purpose. It belonged to the late Marquis of Dalhousie, Governor-General of India, and was probably brought from Persia. Sometimes two thimbles are worn for this purpose on the first and second fingers of the right hand.) Upon the inside of this ring, which projects half an inch, the string rests when the bow is drawn; on the outside it is only half that breadth, and in loosing the arrow, the archer straightens his thumb, which sets the arrow free. These rings with a spare string are usually carried in a small box suspended at the bowman's side. (*The Book of Archery*, p. 135.) A leathern sleeve called "Godha" is worn on the left arm.—(*Ward.*)

---

[1] Oriental Memoir, Vol. II.
[2] Summary of the Mahratta and Pindaree Campaign, 1820.
[3] Sketches of India, by an Officer, 1825.
[4] Duff, Vol. III., p. 325.

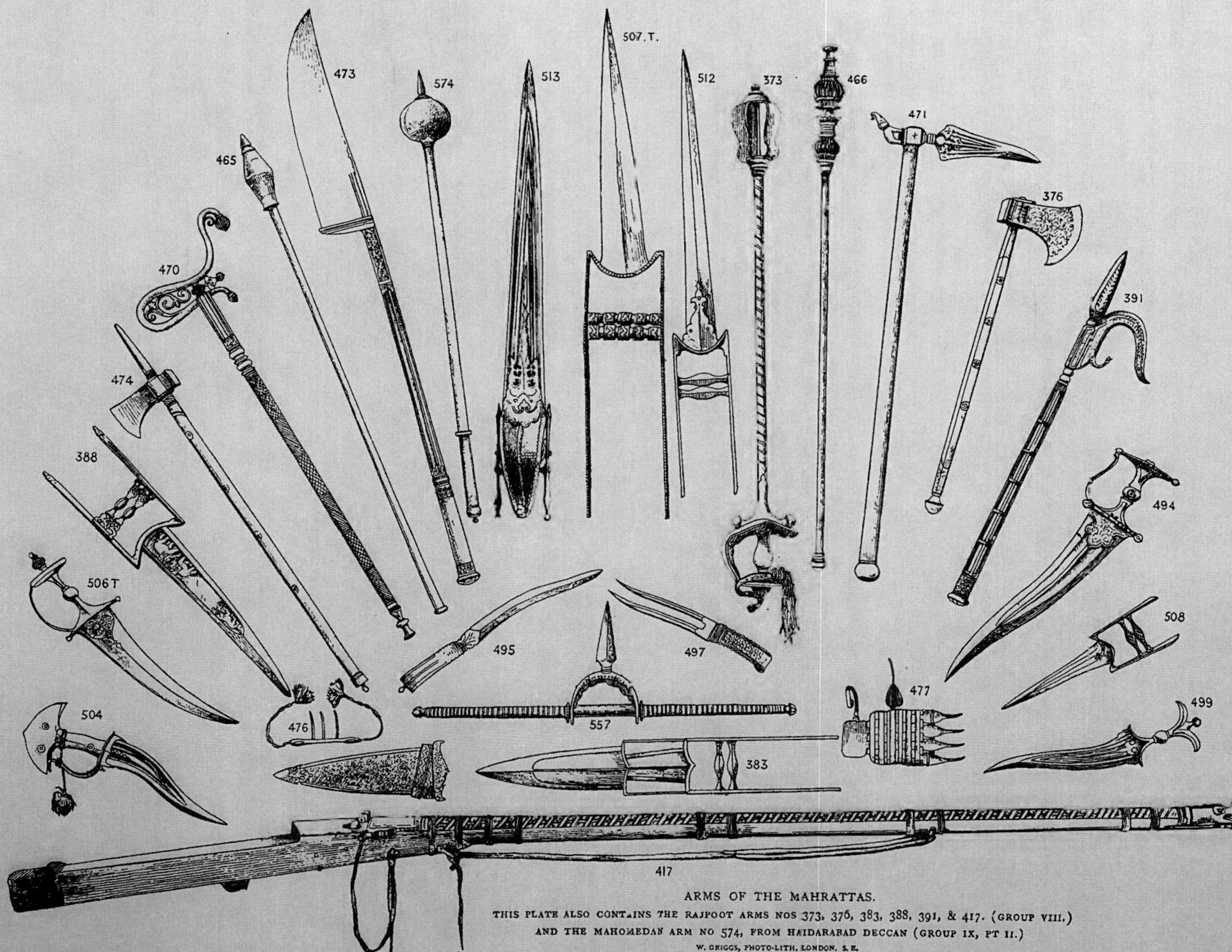

ARMS OF THE MAHRATTAS.

THIS PLATE ALSO CONTAINS THE RAJPOOT ARMS NOS 373, 376, 383, 388, 391, & 417. (GROUP VIII.)
AND THE MAHOMEDAN ARM NO 574, FROM HAIDARABAD DECCAN (GROUP IX, PT II.)

W. GRIGGS, PHOTO-LITH. LONDON. S.E.

458. Bow; "Kamán;" curved Parthian shape. Of horn, lacquered and painted in brown and gold. Gut string bound with silk. *Ahmednugger.* (6553.–'67.)

459. Bow; "Kamán;" Parthian shape. Horn lacquered and gilt. *Indore.* L. 4 ft. (7418.–'67.)

460. Quivers and Arrows. Leather.

461. Spears (2); "Sángu; long slender quadrangular heads; steel shafts; the grip covered with velvet. *Vizianagram.* L. 7 ft. 11 in.; L. of bl. 2 ft. 6 in. (8836.–'55.)

The Mahratta lance is called "Birch'há."—Tod, Rajputana.

462. Spears (3). Small blades, flexible shafts, painted green. *Gwalior.* (12713.)

463. Spears (2); "Bhálá." Small blades. Long bamboo shafts. Used by Mahratta horsemen. *Gwalior.*

464. Spear-Butts (3). Steel; curiously wrought brass mounts. *Gwalior.* L. $12\frac{1}{2}$ in. to 19 in. 12680 (7452.)

465. Mace. Persian type. Spindle-shaped head Gold damascened enrichments. *Sattara.* L. 3 ft. 6 in. (Pl. X., No. 465.) (12602.–'69.)

466. Mace; "Garz;" many-bladed double head; the shaft encircled by small sliding rings. L. 2 ft. 7 in. *Indore.* (Pl. X., No. 466.) (7367.–'55.)

467. Mace; "Gargaz;" of steel. Seven-bladed head with basket hilt. Engraved shaft. *Sattara.* L. 2 ft. 4 in. (8654.)

468. Mace; "Dhara;(?)" steel embossed and damascened with gold, six-bladed head. Octagonal shaft. Basket hilt. L. 2 ft. *Kolapore.* (8653.–'55.)

Fig. 26. Axe called Ravensbeak. (E. Coll.)

469. Mace; "Gargaz;" of steel. Eight-bladed head with basket hilt. *Kolapore.* L. 2 ft. 10 in. (8649.–'55.)

470. Mace; "Khúndlí P'hansi;" curiously shaped head of open steel scroll-work. The shaft, ornamented with incised spiral and lozenge pattern is hollow and contains a narrow quadrangular blade attached to the pommel which unscrews. Probably a Bairagi Crutch. *Kolapore.* L. 19 in. (Pl. X., No. 470.) (8650.)

471.* Crow-Bill; "Buckie (?);" curved dagger-like blade fixed to a plain wooden shaft, on the opposite side of which is a small elephant figure with up-lifted trunk. *Kolapore.* (Pl. X., No. 471.) (8651.–'55.)

One in the E. Coll. is called Ravensbeak, "Tabar-Zaghnol."

472.* Crow-Bill; "Hoolurge (?);" curved peas point blade, springing at right angles from the shaft which is silvered and terminates in an elephant's head damascened in gold. The shaft is hollow and encloses a dagger attached to the pommel or butt end which unscrews. *Datiah.* L. 13 in. (7419.–'67.)

473. Battle-Axe; "Buckie;" of steel, in one piece. Broad, slightly curved, pointed blade, $13\frac{1}{2}$ inches in length, springing from a ribbed and engraved shaft. Used on state occasions. *Kolapore.* L. 2 ft. 10 in. (Pl. X., No. 473.)

474. Battle-Axe; "Buckie;" with spear poin and hammer head. Ebony shafts studded witl brass bossettes. *Kolapore.* L. 2 ft. 1 in. Bl. $4\frac{1}{4}$ in. by $2\frac{1}{4}$ in. (Pl. X., No. 474.) (8652.–'55.)

475.* Battle-Axe. The blade is ornamented with flowers chiselled in low relief, set with turquoises and damascened in gold. The shaft is of steel damascened in gold, partially covered with velvet. *Kolapore.* (Pl. XV., No. 475.)

476. Tiger-Claws; "Bág'hnak;" consisting of three connected steel claws about 2 inches in length, sharpened on their inner edges, with side rings for the insertion of the first and fourth fingers. Crimson silk tassel attached. *Sattara.* (Pl. XV., No. 476.) (8457.)

The Baghnakh is carried concealed in the hand, and when about to be used, the claws project from the closed fingers like the claws of a tiger. It was with the identical weapon here shown that Sivaji, the founder of the Mahratta Empire, is said to have killed his enemy Abdalla Khan.—Cf. *Historical Sketch*, p. 21.

477. Tiger-Claws; "Bág'hnak." In this case the claws, five in number, are attached to jointed plates of steel lining the palm of the hand, to which the weapon is fastened by rings at the wrist and fingers. *Sattara.* (Pl. X., No. 477.) (845.–'55.)

478. Tiger-Claws; "Bág'hnak;" secured to the hand by two rings, through which the first and fourth fingers pass. *Kolapore.* (8454.–'55.)

479. Tiger-Claws (2); "Bág'hnak." *Gwalior.* (8456.–'55.)

480. Dagger; "Bánk;" sickle-shaped; polished steel blade, of semicircular outline, mounted on a straight hilt of dark wood, studded with floriated silver bosses; crimson velvet sheath, tipped with silver. *Indore.* (7427.–'67.)

481. Dagger; "Bánk;" crescent-shaped; curved blade of burnished steel; hilt of dark wood, continuing the curve of the blade, and together forming an exactly semicircular outline. *Kolapore.* (8642.–'55.)

482.* Dagger; composed of two blades, which, when united, form a pair of scissors; one of the blades is roughened, to act as a file; ivory handles; sheath of green velvet, silver mounted. *Datiah, Central India.* (7431.–'67.)

483.* Dagger; "Ch'hurá-káṭi;" small pointed blade, of dark steel; ivory hilt, with silver-gilt mounts; conical sheath of silver, embossed and gilt. *Vizianagram.* Presented by the Rajah of Vizianagram. (8710.–'55

484. DAGGER; "Peshkabz;" doubly-curved blade; buffalo-horn hilt; red leather sheath. *Vizianagram.* L. 12 in. (7308.–'67.)

485.* DAGGER; "Peshkabz;" one-edged blade; broad, slightly curved back; ivory hilt; crimson velvet sheath, silver-gilt mounts. *Vizianagram.* (8716.–'55.)

486.* DAGGER; "Jambiya;" bright curved blade, with strong central rib; hilt of horn, ornamented with Venetian sequins, and encircled by an embossed band of gold; silver sheath, chased and embossed. An Arab weapon. *Haidarabad, Deccan.* ('51.)

487.* DAGGER; "Jambiya;" bright curved blade; hilt of copper, engraved and parcel-gilt; silver sheath, richly chased and embossed. *Haidarabad, Deccan.* (11906.–'67.)

488.* DAGGER; "Jambiya;" short curved blade, with strong central rib; ivory hilt, with silver mounts; blue velvet sheath, tipped with silver, *Haidarabad, Deccan.* ('55.)

489.* DAGGER; "Jambiya;" bright curved blade; ivory hilt, studded with silver-gilt bosses; yellow velvet sheath. *Gwalior.* (8722.–'55.)

490.* DAGGER; "Bich'hwá;" doubly-curved blade; hilt with knuckle-guard; yellow velvet sheath. *Gwalior.* (8723.–'55.)

Cf. Tayler Collection and 344, Additional Tower Collection.—Bichwa (Scorpion) so called from its likeness to a scorpion sting; small crooked dagger, worn generally by common people in Mysore and Hyderabad, concealed in the sleeve within a sheath. Blade of common steel; handle of plain iron, or ornamented with silver or brass, plain or figured. Made for right or left hand, with double blade.—"Vinchu," Marathi.

491.* DAGGER; "Bich'hwá;" bright blade, doubly curved; guarded hilt, damascened with gold and silver; blue velvet sheath, with embossed silver-gilt mounts. *Gwalior.* (7448.)

492. DAGGER; "Bich'hwá;" straight blade; loop hilt. *Mourpore.* L. 13 in. (7321.–'67.)

493.* DAGGER; "Bich'hwá;" doubly curved blade; hilt with knuckle-guard; velvet sheath, tipped with silver. *Kolapore.*

494.* DAGGER; "Bich'hwá;" doubly curved blade, deeply grooved; steel hilt, damascened in gold with ornaments and inscriptions; green velvet sheath, tipped with gold-damascened steel. *Haidarabad, Deccan.* (Pl. X., No. 494.) (7439.–'67.)

495, 496. DAGGERS; "Bich'hwá;" doubly curved blades: guarded hilts; one is for the right hand, the other for the left. *Satara.* L. 13 in. (Pl. X., No. 495.) (8724.–'55.)

497. DAGGER; "Bich'hwá;" forked blade, slightly curved; guarded hilt, inlaid with brass. Taken at *Lucknow.* L. 10½ in. (Pl. X., No. 497.) (8766.–'55.)

498.* DAGGER; "Bich'hwá;" small, doubly-curved blade of Damascus steel; ivory hilt; purple velvet sheath. Presented by Col. Hamilton. (11,498.–'67.)

499.* DAGGER; "Chilanum; (?)" doubly curved blade; hilt silvered; sheath velvet-covered and tipped with silver. *Vizianagram.* (Pl. X., No. 499.) (8717.–'55.)

500, 501. DAGGERS; "Khanjarli;" doubly-curved blades; ebony hilts, with broad lunette-shaped pommels. L. 12½ in. *Vizianagram.* (7307, 7311.)

The Zarkoe Selo Catalogue, p. 276, describes one like that from Vizianagram, with closed guard to hilt, and ivory mounts. These are rivetted by eight coins of the Great Mogul Shah Alum-Gir, in the sixth year of his reign, 1758, struck at Arkâti, (Arcot) in the Madras Presidency, as an Arabic inscription on them denotes.

502. DAGGER; "Khanjar;" doubly-curved two-edged blade; protected hilt of buffalo horn and steel; red leather sheath. *Vizianagram.* L. 12 in. (7307.–'67.)

503. DAGGER; grooved flamboyant blade; ebony hilt, provided with steel knuckle-guard; broad lunette-shaped pommel. *Vizianagram.* L. 12 in.

504.* DAGGER; "Khanjar;" Damascus blade, doubly curved and fluted; ivory hilt, with knuckle-guard and large lunette-shaped pommel studded with gilt bosses; velvet sheath, with silver-gilt mounts. *Vizianagram.* (Pl. X., No. 504.) (8714.–'55.)

505.* DAGGER; "Khanjar;" doubly-curved grooved blade, with strong central rib; ivory hilt, with large lunette-shaped pommel, studded with gilt-headed nails. *Vizianagram.* (8715.–'55.)

506 T.* DAGGER; "Khanjar." *Indore.* (Pl. X., No. 506 T.) (101.)

507 T. DAGGER; "Kaṭár." (226, Additional Collection.) (Pl. X., No. 507 T.)

508. DAGGER; "Kaṭár;" blade thickened at the point; straight guards; transverse hilt. *Maharapore, Gwalior.* L. 11 in. (Pl. X., No. 508.) (8727.–'50.)

509. DAGGER; "Kaṭár;" broad triangular blade. *Vizianagram.* L. 18 in.; L. of blade, 9 in. (7352.–'67.)

510. DAGGER; "Bundí Kaṭárí;" narrow grooved blade; transverse hilt, once silvered; red velvet sheath, with silver mounts. *Vizianagram.* L. 19 in. (8712.–'55.)

511. DAGGER; "Sítárámpúrí Kaṭárí;" Damascus blade; hilt and side-guards roughly gilt; velvet scabbard, silver-gilt mounts. *Vizianagram.* (8713.–'55.)

512. DAGGER; "Pattaní Jamdádú" (death-giver); an elongated form of the preceding weapon; hilt roughly silvered; sheath covered with purple velvet, and capped with silver mounts. *Vizianagram.* L. 2 ft. 3 in.; L. of blade, 18 in. (Pl. X., No. 512.) (8786.–'55.)

513. DAGGER; "Bara Jamdádú;" fluted blade, an elongated form of the Kutar, with small hand-guard, gilt and lined with velvet; sheath of purple velvet, with silver and gilt mounts. *Vizianagram.* L. 2 ft. 3 in. (Pl. X., No. 513.) (8758.)

514. DAGGER; "Bara Jamdádú;" thin rapier blade; an elongated form of the Kaṭár, with small hand-guard, showing the transition between that weapon and the gauntlet sword (Paṭá). *Vizianagram.* L. 2 ft. 4 in. (8720.–'55.)

515. GAUNTLET SWORD; "Paṭá;" highly-polished flexible rapier blade of Spanish manufacture; gauntlet hilt of polished steel, padded and lined with velvet; green velvet scabbard. Used by professional swordsmen. *Indore.* L. 3 ft. 11½ in.; Bl. 3 ft. (6459.–'67.)

516. SWORD-STICK; "Gupti" (*i.e.* "concealed"); a long, fluted, flexible, and very slender blade, fitting into an ebony stick sheath. *Vizianagram.* L. 3 ft. 2½ in. (8708.–'55.)

517. SWORD; "Gupti;" long narrow blade; red leather scabbard. *Vizianagram.* L. 2 ft. 10 in. (7315.–'67.)

Cf. from Codrington Collection.—Gupti; sword stick, long, narrow, two-edged blade of elastic steel; plain handle; round scabbard. Malabar. Taken at Seringapatam.
"Gupti;" steel; handle curiously figured.—(Nurwul, 1700.)
Do. Solingen blade (Germany, 1650), with basket handle.

518, 519. SWORD-STICKS; "Gupti;" sheaths of wood, painted and lacquered. *Bombay.* L. 2 ft. 5 in. and 3 ft. 4 in. (9151.–'74.)

520. *SWORD; "Khándá;" straight Damascus blade, widening towards the point, strengthened by side plates of perforated steel damascened in gold with flowers and animals; basket hilt, with spiked pommel of steel similarly ornamented; attached is a knotted waist-belt of many-coloured silk; scabbard of blue velvet, with repoussé and engraved mounts of pure gold. The national sword of Orissa. Presented by H.H. the Maharajah Holkar. *Gwalior.* L. 3 ft. 6 in.; W. 1½ in. to 2½ in. (8683.–'51.)

Cf. Musée Z. S., Pl. clxvii. 2; also 257–280.—"Khanda;" also worn by Rajpoot chiefs. The spike of the pommel is curved over, so that the hand may keep up the sword by resting on it, as shown in the portraits of many Hindoo Rajahs.

521.T* SWORD; straight blade, the back and lower part of which is strengthened with perforated steel supports enriched with gold damascening. *Indore.* (Fig. 24, No. 521 T.) (100.)

522. *SWORD; straight burnished blade, strengthened by perforated steel supports at the back; basket hilt, with spiked pommel of steel damascened with silver; crimson velvet scabbard. *Indore.* L. 3 ft. (7433.)

523. SWORD; "Farang," or "Firangi" (Mahrathi). Introduced by the Portuguese (Firingis). Straight blade of fine Damascus steel, slightly widening towards the point, and strengthened at the back; silvered basket hilt, padded, with spiked silver pommel; scabbard covered with purple velvet. Worn by men of rank at the end of the 18th century. *Lahore.* L. 3 ft. 6 in.; W. 1½ in. (Fig. 24, No. 523.) (8505.–'55.)

Cf. from Codrington Collection.—"Farang;" straight, long, narrow sword; grooved French blade, set at Gwalior 1800. Taken from Holkar's army, 1817.
"Farang;" plain, narrow sword, of fine elastic steel (Nitsia).
Do.; straight sword, with jagged edge. Hindostan, taken at the siege of Seringapatam; plain iron handle. Tower Additional, 333.
"Farang;" light thin sword, plated handle.
Do.; steel handle, slightly ornamented with gold; the blade bears the initials of Hyder Ali.
This is chiefly used by good swordsmen of cavalry, and occasionally by men of high rank; a favourite weapon with good soldiers.

524, 525. SWORDS; similar to No. 523. The hilt of one of these swords is plated with silver ornamented in niello. *Bijnur.* L. 3 ft. 3 in. and 3 ft. 4 in. (7432.–'67.)

526.* SWORD; "Paṭṭisa;" broad, straight, two-edged blade, widening towards the point; hilt damascened with gold, attached to the blade by long steel processes running up the middle of the blade on each side; crimson velvet sheath. *Central India.* Presented by Col. Sir H. Worsley. L. of blade, 3 ft.; W. of blade, 1½ in. to 2 in. (Fig. 24, No. 526.) (8680.–'51.)

Cf. flexible sword in Guthrie Collection, which could be worn in the girdle, bent round the body.

527.* SWORD; Spanish or Portuguese blade; long, straight, two-edged, and flexible, of burnished steel, bearing incised Latin inscriptions near the hilt; large padded basket-hilt with spiked pommel of steel damascened with gold; crimson velvet sheath. (8512.–'55.)

Cf. "Dhoup;" straight blade. Used by most of the Deccanees.—*Ain-i-Akbari.*
Sivajee's sword is an excellent Genoa blade of the first class, called "Bhavani." It is preserved by the Rajah of Sattara.

528.* SWORD; slightly incurved, one-edged blade of dark tinted Damascus steel; hilt with knuckle-guard of steel damascened with gold; gold tassel pendent from pommel; green velvet sheath. *Haidarabad, Deccan.* L. 2 ft. 9 in. (Fig. 24, No. 528.) (7434.–'67.)

529.* PISTOL-SWORD; straight blade of burnished steel; basket hilt of steel, armed with a pair of pistols projecting one on each side of the blade, the triggers being concealed within the sword hilt. *Datiah, Central India.* L. 2 ft. 11½ in. (7435.–'67.)

530 T.* SWORD; broad blade; hilt damascened in gold. (Fig. 24, No. 530 T.) (203.)

531. SABRE; grooved blade; guarded and padded hilt of steel inlaid with gold; spiked pommel. *Gwalior.* L. 3 ft. 6 in. (Fig 24, No. 531.) (8684.–'55.)

532.* SABRE; broad fluted blade, slightly recurved; basket hilt, with spiked pommel of steel damascened with gold; grip bound with silver wire; green velvet scabbard. L. 3 ft. 6 in. (8681.–'55.)

The long spike proceeding from the hilt (kubja), s useful both for guarding the arm, and for a grasp for the left hand in a two-handed stroke.—*W. F. Sinclair, B. C. S.*

533. SABRE; "Talwár;" slightly recurved blade, grooved and burnished. Hilt with knuckle guard, of steel damascened with gold. Blue velvet scabbard attached to velvet waistband studded with gilt-headed nails. *Indore.* L. 3 ft. 2 in. (7437.)

534 T. SABRE; "Nímcha or Teghá;" iron hilt. Date about 1780. "Used chiefly by men of high rank." (335.)

535. SABRE; "Nímcha;" grooved blade; steel hilt; red leather scabbard. *Vizianagram.* L. 2 ft. 8 in. (7313.–'67.)

536. SABRE; "Teghá;" broad blade; bright steel hilt with knuckle guard. *Vizianagram.* L. 3 ft.; Bl. 2 ft. 6 in. by 2 in. (7314.–'67.)

Cf. from Codrington Collection.—"Teghá;" short, broad, heavy sword. Very superior blade with two grooves. Handle and ferrule richly ornamented with gold. Used by all ranks.

537, 538. SABRES; "Farang Katti"; channelled blades; steel hilts; red leather scabbards. L. 3 ft. 1 in. *Vizianagram.* (7316.–'67.)

539, 540. SABRES; "'Abbásí"; deeply curved blades; steel hilts; scabbards of red leather. L. 3 ft., and 3 ft. 2 in. *Vizianagram.* (7349.–'67.)

Cf. from Codrington Collection.—"'Abbási;" scimitar of superior steel; handle of ivory and iron inlaid with gold, said to have been invented by Abbas the Great.

This steel is exceedingly hard and brittle and gives a severe cut. Made at Khorassan. Worn by Persians and Mogulyes of high rank.

"'Abbási;" handle of elephant's head pattern gilt.

Do.; handle and mounting of copper deeply carved and gilt.

Do.; nearly straight (Poonah). Time of Hyder Ali.

Cf. sword which belonged to Holkar, now at Windsor. The scabbard and hilt is inlaid with rubies, pearls and emeralds.

Another similar to it was presented by Holkar to Sir John Malcolm, after the battle of Mahidpur, and is now in the possession of General Malcolm.

541, 542. SABRE BLADES; one of native, the other of English manufacture, the latter bearing the Hon. E. I. Co.'s mark, and the date 1823 inlaid in gold. *Deccan.* L. 2 ft. 11 in., and 3 ft. 1 in.

543. *MATCHLOCK; "Toradár;" fine wire-twist barrel damascened at the mouth and breech with gold enrichments. Stock slightly curved of red wood. Capped with ebony and strengthened with side plates of steel richly damascened with gold ornaments. *Indore.* L. 5 ft. 10 in. (8660.–'55.)

544. *MATCHLOCK; "Toradár;" barrel decorated throughout its entire length with panels in damascening. Stock slightly curved, of red wood and ebony ornamented with repoussé and perforated silver work, and attached to the barrels by bands of the same. *Indore.* (Pl. IV., No. 544). (8657.–'55.)

545. *MATCHLOCK; "Toradár;" barrel richly ornamented throughout with floral damascenings in gold. Stock of red wood; butt slightly curved, mounted with ebony and silver. *Indore.* L. 5 ft. 3 in. (8665.–'55.)

546. *MATCHLOCK REVOLVER-GUN; four chambers. The barrel and chambers ornamented throughout with floral damascenings in silver, bearing here and there traces of gilding. Heavy wooden stock; a supply of match cord is wound round the butt. *Indore.* Presented by Sir Robert Hamilton. L. 5 ft. 10 in. (Pl. IV., No. 546).

547. MATCHLOCK; "Toradár;" watered steel barrel damascened with gold at the breech and terminating in a spirally-twisted muzzle. Stock of dark wood capped and mounted with ivory. (8862.)

548. MATCHLOCK; "Toradár;" octagonal barrel damascened in gold and silver, particularly at the breech and muzzle, and attached to the stock by bands of steel perforated and silvered. Stock of red wood, capped and mounted with ivory. *Indore.* L. 5 ft. 11 in. (11715.–'67.)

549. MATCHLOCK; "Toradár;" bright steel barrel with minutely grained surface, bell-shaped muzzle. Stock slightly curved, of polished red wood and ebony. *Bareli.* L. 6 ft. (8670.–'55.)

550.* MATCHLOCK; "Toradár;" octagonal barrel attached to the stock by numerous silver bands. Stock, similar to that of Kurg gun, No. 138, of a kind of jackwood (*Artocarpus sp.*) studded with small silver bosses. *Belgaum.* L. 5 ft. (8658.–'55.)

551 T. MATCHLOCK; barrel 7 feet long. Fired from a rest. Left trophy. *Oude.* (258.)

552.* MATCHLOCK; "Toradár;" square barrel with square bore, the sides damascened in gold, throughout their entire length with running scroll and other ornaments. Stock capped with iron, and mounted with chased silver. *Mahratta.* L. 5 ft. $7\frac{1}{2}$ in. (Pl. IV., No. 552). ('51.)

One in the E. Collection has a square barrel with circular bore.

553.* MATCHLOCK ACCOUTREMENTS; consisting of a massive silver-plated belt studded with bosses, to which are suspended powder and priming horns, both ornamented with chased silver mounts. *Haidarabad, Deccan.* Worn only by Arabs in the service of the Nizam. (7428, 7429.)

554.* MATCHLOCK ACCOUTREMENTS; leather plated with richly embossed silver set with cornelians. *Haidarabad, Deccan.* Used by Arabs in the service of the Nizam. (7333.–'55.)

555.* ACCOUTREMENTS; consisting of pouch attached to belt of green velvet embroidered with gold thread.

556.* GUN ACCOUTREMENTS; "Kamr basta," consisting of powder-horn, various pouches, hunting-knife, &c., all attached to a leather belt covered with gold-embroidered velvet. *Sawantwari.* Worn by the Sirdars of the Deccan. (8640.–'55.)

557.* PARRYING SHIELD; "Saintí;" consisting of a ringed shaft of steel, 22 inches in length, which is held in the middle; the grip is protected by a padded basket of steel, from the centre of which projects a small dagger. *Vizianagram.* (Pl. X., No. 557.) (8452.–'55.)

This weapon was introduced into Spain by the Arabs, an example of it is found in the Armeria Real de Madrid, dating from the 15th century.

558. SHIELDS (2); "Ḍhál;" circular and convex; black rhinoceros hide, with four perforated steel bosses. *Indore.* Diam. 2 ft. (7324.–'67.)

559 T. SHIELD; black buffalo hide, with gilt bosses. *Indore.*

560. SHIELD; black rhinoceros hide, with four iron bosses. Diam. 18 in.

561, 562. SHIELDS; "Ḍhál;" circular and convex; prepared rhinoceros hide of a light-brown tinge and semi-transparent surface, ornamented with a centre and border of painted gilt enrichments, the central rosette surrounded by four floriated gilt bosses. *Haidarabad, Deccan.* Diam. 18 in. (8785.–58.)

563. HELMET; "Tóp;" of damascus steel, embossed and parcel-gilt. It consists of a recurved pointed cap of steel springing from a circlet of conventional gilt leaves. The front is occupied by a sliding noseguard, which is prolonged under the chin, flanked by a pair of port-

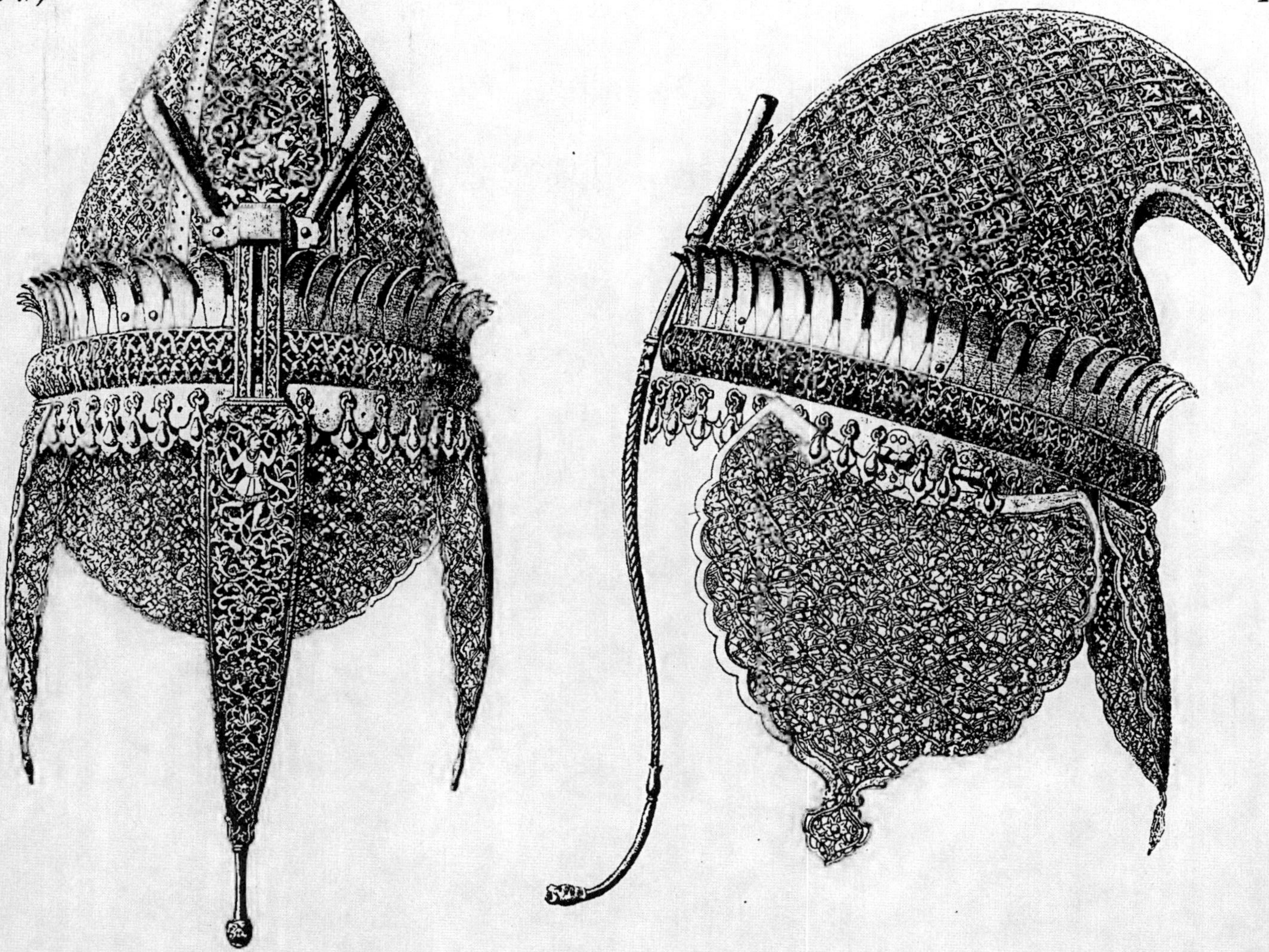

MAHRATTA HELMET

PIERCED IRONWORK GILT. (ZARKOE SELO COLLECTION)

W GRIGGS, PHOTO LITH. LONDON. S. E.

aigrettes. Originally, a coif of chain-mail was suspended from the sides of the helmet as evidenced by the holes drilled in them for that purpose. *Gwalior.* H. 9 in. (Fig. 27.) (8699.–'55.)

Fig. 27.—Mahratta Helmet (No. 563).

Cf. Z. S. Collection.—Hindoo armour and helmet. Four plates with vambraces, the ornament in raised work, and gauntlets with jazerant work on red velvet. The helmet (Pl. XI.) is peculiar, resembling in gilt metal the general outline of the Phrygian or Doge's cap. The point of the bonnet is curved back, and round the base is a sort of crown formed of a row of leaflets curving outwards; four moveable pieces of pierced tracery are hung from the helm so as to cover the ears, back of the neck, and face as far as the eyes. Gilt pendants formed of stones like a turquoise run round the helmet, and a curved nose piece descends in front of the face; this has raised figures of Hindoo gods, one mounted on a griffin, another dancing, and at the base a dog's head. —*Z. S. Cat.*

564. HELMET; "Tóp;" steel, damascened with gold. Hemispherical with plume-holder, porte-aigrettes, and sliding noseguard, the latter terminating at its upper end in a pine shaped ornament of perforated steel. Attached is a coif of fine mail (unriveted) falling in points on the shoulders, and composed of steel and brass rings in alternate zigzag stripes. *Gwalior.* (Fig. 28.) (8581.–'55.)

565.* HELMET; "Tóp;" steel damascened with gold; hemispherical, with jewelled noseguards plume of heron's feathers, porte-aigrettes and coif of mail, the latter of brass and steel in lozenged designs. *Gwalior.* Depth, 4½ in. (8583.)

566.* HELMET; "Tóp;" hemispherical, surmounted by a quadrangular arrow-head of steel; sliding noseguard flanked by porte-aigrettes; short coif of mail falling in points, the links of brass and steel in zigzag stripes. The body of the helmet is covered with rich floral arabesques chiselled in low relief; a broad band of damascened ornaments encircles the base, and the porte-aigrettes, noseguard, &c. are covered with similar enrichments. *Gwalior.* (8647.–'55.)

567.* HELMET; "Tóp;" similar in all respects to the preceding example, No. 566. *Gwalior.* (8697.–'55.)

Fig. 28.—Mahratta Helmet (No. 564).

568.* COAT OF MAIL AND ARMGUARDS. Presented by Lord Frederick Fitzclarence, to whom it was presented by the Maharajah Holkar. *Gwalior.* (8646.)

The coat is composed of unriveted links of steel and brass, alternating in lozenge patterns. Collar and facings of brocade with massive ornaments of silver-gilt, repousée, and perforated.

The arm guards are of silver-gilt richly embossed and further ornamented by little patches here and there of brilliant-coloured translucent enamel. They are lined with velvet, and terminate in open gauntlets of dark blue velvet embroidered with gold.

569 T.* CUIRASS; "chár aína;" composed of four plates of damascus steel with floral border in low-relief and gilt. *Gwalior.*

570. CUIRASS AND ARMGUARDS. The cuirass, of four pieces ("chár aína, or the four mirrors)," breast, back, and side plates; connected by straps and buckles, and lined with velvet. Each plate, oblong in form, is composed of cloudy yellow steel, enriched with a broad border of running floriated scrolls damascened in gold, and a central star-shaped ornament of uncut rubies. Breast and back plates, 9 in. by 11½ in. Side plates, 7½ in. by 9½ in. (12575.–'69.)

The Arm guards are of steel damascened with gold, and enriched with star-shaped ornaments of uncut rubies and diamonds (in one guard wanting; padded and lined with velvet. Attached to the wrist ends are open gauntlets of purple velvet, studded with small gilt-headed nails disposed in a lozenged diaper. L. 20 in. (12576.-'69.)

571. COAT OF CHAIN MAIL; "Zirah-baktar." The links composing it are small, not riveted, of brass and steel alternating in zigzag stripes. The collar is of purple velvet, studded with small gilt-headed nails, arranged in a lozenged design. *Gwalior.* (8647.)

Cf. Tower Collection. Class 15, No. 10 from Gwalior. "BAKTAR ZILLO;" jacket of iron scales and short chain sleeves ornamented with brass lingams. Made at Poonah or Sattara about 1750. Probably worn by Hindoo officer.

572 T.* SUIT OF ARMOUR; consisting of a coat of steel mail, pair of arm guards of embossed steel, and a cuirass or broad belt composed of strips of steel, hinged together and silvered on the outside. *Indore.*

573.*CUIRASS; "Petí;" for the protection of the body and neck; composed of hide covered with crimson and green velvet studded with gilt-headed nails (Jazerant work.) When open this coat is rectangular in shape; it is provided with armholes at the sides, and an attached piece at the back, forming an ample protection for the neck. *Indore.* (Fig. 29.)

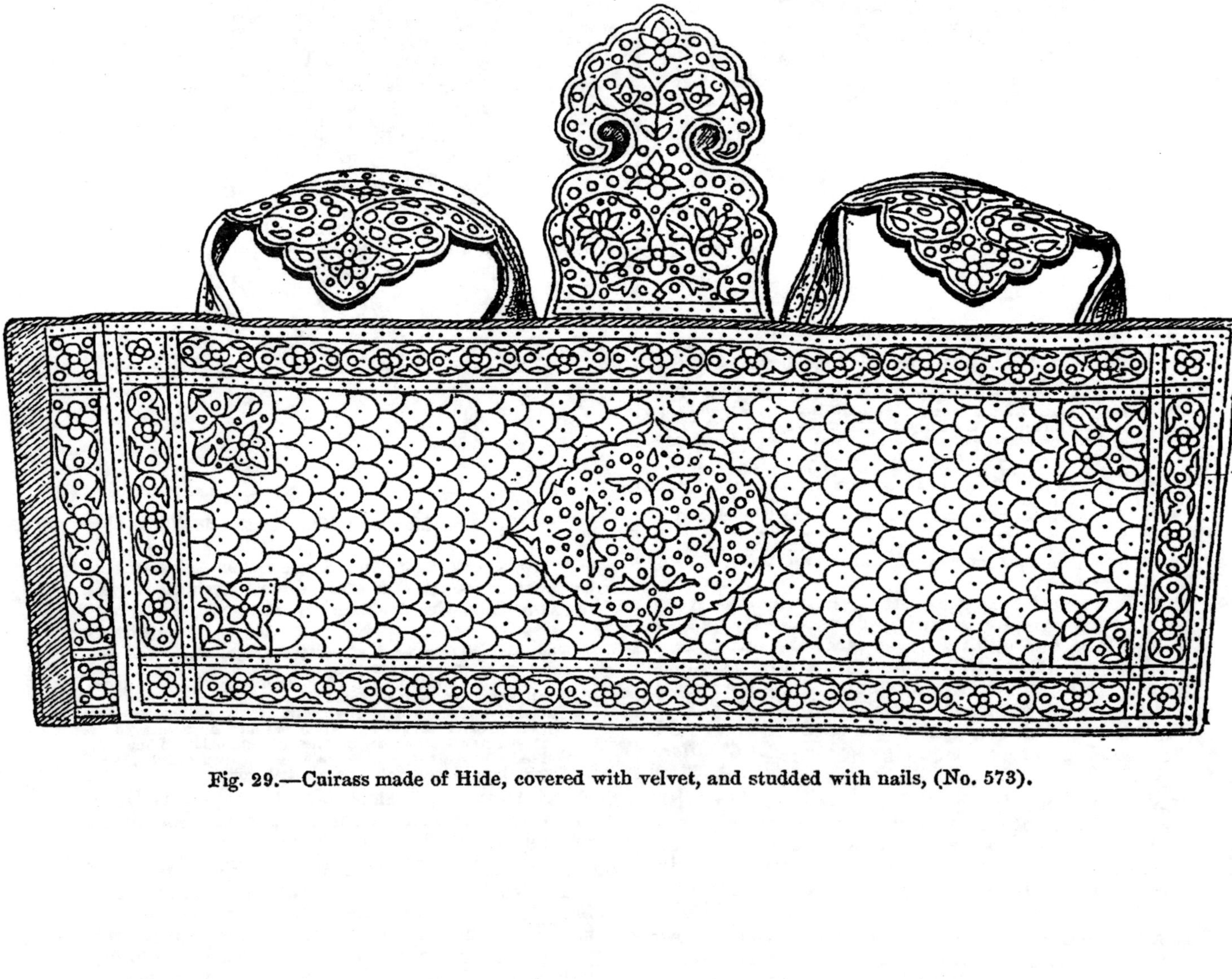

Fig. 29.—Cuirass made of Hide, covered with velvet, and studded with nails, (No. 573).

GROUP IX.

Part II.—MAHOMEDAN ARMS OF THE DECCAN AND MYSORE.

Most of the arms in this group may be traced to the time of Hyder Ali and his successor, both of whom by their military power influenced the whole of Mysore and Southern India. They were at great pains to get the best possible arms, and to adopt European improvements in them. The confidence of Sultan Tippoo was placed chiefly on his artillery and musquets. His manufactories,[1] called Tárá Mandal, were established in four places: Seringapatam, Bangalore, Chital Drúg, and Nagar. He sent an embassy to the Sultan of Rúm (Constantinople) with a present of musquets, rockets, and valuable cloths and jewels. The Sultan returned him a present of a sword and shield ornamented with jewels. It was after this that he had his tiger throne made of gold and jewels.

The Army of Hyder Ali was composed of 20,000 cavalry, 30,000 Sepoys, and 4,000 Topasses (artillerymen.) The gorgeous military pageants in which he delighted are graphically described in the history of his life,[2] from which the following extracts are taken:—

"Hyder marched in procession every day to Seringapatam. Five hundred couriers, well clothed and mounted on dromedaries, headed the procession; next followed regiments of cavalry. Two elephants, bearing the great standards of the 'Sawárí,' embroidered in gold on a blue ground, one representing the sun and the other the moon and the stars, headed the line of elephants. One of the latter carried the great timbals, by means of which the orders of the general are communicated; these are sounded continually during the march, and may be heard more than a league off. After this came four others carrying thirty-two musicians playing the music of the Sawárí, their instruments being small timbals, hautbois, flutes, and trumpets. These were succeeded by five elephants bearing golden towers or chairs of an octagonal shape, firmly fixed to their saddles by means of straps and silver chains.

"Each of these chairs contained six warriors, clad in musket-proof armour, and armed with 'fusils,' a species of blunderbuss of a very large conical bore, capable of discharging a whole handful of balls at once. One of these elephants is intended for the Nabob, but he never makes use of it in any battle. Two regiments of Caffres or Abyssinian horse came next. The men bore lances and were completely armed, one regiment having their arms polished, the other bronzed, and both had large plumes of red and black ostrich feathers attached to their helmets and hanging down their backs; the harness of their horses was red with black silk fringes. The cavalry was followed by a number of men on foot, almost naked, with large silk scarves and tight drawers reaching to the middle of the thigh; they carried long lances ornamented with ostrich feathers, and small bells that sounded as they marched. These were succeeded by a body of men carrying small banners or flags of a red ground embroidered with flames of silver.

"The lance bearers usually follow the prince to the chase. The bearers of the small standards are sent as safeguards to towns, villages, or castles; the appearance of these colours is sufficient to prevent the soldiery from entering any place, but the authorities of the place are bound to attend at the gates to furnish the army on payment with everything they want.

"After this crowd of people on foot came the nobility, following the court without distinction of rank. Nothing could be more brilliant than this troop. They were armed from head to foot and mounted on the most beautiful horses; their arms were damascened and encrusted with gold and silver; many had their casques ornamented with aigrettes of pearls and precious stones, and great numbers had coats of mail gilt and enameller.

---

[1] Mir Hussein, 145.

[2] Life of Hyder Ali, p. 155, Thacker, 1855.

The bridles of their horses were enriched with pearls and other valuable stones, and with plumes of feathers. They all had 'áftábgírs,' or parasols, formed of rich brocade, carried by men on foot at the end of a long staff, covered with gold or silver.

"The eight huntsmen of the Nabob, mounted, and twelve grooms on foot, each leading one of the Nabob's horses, richly caparisoned, followed the nobles.

"After them followed a troop of running footmen with black staves headed with gold, and twelve ushers, or 'Sanguedars' [sángdár?] on horseback, carrying gold and silver maces tipped with small crowns.

"The grand officers of the household, each with a large collar or chain of gold depending on his breast as insignia of office, preceded the grand almoner, or 'Pírzádah,' who, mounted on an elephant covered with green, marched alone. He was immediately followed by the Nabob himself, who rode on a white elephant decked with rings and chains of silver. The pavilion in which the Nabob sat was covered with yellow stuff, and was ornamented with four small globes of silver. Attached on each side by silver chains hung small hatchets, such as the 'Samorin' has carried before him. (It is the custom of the Indians to assume the marks of honour of those they have vanquished.) The elephant bore on his head a kind of buckler of gold, representing a sun.

"About two hundred elephants, marching in pairs, followed the Nabob. Their trappings and the pavilions they bore varied in colour and magnificence. Some were bordered with gold and silver lace. Many of the pavilions were composed of wrought silver or enriched with precious stones.

"The last five elephants carried the 'honours,' which are allegorical and expressive of the virtues a sovereign ought to possess. The first carried a mosque of gold. The second, at the extremity of a red staff the head of a fish, whose scales were formed of jewels and enamel. The third carried a large flambeau of white wax in a chandelier of gold. The fourth bore two small pots of gold called 'chambú' at the end of a large red staff. Lastly, the fifth was surmounted by a round chair without a canopy, covered on the outside with ivory inlaid-work, and ornamented with gold.

"After the 'honours' followed two regiments of Abyssinnians on horseback, like those in front, and the procession was closed by 200 Caffres on foot, clothed in scarlet with silver collars, and armed with lances varnished black and interspersed with silver gilding. The whole train was enclosed between a double rank of men on foot, clothed in white silk and bearing lances; the latter were about fourteen feet long, varnished black, and adorned with plates of silver; from their armed ends depended small red streamers ornamented with silver flames."

The artillery of Hyder Ali included, in addition to that of native manufacture, at least 30 French pieces cast in the reign of Louis XIV. which had been recovered from the wrecks of the squadron of M. de la Haye, lost in the roads of Masulipatam.

At the capture of Seringapatam a great variety of arms were taken. These were sent home by the East India Company, and many of them presented as trophies to distinguished persons. Hence most collections contain some arms of that period. The tiger ornament, whether applied to the hilt of a sword in the shape of a tiger-head pommel, or inlaid in gold on the blade of the weapon, is one of the most characteristic features in Tippoo's arms. Most of the cannon cast during the reign of Tippoo, writes Forbes,(1) were ornamented with the representation of a tiger devouring an European.

Tippoo lived in constant fear of assassination, and lest any person should fall upon him in bed, slept in a hammock which was suspended from the roof by chains in such a situation as to be invisible through the windows. After the capture of Seringapatam there were found in the hammock a sword and a pair of pistols.

The Nizam,(2) whose capital is Haidarábád, is now the chief representative of the Mahomedan rule in India, and holds a leading position among the native States.

1 Forbes' "Oriental Memoirs," Vol. IV., p. 190.

2 The Nizam ul Mulk was in 1712 appointed Subadar of the Deccan by the Emperor of Delhi.

(Group IX. part II.) Plate XII.

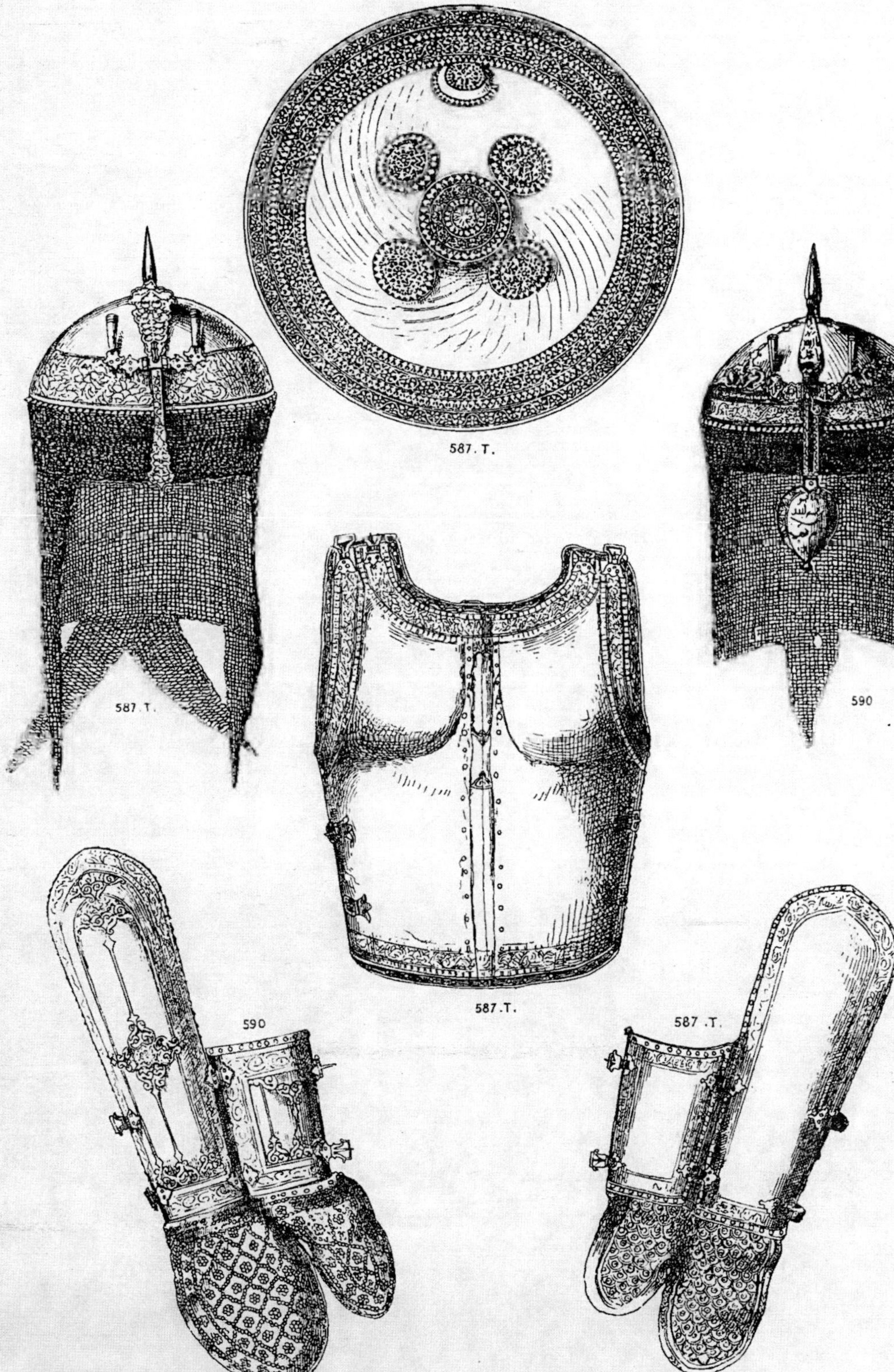

MAHOMEDAN ARMS OF THE DECCAN AND MYSORE.

W. GRIGGS, PHOTO LITH. LONDON. S. E.

A recent traveller to Haidarábád, Mrs. Burton, tells us of the armouries of Sir Salar Jung, G.C.S.I., and of Wikar Shums ool Umara, K.C.S.I.,(1) and the way in which every respectable person wears weapons, matchlock, sword and pistol in the streets.

To the court of Haidarábád is attached a corps of mercenaries, Arabs, Sidis, and Afghans, about 6,000 in number, each with their own peculiar weapons. In former times they were even more numerous in that part of India.

Most of these arms will be found in Case 54, a few in the small trophy on the left of the large screen.

The following notes from the Codrington Collection illustrate the type of bow and lance peculiar to Mysore in the time of Hyder Ali and Tippoo.

"Kamán." Bow made of buffalo-horn and bear-wood, painted and varnished, with silk string.—"Mysore." The quivers "Turkass" are of leather, either plain red, or covered with silk or velvet, figured with tinsel spangles, sometimes of leopard skins.

"Bhálá." Used by officers of light cavalry in the Hyderabad country, 1807. Shaft, 11 ft. 2 in. long, of bamboo painted green with an iron ferrule; the head is of steel overlaid with silver.

"Bhálá." 13 ft. 11 in. long (Mysore '49). Used by irregular infantry; the shaft of bamboo painted red with brass rattle middle.

"Ballam." Short spear with broad head ornamented with brass. Shaft painted. Used by infantry. Hyderabad, 1800.

"Birch'há." Heavy spear of good steel overlaid with silver; shaft painted; ferrules ornamented with silver. Used at Seringpatam in the time of Tippoo Sultan. (Tower Collection, Class 15, No. 20.)

"Birch'há." Heavy spear of good waved steel figured and slightly curved. Used by Southern Polygars. Tinnevelly, 1750.

"Laange.[2]" Used by horse and foot soldiers of all ranks at the siege of Seringapatam. Iron head, four-cornered. The shaft hollow, figured and partly plated; silver ornamented ferrules.

The body guard of the Rajah of Mysore use a lance, the head of which is about 30 inches in length.—*Sir W. Denison's Letters*, 1863.

574. Mace; "Garz;" Globular head of steel (3 in. in diam) surmounted with gold damascenings and surmounted by a quadrangular arrowhead of steel. Shaft of gilt steel. *Haidarábád. Deccan.* L. 2 ft. 2 in. (Pl. X., No. 574.) (7516.)

575 T. Mace; steel damascened with gold; six-bladed head, the edges of the blade escalloped; ribbed shaft; basket hilt. *Haidarábád.* (Pl. XV., No. 575 T.) (111.)

576 T. Sword. Straight blade, bearing a rudely engaved tiger. Plated hilt. *Mysore.* (Fig. 24, No. 576 T.) (411.)

577 T. Two-edged Sword; "Khanjar;" iron hilt. Time of Hyder Ali, "seldom used by Hindoos, and never by Mogulyes. Said to have been invented by the Syrians." (334.)

578 T. Sword; "Sosunpattah;[3]" broad blade. Padded basket hilt ornamented with bidri work. Time of Tippoo Sahib. (Fig. 24, No. 578 T.) (337.)

579 T. Sword; "Firangi;" straight blade with scalloped edge. Basket hilt padded; spiked pommel. Time of Hyder Ali Khan. Taken at the siege of *Seringaptam.* (Fig. 24, No. 579 T.) (333.)

580. Sword; "Katti Talwár;" slightly incurved, channelled blade; guarded hilt with short spike projecting from the pommel. L. 3 ft. 5 in. L. of blade, 2 ft. 9 in. (Fig. 24, No. 580.) (8795.–'55.)

Cf. incurved blade from Haidarabad in Tayler Collection.

581. Sabres (2). Grooved blades; basket hilts with spiked pommels. Leather sheaths. *Tinnevelli.* L. 3 ft. 8 in. to 3 ft. 9 in. (Fig. 24, No. 581.) (8871.–'55.)

The following notes of swords and daggers are taken from the Tower, the Codrington, and other collections:—

"Sultáni." Very heavy clumsy sword of coarse waved steel. Plain handle. *Seringapatam.* Time of Tippoo. Invented by him for the use of officers in his service. 338, Tower, Additional Collection. The blade is slightly curved and has inscriptions in tiger stripes.

"Jumgheerdha(?)" Long, narrow, straight sword attached to a kind of basket-handle slightly plated. Time of Hyder Ali. Worn by the Polygars of *Nugger.*

"Goliah." Heavy sword, slightly bent, made of fine waved steel, back and handle inlaid with silver. Hindostan and Lahore, 1780. Taken at the Siege of *Seringapatam.* Used by men of rank.

"Kassidgode." Sabre of fine waved steel, blade grooved; handle and ferrule ornamented with gold. Hindostan, 1794. Taken at the siege of *Seringapatam.*

"Lall-i-wall." Narrow curved sword, made of waved steel, with very broad back and gilt hilt. Hindostan. Tippoo Sultan's time.

"Mahmúd Bandar." Large broad sword slightly curved, with two wide grooves of very fine waved steel with old plated handles. Used by men of rank in Tippoo's time.

"Nimcha" or Teghá or Goliah. Small light sword slightly curved made of hard waved steel (pigeon's eye); plain handle. Hindostan, 1780. Boorhampore. Taken at *Seringapatam.*

"Nimcha." Handle ornamented with silver. *Malabar* 1770.

"Teghá." The handle ornamented with tiger-stripes in Persian character inlaid with gold. Each Persian word describes an attribute of the deity, and is considered a talisman too sacred for infidels to view. Therefore the Mahomedans say the handle should be kept covered, and never be touched unless the hands are previously washed. Probably worn by Tippoo.

"Sháh Nawáz Kháni." A broad heavy sword of coarse waved steel. Scythe shaped, figured iron handle.

"Sháh Nawáz Kháni." Point inclined downwards. Plain handle.

"Sháh Nawáz Kháni." Handle of watered steel. Back strengthed by plates of figured iron, ornamented with gold and silver. This weapon taken at Seringapatam was invented by a Persian officer of Hyder's army (Nawáz Khán) whose name it bears. It was used chiefly by men of rank.

"Alamáni." Shaped liked the old German Hussar sabre. Hence probably its name. Fine, hard, clouded steel; gilt handle. *Guzerat*, 1600. Used probably by Hyder's German cavalry.

"Saif." Long, heavy, two-edged sword of good waved steel. Plain handle.

---

1 This gentleman possesses a coat of mail, belonging formerly to his great-grandfather, every link and ring of which is engraved with a verse from the Koran.

2 Probably a corruption of "lance."

3 Query? Súsan-pattá.—lily-leaf.

"Sosunpattah." (See 578T.) A short, broad, heavy sword, slightly bent, point inclining upwards. Back of handle and ferrule richly ornamented with gold and silver. Worn by all ranks in Hindostan. Time of Tippoo. Tower, 337. Additional Collection.

"Tippoo Sahib's sword." Very large blade with inscriptions on both sides. On the right "Tippoo Sultan." On the left "Victory of Hyder" alluding to his father Hyder Ali, or perhaps also to Hyder Allah, the Lion of God, one of the titles of Ali. Z. S. Collection.

"Asil." Slightly curved sword of watered steel with two grooves. Plain handle. Time of Tippoo.

"Tooroom." (Turup?) A long broad dagger of good steel with many grooves, attached to a kind of basket hilt, ornamented with silver ferrules. Worn by irregular infantry of Rajpoots and Mahrattas of all ranks in southern India. Time of Tippoo.

'Saffdara." Narrow two-edged knife of good waved steel; iron handle inlaid with silver (Arabic inscription in tigers head); ferrules ornamented with silver. Made at *Seringapatam* by Tippoo Sultan's order. Worn by men of high rank.

"Saffdara." Handle ornamented with tiger stripes inlaid with silver.

"Peshkabz." Broad knife of waved steel, back slightly ornamented with gold. Handle of rhinoceros ivory. Silver ferrules. Hindostan. Time of Tippoo.

"Jambiya" or curved knife. Watered steel, ivory handle. Worn by Arabs, chiefly men of rank. Mysore, 1846.

"Jambiya." Ivory hilt. Gilt and embossed ornaments. From Deccan. Tower Collection 5. The curved dagger "Jambiya" is now used near Aden by the Arabs, and was probably imported by them into India.

"Bánk." Curved dagger. Watered steel blade, figured copper handle and finger guard. Worn by common people among the Mogulyes and people[1] of the Rajwar caste throughout India. Tower. 341, Additional Collection.

"Bánk." Good steel blade; iron handle ornamented with brass. Mysore. Time of Tippoo.

"Bánk." Common steel blade, iron handle. Carnatic Worn chiefly by irregular infantry.

Cf. in British Museum, Henderson Collection. A dagger of Hyder Ali from Sir H. Munro, handle in jade, carved horse's head, and rich enamelled sheath.

Two swords of Tippoo are preserved at Windsor; one with a tiger's-head pommel (*vide* Fig. 3.), the other with sentences from the Koran engraved on the blade, and raised gold-work on the hilt.

582. MATCHLOCK PISTOLS; "Tamancha;" hilts of dark wood, shaped like miniature gun-stocks and terminating in knobs. *Mysore.* L. 19 in.

Cf. Codrington Collection. Matchlock of brass, time of Hyder Ali, used by irregular infantry.

583. MATCHLOCK; "Toradár;" the barrel covered with a lozenge-diaper ornamentation, hammered in low-relief, and attached to the stock by leather strips; stock strengthened with side plates of Damascus steel. *Mysore.* L. 5 ft. 3 in. (8661.–'55.)

584 T. MATCHLOCK; the barrel and side-plate chased, and at the mouth and breech ornamented with low-relief gilt enrichments; on the trigger is the figure of a tiger. *Mysore.* (409.)

585. MATCHLOCK; very long barrel. Taken at the siege of Seringapatam. (351.)

Notes from Codrington Collection:—"Bukmár;" musquetoon with bell mouth: tiger pattern. Taken at Seringapatam. Used by officers of camel corps.

"Karol."—Heavy carbine used by cavalry in the time of Hyder Ali.

"Bandúq." Long matchlock of good iron twist. *Carnatic*, 1800.

"Jazá'il;" heavy wall piece 8 ft. long matchlock.

Dc., 7 ft. long. Barrel taken at Seringapatam.

586 T. MUSKET BARREL, with small bayonet ("Sangin") attached; engraved with figures of tigers and tiger-stripes, and inscribed in Arabic, "Matchless musket of the Ruler of India. "May it be like burning lightning!" In the tiger-stripe near the centre of the barrel is written "Royal Manufactory." Used by the guard of Tippoo Sultan. Trophy on the left (408).

587 T.* SUIT OF ARMOUR; of steel richly damascened with gold. *Haidarabad.* (Pl. XII., No. 587 T.) It comprises the following pieces:—

1. Helmet with coif of mail and sliding nose-guard, the latter inscribed with a verse from the Koran, "Assistance from Allah and approaching victory."

2. Cuirass, resembling in shape those worn in Europe during the Middle Ages, and composed of breast and back-plates, with moveable shoulder pieces.

3. Arm-guards.

4. Shield, circular and convex of embossed steel, elaborately ornamented with pierced and gilt metal work on a ground of crimson foil. Lined with velvet studded with gilt-headed nails. (Jazerant work.)

588 T. QUILTED HELMET AND BELT. The helmet, a kind of cap with flaps at the sides and back, is covered with crimson velvet richly embroidered with gold, and encircled by a green muslin turban. The broad quilted belt is also covered with crimson velvet similarly ornamented. Belonged to Tippoo Sultan, and subsequently in the collection of the Duke of York. (406–7.)

589. QUILTED HELMET AND CUIRASS. Worn by Tippoo Sultan. The helmet, which is very large and provided with flaps at the back and sides, is composed of many thicknesses of a coarse cotton fabric compactly quilted together. It is covered with dark green silk or satin, and lined with velvet of the same colour. On the inside of the flap at the back is embroidered an inscription to the effect that the helmet has been dipped in the holy well of Zam-Zam at Mecca, and is therefore impenetrable.

The cuirass, nearly an inch in thickness, is composed of the same material, covered with green velvet. It is fastened by lacing in front. and is provided with armholes and epaulettes at the sides. Presented by the besiegers of *Seringapatam.* (1163.)

There are at Windsor two suits of quilted crimson velvet embroidered with gold, which belonged to Tippoo. Also a bell-mouthed carbine, and a gauntlet sword, terminating above the blade in a tiger's head, from which proceed elephant's tusks with rubies and diamonds.

590. SUIT OF ARMOUR, consisting of helmet, coat, and arm-guards. Once belonged to Tippoo Sultan. Taken at the siege of *Seringapatam.* (8580.)

The helmet (Pl. XII., No. 590) is of steel, damascened with gold; hemispherical, surmounted by a quadrangular gilt arrowhead, and encircled at the base by a broad band of damascened foliage; sliding nose-guard, flanked by porte-aigrettes; coif of mail (brass and steel alternately) falling in points on the shoulders.

The coat is composed of unriveted links of steel and brass, the latter in intersecting diagonal stripes; velvet collar, studded with a lozenge diaper of gilt-headed nails.

The arm-guards (Pl. XII., No. 590) of steel, ribbed, and ornamented with delicate gold damascening; open gauntlets of velvets, studded with gilt-headed nails.

591T. HELMET; "Tóp;" composed of plate and chain mail, and armed with a large crescent-shaped nose-guard of steel, sharpened on its lower edge. Taken at the siege of Seringapatam. Worn by Mogulye heavy cavalry in the time of Hyder Ali Khan. Tippoo Sahib retained only 1,000 men thus armed as a body-guard. (Fig. 30.)
Screen on the left (364).

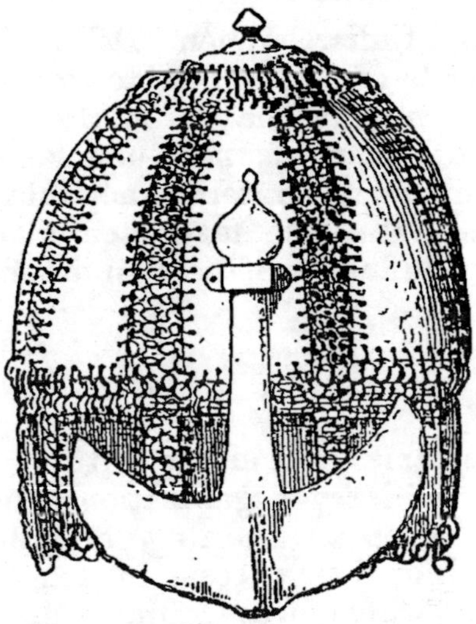

Fig. 30.—Helmet worn by Mogul Cavalry (No. 591T).

These large and heavy helmets were probably introduced before the time of the Mogul Emperors.

Cf. large iron helmet formerly in Meyrick Collection, now in British Museum.

In the Tarik-i Tahiri, we are told that on the first invasion of the Moguls into India the women miscarried at the very sight of the Moguls with their terrific head-pieces. —*Elliott*, Vol. I., p. 533.

The helmet was sometimes replaced by a nasal guard, which protected the face and forehead. There is one in the Henderson Collection, British Museum, which is 11 inches long and 7 inches broad, with two trefoiled openings on each side, into which the twisted folds of the turban were inserted. Cf. plate representing the dynasty of Beejapore, Langlès, Vol. I., p. 235.

The following armour and accoutrements from Mysore are described in the Codrington Collection, dated 1850:—

"Zirah baktar." Coat of mail reaching to the knees, made of iron chain plates and scales, two rows plain, one scalloped. Made at Seringapatám, in the time of Hyder Ali Khan. Used by Mogulye heavy cavalry in the time of Hyder. (Tippoo Sultan retained only 1,000 as body guard.)

"Zirah baktar. Fifteen rows plain narrow scales, with chain skirt. Worn by officers of high rank. Taken at the siege of Seringapatam.

"Zirah-baktar." Jacket of scales shaped like a leaf, and coarse chain.

"Zirah-baktar." Coarse chain and plates. All taken at the siege of Seringapatam.

These were worn with quilted cloth underneath, and bound with cotton velvet.

"Kurtani." Coat of coarse chain mail.

"Ranjakdán." Small powder horn of carved antelope horn. *Mysore.*

"Collery" Horn. Made of copper ornamented with brass, silk cord, tail of yak, and strips of coloured cloth attached. *Mysore*, 1840. Blown to call troops together.

"Ch'hátá." Red cotton velvet parasol, embroidered with gold. *Mysore*, 1850. This is only permitted to be worn by such persons as have been presented with it by their prince.

The largest shields, of raw hide of elk or bison, were made at Sylhet, in Eastern Bengal, and are 2 ft. in diameter. They are painted black, and ornamented with brass bosses or crescents, and were used by Tippoo's army.

Tippoo's tent of red cloth, embroidered with silver and gilt thread, is still preserved at Windsor.

Tippoo's saddle is at Zarkoe Selo.—*Rockstühl*, Pl. 92-4. The peak terminates in a swan's neck. It is of silver repoussé work, and chiselled with representations of the wild animals of the chase. The stirrups are of silver gilt, and enriched with flowers in enamel.

The harness belonging to Tippoo's saddle is composed of head-piece, breastplate, and crupper in silver gilt, a chabraque of red silk covered with gold embroideries and tassels of gold.

The following is a description of the horse furniture in the Codrington Collection:—

"Bálá-tang." Surcingle of silk.

"Dumchi." Crupper of leather covered with velvet and small metal bosses.

"Gulú-Band." Strips of velvet flowered with silk, for mane.

"Khogir." Saddle, red velvet.

"Kafal Posh." Loin-covering, of black velvet.

"Unniannau (?)." Reins of rope covered with velvet.

"Pultah." Headstall covered with velvet and ornamented with metal.

"Oostuck (?)." Saddle cloth, to be worn over saddle.

"Lagseam." Mogul bit.

"Shikárband" (*i.e.* game-straps). Bunches of string covered with velvet, to be fastened to corners of saddle.

"Zerband." Martingale of red silk net.

"Rikáb." Iron stirrups.

"Turrah." Ornament for the head of feathers and gold.

"Padak," "Málá." Ornament of metal for neck.

"Kolda." Whip.

"Sulimáni manká." Amulet of stones and shell for neck.

"Ghagri." Rattle of metal tied on to the leg

GROUP X.

ARMS OF NORTH-WESTERN INDIA.

This group comprises the arms of North-Western India. When Delhi was the seat of empire of the "Great Mogul," his rule extended beyond the Punjab to Cashmere, Afghanistan, Beluchistan, and Sind, the arms of which countries may properly, therefore, be included in those of our Indian empire. The best artificers of India and Persia were attracted at this period to the court of Delhi, and the finest decorated arms inlaid with gold, silver, and jewels were manufactured in the capital. The far-famed blades imported from Khorassan received Indian mounts, and the influence of Persian art extended over the whole of the north-western frontier of India.

PART I.—PUNJAB.

The *Sikhs*, the latest military power of India which came in contact with our arms, may also claim to have possessed the most perfect military organization. They, of all the Indian races, have most profited by that European training and discipline which they were one of the first to appreciate. Much of their success in arms is due, however, to the half military, half-religious system which was founded by Nának Sháh (1469–1539), and continued by his successors the Gurus. The rise of the Sikh power was owing to Govind, the tenth and last leader or Guru, who, when the Sikhs were persecuted as infidels by Aurungzebe, formed the bands of that sect into a religious and military commonwealth, or Khálsa, animated with undying hatred to the Mahomedans. The Gúrú Govind was murdered, and after his death was venerated as the chief apostle of that religion. The religious element of Sikhism was represented by the "Akálís." They were "the immortals" or soldiers of God, who claimed for themselves to have been instituted by Govind Sing. Instead of practising the inert asceticism of the Hindu sects, they were called upon to leave their homes and devote themselves to the profession of arms, in defence of their faith.

After the death of Aurungzebe, the power of the Sikhs again revived, and although once more almost exterminated under Farrukhsiyar at the beginning of the 18th century, they retained their hold on the country, not only under the weak Mogul Emperors, but also when, after 1748, the Punjab passed under the rule of the vigorous Afghan leader Ahmad Sháh 'Abdali, the conqueror of the Mahrattas in the great battle of Pánipat. They established themselves in petty isolated forts, under the cover of which they gave constant employment to the governors of Lahore and Sirhind.

In 1762 they held their first public assembly "Sárbat Khálsa," in Amritsir, but Ahmad Sháh returned to India, to avenge the defeat of his lieutenants, destroyed their sacred temple at Amritsir, and polluted it.

The insurgents fled before him to the desert near Rajpútáná, but returned in 1764 as soon as Ahmad Sháh had retraced his steps; and when he returned to the Sutlej the Sikhs again dispersed before his army. But finally, Ahmad Sháh was compelled to leave the Sikhs in virtual possession of the Punjab and Sirhind, though he still retained the nominal sovereignty.

The Sikhs at this period were not governed by any one prince, but were divided into twelve fraternities called "Misl," each one acting according to its own interest and way of thinking. Twice in the year, at the anniversary of the great festivals of the "Báisákhi" in April, and of the "Dewáli" in October, the Sikhs hold a *gurumátá* or general council,

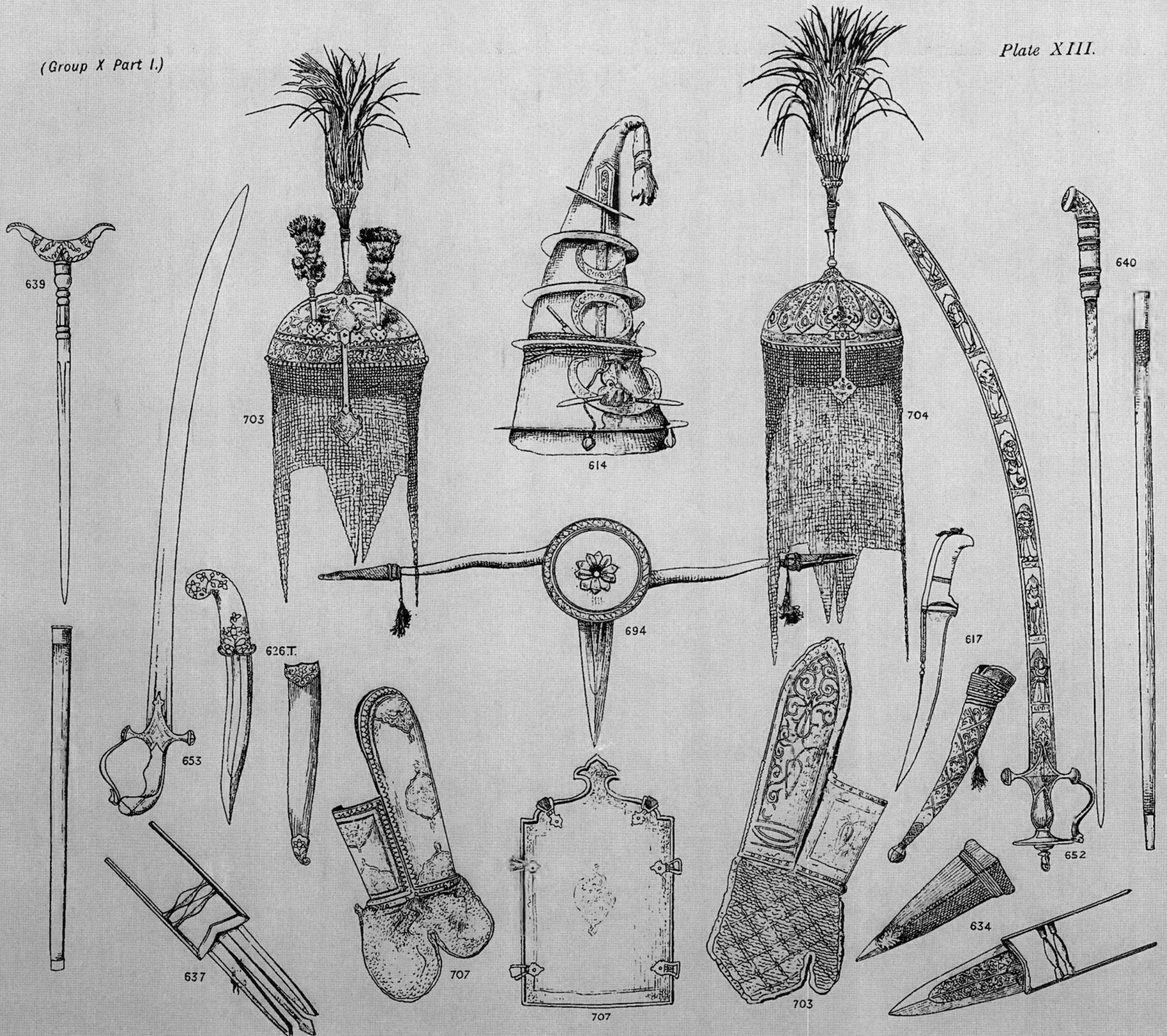

ARMS OF NORTH-WESTERN INDIA.

W. GRIGGS, PHOTO-LITH LONDON, S.E.

at which their future enterprises are resolved upon, and, according to their importance the co-operation of the whole brotherhood or of one or more divisions called for.

The twelve "misls" were named and constituted as follows:—

1.	Bangí	10,000	armed horsemen.
2.	Rámgarhí	3,000	do.
3.	Ghanaiya or Kanaiya	8,000	do.
4.	Nakaiya	2,000	do.
5.	Alúwálá	3,000	do.
6.	Dalawálá	7,500	do.
7.	Nishánwálá or Nisbániya	12,000	do.
8.	Faizullapúriya	2,500	do.
9.	Krora Singhiya	12,000	do.
10.	Shahid and Nihang	2,000	do.
11.	Phulkiya and Bhekiya	5,000	do.
12.	Sukar Chakiya	2,500	do.
	A total of	69,500	do.

Among their prominent leaders at that time, and the founder of the last Misl, was Charat Singh, the grandfather of Ranjít Singh. He was one of the first to build a "garhi" or fort as a storehouse for his booty. When his fortress of Gujráoli (now Gujránwálá) was besieged by the viceroy of Lahore, the Sikh mercenaries who served under him went over to their brethren in the fort, upon which the Mahomedan army took to flight. His son, Mahá Singh, increased the power of the family by taking Jámú from Jai Singh, and in 1798 his grandson, Ranjit Singh, when only 18 years of age, was appointed Governor of Lahore by Zaman Sháh the grandson of Ahmad Sháh.

The rapid rise in the power of the Sikhs was to a great extent due to the adoption by them of improved weapons and methods of warfare. In 1800 they had 40 pieces of field artillery. Cunningham[1] gives the following graphic account of the character of the Sikhs as infantry, and compared with the other fighting races of India:—

" The Rajpoot and Pathan will fight as Pirthee Raee and Jenghiz Khan waged war. They will ride on horses in tumultuous array, and they will wield a sword and spear with individual dexterity; but neither of these cavaliers will deign to stand in regular ranks, and learn, as the Sikhs have learned to handle the musquet of the infantry soldier, although the Mahometan has always been a brave and skilful server of heavy cannon. . .

" The early force of the Sikhs was composed of horsemen, but they seem intuitively to have adopted the new and formidable matchlock of recent times, instead of the ancestral bow, and the spear common to every nation. Mr. Forster noticed this peculiarity in 1783, and the advantage it gave them in desultory warfare. . . .

" In 1805, Sir John Malcolm did not think the Sikhs better mounted than the Mahrattas. . . . The peculiar arms of the contending nations of the last century passed into a proverb, and the phrase 'the Mahratta spear, the Afghan sword, the Sikh matchlock, and the English cannon' is still of common repetition."

The Mahrattas kept the Sikh States in submission till they were defeated by the English forces under Lord Lake. In 1799 Ranjít Singh assumed the title of Rajah. In 1809 he signed a treaty with the English, which defined the territory of the Sikh chiefs south of the Sutlej, while it did not interfere with the limits of the Sikh States, north of the Sutlej.[2] During the same year he commenced the reorganisation of his

[1] Sikhs, p. 182.   [2] Treaties and Engagements with India, Vol. III., p. 14. Edited by Lieut. Talbot.

army on the English model, being much impressed by the superiority of the disciplined troops of Mr. Metcalfe's escort against the Akális in a fanatical outbreak of the population of Amritsir. With this view he endeavoured to obtain subalterns from the Company's army to discipline his own. He divided his infantry into battalions of three or four hundred men each; the artillery formed a separate corps under a "Darogha" or Commandant; and the cavalry remained under his own command.[1]

In 1822 Allard and Ventura entered Ranjít Singh's service and disciplined his army. In 1832,[2] Captain Murray states that Ranjít Singh's army numbered 80,905 men, of whom the élite were:—

The French legion, 8,000 men.

The Ghurchaṛh'as and Ghurchaṛhkhás, cavalry clad in armour and carrying musquets, 4,000. These were supported[3] by territories which brought them in a revenue of 3,000 or 4,000 rupees a piece; their horses and entire equipments were their own property.

Their uniform consisted of a velvet coat or gaberdine, over which most of them wore a shirt of mail. Others had this shirt made to form part of the tunic. A waist belt richly embroidered in gold, supported the powder horn covered with cloth of gold, as well as the Persian Kaṭár, and the pistols which many of them carried. Some wore a steel helmet inlaid with gold, and surmounted by the "Kalghí" a black heron's plume. Others wore a cap of steel worked like the cuirass in rings. The left arm is often covered from the hand to the elbow, with a steel cuff inlaid with gold. The round Sikh shield hangs at the back, and is fastened by straps across the chest. A quiver at the right side, and a bow slung at the back complete the equipment.

The remaining forces were:—

3. Disciplined battalions, 14,941.
4. Infantry regiments variously equipped, 23,950.
5. Cavalry, 3,000.
6. Sirdars contingents, cavalry, 27,014.
7. Elephants, 101.

Captain Murray calculates the artillery, which was miserably organised and served, except that portion attached to the French legion, as composed of 370 guns and 370 "Jinjáls." Of the whole number probably not 50 would be reckoned serviceable by us.[4]

"Ranjít Singh's force" writes Masson,[5] "consisted of perhaps 20,000 troops trained after "the French or European methods of discipline, and 50,000 Sikhs or Gorkhas. Each "regiment wore a 'pagri' or turban of distinguishing colour."

"The Sikh irregular cavalry," remarks the same writer, "have a peculiar exercise at "which they are very expert. In action they advance upon their enemies until their "matchlocks can take effect, discharge them, and then precipitately retreat to reload and "repeat the same manœuvre."

"The Sikh soldiers" writes Captain Mundy,[6] "dressed (1827) in tunics of quilted cotton "or silk with a peculiar shaped red turban and cummerbund of the same colour.[7] Their "legs were bare below the knee, and they were all armed with a spear or sword and "black shields of buffalo hide studded with brass." But the arm that is exclusively peculiar to this sect is the quoit. It is made of beautiful thin steel, sometimes inlaid with gold; in using it the warrior twirls it swiftly round the forfinger, and raising his hand over his head, launches it with such deadly aim, as according to their own account to be sure of their man at 80 paces. The quoit is worn only by the Akális, who are armed to the

---

[1] Baron Hügel's Cashmere, p. 367. [2] Ibid. p. 379. [3] Ibid. p. 330–404.
[4] Treaties and Engagements with India, Vol. III., p. 404. Edited by Lieut. Talbot.
[5] Journey in Afghanistan, 1842.
[6] Journey of a Tour in India, p. 131, 1827.
[7] They now generally wear tight fitting trowsers of silk or cotton.—W. E.

teeth. They wear, in obedience to their founder, the tenth Guru, Govind, nothing but steel and blue cotton cloth, steel bow, sword, shield, brace of horse pistols or collection

Fig. 31.—A Sikh throwing the Quoit.

[1] Fig. 32.—Sikh Quoit from Lahore. (E. Coll.)

of daggers, and sometimes as many as six war quoits round the arm and on the top of their high conical turban.

The Sikhs attained their greatest power under Ranjít Singh. It is unnecessary to recall their gallant defence of the Punjab, and their loyalty in later days, to show that under European discipline they have not lost their ancient courage and vigour.

In the south-west of the Punjab lies the district of Multan inhabited by the *Jats*, the descendants of the Scythian invaders of India. To the successive Mahomedan invaders of India, the Jats have always offered a strenuous resistance. At the end of the last century they were under Afghan rule till Ranjít Singh annexed the province of Multan to his kingdom. Their arms do not differ from those of the Punjab or Rajputana.

The Mekránís, inhabitants of the country west of Sind, used to migrate into Central India in quest of employment in a quasi-military capacity. They are expert marksmen and good swordsmen.

The arms of the *Bilúchís* do not appear to have any special character. They are not represented in this collection. Pottinger in his travels (1816) says, "The Beloochee "soldier carries a matchlock, sword, spear, dagger, and shield, besides a number of powder "flasks, priming horns and pouches. They are all capital marksmen. They get their "arms from Persia, Khorassan, and Hindostan, their spears from Sinde. At Khelat "there is an armoury belonging to the Khan, but the workmanship is clumsy. In firing "at a mark I am assured they can hit a mark six inches square when riding at full "galop, and they kill small birds with a single ball at 60 yards." They are equally good shots with a Snider carbine.[2]

---

[1] The quoit illustrated in Fig. 32 was probably made at Lahore for a Mr. Hamilton, and is thus described by Mr. Poole, of the British Museum:—Inscription on a steel quoit, inlaid with silver: on one side a floral pattern; on the other a similar pattern, but the flowers replaced by cinq foils, derived, no doubt, from the arms of Hamilton, gules, three cinq foils ermine; on this side a panel occurs with the inscription,

"The possessor of it [is] George, son of Daniel, the Hamiltonian."

[2] Cf. V. Ball, "Jungle Life in India," pp. 444–8. 1880.

NOTE.—*The more ornamental arms will be found in Cases 45 and 69 (the latter fire-arms).*

592.* Bow; "Kamán;" made of prepared horn, lacquered and gilt; strings of spun silk; bow-cover crimson velvet embroidered with gold. *Delhi.* (8589.–'55.)

593.* Bow; "Kamán;" made of horn, lacquered and painted with floral arabesques in gold and colours; silken string. *Lahore.* L. 4 ft. (8594.–'55.)

594. Bow; "Kamán;" curved Parthian shape, probably of buffalo horn, painted and lacquered in red, green, and gold; string of spun silk. *Delhi.* L. 4 ft. (8591.–'55.)

595. Bow; "Kamán;" horn painted and gilt. *Delhi.* L. 4 ft. (8590.–'55.)

596. Bows; "Kamán;" horn, painted and lacquered. (8850.)

597. Bow; "Kamán," and arrows (12); steel, painted. Presented by Dr. Nicholson. *Cambay.* L. 4 ft. ('62.)

598. Bow; "Kamán;" steel, very elastic, painted with floral arabesques. Taken at *Lucknow.* L. 3 ft. 5 in. (8761.–'70.)

599.* PELLET-BOW; "Gulel;" bamboo, painted in green and gold; ivory mounts; double string. *Lahore.* L. 4 ft. 10 in. (8638.–'55.)

The pellet is held in a small web of silk attached at each end to one of the strings.

600.* PELLET-BOW; "Gulel;" bamboo, ornamented with gilt pines painted on a red ground; double string. *Lahore.* L. 4 ft.

601.* QUIVERS (2); "Tarkash;" long, cylindrical, covered with crimson velvet; *Lahore.* (8588.–'55.)

602.* QUIVERS (2) AND ARROWS; "Tír-o-tarkash;" the quivers of crimson velvet, embroidered on one side with gold. *Lahore.* (8688.–'55; 8587.–'55.)

603.* ARROWS; "Tír;" black reed shafts, painted and gilt, and tipped with ivory; flat points of perforated steel-work. *Lahore.* (8772.–'51.)

604.* ARROWS; "Tír;" reed shafts, painted and gilt at the feathered ends; various shaped points, with ornamental mounts of steel inlaid with brass and copper. *Lahore.* L. 2 ft. 4 in. (8588.–'55.)

605. ARROW. Unfeathered shaft notched at the end; broad, leaf-shaped blade. *Lucknow.* Taken at the mutiny. L. 6 ft.

606. SPEAR. Palmwood shaft; small triangular head with thickened point. *Jind.* (12716.–'55.)

607–609. SPEARS. Long bamboo shafts; small heads: heavy bossed butts. *Lahore.* L. 12 ft. to 15 ft.

610. SPEAR. Long shaft painted with hunting scenes, wild animals, &c., on a green ground. Small head decorated with a tuft of black silk threads. Bossed butt. *Lahore.* L. 13 ft. 6 in.

611. SPEAR; "Neza;" the shaft lacquered with floral arabesques in gold on a crimson background; the point long, slender, and quadrangular, plated with gold ornamented in niello. The pointed butt-end is similarly treated. *Lahore.* L. 8 ft.; point, 16 in. (8834.–'55.)

612. SPEARS, (2) "Neza;" long slender blades; metal mounts. Used by horsemen. *Jind.* L. 9 ft. and 9 ft. 3 in. L.; of head, 21 in. (8863.–'55.)

613. * QUOIT TURBAN; "Dastár Bunggá"; worn by the Akalee Sikhs. The turban is conical in shape, about 20 inches in height, and constructed of indigo-blue cotton cloth twisted round a light sub-structure of cane; encircling it are nine quoits, a tiger claw (wagnuk) and other small weapons, all of steel. *Lahore* Diam. of quoits, 4 in. to 11 in. (8365.–'55.)

614. * QUOIT TURBAN; "Dastár Bunggá;" a conical structure of dark blue cotton cloth, encircled by quoits (5), crescents, small knives and tiger-claws, all of blueish steel damascened with gold. *Lahore.* (Pl. XIII., No. 614.) (8569.–'51.)

615. QUOITS; "Chakram;" flat steel rings, of various sizes, sharpened on the outer edge. Used by the Akalee Sikhs. *Punjab.* Presented by Major, afterwards Sir Herbert, Edwards. Diam. 5¼ in. to 11 in. (8601.–'55.)

616. MACE; "Garz;" steel damascened with gold; six-bladed head of blueish steel; shaft sparingly ornamented with gold damascenings, *Lahore.* L. 2 ft. 2 in. (8556.–'55.)

617. * DAGGER; "Peshkabz;" curved blade, ribbed, and thickened at the point, and damascened with gold near the hilt; hilt of walrus ivory, and gold-damascened steel. Embossed black leather sheath, silver-mounted. *Peshawur.* (Pl. XIII., No. 617.) (8526.–'55.)

618. * DAGGER; "Peshkabz;" blade damascened with gold; ivory hilt; velvet scabbard with gold-damascened steel mounts. *Peshawur.* (8535.–'55.)

619. * DAGGER; "Peshkabz;" one-edged pointed blade of Damascus steel; hilt covered with rock crystal beneath which are seen native paintings of mythological subjects; the rivet heads attaching the crystal to the hilt are concealed by rubies. *Lahore.* (8528.–'51.)

620.* DAGGER; "Peshkabz;" Damascus blade, ornamented with chiselled and gilt floriations; walrus ivory hilt. *Lahore.* (8540.–'55.)

621.* DAGGER; "Peshkabz;" pointed one-edged blade with broad, straight back; ivory hilt, crimson velvet sheath, silver mounted, with gold tassels attached. *Lahore.* (8520.–'55.)

622.* DAGGER; "Peshkabz;" blade of yellowish steel, sparingly ornamented with gold damascenings; hilt of walrus ivory, with gold damascened steel sides; dark brown leather sheath. *Lahore.*

623.* DAGGER; "Peshkabz;" curved blade, with broad back ornamented near the hilt with arabesques chiselled in low relief and partially gilt; hilt of walrus ivory and embossed steel; sheath of black leather embossed and tipped with gold. (8538.)

624. DAGGER; "Peshkabz;" ivory hilt, brass mounts; velvet sheath with elaborately chased and perforated brass mounts. *Bánú.* (Pl. XIV., No. 624.) (6550.)

625.* Dagger; "Peshkabz;" blade damascened with gold at the hilt; hilt of walrus-ivory and steel damascened with gold; embossed black leather, sheath with silver mounts. *Bijnur.* (7430.–'67.)

626.* Dagger; "Khanjar;" two-edged doubly curved blade of Damascus steel; pistol-hilt of green jade set with diamonds and rubies. *Lahore.* (8525.–'51.)

626.a* Dagger; "Khanjar;" hilt of white jade encrusted with large flat diamonds, rubies, and emeralds, in floral designs. Green velvet sheath with white jade mounts similarly ornamented. Presented by the Marquis of Hastings. (Fig. 13, No. 1.) (8524.–'50.)

627.* Dagger; "Khanjar;" pistol-hilt of mottled jade ornamented with low relief foliated carvings; sheath covered with kincob and mounted with gold. *Lahore.* (8536.–'55.)

628.* Dagger; "Bich'hwá, or Scorpion;" doubly curved small blade of Damascus steel; walrus-ivory hilt; purple velvet sheath. *Punjab.* Presented by Col. Hamilton. (11,497.–'67.)

629.* Dagger; "Kaṭár;" broad Damascus blade ornamented with a foliated central rib chiselled in low relief, and bearing on both sides inscriptions inlaid in gold; the hilt and sideguards are gilt, embossed and delicately chased with running foliated scroll ornaments; green velvet sheath tipped with gold. *Lahore.* L. 17½ in. (8548.–'51.)

630. Dagger; "Kaṭár;" damascus blade of yellow-tinted steel, ribbed, and thicked at the point. Transverse hilt plated with silver. *Lahore.* (8544.–'55.)

631.* Dagger; "Kaṭár;" polished, grooved blade. Hilt and guards damascened with gold ornaments and inscriptions. *Lahore.* (8543.–'51.)

632. Dagger; "Kaṭár;" blade enriched with conventional honey-suckle floriations chiselled in low relief and gilt. *Punjab.* L. 15 in. (11,499.–'71.)

633.* Dagger; "Kaṭár;" narrow, deeply-grooved quadrangular blade. The steel hilt and sideguards completely covered with inscriptions damascened in gold. Crimson velvet sheath with perforated gold mounts. A Sikh weapon. (12,574.)

634. *Dagger; "Kaṭár;" broad blade ornamented with a diaper of birds and flowers, cut in low relief, the back ground filled in with some black composition. The hilt and sideguards are ornamented with little scenes of houses, trees, flowers, &c. inlaid in brass. Crimson velvet sheath tipped with silver. (Pl. xiii. No. 634.) (8711.)

635.* Dagger; "Kaṭár;" gold-damascened side guards. Gold and silk cord with tassel. Green velvet sheath. *Lahore.* (8547.–'55.)

636.* Dagger; "Kaṭár;" deeply grooved blade of damascus steel. Hilt and guards gilt, and ornamented with incised scrolls of birds and flowers. Purple velvet sheath. *Punjab.* Presented by Col. Hamilton. L. 16 in. (11,500.–'67.)

637.* Dagger; "Kaṭár;" with five blades, which spring open on pressing together the bars of the hilt. Hilt and sideguards damascened with gold. Crimson velvet sheath with gold mounts. *Pattiálá.* (Pl. xiii. No. 637.) (8542.–'51.)

638.* Dagger with Pistols; the dagger is of the ordinary Kaṭár type, the blade enriched with foliated ornaments chiselled in low relief. The side guards are continued into pistol barrels, one on each side of the blade, the triggers lying within the side-guards; the barrels are made to unscrew and may be removed at will. The hilt, sideguards, and pistol-barrels are of gilt steel. *Lahore.* (8549.–'55.)

639. Crutch Dagger; crutch shaped hilt, of carved jade and crystal, short blade; stick sheath. (Pl. xiii. No. 639.) (8519.)

640. Sword-hilt and Scabbard Mounts; steel damascened in gold. *Lahore.* (Pl. xiii. No. 640.) (8605.–'51.)

641.* Sword-stick; "Gupti;" highly burnished rapier blade, enriched with gold damascenings at the hilt. Pistol-hilt of ivory carved with low-relief floriated ornaments, painted and gilt. The stick-sheath is painted with floriated arabesques in gold on a dark blue ground. *Lahore.* L. 2 ft. 11 in. (8557.–'55.)

642. Sword-sticks (2); "Gupti;" pistol hilts of wood. (12,613) (12,594.)

643. Gauntlet-sword; "Paṭa;" straight rapier blade; long gauntlet hilt of steel mounted in brass with simple zigzag ornaments and two small fish figures. *Punjab.* (12,531.)

644.* Sabre; "Talwár;" heavy, burnished damascus blade bearing an inscription incised in the steel. Hilt with double handguard for the knuckles and back of the hand, thickly plated with gold. Scabbard of purple velvet. *Lahore.* Presented to the Governor-General of India by the Maharajah Nownchall Sing in Durbar. L. 2 ft. 10 in. (8510.–'50.)

645.* Sabre; "Talwár;" finely watered dark steel, guarded hilt richly damascened in gold. Scabbard covered with gold brocade enriched with massive gold mounts, perforated and embossed. *Lahore.* L. 3 ft. 1 in. (8501.–'55.)

This sword belonged to the late Raja Suchet Singh, by whom it was presented in Durbar to the Governor-General of India.

646.* Sabre; "Talwár;" heavy polished blade of damascus steel. Guarded hilt enriched with bas-relief floral ornaments gilt and panelled. Crimson velvet scabbard gold-mounted, with brocade waistbelt attached. *Lahore.* L. 2 ft. 7½ in. (Pl. xiv. No. 646.) (8515.–'50.)

The sword of Rustum, an heir-loom of the Durrani family. Procured by the Maharaja Runjit Sing from Shah Shuja-ul-Mulk, the last of the race.

647.* Sabre; "Talwár;" the blade is covered on both sides with representations of hunting scenes and various animals and birds; the figures are chiselled in low relief and the outline damascened with gold. Hilt with tiger-head pommel, of steel sparingly ornamented with gold damascenings. *Punjab.* L. 3 ft. 1 in. (12,640.–'25.)

648.* SABRE; "Talwár;" heavy damascus blade, polished, and fluted. Guarded hilt with low-relief floriations, chiselled and gilt. Scabbard of yellow velvet, with a waistbelt of yellow silk brocaded with silver attached. *Lahore.* L. 3 ft. 1 in. (8506.–'55.)

649. SABRE; "Talwár;" Persian blade of soft steel damascened with gold near the hilt. Guarded hilt of steel. *Punjab.* L. 3 ft. 3 in. (8739.)

650.* SABRE; "Talwár;" burnished blade with waved edge; hilt with knuckle guard of steel damascened with gold; green velvet scabbard. *Lahore.* L. 3 ft. (8507.–'51.)

651.* SABRE; "Talwár;" fine damascus blade, damascened with gold at the hilt and along the back, and bearing an inscription inlaid in gold. The hilt, with triple handguard and globular pommel, is of steel damascened with gold and enriched with rubies, turquoises, and other stones.

652.* SABRE; "Talwár;" each side of the blade is divided into seven compartments filled with representations of the incarnations of Vishnu and other mythological subjects chiselled in low relief and gilt. Beneath each panel is an explanatory inscription damascened in gold. The hilt, with knuckle-guard and broad circular pommel, is similarly ornamented. L. 3 ft. 3 in. *Lahore.* (Pl. xiii. No. 652.) ('55.)

Cf. Musée Z. S., Pl. viii.—"JOHUR (jauhar)." The blade is covered with figures in relief damascened in gold; among them an elephant, tigers, antelopes, and a horseman facing a lion. The hilt ornamented with trees, flowers and hunting scenes.

653.* SABRE; "'Abbási Talwár;" slightly recurved fluted blade of bright steel; hilt, with knuckle-guard and griffin-head pommel, of steel damascened with gold and set with turquoises. Crimson velvet scabbard with gold damascened steel mounts. *Gujerat.* L. 3 ft. 1 in. (Pl. xiii. No. 653.) (8508.–'55.)

654.* SABRE; "Shamsher;" the blade is ornamented on both sides with numerous figures of animals (tigers, antelopes, rabbits, &c.), incised and damascened in gold. Hilt of ivory and damascened steel. Scabbard of embossed black leather, attached to leather waist-belt with damascened steel mounts. *Lahore.* L. 2 ft. 11½ in. (8502.)

655, 656. SABRES; "Shamsher;" cloudy yellow blades of Damascus steel bearing incised inscriptions; hilts of walrus-ivory and gold-damascened steel; scabbards of black morocco leather, embossed, with steel mounts. *Lahore.* L. 3 ft. 6 in. (11,910.–'73.)

657.* SABRE; "Shamsher;" hilt of ivory and gold-damascened steel; leathern scabbard embossed and gilt, with gold damascened steel mounts. *Delhi.* L. 3 ft. 2 in. (8872.–'55.)

658.* SABRE; "Shamsher;" fine Damascus blade with waved edges, enriched with gold damascenings at the hilt and point, the latter bi-furcated for about 4½ inches; hilt of walrus-ivory; cross-guard and pommel of steel damascened with gold; black leather scabbard with gold-damascened steel mounts. *Peshawur.* (Pl. xv. No. 658.) (8503.–'55.)

659.* SABRE; "Shamsher;" Khorassan blade; hilt of ivory and gold-damascened steel; scabbard of leather, embossed and perforated. *Peshawur.* L. 3 ft. 6 in. (Pl. xv. No. 659.) (8504.–'55.)

660.* PISTOLS (a pair); "Tamancha;" octagonal barrels, damascened in gold with flowing open scroll ornaments; side-bar locks; roughened hilts with hollow pommels for storing shot or caps. *Lahore.* (8564.–'55.)

661. PISTOLS (a pair); "Tamancha;" plain burnished barrels with flint locks, After an English pattern. *Lahore.* L. 17 in. (8562.–'55.)

662. PISTOLS (a pair); Damascus barrels; chased steel mounts; flint locks. L. 20 in. (12,598.–'69.)

663. MOUNTAIN GUN OR WALL PIECE; "Sher bacha;" rifled Damascus barrel; massive wooden stock provided with steel supports; powder horn and bullet mould attached. Presented by H.H. Gulab Singh. *Lahore.* L. 3 ft. 1 in. (8536.–'55.)

664.* MATCHLOCK; "Toradár;" octagonal barrel of dark-tinted Damascus steel, ornamented with gold damascenings at the mouth and breech; dark wood stock; straight butt, with ivory and silver mounts. *Lahore.* L. 5 ft. 3 in. (8625.–'55.)

665.* MATCHLOCK; "Toradár;" Damascus barrel with gold Damascened ornaments at the mouth and breech; stock strengthened by side-plates of damascened steel; butt straight and slender. *Lahore.* L. 5 ft. 10 in. (7492.–'67.)

666.* MATCHLOCK; "Toradár;" barrel damascened with gold at the muzzle and breech; light wood stock with steel side-plates also damascened. *Lahore.* L. 5 ft. 3 in. (8623.–'55.)

667.* MATCHLOCK; "Toradár;" burnished barrel damascened with gold at the muzzle and breech; teak-wood stock strengthened with side-plates of Damascus steel. *Lahore.* L. 5 ft. 8 in. (8630.–'55.)

668. MATCHLOCK; "Toradár;" fine Damascus barrel, with gold enrichments inlaid at the muzzle and breech; stock very slender, of dark wood curiously painted with hunting scenes, foliage, &c. on a gold back ground. *Lahore.* L. 5 ft. 6 in. (8625.–'55.)

669. MATCHLOCK; "Toradár;" barrel is covered with incised foliated ornaments, evidently intended to be filled in with gold; stock painted with arabesques of birds and flowers on a dark green ground. L. 4 ft. 5 in. (12,532.–'69.)

670.* MATCHLOCK; "Toradár;" rifled barrel of Damascus steel, with gold enrichments inlaid at the mouth and breech; stock of dark wood, attached to the barrel by five perforated silver bands; butt, slender and straight; heavily plated with silver, ornamented in niello. *Lahore.* L. 5 ft. 6 in. (8627.–'55.)

671. MATCHLOCK; "Bandúq Toradár;" a wall piece provided with forked steel supports. A supply of match-cord is wound round the butt end. Presented by H.H. Golab Singh. *Lahore.* L. 6 ft. 5 in. (8629.–'51.)

672.* MATCHLOCK; "Toradár;" Damascus barrel with gold damascenings at the mouth and breech; stock straight and slender, of red wood mounted with ivory, and strengthened by side-plates of chased silver. *Lahore.* L. 5 ft. 8 in. (8628.–'55.)

673. MATCHLOCK; "Toradár;" teak-wood stock; butt straight, and very slender, capped with ivory, and mounted with plates of engraved brass. *Punjab.* L. 5 ft. 6 in. (8624.)

674. MATCHLOCK; the brecch inlaid with gold enrichments; stock of dark wood with brass and ivory mounts. *Punjab.* L. 5 ft. 7 in. (12,535.–'69.)

675. MATCHLOCK; inlaid with gold at the brecch; stock of dark wood, strengthened by side-plates of steel, and mounted with ivory. *Punjab.* L. 5 ft. 9 in. (12,537.–'69.)

676.* MATCHLOCK; "Toradár;" barrel damascened with silver throughout its entire length; straight slender stock, with side-plates of chased silver, attached to the barrel by three silver bands. *Punjab.* L. 4 ft. 7 in. (12,539.–'69.)

677.* MATCHLOCK; "Toradár;" octagonal barrel of burnished steel, damascened with gold ornaments at the mouth and breech; stock painted with floral arabesques in gold and colours; butt straight and slender. *Delhi.* L. 5 ft. 3 in. (4404.–'55.)

678. MATCHLOCKS (2); "Toradár;" very small, the barrels damascened with silver ornaments throughout their entire length; the stocks are inlaid with ivory in a lozenge diaper of small quatrcfoils dotted with red, and braced by side-plates of engraved brass. A lady's gun. *Gujranwala.* L. 2 ft. 9 in. and 3 ft. 1 in. (8558–9.–'55.)

Miniature arms are made not only for women, but also for boys as young as five years old. "Voyage dans l'Inde," p. 174, Prince Soltykoff.

Cf. Sword made by Asad Ullah for a child.—Cat. Z.S. Coll., p. 312.

679.* MATCHLOCK; "Toradár;" barrel of blueish steel, enriched with silver damascenings at the mouth and breech; attached to the stock by bands of brass; stock of dark wood, with massive brass mounts and incrustations of embossed silver. *Gujranwala.* L. 5 ft. 7 in. (8621.–'55.)

680.* FOWLING GUN; "Bandúq;" imitation twist barrel; side-bar lock; copy of English work. *Gujranwala.* L. 4 ft. 1 in. (8635.–'55.)

681.* PERCUSSION GUN; "Bandúq;" fine Damascus barrel, with gold enrichments at the mouth and breech; bar lock; stock lacquered red, with engraved steel mounts, attached to barrel by capucines of steel damascened with gold; from an English pattern. *Lahore.* L. 5 ft. 3 in. (8620.–'55.)

682.* PERCUSSION GUN; "Bandúq;" octagonal twist barrel, burnished. Made from an English pattern. *Lahore.* L. 3 ft. 9 in. (8634.–'55.)

683.* MATCHLOCK ACCOUTREMENTS; "Kamr;" consisting of powder-flask, pouches, priming horn (singra), match cord, flint and steel, &c.; attached to a belt, which, together with the pouches, is covered with green velvet embroidered with gold. *Lahore.* (8574.–'55.)

684.* MATCHLOCK ACCOUTREMENTS; "Kamr;" powder-flask, pouches, and belt of light brown leather. *Lahore.* (8570.–'55.)

685.* MATCHLOCK ACCOUTREMENTS; "Kamr." *Lahore.*

686.* MATCHLOCK ACCOUTREMENTS; "Kamr;" pouches, powder-flask, &c., covered gith velvet richly embroidered with gold. *Hazára.* (8572.–'55.)

687.* MATCHLOCK ACCOUTREMENTS; "Kamr." *Hazára.* ('55.)

688.* POWDER-FLASK; made from the shell of the Pearly Nautilus; red silk cords attached. *Lahore.* (8373.–'55).

689.* POWDER-FLASK; cylindrical; ebony, with ivory and silver mounts.

690. PARRYING SHIELD; "Márú;" consisting of a pair of antelope horns, tipped with small steel points, and united vertically at their butt ends, the point of junction being covered by a small circular and convex hand-guard of steel, ornamented with four bosses and a crescent of perforated steel. *Delhi.* L. of horns, 3 ft.; Diam. of guard, 8 in. (8798.–'55.)

691. PARRYING SHIELD; "Márú;" antelope horns, tipped with steel; hand-guard of steel, enriched with silver mounts. *Delhi.* L. 3 ft. 6 in.; Diam. of guard, 8 in.

692. PARRYING SHIELD; antelope horns, tipped with steel; hand-guard of steel, bossed and damascened with gold. *Punjab.* L. 3 ft. 5 in.; Diam. 7 in.

693. PARRYING SHIELD; "Márú," or "Mádú;" antelope horns, tipped with steel; hand-guard of brass, bearing four bosses and a crescent. *Benares.* L. of horns, 2 ft. 9 in.; diam. of guard, 9 in. (8799.–'55.)

694. PARRYING SHIELD; "Mádú," or "Márú;" black buck horns, tipped with steel damascened with gold; small circular hand-guard of steel damascened with gold and bearing a large central gilt boss; grooved dagger blade projecting from under-guard. *Datiah.* (Pl. xiii. No. 694.) (7443.)

695. SHIELD; steel damascened with gold; circular and convex. The centre is occupied by a rayed head, symbolic of the sun, surrounded by four damascened bosses and a Mahommedan crescent. A broad border of richly foliated damascening surrounds the shield, while the rest of the surface is filled in with interlacing arabesques of gold. *Lahore.* (8577.–'55.)

Cf. with the following, the two finest shields in tho Z.S. collection. Lahore and Delhi vied with each othor in supplying the Mogul emperors with arms.

Large shield of Delhi, of Damascus steel, belonging to the Emperor Bahadur Shah. On the 24 cartouches along the border of gold inlaid work are the names of Allah. Mahomet, and the four first Caliphs, Tamerlane and his descendants, Baber and his successors on the throne of Delhi up to the reigning sovereign in this century. In the 12 cartouches in the centre are the following flowery verses in Arabic, which shows it to be the work of a Mahomedan armourer:—

"The shield above the head of this illustrious person is like a rainbow by the side of the sun.'

"O King, Saturn (!) does not reach the height of your court, and heavenly kindness does not attain the height of your abode."

"The moon has reached a pitch which the effort of man's imagination cannot reach."
"There is not a spot in the regions of East and West which an order sent from you does not reach."
"There is not a day when in a thousand ways eloquent poets do not bring you the tribute of their praises."
"There is not a man sufficiently versed in the science of algebra to commemorate all your virtues."—Zarkoe-Selo Catalogue, p. 313.

Shield of Báhádur Shah. This is remarkable, for the inside as well as the outside is damascened in gold. The Suni crescent engraved on it shows it was made for a Mahomedan. It has a long inscription in Hindustani to this effect:—

"You are a Nawab whose power is heavenly, and whose escort is the sun. To Arabia and Persia your power extends. You are the lion of the desert on the field of battle. When Rustam comes, the falcon swims like a fox. God has exalted you; you have conquered the terrestrial globe, and for shame the earth has become the arid soil of Shám (*i.e.* Syria). Such goodwill has befallen the world that the lion has become as the shepherd, or like the kid. The torch of the sun is above the firmament. Your hand scattering good absorbs the dawn's light. But I ask you, if you are pleased with me, who is in your service, cast a little look upon me from your throne."—p. 327.

696. SHIELD; "Ḍhál;" of Damascus steel, richly damascened in gold. The ornaments are, at the centre, a conventional representation of the sun surrounded by four bosses; at the circumference, a deep border of floriated scroll-work. The shield bears, in addition, an Arabic inscription inlaid in gold. *Lahore.* Diam. 15 in. (8691.–'55.)

697.* SHIELD; "Ḍhál;" of bluish steel, chiselled in low relief and damascened with gold. A rosette of floriated ornaments, surrounded by four hemispherical bosses encrusted with diamonds, occupies the centre. The body of the shield is covered with outline arabesques chiselled in low-relief and gilt, while the interlinear spaces are filled in with birds, beasts, and other subjects damascened in gold. *Lahore.* Presented by H.H. the Maharajah Suchet Sing. Diam. 18 in. (8616.–'50.)

698. * SHIELD; "Ḍhál;" Circular and convex with recurved edge. Of bluish steel damascened with gold. Modern work. Round the centre are grouped four hemispherical, damascened, bosses with perforated edges. The background is covered with a diaper of floral ornaments: Near the centre is fixed a gilt lion or tiger, and on the left of the shield a crescent with perforated margin. *Sialkot, Punjab.* Diam. 18 in. (7361.–'67.)

699. SHIELD; "Ḍhál;" black buffalo hide, varnished, and ornamented with four bosses of steel damascened with gold. Gold tassel attached, Diam. 21 in. (8602.–'55.)

700. SHIELD; "Ḍhál;" buffalo hide. Four gilt bosses. *Lahore.* (8593.–'55.)

701. SHIELD; "Ḍhál;" buffalo hide. Copper bosses. *Punjab.* Diam. 18 m. (12,502.–'69.)

702. SHIELDS. Translucent rhinoceros hide, enriched with painted gold ornaments and four petaloid metal bosses, once gilt.

703. * SUIT OF ARMOUR, consisting of helmet, cuirass, armguards and shield of steel damascened with gold. Worn at the Court of Ranjít Singh. *Lahore.*

1. The helmet (Pl. xiii. No. 703) of the usual hemispherical shape is surmounted by a plume of heron's feathers, and furnished with a sliding noseguard flanked by aigrettes of coloured feathers and tinsel. The surface is covered with interlacing arabesques, and the base of the helmet is encircled by a band of boldly-designed floriated scroll work, the ornaments being chiselled in low relief and gilt. The nose guard and porteaigrettes are damascened in the usual manner. Attached is a coif of mail falling in points on the shoulders and composed of brass and copper, the links alternating in the formation of lozenged designs. Depth 4 in. (8585.–'55.)

2. The Cuirass is composed of four plates. (Char aina or the four mirrors.) Each plate is covered with open foliated arabesques damascened in gold, enclosed by a diaper border of quatrefoil lozenges, also in gold. L. 11 in. by 7 in., 10 in. by $6\frac{1}{2}$ in. (8576.–'55.)

3. The arm-guards (Pl. xiii. No. 703) of the usual shape are lined with velvet, and terminate in open gauntlets of chain mail, the links (unrivetted) of steel and brass disposed in a lozenge design. Ornamentation similar in character to that of the other parts of the suit.

4. The shield has been described above (No. 695.)

703A T. HELMET; small, shaped like a Turban with coif of mail; gold-damascened enrichments. *Lahore.* (198.)

Cf. Helmet in the Z. S. Collection (Pl. XIV., Vol. iii.), formed like a low-crowned, broad-brimmed hat, perhaps

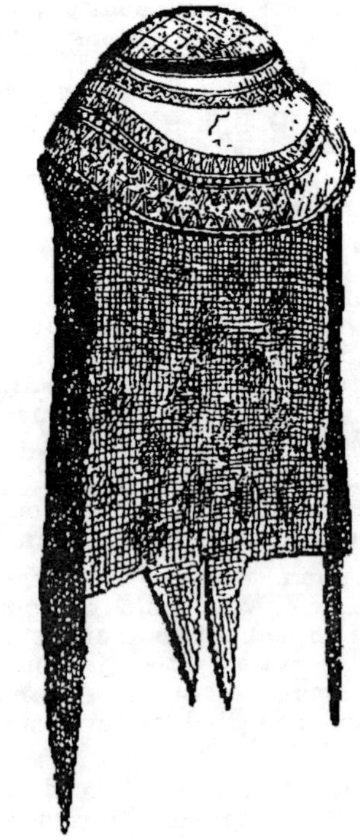

Fig. 33.—Helmet from Lahore, No. 703A T.

copied from the "eisen-hut," used as a military head-dress in the 16th and 17th centuries in France and Germany. It has a chain mail coif, and plume-holder. The steel is of the finest quality, and of a cloudy-yellow colour. The damascened gold work is of 17th century style. The cartouches contain invocations to Ali in Arabic. It probably belonged to a Persian, and was made for him at Delhi.

704.* Helmet; "Tóp;" hemispherical, of steel covered with gold damascenings. It is furnished with a sliding nose-guard, the extremities of which are set with moonstones, and is surmounted by a plume of heron-feathers springing from a porte-aigrette similarly ornamented; from the latter proceed radiating lines dividing the helmet into raised and fluted segments in each of which is set a pear-shaped moonstone. A long coif of mail descends from the base of the helmet falling in points on the shoulders; in the links of which it is composed, steel, brass, and copper alternate in the formation of a lozenge pattern. *Lahore.* (Pl. xiii. No. 704.) (8584.)

705.* Suit of Chain Mail consisting of a helmet, coat and pair of trousers. *Lahore.* (8599.)

1. The helmet consists of a long coif of unriveted steel mail falling squarely on the shoulders, and surmounted by a large gilt plume holder. A triangular opening is left for the face, but if required this can be closed by a pointed flap attached, when open, to the plume holder.

2 and 3. The coat and trousers are lined with crimson silk, which trimmed with gold braid forms the collar and facings of the coat. The links are riveted, and are of steel alternating at the borders with links of brass in the formation of a lozenged design.

706.* Coat and Trousers of Mail. Presented by the Raja Suchet Sing. *Lahore.*

The coat is composed of extremly fine and light mail covered with green velvet, richly embroidered with gold.

The trousers are made of very large riveted links of steel.

Note.—Cf. with the following examples of chain-armour from the Cod. and Z.S. Collections:—

"Tóp." Cap of chain and plates; crescent visor; and chain curtain for breast and back.

"Tóp." Scales and chain to match.

"Tóp." With large plates and chain with crescent visor.

"Tóp." With scales and chains for breast and back.

"Tóp." Zirrah buktur." Made of iron chains, plates and five rows of scales. Vandyke pattern (Grey).

"Zirah baktar." Five rows of scales of scallop pattern.

"Zirah baktar." Reaching to the waist.

"Zirah baktar." Coat worn by officers made of very fine perforated scales; scalloped pattern joined with chains.

"Zirah baktar." Coat of strong chains; two rows plain and one scalloped.

"Zirah baktar." Three rows scalloped, two plain; fine chain.—*Cod. Coll.*

Coat of chain mail. The body of the coat is formed of large rings of rivetted steel, each bearing the inscription "Allah, Mohammed, Aly, Fatima, Hussain, Hassan" in Arabic. This has therefore been made for a Shiah Mussulman. or follower of Ali. The fastening at the neck is enriched by a heart-shaped pendant of jade encrusted with rubies, and with two hooks in silver gilt, each representing an elephant with eyes of diamonds, the howdahs being of turquoise. Similar pendants hang on each side of the breast. — *Rockstühl Cat. Z. S., Pl.* lxvii. *p.* 255.

Coat and helm of mail, formed of rings of steel and brass not rivetted, so that the two colours form a design, which they say typifies the mixture of the white waters of the Ganges with the yellow waters of the Jumna, the two sacred rivers. It is, therefore, called "Zirah Kortah Sakton."—*Cat. Z. S., Pl.* clxiii.

707. * Cuirass and Arm-guards; steel damascened with gold. *Lahore.* (Pl. xiii. No. 707.) (8578.–'55.)

The Cuirass, in four pieces "Chár áína;" padded and lined with crimson velvet. Each plate is enriched with a broad border, and central cartouche of conventional floriations damascened in gold.

The Arm-guards, lined with velvet, terminating in open gauntlets of brocaded crimson silk.

708. * Helmet and Arm-guards. *Jind.* The helmet, of steel damascened with gold, is hemispherical, surmounted by a damascened plume-holder from which radiate lines connecting it with a festooned band of damascened ornaments at the base. Sliding nose-guard flanked by aigrettes of tinsel and coloured feathers. Coif of mail, falling in points on the shoulders, the links composing it of steel and brass alternating in the formation of transverse zigzag stripes. (8579.)

The Armguards. Steel damascened with gold, and terminating in an open gauntlet of chain-mail, the links composing which are of brass and steel alternately. Padded and lined with velvet. (8582.–'55.)

709. * Coat of Mail; composed of large riveted links, each of which bears an Arabic inscription produced by means of a punch. The links are of steel, with the exception of those at the edges and the ends of the sleeves which are of copper or brass, forming a border two inches in width round the coat.. *Punjab.* Presented by Col. S. W. Hamilton. (11,496.–'67.)

Note.—Rockstühl thus describes the dress of a chief of the Mohammedan guard of the Great Mogul (Pl. 91-92.) The steel plates, richly gilt, are worn on a quilted jacket with four flaps which fold down over the legs. The legs are covered with a pantaloon of black quilted silk and studded with gilt nails. The arms, thighs, knees, and shins are further protected by steel plates.

Part II.—Sind.

The Amírs of Sind were under the rule of Afghanistan till they became independent chiefs, but owing to their treacherous behaviour after the Afghan war, they provoked attack. Sir Charles Napier, in the hard-fought battle of Miani, defeated them and their brave Bilúchí troops, and they all, with the exception of Khairpur, who remained faithful to the English rule, were forced to surrender their country to the English in 1843. it is, therefore, before that time that the best specimens of workmanship in arms are to found such as are mentioned by the writers who visited the courts of the Amírs and saw their splendour.

In the character of their ornament, rather than in their shape, the Sindian arms approach more closely the Persian than the Afghan type. The coloured enamels, the embroidered leather accoutrements, and the chased silver mountings which characterise their swords are of a more decorated style than is usually met with in India.

Postans[1] describes the Sindian arms as being of very superior quality, "particularly the " matchlock barrels, which are twisted in the Damascus style. The nobles and chiefs " procure many from Persia and Constantinople, but nearly as good can be made in the " country. They are overlaid with gold, and very highly finished. The European lock " is attached to the Eastern barrel, and our guns and barrels are only prized for this " portion of their work. The best of 'Joe Manton' and 'Purdy' guns, of which " sufficient to stock a shop have at various times been presented to the Sindian chiefs by " the British Government, share this mutilating fate. The Sind matchlock is a heavy, " unwieldy arm, the stock much too light for the great weight of the barrel.

" The sword blades are large, curved, very sharp, and well-tempered. The sheath also " contains a receptacle for a small knife used for food and other purposes.

"The belts are of leather or cloth, richly embroidered, for which Guzerat has long been " famous.[2] Great taste is also displayed in the manufacture of the pouches, &c. attached to the waist.

" Shields are made from rhinoceros hides, richly embossed with brass or silver. They " are carried over the shoulder, or worn strapped between them.

"A great part of the treasure of the Amírs consists in the rubies, diamonds, pearls " and emeralds with which their daggers, swords, and matchlocks are adorned. One or " two Persian goldsmiths are engaged at court in enamelling and damascening, in which " arts they have attained great perfection.

" The Amírs have agents in Persia, Turkey, and Palestine for the purchase of swords " and gun barrels,[3] and they possess a more valuable collection than is probably to be met " with elsewhere. 'I have had in my hand,' says Burnes,[4] 'a plain unornamented " ' blade which had cost them half a lac of rupees. They estimate swords by their age " ' and watering or temper. One presented to me bears the date 1708, and was valued " ' in Scinde at 2,000 rupees. "Another bore the following inscription:—'Of ancient " ' steel and water, I am the produce of Persia. I am light in appearance, but I am " 'heavy against my enemies. When a brave man wields me with his strength a " 'hundred thousand Hindoos will perish by my edge.'" The verse was written by the Amír's Vizier. The armoury also contains swords worn by Shah Abbas the Great, Nadir Shah, and Ahmed Shah Durrání.

The swords are balanced differently from ours. "I have seen one of the young princes," continues Burnes, "with a single stroke cut a large sheep into two pieces.

"The favourites of the Amírs may be distinguished by gold-mounted swords, which " are the highest honorary distinctions conferred by the Hyderabad Durbar. It is " contrary to the usage of the court to wear side-arms ornamented with any of the " precious metals which are not presented by their Highnesses. For very high services " the Amírs sometimes, though rarely, give one of their valuable blades adorned with " diamonds."

"The Amírs of Sind show their love of sport by taking the field with hawks, dogs, " &c., but they never expose themselves to the sun, but remain under shelter till the " deer or hog is forced to come before them to a small tank or well to drink, when they " shoot him deliberately, and receive the acclamations of their followers."

There is a peculiar Sindian custom alluded to by Sir H. Elliot, and mentioned in the

---

[1] Personal Observations in Sind.

[2] Marco Polo describes the mats in red and blue leather, exquisitely inlaid with figures of birds and beasts, and skilfully embroidered with gold and silver wire.—Book iii. ch. 26.

[3] Those not rifled come chiefly from Constantinople. They are of very small bore, and long in the barrel.

[4] Burnes' Visit to the Court of Scinde.

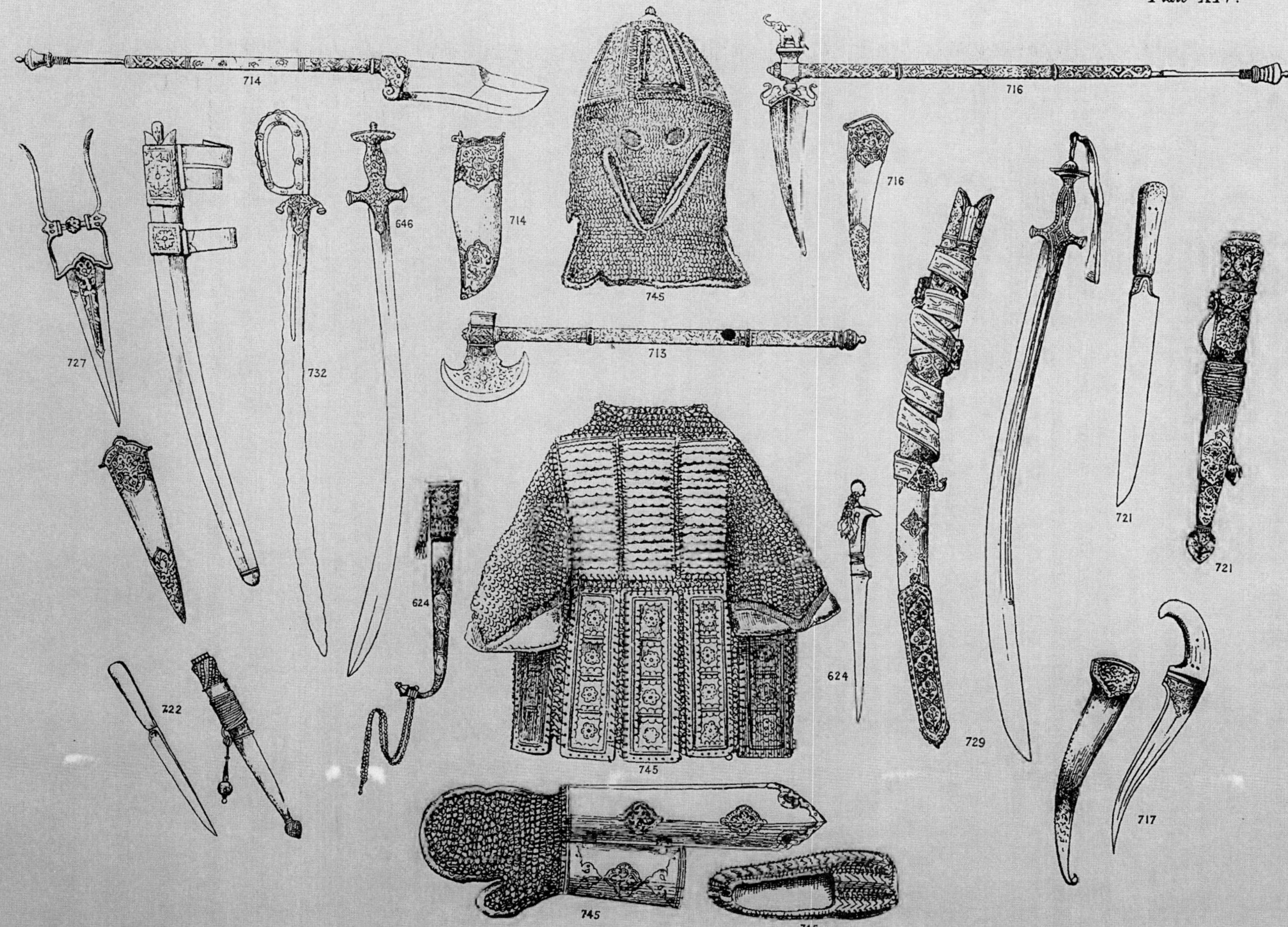

ARMS OF SIND.

W. GRIGGS, PHOTO LITH. LONDON, S. E.

Táríkh-i-Sind (M.S., p. 173):—"When they saw the army of the Moghals, they dis-
" mounted from their horses, took their turbans from off their heads, and, binding the
" corners of their mantles or outer-garments to one another, they engaged in battle; for
" it is the custom of the people of Hind and Sind, whenever they devote themselves to
" death, to descend from their horses, to make bare their heads and feet, and to bind
" themselves to each other by their mantles and waistbands."

Again, p. 194:—"The men under Khangár, having set themselves in battle array,
" dismounted from their horses, locked their shields together, seized their spears in their
" hands, and bound the corners of their waist-bands."

Sir Henry Elliot[1] remarks that the practice of dismounting previous to coming to close combat is of common observance among many of the border tribes between Sind and Rajputana, and is frequently alluded to in their local histories. Indeed, to the present day, the Sindians are, unlike most Asiatic nations, still somewhat repugnant to fighting on horseback, and pride themselves more on being foot soldiers than cavalry.

Kach.

The arms of Kach bear a general resemblance to those of Sind. Postans describes a Kachi horseman armed with a tulwar or sabre sheathed in an embroidered leather scabbard. The characteristic weapon of Kach, however, is an axe, the head of which springs from an elephant's head in high relief, while the handle is hollow, and conceals a pointed dagger. The peculiar Kachi dagger, which is hung with chains to the belt, and drops into a deep sheath, is probably borrowed from the Turks, with whom, in Egypt, there has been constant intercourse by way of trade, or from the Arab mercenaries who have constantly been in the service of the Rao of Kach.

Káthiawár.

The Kattees of Guzerat carry a sword, shield, and spear. The latter is about 8 ft. long, and is made so slender as to break when thrown at the enemy, to whom it thus becomes useless.

Till the establishment of the British supremacy in 1835, no deed or agreement was considered binding unless guaranteed by the mark of the "Kaṭár," and on the failure or breach of a contract they inflicted "trágá," on themselves, (*i.e.*, committed suicide) or, in extreme cases, carried out the murder of relations with that weapon. The Bards of Guzerat were hereditary heralds, and guardians of "trágá." They seldom appeared without the Kaṭár, a representation of which was scrawled beside their signatures, and rudely engraved on their monumental stones.[2]

"Trágá," as generally performed, extends no farther than a cut with the "Kaṭár" in the arm, and those people who are in the habit of becoming security generally have such cuts from the elbow downwards.

The majority of these arms will be found in Cases 49 (*right half*) *and* 67 (*fire-arms*).

The Sindis are very dexterous with the bow and a *blunt* heavy arrow, which they send in a transverse instead of a straight direction, so that the object is struck by the body, not the point of the arrow. Such arrows are used for game, and with them the Sindhis kill partridges flying. Persian arrows are generally used in Sind.

710. Spear. Shaft in two parts, screwing together in the centre, of lacquered black wood, richly mounted with embossed and chased bands of silver-gilt. The point is furnished with a crimson sheath mounted with gold. *Bhúj, Kach.* L. 7 ft. 4 in.; point, 11 in. (7489.)

Cf. "Panjmukh," five-headed spear used by the people of Guzerat.—*Cod. Coll.*

711–712. Battle Axes; "Tabar" crescent-shaped blades, parcel-gilt and chased. Hollow shafts covered with a diaper of chased and gilt ornaments; each shaft contains a dagger attached to the pommel which unscrews. *Kach.* L. 21½ in.; head, 5 in. by 5 in. (8643-44.-'51.)

713. * Battle Axe; "Tabar;" crescent-shaped blade parcel-gilt and richly engraved. The shaft similarly ornamented, is hollow and contains a dagger attached to the pommel which unscrews. *Bhúj, Kach.* L. 23 in. (Pl. xiv. No. 713.)

---

[1] History of India, Vol. I., App., p. 535.

[2] Trans. of the Lit. Soc. of Bombay. 1813. Forbes' Ras Mala; p. 558 (new edition) 1878.

714. Battle Axe; broad, somewhat knife-shaped blade, parcel-gilt and chased, springing from a gilt and jewelled elephant's head which terminates one end of the shaft. The latter finely engraved and parcel-gilt, is hollow and contains a small dagger attached to the pommel which is moveable. Crimson velvet sheath with embossed gold mounts. *Bhúj, Kach.* L. 26 in.; L. of blade, 8½ in. (Pl. xiv. No. 714.) (7411.)

715.* Battle Axe; knife-like blade springing from an elephant-head, gilt and chased, which terminates the shaft. The latter is parcel-gilt and chased, and encloses a dagger as in preceding examples. *Kach.* L. 2 ft. 4 in. (8645.–'51.)

716. Crow-bill; "Hoolurge;" curved spear-point blade, ribbed, thickened at the point, and ornamented at its base with two small lion figures in low-relief, gilt, and chased. As in the preceding specimen, the blade starts at right angles from the shaft, which on the opposite side bears the figure of an elephant with raised trunk, also gilt and chased. The shaft is covered with a diaper of chased and gilt ornaments, and encloses a dagger unscrewing at the butt end. Velvet sheath (for the blade) with embossed and chased mounts of ruddy gold. (Pl. xiv. No. 716.) (7419a.)

717.* Dagger; "Peshkabz;" slightly recurved blade with thickened point, of yellowish Damascus steel. Walrus ivory hilt, with gold-damascened steel mounts. Sheath covered with shagreen similarly mounted. Presented by H.H. the Nawab of *Bhawalpur.* (Pl. xiv. No. 717.) (8527.–'55.)

Cf. with this example, the following from the Z.S. Collection. "Zirah-bhouk" ("mail-piercer;") knife of fine Damascus steel, short with a conical point. It is used for piercing through the rings of a coat of mail. One of these knifes is hollowed out along the back, and the groove filled with small pearls which run backwards and forwards in handling the weapon. It is said in Persian poetry that they represent the tears of the wounded.

In a dagger of the Soltykoff Collection, there is a groove in the blade filled with a number of small rubies, so that when the dagger is raised the stones glitter like drops of blood. India is perhaps of all countries that which has endowed cruelty with the utmost grace. —"Chefs d'œuvres of Industrial Arts. Burty, p. 254."

The handle of these knives is usually of walrus-tooth ivory which is preferred to that of the elephant as being less likely to split. One of them has engraved on the handle in Persian letters: "If this is accepted what "glory and what honour!" It has probably been made by some armourer for presentation to some sovereign. The handle opens with a spring and conceals within it another dagger running down into the hollow of the blade, and this again contains another still smaller ornamented in like manner.—*Cat. Z.S.*, p. 272, 305; pl. cxxvi. 5, 6, 7.

718. Dagger; "Peshkabz;" straight blade of darkened damascus steel. Hilt of mother-of-pearl. Silver sheath enamelled in translucent blue and green. *Sind.* C. 49.

719.* Dagger; "Peshkabz;" dark steel blade. Hilt, gold-mounted with sides of dark green glass. Sheath of embossed black leather with chased gold mounts. *Bhúj, Kach.* (55.)

720.* Dagger; "Peshkabz;" hilt of dark green glass in chased gilt, setting. Sheath of red velvet with repoussé and chased gilt mounts. *Bhúj, Kach.* (7415.–'67.)

721.* Dagger; "Peshkabz;" watered blade of dark steel. Hilt of walrus ivory. Leather sheath embroidered with silk, and enriched with enamelled silver mounts in blue and green. *Sind.* L. 18 in. (Pl. xiv. No. 721.) (8702.)

722.* Dagger; "Peshkabz;" hilt of walrus ivory with enamelled gold enrichments at the sides. Sheath of leather with enamel mounts of turquoise and dark blue on gold. *Sind.* (Pl. xiv. No. 722.) (–'55.)

723.* Dagger; "Peshkabz;" yellow-tinted blade damascened with gold near the hilt. The latter of steel ornamented with gold damascening, is hollow and contains a penknife, toothpick, and other small articles. *Guzerat.* (8523.–'55.)

724.* Dagger; "Peshkabz;" blade damascened with gold near the hilt. Buffalo horn hilt. Crimson velvet sheath with gold damascened steel mounts. *Guzerat.* (8529.–'55.)

725.* Hunting Knife; broad straight blade with an inscription inlaid in gold on the back. Guarded hilt of ivory and black buffalo-horn with gold damascened steel mounts. Crimson, velvet sheath, silver mounted. *Khairpur, Sind.* (7450.–'67.)

726.* Hunting Dagger; bright steel blade, the back bearing inscriptions inlaid in gold. Hilt of ivory and horn. Velvet sheath with silver mounts. *Khairpur, Sind.* (7450.–'67.)

727.* Dagger; "Garsoee Katár;" bright steel blade with a perforated and gilt central rib. Hilt chased and gilt; curved sideguards. Velvet sheath with embossed and gilt mounts. *Bhúj, Kach.* (Pl. xiv. No. 727.) (7413.–'67.)

728.* Sabre; "Talwár;" Fine Khorassan watered blade. Hilt thickly plated with gold, embossed and chased. Velvet scabbard attached to a silk embroidered leather belt, both enriched with medallions and plaques of enamelled gold; the designs consist of flowers and birds in raised enamels. Attached in a pocket sheath at the side of the scabbard, is a small knife with walrus-ivory hilt. *Haidarabad, Sind.* L. 3 ft. 2 in. (8690.–'55.)

729.* Sabre; "Talwár;" polished fluted blade. Hilt plated with gold. Scabbard of leather embroidered with silk, and enriched with blue and green enamelled silver mounts. Waist belt similarly ornamented. A small knife with walrus-ivory hilt is carried in a sheath at the side of the scabbard. *Haidarabad, Sind.* L. 2 ft. 11 in. (Pl. xiv. No. 729.) (–'55.)

730.* Sabre; "Talwár;" bright blade, guarded hilt of steel, parcel-gilt and engraved. Crimson velvet sheath with embossed gold mounts. L. 3 ft. *Bhúj, Kach.* (7410.–'67.)

731.* Sabre; "Shamsher;" watered blade. Hilt mounted with horn. Blue velvet scabbard with gilt metal mounts. *Sind.* L. 3 ft. 4 in. (12605.)

732.* Sword; burnished blade, with waved edges; guarded hilt of black buffalo-horn, studded with gilt bosses; black leather scabbard, with small brocaded side-sheath attached, containing an ivory-handled knife. *Sind.* L. 2 ft. 7 in. (Pl. xiv. No. 732.) (8531.)

733.* Flint-Lock Gun; "Bandúq Jauhardár;" Damascus barrel of splendid workmanship, with gold enrichments damascened at the mouth and breech, the latter inlaid also with Arabic inscriptions; ebony stock, attached to the barrel by four bands of enamelled gold; butt of the curved Afghan shape, inlaid with medallions and plaques of translucent enamels on gold. *Haidarabad, Sind.* L. 5 ft. 5 in. (Pl. iv. No. 733.) (8674.–'55.)

734.* Flint-Lock Gun; "Bandúq Jauhardár;" finely-worked Damascus barrel, with massive gold enrichments at the mouth and breech. Near the latter is an inscription inlaid in gold. Stock of dark wood, curved and very broad at the butt (Afghan shape), inlaid and mounted with plaques of translucent blue and green enamel on silver, and attached to the barrel by four narrow bands of the same. *Haidarabad, Sind.* (8675.–'55.)

735.* Gun Accoutrements; "Kamr;" consisting of a silk-embroidered leathern belt, to which are attached bullet-boxes (2), wad-box, powder horn and priming horn of leather and steel enriched with blue and green enamelled silver mounts. *Haidarabad, Sind.* (8686.)

736.* Rifle; "Bandúq Jauhardár;" Damascus barrel of exquisite workmanship (small bore), damascened with gold at the breech and mouth; tiger-head muzzle set with rubies and emeralds; flint lock; broad, curved butt (Afghan shape) of ebony inlaid with medallions and plaques of gold enamelled in low-relief with flower forms (iris, rose, &c.); stock attached to the barrel by three bands of enamelled gold. Presented by H.H. the Nawab of *Bhawalpur.* L. 4 ft. 10 in. (Pl. iv. No. 736.) (8619.–'55.)

737.* Rifle Accoutrements; "Kamr;" consisting of a powder-flask, patch-box of steel damascened in gold with inscriptions, a priming horn, and various black leather pouches embroidered with silk, all attached to a white cotton kummerbund embroidered with gold. *Bhawalpur.* Presented by the Nawab of Bhawalpur. (8571.–'55.)

738.* Flint-Lock Gun; "Bandúq Jauhardár;" Damascus barrel, inlaid and plated with gold at the muzzle and breech, and bearing an inscription also inlaid in gold; the muzzle set with nine uncut rubies and an emerald, the latter forming the "sight;" rosewood stock, attached to the barrel by three perforated and engraved gold bands; curved and broadly expanding butt, enriched with engraved gold mounts; red leathern belt. *Sind.* L. 5 ft. 4 in. (7496.–'67.)

739.* Gun Accoutrements; "Kamr;" consisting of various pouches and a powder-horn, all covered with silk-embroidered velvet, and a priming-horn ornamented with gold lacquer-work. *Jacobabad, Sind.* (6559.–'67).

740.* Shield; "Ḍhál;" circular and convex; papier-mâché, lacquered and gilt. The body of the shield is blue, with a floral diaper; this is surrounded by a painted border of gold, green, and red on a white ground. The centre is occupied by a rosette of similar character, surrounded by four conical brass bosses. *Ahmedabad.* Diam. 15½ in. (7381.)

741.* Shield; "Ḍhál;" papier-mâché, lacquered and gilt. The body of the shield is a foliated diaper in dark red, surrounded by a border of gold, red, and green, on white. The centre is occupied by a rosette of similar character enclosed by four conical bosses of brass. *Ahmedabad.* Diam. 21 in. (7382.–'67.)

742.* Shield; "Ḍhál;" circular and convex, with recurved edge; prepared rhinoceros-hide, translucent and of a light brown tint. The centre is occupied by a rosette painted in white, gold, green, and red, surrounded by four large copper-gilt bosses, repoussé, chased and jewelled. A fifth boss of different shape ornaments the upper part of the shield, which is encircled by a narrow border similar in character to the rosette at the centre. *Bhúj, Kach.* Diam. 21 in. (Pl. xv. No. 742.) (7380.–'67).

743.* Shield; "Ḍhál;" prepared rhinoceros-hide, semi-translucent, with dark red diaper ground. The centre is occupied by a closely-foliated rosette painted in gold, surrounded by four ornamental gilt bosses. The outer border is of similar character, on a white ground. Diam. 21 in. (8615.)

744.* Shield; "Ḍhál;" circular and convex, with recurved edge; of prepared deer-skin, translucent and of a yellowish-brown tint. The centre is occupied by a rosette painted in gold, surrounded by four gilt bosses with perforated margins, and a crescent. A border, similar in character to the rosette, surrounds the shield. *Bhúj, Kach.* Diam. 21 in. (8622.–'55).

745. Suit of Chain and Plate Armour; comprising a helmet, corslet, trousers, arm-guards, and shoes. *Bhúj, Kach.* (Pl. xiv. No. 745.) (8641.–'55.)

1. The helmet is composed of padded chain mail strengthened by wedge-shaped plaques or embossed brass, and is surmounted by a small boss or button of brass. Attached to the base of the helmet is a coif of padded mail, falling squarely on the shoulders, the back of the neck being additionally protected by overlapping plates of brass and steel; a triangular opening is left for the face, but in case of need this opening can be closed by a fragment of the coif (provided with holes for the eyes), which, when raised, is attached by a hook to the upper part of the helmet.
2. The corslet, a sort of coat with short sleeves, is of riveted chain-mail padded with cotton, and strengthened in front by overlapping scales of brass and steel, and oblong plaques of steel with brass mountings.
3. The arm-guards are of steel, with brass mounts, and terminate in open gauntlets of chain-mail, wadded with cotton.
4. The trousers are of riveted chain-mail.
5. The shoes of wadded leather covered with scalloped scales of brass and steel connected by chain-mail.

GROUP XI.

N.W. FRONTIER, AFGHANISTAN, PERSIA, CHINA, ETC.

Afghanistan.—The Afghans are divided into a number of tribes, who live in constant feuds with one another, among which the Durránís have gained a predominance over the rest. Their history in the present century is made up of a series of revolutions. They are Mahomedans, and with the exception of some Persian colonists, as Kazilbáshís, belong to the Suni persuasion, and are, therefore, bitterly opposed to the Persians as Shiahs. They have a common origin with the Pat'háns, found all over India, who are of Afghan descent, and serve as mercenaries with the Mahomedan princes of India.[1]

The Rohillas, who showed themselves to be sturdy combatants in our campaign against them, are descended from an Afghan colony settled in Upper India.

Elphinstone, in his admirable account of his embassy to Cabul, gives the following description of the arms of some of the tribes at the beginning of the century:—

" The *Ghilzais, Turis, Shinwaris, and Momunds* dwell in Cabul. They wear a curved sabre of the Persian shape, without guard to the hilt, called 'shumsheer,' a long knife in the girdle, a spear, and matchlock. For defensive armour some wear quilted jackets, some plate armour or chain mail, others leathern cuirasses. Indian steel is most prized as the material for swords, but the best swords come from Persia and Syria. The Persian short dagger with thick handle is common. Also one about 14 inches long, tapering to a point, with a round handle. When drawn it is of the shape of a small English carving knife."[2]

The *Hazáras* are good archers as well as good shots. They use a kettle-drum to call their troops together.

The arms of the *Durránis*, who inhabit Kandahar and Herat, consist generally of a Persian sword and a matchlock; a few among them have firelocks. The villagers carry matchlocks with curved stocks; their ammunition is strapped in cartridge cases across the left breast. Pistols[3] are rarely met with except in the possession of the chiefs. A few of the best men have spears, which they put in the rest when they are about to charge. Shields were formerly in use among them, but are now discontinued.

The Durránis never serve as infantry.[4] Moorcroft, in 1824, described their cavalry as consisting of 1,200 horse. "They moved in three bodies, travelling generally at a " quick walk of about 4½ miles an hour. Their baggage was carried on mules or gallo- " ways, and their servants rode on the top of the load. The troopers were variously " mounted, most of them riding strong active horses. Some were armed with swords and " spear heads without shafts; others carried bad pistols stuck in their 'kummerbunds' " (waist cloths); others, again, carried matchlocks, with the 'limak' or crooked stock, or " flint locks. The cannon were about four or five-pounders, tolerably well cast, but " vilely mounted.'

The arms of the *Populzais* are described by Lieut. Macartney as consisting of swords daggers, battle axes, and short matchlocks. Some of the latter have locks like that of a carbine, but are of a larger bore, and some are provided with moveable bayonets.

The *Gholámis* are armed much in the same way, but have more firelocks and spears.

The *Ghilzais* use the same arms as the Durránis, with the addition of a small shield.

The Eastern Afghans wear Hindustani swords, shields, leather cuirasses, matchlocks, and often spears.

---

[1] It was a stipendiary troop of Pathans or Wulaitees, which under the ex-Nawab of Tonk was engaged in the murderous fray with Rajputs, which ended in the death of the Thakoor of Lawa.

[2] Mission to Cabul, p. 271.

[3] The pistols made in Daghestan are most prized, but they are imitated in Kashmír so as not to be distinguishable from the originals.

[4] They held their lands by military tenure, and for every parcel of land demanding the services of a plough, a horseman was to be provided for the service of the State. *Kaye*, Afghanistan, p. 15.

[5] Moorcroft's Travels, p. 351, 1824.

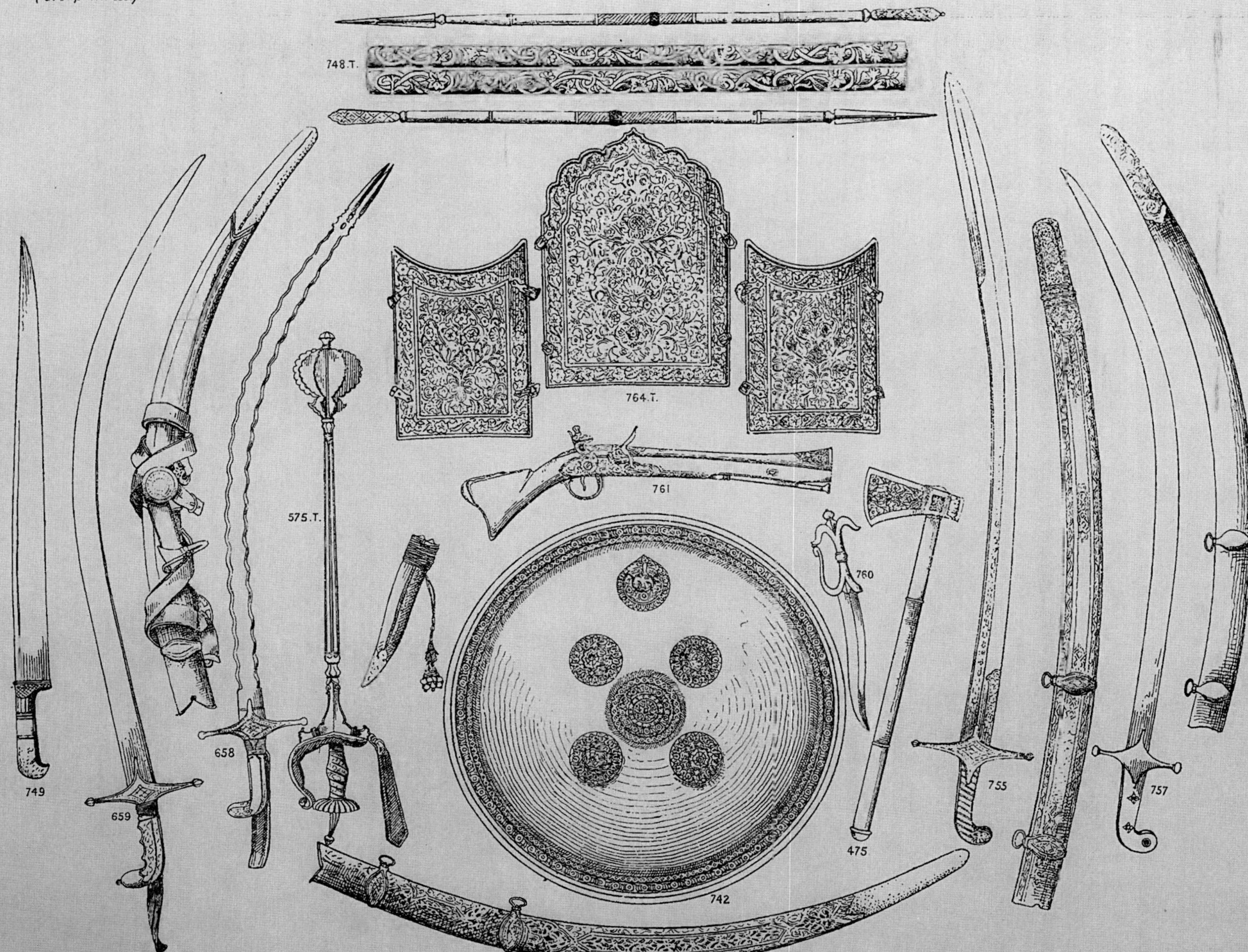

MISCELLANEOUS EXAMPLES OF PERSIAN AND INDIAN ARMS.

W. GRIGGS, PHOTO LITH. LONDON. S. E.

The infantry have generally a sword, a shield, and a matchlock with a rest. Those of the Kohistan of Kabul carry a firelock, pistol, and a short dagger, but no sword. The Ghilzais, the Khyberies, and some other tribes use a knife about 3 feet long (No. 749), which drops into a large sheath and hangs on the thigh. They are made at Jellalabad. Two in the author's collection are decorated near the hilt with gold and silver arabesques, in the Persian style. The handles of these are of walrus tooth. These arms are, no doubt, still generally worn, but the regular regiments, drilled after European fashion by the Amír, have recently been furnished with European arms.

Elphinstone describes[1] a fight between two Afghan tribes, the Bábúzai and Nekpíkhail: "Both sides had some horse and some hundred Jailumees (champions distinguished by a fantastic dress, and bound to conquer or die). The rest were a mob, some in thick quilted jackets, some in coats of mail, and others in leathern cuirasses, all armed either with bows or matchlocks, and with swords, shields, long Afghan knives, and iron spears.

"When the armies came in sight they at first fired on each other; afterwards the Jailumees turned out and engaged with the sword; and at the last the main bodies came into close combat.

"The brave men on each side were mixed together, and fought hand to hand. The cowards, who were by much the greater number, hung back on both sides, but joined in the general clamour. Every man shouted and reviled his adversaries with as loud a voice as he could."

The wild races on the N.W. Frontier *Afrídís, Wazírís and Mahsúds*, &c., who are subdivided into various clans, use the same arms, and fight with great gallantry in their almost inaccessible country. Their matchlocks were, till the introduction of the rifled weapons, much superior to our old "brown bess," and carried up to 800 yards with accuracy.

Kashmír is still famous for the manufacture of sword and gun barrels. Pistols are made in admirable imitation of European work. The Kashmiri swords are frequently ornamented with incised figures in relief of men and animals, and the outline heightened with gold. The Kashmíris are of no account as soldiers.

The *Siaposh Kafirs* are probably a race who have resisted conversion to Mahommedanism, and in blood allied to the people of Chitrál and Dardistán. Their arms exhibited in the India Museum, by Dr. Leitner, consist of bows and arrows.[2]

Persia. Persian arms were generally worn by the upper classes in India, and the blades of swords were often Persian, even though mounted in India. In fact as Persian artificers were frequently employed at the principal native courts, it is difficult sometimes to say whether a piece of armour is Persian or Indian. The coats of mail and armour are now no longer worn in that country, except to add to the pageant of their religious processions held annually in the month of Muharram to commemorate the death of Hassan and Hussain, the Shiah martyrs. Many that are of modern manufacture have been made for ornament rather than use, and betray in their style the decline of the art. The best period seems from the examples preserved to have been from the time of Shah 'Abbás to that of Nádir Sháh.

Chardin gives a detailed account of the organization of the first standing army in Persia at the time of Abbas I. It consisted of two corps, the first, 12,000 musqueteers on foot, and intended to oppose the Turkish Janissaries, and the second, cavalry numbering 10,000. These were in addition to the ordinary levies or "Kazilbáshes" (red caps). The Ṣufís were a body guard of 200 men, armed with sabre, dagger, and an axe on the shoulder. The Ja'zá'írí, or guards of the palace, were raised by 'Abbás II. They carried a large musquet, which as well as their swords, daggers, and powder flasks were mounted in silver. They fired the musquet off from a wooden fork about two feet long placed on the ground to serve as a rest.

There is in the Munich Library an illuminated MS. of the Shah Nameh, repre-

[1] Mission, p. 342. [2] Cf. Masson Journies in Afghanistan, p. 230. [3] Chardin, vol. iii. pp. 316–22.

senting the costume and arms of the Persians in the 17th century. The Khorassan sword appears to be worn on the left and the dagger on the right side. Maces, both pear-shaped and in the shape of a cow's head, and bows and arrows rather than guns are used. The combatants generally wear conical helmets with solid guards over the neck and ears. The horses as well as their riders have a complete covering of plate mail with alternate rows of gold and silver scales. There is in the British Museum a helmet with vambraces, which belonged to Shah 'Abbás, and is inscribed with his name, and which is of splendid workmanship, with floral ornaments chiselled in relief out of the steel. Of the same character and finish of detail is a set of "chár áína" or breast plates which are only equalled by a set at Windsor. (Fig. 34.) Some fine arms have been presented by the Shahs to the Emperors of Russia.[1]

Fig. 34.—Centre of Persian Breastplate at Windsor.

In a coloured native drawing in the author's possession, Nádir Sháh is represented seated on the ground with his sword lying before him; the hilt of the sword is pistol-shaped and encrusted with large rubies and emeralds. From the time of Nádir Sháh or the middle of the last century the work becomes gradually more florid, and quotations from the Koran or verses of Sa'dí are more liberally distributed over the work in geometrical cartouches.

The blades of later Persian dress swords are covered with ornament. One of about the middle of the last century, in the E. collection, is like a Turkish scimitar with escalloped edge, and inlaid with arabesques in gold and silver. Another more modern has alternate bands of inscriptions and natural flowers raised in low relief. Besides the ordinary curved "Shamsher," the Persians use a straight sword with the quillons downwards. One in the E. collection has the Lion and Sun engraved on the blade near the hilt and a raised serpent runs down the middle to the point.

The helmets are of a pear shape and as well as the shields and breastplates (*char aina*) are richly ornamented; and the shields of rhinoceros hide imported from India are frequently transparent and painted with elaborate designs added by the Persians. There is one in the Zarkoe Seloe collection, of wood covered with gold brocade encrusted with silver gilt plaques, and with turquoise studs. The hexagonal boss in the centre is ornamented with jade inlaid with emeralds, turquoises, and carbuncles. The style is of the early part of the 17th century.—(*Vide* Cat. Z.S. Coll., Vol. iii., Plate iii.).

[1] Vide Chapter on decoration.

The Persian dagger has usually a fiddle-shaped hilt and stiletto blade, though sometimes the hilt is long and narrow. Ivory, enamel, and chiselled steel are the usual materials of which the hilts are composed. The blades are generally engraved and inlaid near the hilt with floral patterns in gold. In the Caucasus on the Circassian frontier a straight dagger or short double-edged sword, "qáma," is commonly used.

The javelins in this group are carried in sheaths which hold two or three. The spear heads are long and thin. They are frequently for ornamental purposes made with two or three prongs, and generally have a slighter shaft, and lighter appearance than the Indian

The *Abyssinian* and *Arab* arms deserve mention, as they were introduced by the mercenaries who have been mentioned as serving in some of the courts of Southern India. The curved dagger of the Arabs, the Jambiya, has long been naturalized in Central India.

The Abyssinians have long held a footing in the country. An Abyssinian Sídí held jaghírs from the Kings of Bíjapur, and was Admiral of the Mahomedan fleet. For many years the Sídís[1] stood sieges against the Mahrattas in their stronghold of Janjíra. In 1733 the Abyssinian (Habshi) Sídí signed an offensive and defensive treaty with the Government of Bombay, and ever since his successors have in their piracies spared British ships. The present representative of that race and dynasty is the Nawab of Janjíra.

In *China* until the introduction of European arms, the native weapons do not seem to have much changed from the earliest times. The Chinese commonly use the straight sword, which resembles the Tibetan, the spear, and bows and arrows. Their casques are of Mongolian type.[2]

The manufacture of iron is carried on in China by rude processes which are described as similar to the Catalan process known in the Pyrenees. Their steel is made by placing the raw iron and the pig iron in bands together in a brick furnace between two layers of burning coal. When it is molten it is well hammered several times. They also harden steel by dipping it when red hot in oil.[3]

The *Japanese* arms differ entirely from the Indian, but resemble the Burmese in the shape of their swords, though they are far superior in quality. The Japanese derived from China the Buddhist religion, and with it probably the grotesque forms which characterise some of their helmets, such as those surmounted by a dragon or other crest.

Many of their swords are of great antiquity and much prized when the work of celebrated makers such as Ama Kumi and Shin Soku. The former dates from about A.D. 700. They are handed down as heirlooms in families, and are acquired with difficulty.

In the catalogue of the collection belonging to Mr. W. J. Alt, exhibited in the Bethnal Green Museum, 1876, a full description is given of the different weapons, sword, spear, and bows and arrows used by them. In their ornament the extensive use of lacquer, and mother-of-pearl distinguishes them from any other Oriental nation. They are equally skilled in the working of silver, bronze and enamels. Dragons, verses and mottoes in Chinese, and even occasionally Sanscrit letters are engraved on the sword blades. Their sword hilts are richly inlaid with gold and silver so as to present scenes in war and the chase or landscapes.

---

1 Moral and Material Progress Report, 1874. By Clements R. Markham.

2 Cf. Casque worn by Emperor of China. Musée d'Artillerie, Paris.

3 Stanislas Julien, p. 57.

AFGHANISTAN, KASHMIR, AND PERSIA.

Mostly in Case 49 (left half), a few in Group X.

Note on the bows of Persia.—The bows and arrows of Persia are celebrated throughout the East. The Persian bows, says Chardin, are the most esteemed in the East. The concave side of the bow (convex when strung) is lined with several strings of thick catgut, to give it elasticity and force. The material of which the belly of a Persian bow is made is buffalo or wild goat's horn, jet black, and of a fine polish; glued to this is a thin slip of some hard wood little inferior in toughness, which serves for the back. The extreme points are fashioned to resemble a snake's head, the loops of the cord having the appearance of being held within its extended jaws. The horn is left plain, while the wooden back is decorated with rich arabesques. Birds, flowers, and fruit are represented on its surface in varied colours intermingled with gilding, and the grip of the bow is marked by broad bands of the same metal, separated by figured of flowors and fruit.

The string is composed of strong silken threads laid together until the whole is of the thickness of a goose-quill. Whipping of like material is then bound firmly for about 3 or 4 ins. at the centre, and large loops of scarlet or other colour are attached to this middle-piece by a very curious knot. The contrast between the pure white silk and the gaudy loops is very striking.—*Hansard, Manufacture of Bows*, p. 133.

746. BATTLE AXE; "Tabar;" The shaft is hollow and divisible into three parts, to each of which is attached a small dagger. Presented by Maj.-General Sir F. J. Goldsmid. *Seistan, Afghanistan.* Blade, 5½ in. by 3½ in. (12,042.–'72.)

At Windsor there is a fine battle-axe with enamelled handle inlaid with jewels, which belonged to Nadir Shah. The large two handed battle-axe "Tabar-i-zin" (saddle-axe) is commonly used by Afghans.

747. PAIR OF JAVELINS; of steel; spirally twisted in the middle, where they are held. L. 2 ft. 7 in. (12,599.–'69.)

748 T. PAIR OF JAVELINS; of steel embossed and damascened with gold; with case of crimson velvet richly embroidered with gold. *Persian.* (Pl. xv., No. 748 T.) (516.)

749. SWORD; "Salawár Yataghán, or Khyber Knife;" yellowish tinted damascus blade, richly damascened with gold ornaments; broad straight back, towards which the cutting edge slopes gradually. Hilt of walrus ivory, unguarded. Sheath enclosing both blade and hilt, of black leather capped with brass. *Peshawur.* L. 2 ft. 6 in.; Bl. 2 ft. 1 in. (Pl. xv. No. 749.) (8532.–'55.)

750. SWORD; "Salawár Yataghán, or Khyber Knife;" Kara (black) Khorassan blade. Hilt of walrus ivory mounted with brass. Black leather sheath with embossed brass mounts. *Peshawur.* L. 2 ft. 6 in.; Bl. 2 ft. 1 in. (8533.–'55.)

Cf. "Ch'hurá," made in Khorassan, Kabul, and Jellalabad. A strong heavy knife.

Ghammaad (Qáma), heavy two-edged knife of very hard waved steel, deeply grooved and slightly ornamented with gold; horn handle. Daghestan, 1820. Worn by Persians of all ranks; used as hatchet, sword, and knife.

751. SABRE; "Shamsher;" fine blade; hilt of walrus ivory and steel damascened with gold, bearing inscriptions in low relief; scabbard of embossed black leather, with steel mountings damascened in gold, and bearing inscriptions carved in low relief. Used chiefly in Persia and Afghanistan. Presented by Sher 'Ali, Amír of *Kabul.* L. 3 ft. 5 in. (11,694.–'70.)

752. SABRE; "Shamsher;" dark-tinted damascus blade; hilt of walrus-ivory and steel, the latter damascened with gold; scabbard of embossed black leather with gold-damascened steel mounts. Presented by Sher 'Ali, Amír of *Kabul.* L. 3 ft. 3 in. (11,696.–'70.)

753.* SABRE; "Shamsher;" fine watered blade, bearing an inscription inlaid in gold; scabbard of embossed black leather. Presented by Sher 'Ali, Amír of *Kabul.* L. 3 ft. 7 in. (11,693.–'70.)

754.* SABRE; "Shamsher;" fluted Damascus blade; walrus-ivory hilt; cross-guard and pommel of steel damascened with gold; embossed black leather sheath with steel mounts. Presented by Shere Ali, Ameer of Kabul. *Kabul.* L. 3 ft. 5 in. (11,695.)

Cf. from Codr. Coll. "Allemanee." Plain handle. German cavalry blade? Afghanistan, 1780.

755.* SABRE; "Shamsher;" slightly recurved Damascus blade covered with inscriptions of a genealogical nature inlaid with gold; hilt of walrus-ivory and gold damascened steel; scabbard of embossed black leather, with steel and silver mounts, the latter ornamented in niello. Presented by Col. Pennington. *Lahore.* L. 3 ft. 6 in. (Pl. xv. No. 755.) (1511.–'55.)

756.* SABRE; "Shamsher;" watered blade of very dark steel bearing an inscription inlaid in gold; hilt of walrus-ivory and steel; black leather scabbard with steel mounts. C. 49.

757.* SABRE; "Shamsher;" Damascus blade; buffalo-horn hilt, with gold mounts; blue velvet sheath with gold-damascened steel mounts. (Pl. xv. No. 757.) (12,605.)

758. SABRE; "Shamsher;" small blade; hilt of ivory and steel damascened with gold; green velvet sheath with embossed and gilt steel mounts.

759 T. SABRE; "Shamsher;" the hilt and scabbard covered with embossed and gilt leather, with metal mounts ornamented with pounce work. The blade is inscribed "Made by Asad Ullah, of Ispahan."

760. DAGGER; "Peshkabz;" two-edged doubly-curved Damascus blade; carved jade hilt, with knuckle guard; green velvet sheath, with gilt mounts, gold cord and tassels. Presented by H.H. Gulab Sing. *Kashmir.* (Pl. xv. No. 760.) (8522.–'55.)

761, 762. MUSQUETOONS (2); "Sher bacha (young tiger);" Damascus barrels, with chiselled and gilt floriations at the mouth and breech; flint locks; stocks coloured red and black respectively. Presented by H.H. the Maharajah Gulab Sing. *Kashmir.* (Pl. xv. No. 761.) (8561.–'55.)

Note.—"Zambúraq" ("Little Wasp"). Camel swivel gun used by the Persians.—*Malcolm's Persia.*

763 T. HELMET; hemispherical, surmounted by a steel ball perforated to hold a plume. *Persia.* (505.)

764 T. CUIRASS; "Chár áina," or "the four mirrors," composed of four plates; ornamented with floriated arabesques in red and green enamel, on a copper background, partly gilt. One of the plates is inscribed in Persian, "The noble Ghulám 'Alí Khán. Made by the "humble Mohammed 'Alí of Ispahan, in the "month of Shábán in the year 1213 (Hegira)." *Persia.* (Pl. xv. No. 764 T.) (506–9.)

Cf. Cuirass in S. K. Museum, with diagonal chevron pattern, alternately floriated, and plain damascene work; also plate armour formed of six pieces hinged together to fit the body more exactly.

765. COAT AND TROUSERS OF MAIL. Presented by the Maharajah Naonihál Sing. *Lahore.*

The coat is composed of very fine mail, covered with gold-brocaded green silk (Kincob). (8597.–'50.)

The trousers are of riveted steel links; padded crimson silk waistband. (8600.–'50.)

766. COAT OF MAIL; "Zirah baktar;" the links of which it is composed are small, and unrivetted, of brass and steel, in alternate zigzag stripes; the collar and border are of crimson-brocaded silk (Kincob), edged with gold braid. *Lahore.* (–'55.)

CHINESE, ABYSSINIAN, AND ARAB.

Group on the right, facing the large screen.

CHINESE.

767. GLAIVE; sabre blade (2 ft. 1 in. long), attached to a long shaft (4 ft. 7 in.), painted red, and tipped at the butt-end with iron; *China.* L 6 ft. 8 in.

768. SWORD; long, slightly re-curved blade (3 ft. 7 in.), attached to a hilt (1 ft. 7 in.) of wood, bound with bamboo, and painted red; circular guard. *China.* L. 5 ft. 2 in.

769. SWORD; slightly re-curved blade; wooden hilt; small circular guard. *China.* L. 2 ft. 6 in. (12,610.)

770–771. SWORDS; straight blades; sheaths of tortoise-shell, and green painted wood respectively; embossed brass mounts to hilt and sheath. *China.* L. 22 in. and 28 in. (12,606.)

772. SWORD; straight blade; brass mounts to hilt and sheath. *China.* L. 2 ft. (12,606.)

773. SWORDS (A PAIR) the blades fitting into one sheath; the quillons of the hilt are turned, one towards the blade, the other to the hilt to form a knuckle-guard. *China.* L. 20 in. (12,589.)

774–777. SWORDS Fitting in pairs into two sheaths. Leather covered hilts. Embossed brass mounts. Sheaths of leather and tortoise-shell respectively, with embossed brass mounts. *China.* L. 22 in. by 24 in.

778. SWORD. Grooved blade, hilt covered with interlaced strips of leather. Embossed brass mounts. Shagreen-covered sheath with embossed brass mounts. *China.* (12,609.)

779. DAGGER OR SHORT SWORD. Wooden hilt; quillons turned in opposite directions, one of them forming a knuckle guard. *China.*

780–782. MACES. Shaped like daggers except that in place of the blade there is a tapering octagonal shaft of steel. The quillons are large and turned towards the shaft. L. 17 to 19 in. *China.* (12,594, 12,617, 12,628.)

783. TRIDENT SPEAR. Long wooden shaft painted red. *China.* L. 5 ft. 8 in.

784, 85. MATCHLOCK GUNS. Very rough construction. Stocks painted red.

786 T. MATCHLOCK. Massive carved stock. *China.*

787. MATCHLOCK. Fine barrel. Small bore. Broad flat butt of light-coloured wood. *Burmah.* (12,533.–69.)

ABYSSINIA.

788, 789. DAGGERS. Broad blades. Unguarded wooden hilts. Leather sheaths. *Abyssinia.* L. 16½ in. Bl. 1½ by 2½ in. wide.

790–792. SWORDS. Straight blades. Two with fluted ivory hilts, the third with wooden hilt, all unguarded. *Abyssinia.* L. 2 ft. 1 in.

793–797. SABRES. Deeply curved blades, cutting with either edge. Plain unguarded wooden hilts. *Abyssinia.*

ARAB (DECCAN).

798, 799. DAGGERS. "Jambiya." Abruptly curved, strongly ribbed blades. Wooden hilts, with embossed and chased silver mounts. *Deccan.* L. 12 in. (12,569.–'69.)

TURKISH or ALBANIAN.

800. DAGGER Long blade. Gold mounted hilt, the pommel enriched with a carbuncle. Sheath covered with embossed silver plate. Presented by Claude Russell, Esq. (8459.–'50.)

The following few specimens cannot be strictly included in any of the groups in this collection, but are introduced here as examples of native imitation of European work. Some of the leading native states have now workshops and foundries for the manufacture of arms and artillery.

***801.** TWO GUNS, "Bandúq doráha;" one completely enclosed within the other. The outer gun is provided with a flint lock, the inner one with a percussion lock. Presented by H.H. the Maharajah of *Alwar, Rajputana.* L. 3 ft. 7 in.

***802.** BRACE OF PISTOLS. Stubb-twist barrels. *Agra.* (8563.–'51.)

***803.** MODEL OF A FIELD GUN WITH CARRIAGE. Of brass and steel. Made by a native from an European pattern. *Haidarabad, Deccan.* (8450.–'55.)

804. HUNTING KNIVES (2). Polished blades with side springs; stag-horn hilts; leather sheaths. *Salem, Madras.* L. 12 and 18 in. (8887.–'55.)

GROUP XII.

ARMS USED FOR ATHLETIC AND SACRIFICIAL PURPOSES.

Gladiatorial Contests, Military Games, and Festivals.

The martial exercises of the Indian people have never been carried to the extreme length of the gladiatorial games in which the Romans during the zenith and decline of their empire delighted; nor have they imitated the polished tournament of mediæval feudalism; but while they have combined some of the advantages and disadvantages of both systems, they have often in the trials of personal strength and dexterity in the practice of arms approached the spirit that animated the knights of chivalry in its best days. The courts of the native princes were the scenes of these games.

The Ain-i-Akbari gives us an account of the fighting gladiators who were kept at the court of the Great Mogul to form a pastime in the intervals of the warlike expeditions which formed the principal occupation of the rulers of India:—

"The *Shamsherbáz* or gladiators are of various kinds. Some of them use shields in fighting, others use cudgels. The latter are called *Lakráit*. Others again use no means of defence, and fight with one hand only; these are called *yak-hát'h.* Those who come from the eastern parts of Hindostan use a small shield called *"chirwah."* Those from the southern provinces have shields of such magnitude as to cover a man and a horse. This kind of shield is called *tilwah.*

"Another class, called *P'haráits,* use a shield somewhat less than the height of a man, and one *gaz* in breadth.

"Some again are called *Banáits.* They use a long sword, the handle of which is more than a *gaz* long; holding it with both hands they perform extraordinary feats of skill.

"There is another famous class called *Bankúlis.* These have no shield, but make use of a singular kind of sword, which, though bent towards the point, is straight near the handle. They wield it with great dexterity.

"Others are very skilful in fighting with daggers and knives of various forms; of these there are upwards of a hundred thousand. . . . . .

"There are many Persian and Túráni wrestlers and boxers (*Pahluwáns*) at court, as also stone-throwers, athletes of Hindostan, expert slingers (*Mals*) from Gujrát, and many other kinds of fighting men. Every day some of the above combat together and receive various rewards."[1]

The same taste pervaded all the martial races of India, and the accounts given at different times show how popular such entertainments were, and how, by means of them their martial spirit, and their bodily strength and dexterity in the use of arms were kept up in times of peace. The Rajput princes especially delighted in the exhibition of *Jaṭṭhís* or wrestlers. Every prince or chief entained a certain number of these champions, and the combats were looked forward to with great anxiety.

During the festival of the Dussera, Hyder Ali and Tippoo we are told used to amuse themselves with combats of animals, (such as tigers, buffaloes, and rams) and the boxing of prize fighters called in the Deccan *Jaṭṭhí.* Abyssinians dressed in woollen armour, and furnished with staves of sandal wood were set to fight with bears. In the combat between a man and a lion or tiger, the Nawáb delighted to show his skill with the matchlock. In the midst of the circle a plantain tree was placed under cover of which the man was ordered to attack the animal. If the tiger overthrew the man, the Nawáb fired with such unerring aim that the ball passed through the tiger's head, and the man rose up uninjuréd. If the man slew the tiger, he was richly rewarded.

Their games[2] were continued for ten days in succession. Some of the combatants or "*jaṭṭhís*" were natives of Madagascar, who were trained from their infancy to fight together. They had on their right hands the "woodguamootie,(?)" or four steel talons

[1] Ain-i-Akbari, Gladwin, Vol. I. 226. Blochmann.

[2] Captivity of James Scurry. London, 1824.

which in the nature of a gauntlet were fixed to the back joint of their fingers, and had a terrific appearance when their fists were closed. Their heads were close shaved, their bodies oiled, and they wore only a pair of short drawers. On being matched, at a signal given from Tippoo, they began the combat by throwing the flowers which they wore round their necks, in each others faces; watching an opportunity of striking with the right hand on which they wore this weapon, which never failed to lacerate the flesh and draw blood copiously. They would frequently break each others arms and legs, and unless completely crippled, fought as long as Tippoo pleased.

One of these men challenged another from Tanjore to fight with "krises" (about sixteen inches long, sharp and taper at the end, and four inches wide towards the handle). They stood fronting each other till Tippoo finding them both staunch, relented, and ordered them to withdraw.

Marco Polo[1] mentions a curious custom prevalent on the Malabar coast. At Kail a port in the Tinnevelly district, if any one is insulted by the juice of the betel being spat in his face, he goes to the king, relates the insult that has been offered him, and demands leave to fight the offender. The King supplies the arms which are sword and target, and there the two fight till one of them is killed. They must not use the point of the sword, for this the king forbids. Barbosa,[2] speaking of the kingdom of Battecala in Canara, says of the same customs, "They engage without armour, only from the waist " upward they wear a tight jacket, and have a quantity of cotton cloth wrapped tight " round the chest and shoulders."

The training of these professional wrestlers is described by Broughton as part of a Sepoy's duties in a Mahratta camp, "The Sepoys in the rainy season perform athletic " exercises, which are conducted with a certain ceremonial. A sufficient space is marked " out and called 'Akhárá,' and is held sacred, no one entering with his shoes on. At one " end a small heap of earth is raised to which each one as he enters makes obeisance, and " adds a handful of earth. The most skilful performer is "Khalífa" or superintendent " for the season, and instructs the young 'Paṭṭhá' scholars. The first exercise is the " Dhun which consists in raising the body from the hands and feet, with the chest three " or four inches from the ground in a horizontal position, and continually repeating the " movement as long as the strength will permit. The next exercise is 'kooshtee' or " wrestling, at which they exhibit great dexterity. Those who attain a certain degree " of skill are dignified by the appellation of 'Puhlwan,' and are taken into the service " of the great men in India."[3]

The Sepoys also exercise with "Mugdars" and "Lezam;" the former are thick clubs of hard wood, about two feet or more in length, and from 14 to 20 pounds in weight, which are wielded like dumb bells. The "Lezam" is a stiff bow of bamboo, bent by a strong iron chain to which a number of small round plates of iron are affixed to increase the weight and make a jingling noise. The bow is used by stretching out the right and left arms alternately to the utmost extent.

The Mahrattas use the spear with remarkable dexterity. Sometimes in full gallop, grasping their spears short, they strike the point quickly into the ground, and still holding the handle, they turn their horse suddenly round it, thus performing on the point of a spear as on pivot, the same circle round and round again.

The "Dusséra"[4] or military festival among the Mahrattas used to take place after the S.W. monsoon about the end of September and the beginning of October, when the time is favourable for the movement of troops. The "Jhanḍá" or great standard of the Prince was hoisted, and a camp was formed in Poona. The first nine days, "Naurátra" or festival of nine nights, consecrated to the goddess Durga were employed in the worship of the horses and arms. Swords, guns, and shields carefully cleaned were placed on the altars and blessed by the Brahmins. The horses were decorated with garlands of flowers and paraded in the streets. After the damp of the monsoon this worship of the arms is

[1] Colonel Yule, Marco Polo, Vol. II., p. 307–311. [2] Ramusio, Vol. I., p. 300, quoted by Colonel Yule.
[3] Broughton's Mahrattas, 1809. Cf. coloured native drawing of wrestlers in the India Museum.
[4] Dussera = tenth day, properly "Dasahrá."

peculiarly appropriate. The cannon were the most appropriate emblem of Durga; her trident was marked upon them, and the representation of her shrine was raised before them and surrounded with lamps. One of the chief religious acts in this festival is the capture of Lanká (*i.e.*, Ceylon) which is represented in honour of Ráma. Lanká is represented by a spacious castle with towers and battlements, which is assailed by an army dressed like Ráma and his followers, with Hanumán and his monkey allies. The combat ends in the destruction of Lanka amidst a blaze of fireworks. The Mahrattas at the same time commemorate Ráma's devotions, and his plucking a branch from a certain tree before he set out on his expedition.

At the close of the festival the Peshwa marched out of the city accompanied by the nobles, and preceded by the state equipages of elephants and led horses. On this occasion the Mahrattas went through the ceremony of plundering a field. The Peshwa led the way by tearing up a handful of corn, and his example was followed by all present, thus reminding themselves of their predatory origin. At the Dussera, the Rájpút chiefs worship the Samí tree (*Mimosa suma*) to commemorate the worship of Arjuna and his brothers who hung up their arms upon it. They address the tree under the name of "Asurájitá," the invincible goddess. On the same evening they worship the goddess "Gaḍhechí" the "fort protectress," and on their return join together in bands, brandishing their spears and galloping their horses, as in time of war.[1]

The irregular cavalry, under the East India Company, no less than at the present time, were proficient in martial exercises. Captain Mundy thus describes one of their tournaments:—

"The spearmen of Skinner's horse played their elegant exercise before us with long lances, tipped like foils with a button. Sometimes one fellow retreated at full speed, trailing his long spear after him with the point on the ground, and skilfully warding off the thrusts aimed at himself or his horse by his pursuer; then when he thought his assailant was off his guard, he would make a sudden wheel and assume the offensive, and in the midst of a cloud of dust, the too confident pursuer was thrust from his saddle, and rolled on the ground.

"One of Dongan's native irregular horse performed one of the most difficult feats with the spear. It is called *Nezah Bazee* or spear play. A tent peg is driven by a mallet some 8 or 10 inches into the earth, so firmly that the strength of two men would not suffice to draw it out. The horseman, holding his spear reversed in the rest, rides at full speed past the object, drives his weapon into the tough wood, drags it out of the earth, and brandishes it aloft; if he fails, the ferrule of the spear plunges deep into the earth, whilst the reverse end strikes the rider a violent blow at the back of the head. The greatest adept at the exercise only succeeded twice in five courses.

"At the camp of Scindia, two parties of Mahratta officers, showily attired, and mounted mostly on beautiful Deccanee horses, were ranged opposite each other on either end of a level piece of ground. Each man carried a lance made expressly for practice, much longer than the war spear, and pointed with a ball of cloth. The two adverse troops soon came into action, one retreating and defending themselves, the other pursuing and attacking. Or, a warrior dashed forth from one of the groups, and curvetted about till one of the opposite side accepted his challenge and spurred to the encounter.

"On another occasion in Cuttack the sword-players were selected from the Sepoys of the 39th infantry. They were entirely naked with the exception of a cloth bound tightly round the waist, and reaching a few inches down the thighs. The combatants were armed with a species of single stick, covered with leather to qualify the effect of the blow, and in their left hands they carried a small leathern buckler about the circumference of a dinner plate. After a smiling salaam they approached each other very cautiously, circling round at the respectful distance of 10 feet, and using the most extraordinary and extravagant gestures, which an old Jemadar near me described as useful to awe and distract the attention of the antagonist and to gain the sun of him.

[1] Elphinstone, Vol. I. 337; Forbes, Ras Mala.

When they at last came to blows, they laid about them in real earnest, striking with all their might and often with both hands. The extreme dexterity which they displayed in warding, with the little shield, their crafty feints, and the immense springs they occasionally made to avoid or surprise their adversary, drew loud plaudits. Towards the end of the combat, one of these supple fellows suddenly threw himself upon his knees, in order to cut at the legs of his opponent, and from that apparently helpless position, with the quickness of lightning, sprang back six or eight feet to escape the stroke that was descending on his head. The other in attempting to retort the same manœuvre, received a blow on the shoulder that echoed through the field, upon which the contending couple struck their swords and bucklers together, salaamed in token of amity, and swaggered out of the ring."

"The gauntlet sword whose blade is full five feet long, in the hands of a practised swordsman appears a terrible weapon, though to those unaccustomed to its use, it is but an awkward instrument. After a display of sundry sweeping and rotary cuts that would have severed a bullock's neck, four small limes were placed on the ground, equi-distant round the circle, and the performer describing a variety of evolutions not unlike an exaggerated waltz, approached them alternately and without pausing in his giddy career, divided each of them in two with a well aimed horizontal cut."[1]

Sword dances are common over the whole of India. In Coorg something of the nature of single-stick play is followed. It is called Kol Peria, or stick and shield play. Two men enter the arena, each armed with a long switch in the right hand, and a shield or a handful of whisks in the left; after defying one another, and jumping about in a strange manner, they slash at their adversaries' ankles and legs with the swish in their right hand. Hard blows are dealt out, but they are good-natured fellows, and the performers always embrace each other at the end of the play.

Part of their national dances is called *Kolhata,* or "strike," another stick dance, in which each man is provided with a couple of sticks just like those used at "La Grace." They move round and strike them alternately on those of their neighbours, all the dancers singing as they move.[2]

Before the introduction of rifled weapons into our army, the matchlock was superior both in accuracy and length of range to our musquet, and. as the following quotation will show, was well handled by some native troops. The competitors for the matchlock prizes in Skinner's Horse, thus conduct their exercises :—"A bottle is placed on the ground, or "suspended from a gibbet, and the column of mounted marksmen is formed up at right "angles with the spectators. At a signal from the officer one of the party gallops forth "at full speed, with his matchlock suspended across his bridle arm, darting past the "object at the distance of 15 or 20 yards. Just as he passes the rein drops from his hand, "the matchlock is raised, makes a short horizontal sweep, the ball is sped, and the bottle "flies into a thousand atoms."

The Mahomedans have a special season devoted to martial exercises and pageants. At the time of the festival of the "Muharram," around the Ta'ziyas—light frames of split bamboo, covered with gilt paper so as to represent the tomb of Hussain—a number of long poles are placed, to which are attached extended hands emblematic of the five holy personages of the prophet's family, and naked scymitars representing Zu'lfiqár, the double-pointed victorious sword of Ali.

At the anniversary of Hussain's death a procession by night is formed, and among the crowd some fire off matchlocks, others exhibit their skill in flourishing swords, sometimes singly or in mock combat with each other. One man stands up with a flag in his hand; about one hundred others form a circle, three or four deep, and keep prancing round and round in a strange measured step, brandishing their naked swords, and calling out the names Mahomed, Ali, Hussain.

The Himalayan mountaineers[3] have also their mimic fights. The 1st of April (Bysakh)

[1] Capt. Mundy. Journal of a tour in India, 1827. Vol. ii, p. 143–280.
[2] Bowring. Experiences of a Planter in the Jungles of Mysore.
[3] A Summer Ramble in the Himalayas. Edited by "Mountaineer," 1860. p. 195.

is attended with peculiar ceremony in the Hindoo villages of the Garhwális in the Himálayas. The men from each side of the valley assemble by the river in opposite bodies, each on their own bank, armed with slings and blunt arrows. Each party with their "deptas," and the ark or dwelling place of the Deity, approach the river, and a mimic battle commences between the two, stones being slung and arrows discharged with all the skill and strength of the combatants, who encourage each other by shrill whistles and loud shouts. The "Deptas" must be brought down to the river and sprinkled with water, and when either party attempts to do this, the opposite one directs a shower of stones and arrows upon it, and often succeeds in driving back their opponents several times before they can accomplish their object.

In one of their religious ceremonies the "Pundap natch" or dance, the men strip to their waists, and daub their faces and bodies with "pitace," a yellow powder made from pine tree flowers. A club ("dángrá"), a bow and quiver, or some other weapon is flourished about by the male performers. Others walk bare-foot on the sharp edges of a long line of dangras, hatchets, and other weapons, held with their backs to the ground. These antics are performed in accordance with the character of the spirit supposed to have entered into them, and they will point to the handling of red hot iron without being burnt, and the walking on the blades of sharp weapons without being cut, as proof of the reality of the inspiration.

Besides these military games, the Bilúchís practise the Jarid Bází, "spear-play," which is also common among all classes in Persia.

It is played by two men on horse-back, with a spear shaft 12 feet long. They gallop after each other, one throwing the Jarid or spear shaft with full force, with the view of hitting and unhorsing his opponent, while he, by dexterous agility, has not only to elude the blow but to seize the weapon in the air and attack in turn.[1]

Group on the left, facing the large screen.

A.—ATHLETIC EXERCISES.

805. CLUBS (a pair); "Mugdar;" of Sissoo wood, weighted with lead. *Lahore.* L. 2 ft. 9 in.

806. DUMB-BELLS; of stone; circular, with transverse hilts. *Lahore.* Diam. 12 in.; weight, about 30 lbs. each.

807. DUMB-BELL; stone; small, circular. *Nepal.*

808. CHAIN-BOW; "Lezam;" bamboo, in lieu of string, an iron chain of very large links, to which are attached metal discs, making a jingling noise when the bow is used. *Lahore.* L. 4 ft. 6 in. (8888.–'51.)

809. GAUNTLET-SWORD; "Paṭá;" flexible rapier blade; gauntlet hilt of steel with brass mounts. Used by Sikhs in their sword-play, and by Mahomedans during the festival of the Mohurrum. *Punjab.* L. 4 ft.; L. of blade, 3 ft. (8874.–'55.)

810. TWO-HANDED SWORD; straight blade, expanding towards the point; long hilt, encircled by three huge brass collars. *Punjab.* L. 5 ft. 3 in.; L. of blade, 2 ft. 8 in. (8888.–'55.)

B.—SACRIFICIAL AND OTHER WEAPONS.

811. SACRIFICIAL AXE; "Kigalee (?)" or "K'harga" (Z. S.); broad and massive blade, about 2½ ft. in length, terminating in an axe-like projection; short wooden handle. *Meerut.* L. 3 ft.; W. 4½ in. to 6 in. (12559.–'69.)

812. SACRIFICIAL AXE; "Kigalee;" similar to the preceding example. *Meerut.* L. 2 ft. 7½ in.; W. 2¼ in. to 5 in. (8825.–'55.)

813 T. STATE SWORD of the executioner of the King of Oude; gigantic and massive blade 3 ft. 3 in. long by 6 in. wide, bearing the arms of the King of Oude inlaid in silver; handle (2 ft. 9 in. long) covered with stamped leather; silver plated mounts. L. 6 ft.

814. EXECUTIONER'S SWORD of the King of Kandy; straight blade; hilt with knuckle-guard, silver-gilt; sheath covered with crimson velvet; silver-gilt mounts. Presented by the Rev. B. V. Layard. From *Ceylon.* (8746.–'51.)

815 T. BROAD SABRES; massive iron hilts, embossed From *Gujerat.* Blades, 3 ft. 4 in. by 2¾ in.

816 T. BROAD SABRE. From *Gujerat.* Blade, 3 ft. 3 in. by 4 in.

---

[1] Pottinger's Travels, p. 190.

ARTILLERY.

NEITHER this collection nor that of the Tower contains any gun larger than a wall-piece, or a swivel camel-gun, which is much used in the north of India; but any account of Indian arms would be incomplete without some mention of its artillery, which has played no inconsiderable part in its warfare. As in the manufacture of matchlocks the breechloading principle shown in No. 546 has probably been known for at least 200 years, so in the casting of guns the principles of construction which have lately been exhibited in the Armstrong gun were anticipated in India at least three centuries ago.

The early firearms or engines of the Hindus, to which allusion has already been made, seem to have been of a nature to send forth explosive missiles, and to have involved some knowledge of gunpowder; but there is great obscurity as to the time when the use of artillery was again revived—engines for throwing stones, "manjanik," and perhaps fiery projectiles are mentioned in the Mahomedan writers in the 8th century, on the invasion of Sind. M. Reinaud has examined the subject, and thrown some light on it from the examination

2. 3.

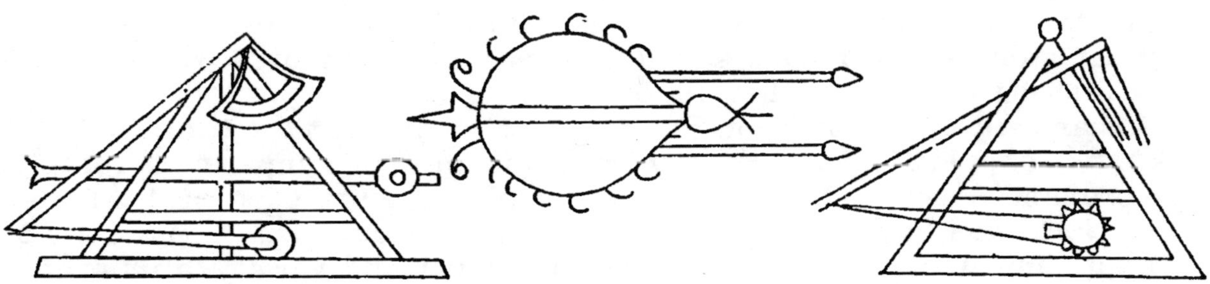

Fig. 35.—1 and 3 Engines, and 2 fiery projectile used by Arabs in the latter half of the 13th century (note 2).

of Arab documents.[1] He has shown that among the Arabs in the 13th century receipts for a mixture of sulphur, saltpetre, and charcoal, which approaches the mixture now known as gunpowder, were common. Also that the Chinese, who had probably imparted their knowledge of saltpetre to the Arabs in the 9th century, had in 1259 a projectile consisting of a nest of grains in a long bamboo tube. But in 1271 the Emperor Kublai had a catapult which was worked by Arab or Western engineers.

In India in the 12th and 13th centuries fire rockets or naphtha balls were used, and Alá-ud-dín when besieging the fort of Rantambhor in 1290 was opposed by a "maghribi"[2] or western engine, which discharged stones and scattered fire from the fort.[3] This engine was probably a large catapult which hurled forth iron or copper balls or pots charged with fire, and like the Arab mangonels was formed of a sling and weighted lever which was moved by men acting together by means of cords.

---

1 Histoire de l'Artillerie, Du Feu Grégeois, Reinaud et Favé. 1845.

2 *Maghrib,* Arabic=West. The Arabs called their countrymen the Moors of Spain, Maghribí "Westerners." Saltpetre was called by the Arabs "snow of China," and when prepared in crystals was called "bárúd" (the word used in Persian and Hindustani for powder), or snow in the form of hail.

3 Elliot, Vol. III., p. 174.

We are told that the King of Pegu advancing in the year 1404 against King Meng Khoung did not dare to land and attack Prome, as it was defended by cannons and muskets.[1] This is a region abounding in petroleum, and the "cannons and muskets" might have been rockets and fire arrows with naphtha.

There is testimony to the use of cannon before the arrival of the Portuguese, and these no doubt were introduced by the Turks or Arabs. In the attack by the Sultan of Guzerat against the pirates of Bulsar, 1482, he embarked gunners and musqueteers from Kambay.

The Portuguese instructed several native princes in the art of casting guns, but it was probably at the time of the Mogul invasion that large guns of European pattern were first used in Upper India. Baber in 1528 used artillery to force the passage of the Ganges at Kanauj. The gun was called Deg Gházi, victorious gun, but he had not many, and the word meaning carriages has been wrongly translated as meaning guns instead of transport waggons. In 1543 Sher Sháh Súr ordered his people to bring all the brass in the camp, and make mortars (degha) of it, to bombard the fort of Raísón, and they brought their pans and made them into mortars. India seems to have adopted freely the new instrument which Persia did not adopt, artillery. In 1549, one of the Jesuit missionaries, writing from Ormus, says of the Soldanus Babylonius "nullis bombardis nec aliis hujus generis tormentis utuntur."[2]

Herbert[3] (1626), speaking of the Malabarese, says, "by long wars they are "grown expert and orderly, yea know how to play with cannons, have as "great store of harquebuzes, and are as well acquainted with the force of "powder as we or any other nation."

Akbar paid much attention to this department. At the time of the Aín-í-Akbari (1556-1605), the artillery in India might compare favourably with the ordnance used at that time in Europe. According to it, "Artillery are "the locks and keys of empires, and, excepting Roum, (*i.e.* Constantinople) no "kingdom can compare with this in the number and variety of its ordnance."[4]

"Some pieces of cannon are so large as to carry a ball of twelve maunds, and others require each several elephants and a thousand bullocks for their transportation. His Majesty has invented several kinds, some of which are so contrived as to take to pieces for the convenience of carriage, and when the army halts they are nicely put together again. Also seventeen pieces are so united together as to be discharged by one match. There are others which can easily be transported by one elephant, called 'gajnál.' Others can be carried by a single man, and are called 'narnál,' (Blochmann)."

In Aurungzebe's time the armoury included 50 or 60 field-pieces of bronze, 70 pieces of cannon, mostly cast, and from two to three hundred light camel guns.

Artillery was not adopted in Persia till the time of Abbas the Great, who formed a corps of 12,000 men which was only kept up till the time of Abbas II. in 1655 who allowed the army to fall into decay.[5] This may account for Kæmpfer in 1692 finding no guns or mortars in that country.

There are accounts of large guns preserved in India, and some of them, even

---

[1] J. A. S. B. Vol. XXXVIII. Pt. 1. 1869, p. 40. [2] Epistola Indica, p. 38. M. Gaspari, Belgæ.
[3] Travels, p. 302. Ed. 1638. [4] Ayeen Akbari, translated by Gladwin, 1783.
[5] Chardin, Voyages on Perse, iii, 316-22. Ed. 1735.

within the writer's recollection, have been made the subject of worship in the Punjab. I have gleaned the following notes of large guns which have been recorded :

Duff[1] mentions the cannon "Malik-i Maidán," the monarch of the plain. It was cast at Ahmadnagar, in 1549, by a native of Cons ntinople named Hüssain Khan. The muzzle is 4 ft. 8 in. in diameter, and the calibre 2 ft. 4 in. There was an inscription put on it by Aurungzebe in 1685 to commemorate the conquest of Bíjapur, where it was preserved and made an object of worship. Wilkinson states that it weighed about 42 tons. An Italian of Otranto, who served in the Mogul armies under the title of Rúmi Khán, had this gun in his park of artillery, and used it in several battles, occasionally firing sacks of copper coins out of it.[2] The Bombay Government in 1823 wished to send it to England, but were unable to transport it!

Dacca had nothing curious to boast of, except a very remarkable piece of ordnance. It was 36 feet long, made of hammered iron, being an immense tube of fourteen bars, with rings driven over them and beaten down to a smooth surface, so that its appearance was very good, although its proportions were faulty (?). By its side lay a stone ball which filled its calibre. Had this ball been of metal it would have weighed 400 lbs. The gun itself must have weighed 64,814 lbs. It was worshipped as a shrine till 1780, when it disappeared; being on an island in the river, it was undermined by the current, and now lies at the bottom of the river.[3]

At Asirgarh there were guns of immense calibre. One of these, an iron gun carrying a ball of 384 lbs., was believed by the natives capable of lodging a shot at Burhánpur, 14 miles distant (!) It was captured in 1818. The garrison was composed chiefly of Arabs and Bilúchís.—*Mill, Notes.*

The brass gun, Maqsad 'Ali, taken at Bhurtpore (1826), was 15 ft. 3 in. in length, 6 ft. in circumference at the muzzle, 9 ft. 9 in. at the breech, while the calibre was $8\frac{1}{4}$ inches.[4]

In Burmah the guns were anciently composed of bars of iron beaten into a cylindrical shape and fastened together. They were raised on a rampart or tower, and threw large stones.

At the capture of Arracan by the Burmese in 1783, a huge piece was found, 30 ft. in length, $2\frac{1}{2}$ ft. in diameter, and 10 in. in calibre.[5]

In England there are but few Indian guns. The most remarkable are the following in Her Majesty's collection at Windsor Castle. A small gun from Seringapatam, of brass and raised silver work, ornamented with arabesques in floral patterns. Two brass Sikh guns taken at Moodkee: the carriages are of teak, inlaid with figures in brass, representing hunting scenes and dragons, in which is introduced "Hanúmán," the Monkey God. The limber of the gun is attached to the back carriage by an elephant's head

---

[1] History of the Mahrattas, Vol. I., p. 112. [2] Wilkinson, Engines of War, p. 53. 1841.
[3] Lives of the Lindsays, Vol. 4, p. 18. Note. [4] Captain Creighton, 1830. Capture of Bhurtpore.
[5] Captain Symes' Embassy to Ava, p. 109. 1800. (This is probably the piece which still lay in the Palace Yard at Amarapura in 1855. See narrative of the mission to Ava under Major Phayre, London, 1858, where a cut is given. The construction is that of the old bombards, longitudinal iron bars girt with a complete coating of thick hoops. The dimensions as given are respectively 28 feet 9 inches, 2 feet 7 inches, and $11\frac{1}{2}$ inches. Note by Col. Yule, C.B.)

and trunk, which is carved so as to connect it. A gun of pale bronze taken from Borneo pirates by Rajah Brooke, and presented by him to Her Majesty. The barrel is 6 ft. 9 in. long, of which the half (3 ft. 1 in.) nearest the breach is octagonal, and the remainder circular. The diameter at muzzle as far as the trunnions is 5 inches, at breach 9 inches. There is on the barrel a raised floral ornament $\frac{1}{4}$ of an inch in relief in triangular panels of a South Indian character. The touch-hole is heart-shaped. The carriage on which the gun is now placed was made at Woolwich.

NOTE.—*The numbers placed opposite the arms refer to the catalogue.* PLATE I.

187

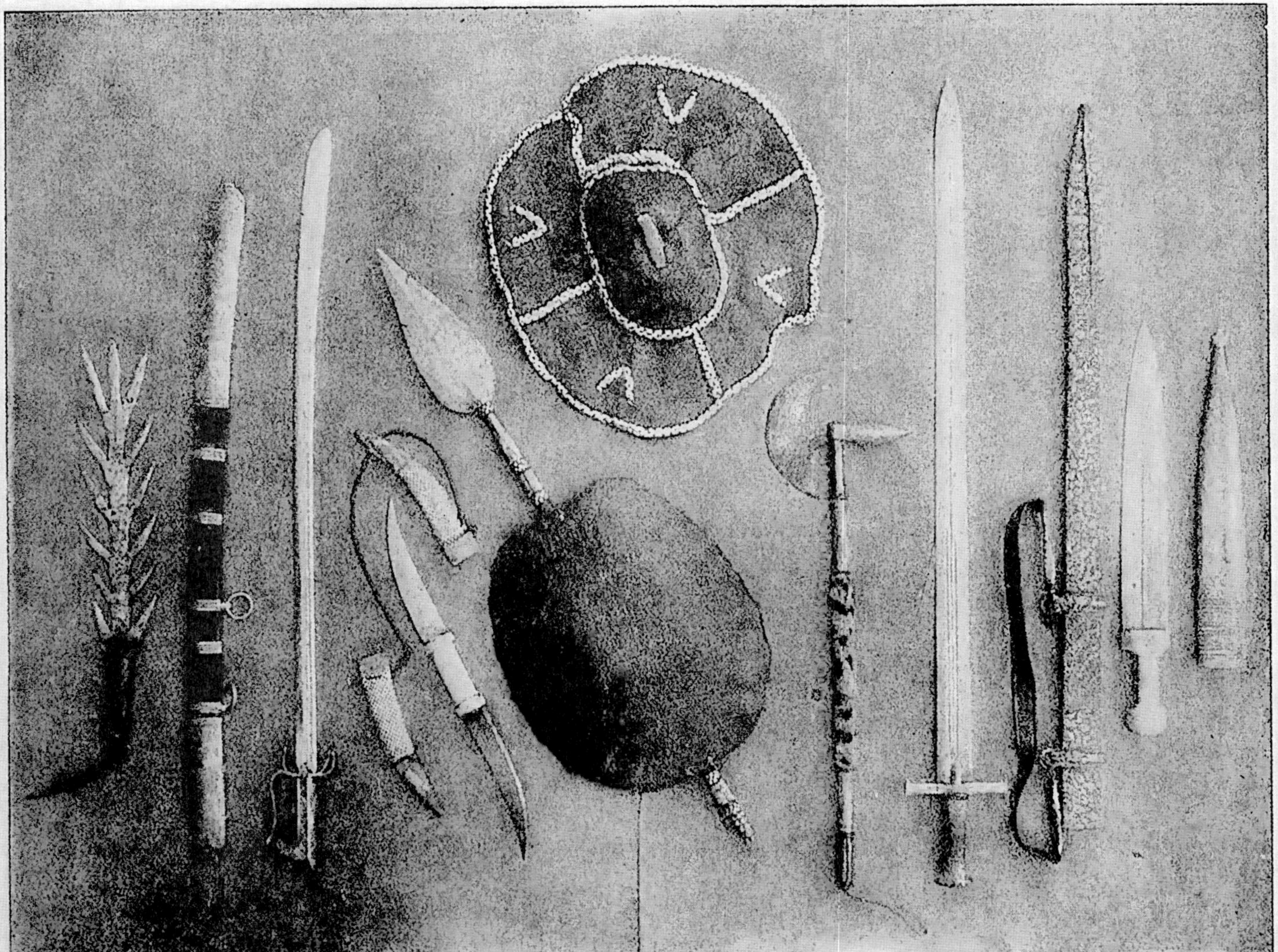

190 194 189 186 193 191 192

GROUP OF ARAB AND SOUDANESE ARMS.

ARAB ARMS.

We have already mentioned how the Arab mercenaries in the service of the Native Courts of Central India brought with them the characteristic dagger "Jambiya," specimens of which are to be seen in our museums with the gold Venetian sequins, nailed into the heavy broad handles, recording the ancient connection of Venice with the East. In a recent visit to Cairo I found these weapons in the bazaars, showing how they had been carried east and west from the shores of Arabia. This leads me, therefore, to mention the characteristics of Arab art as distinguished from that of other countries of the East. The Arabs drew their inspiration for their architecture from the Church of St. Sophia at Constantinople,[1] but the details of their ornaments in their arms and architecture were largely influenced by Persian art. After the conquests of Mahommed and his successors, Saracenic art spread rapidly over Persia, Syria, Egypt, and along the north coast of Africa, as far as Spain, where we find it preserved in the Alhambra, and trace it in the Moorish weapons in the armoury of Madrid.[2]

I propose to confine my remarks to that part of the subject immediately connected with Arabia and Egypt, including the Soudan. We have no authentic arms of the date of the earliest architecture in Cairo of the ninth century, or of the time of Ibn-Tulun, who built himself one of the finest of its mosques and a golden hall.

The Crusaders, in the eleventh and twelfth centuries, came in contact with the Arab troops in Syria and Egypt, and it is said that many of the blades of Arab weapons used in recent wars were handed down from those times. This tradition shows that the keenness of their flexible blades was fully appreciated by their Arab foes. Sir Walter Scott describes Saladin as attracted by the dexterity with which Richard Cœur de Lion wielded his two-handed sword.[3]

In the thirteenth and fourteenth century the Moorish Sultans encouraged art in all its branches. Some, from their martial tastes, were surnamed the "Sword of the Faith," or the "Gunner."

In the reign of Sultan Beybars an Embassy was sent to the Court of Persia taking, among other costly presents,

> "Superb swords with silver hilts, bows from Damascus with silk "strings, pikes of Kana wood with points tempered by the Arabs, "exquisitely fashioned arrows in boxes plated with copper."[4]

Beybars had an important officer called the Silahdar, who carried his lord's armour when he rode out, "a Bedawy sword swung by his side, and a Dawudi cuirass was concealed beneath his vest." "Tabardars carried halberts before

1 Address by Sir H. Howorth, &c., &c., *Archæological Journal*, vol. 51.
2 The latter have already been described in the work, "Armeria Real de Madrid."
3 "The Talisman," p. 291. Ed. 1871.
4 "Art of the Saracens in Egypt." S. Lane-Poole, 1886, p. 28–33.

and behind the Sultan, the State poniards were supported by the 'Polo-master' (Gukandar) in a scabbard on the left, while another dagger with a buckler was carried on the monarch's right."

The chased metal work of Cairo is said by Lane-Poole to have made its first appearance about the end of the last quarter of the thirteenth century, and was brought from Mesopotamia by the Ayubis.

While there is a strong family likeness between Arab and Persian arms, the character of the ornament on Arab arms seems to be different from that of Persian and Indian, in so far as they comply strictly with the law of their religion against the reproduction in art of animate creatures.

The traditions of Persian and Assyrian art have been too strong for the workmen of Mosil and Persia, even when employed in Cairo, and we constantly find animals and sporting scenes, and the combats of animals on the metal work of Cairo as well as Persia. But the Arab swords and daggers with which I am acquainted conform to the general rules of Mahommedan art, and are ornamented either with simple conventional ornaments in plain or twisted plaque work, or are decorated with geometrical cartouches, encircled with floral arabesques, following the patterns used in the mosques and buildings of the best period of Saracenic art.

Lane-Poole, in his admirable work, while he deals with the metal work originating in Persian or Assyrian art which he calls the Mosil style, pointedly omits to mention the Mameluke arms. He seems to think that the armourers of the Arabs in Cairo, during that period, confined themselves to fitting and adapting the weapons and arms of Persia and India, and attributes to a Syrian or Persian origin the arms used in Egypt in mediæval times. Undoubtedly the Damascus blades were largely used by the Arabs, and Arab artificers mounted the European swords, which were much and justly valued in the East when mounted with native hilts and scabbards. But there were fine blades manufactured in Egypt,[1] one is mentioned in the "Armeria Real de Madrid," and I have in my possession one (Catalogue, No. 28) made by Muallein in Egypt, probably in the seventeenth century. At present, certainly, the officials in Cairo and in the Egyptian Army largely use the Turkish scimitar with large pistol-shaped handle. Yet in Zanzibar, where Persian and Indian arms are common, a purely Arab style of hilt is still used, and a large-handled dagger like the "Jambiya."[2] These are mounted in silver or copper and often rudely ornamented with raised work.[3]

The defeat of the Mahdi's Armies and of the Dervishes at Toski in 1889 has brought a good many pure Arab weapons now used in the Soudan into the Bazaars of Assouan and Luxor. The usual sword is a large straight weapon bound round the hilt with silver or brass wire, or more ordinarily with leather thongs and without guard. Some have inscriptions from the Koran engraved on the blades. In the better class of weapons the hilts are of silver with raised arabesque pattern on the grip of the handle and one or more

---

[1] "Spanish Industrial Art Riaño," p. 82. 1879. He mentions Arabic treatise on steel blades in Library of Gotha.

[2] This purely Arab class of weapons is, however, not common in Egypt. The Sirdar of the Egyptian Army, Sir Herbert Kitchener, has two fine specimens in his possession, with silver ornaments.

[3] Those in the Collection of Sir R. Harvey, Bart., from Zanzibar and the neighbouring islands, bear the purely Arab characteristics.

PLATE II.

201
205
204 203 208

202

195

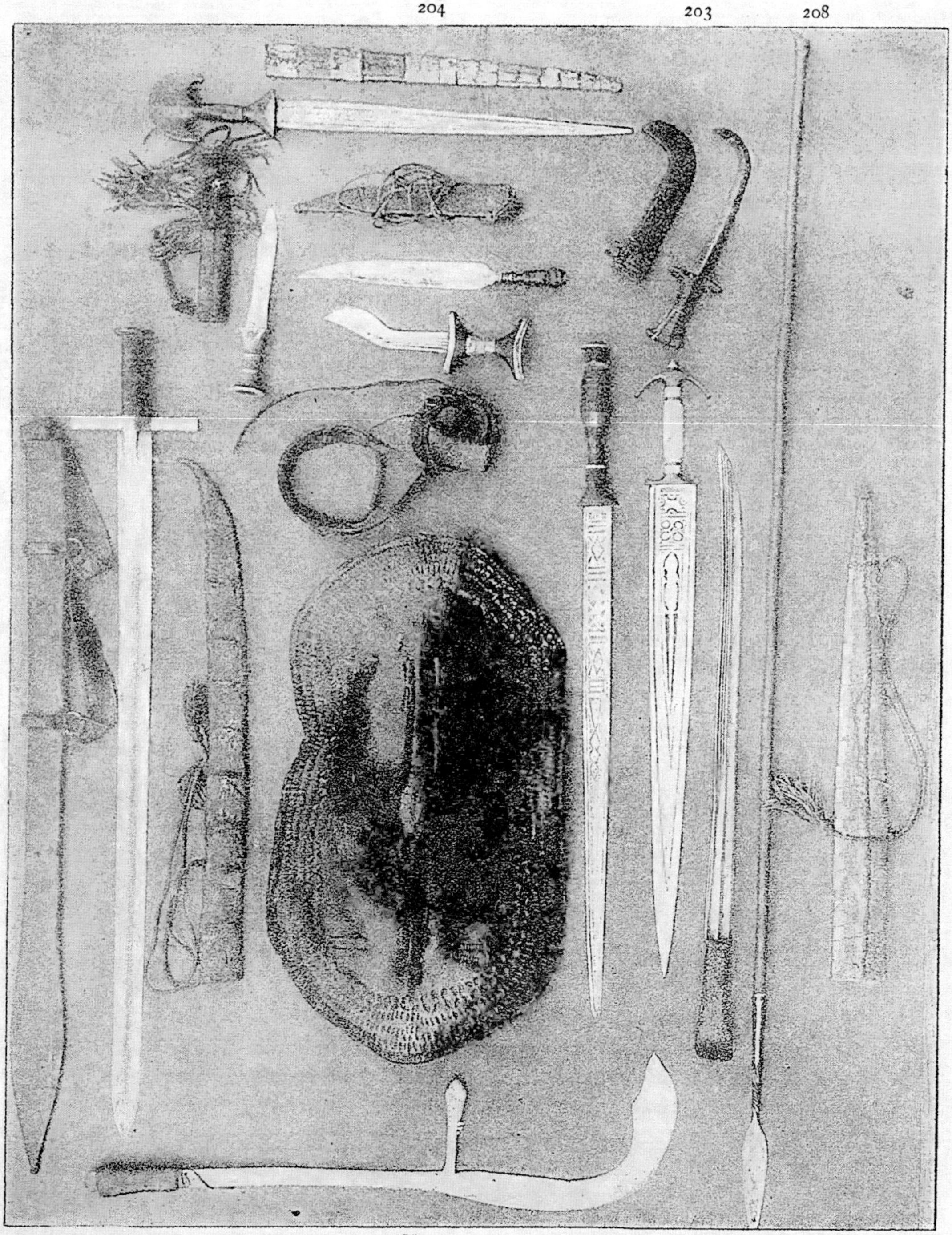

207 188 199 197 198

ARMS OF SOUDAN AND ABYSSINIA.

saucer-shaped pommels above it. In most cases there is a straight crosspiece of steel like a Crusader's sword. The blade is generally flexible, in many cases of Spanish, Italian, or German origin: a wolf or lion is often roughly stamped on it. This may be an old German Solingen mark, but I am assured by Zubeir Pasha that these blades are not, and have not been, manufactured in the Soudan; though some of the European marks have been imitated more or less rudely by native workmen. For instance, a German short sword (Cf. No. 198 in Catalogue) has a Renaissance pattern and figures of the sun and half moon with faces roughly introduced into them. These have evidently been copied and enlarged on another longer blade which has a broad channel down the centre, and has stars and sun and moon with grotesque human faces engraved on them, but without arabesque patterns (Cf. No. 195 in Catalogue).

Weapons vary in character in different parts of the Soudan, but they seem to have been used indiscriminately in the Arab forces of the Dervishes during the wars in the Soudan. Some swords are slightly incurved, like the Turkish "Khanjar," and the hilt terminates in butterfly-shaped ears of the Albanian type. Besides the above a short, curved sword with broad blade is used; some scabbards have raised silver work, while snake and crocodile skins are common. In Dongola we find a long sword-like dagger, the blade tapering to a point, and usually engraved with rude representation of a crocodile, the tail tapering to the point of the weapon. The hilt is made of ivory and ebony and the handle terminates in a crescent-shaped guard of horn curved inwards, and a straight quillon of horn into which the blade is let. This appears to be worn in the girdle, while the long two-handed sword is carried on the left shoulder.[1] In Kordofan a dagger with long horn handle is used, terminating in a half moon curved downwards. The blade is engraved with plain diagonal squares and ovals, and a slight sketch of a crocodile engraved in a very primitive style of art. The sword and dagger with turned ivory handles, and with simple geometrical figures incised, are from Abyssinia.

At Khartoum, incurved daggers are made with plain wooden handles bound with silver plaque work and filigree wire, and a sickle-shaped axe, or sword with points coming out at right angles. The battleaxes and maces, inlaid with patterns in silver wire, are a rude imitation of Persian work. Burckhardt mentions that at Shendy are made the knives, about 8 in. long, and two-edged, which are enclosed in a leather scabbard, and tied over the left elbow (p. 265). He also mentions among the articles of trade with Shendy, sword blades from Solingen, three thousand of which are annually sold at Cairo to the traders from the South (p. 271).

The Arab spear is the usual weapon of the Soudan, both in the shape of the long stabbing spear and the javelin which is thrown; numbers are manufactured for sale to strangers at Assouan, and are of the rudest description—"cheap and nasty." But the best spear-heads are hammered out of a bar of steel, twisted at the base, with a strong and prominent rib running down to a leaf-shaped point.

In the French attack on Egypt in 1799, Denon describes the Arab

[1] See engravings in Father Ohrwalder's "Ten Years' Captivity in the Mahdi's Camp." Plate, pp. 322–7 1893

volunteers from Mecca, who formed the horsemen of the Mameluke forces, as armed with three javelins, a spear, a dagger, two pistols and a carbine. In the Mahdi's army, at the commencement of the revolt, firearms were forbidden, and sticks and lances formed the only arms, thus following in the footsteps of the "Prophet." Before long, Remington rifles were freely used. The Khalifa himself when he reviews his forces wears a suit of mail armour and helmet, and is followed by a body-guard of 200 horsemen, also clad in mail and greaves, their horses protected by brass head pieces.

As a club they use a piece of ebony wood, curved at the end, or a kind of white wood, bound and inlaid with brass wire.

The shields, either circular or oblong, are made of various materials. The Soudanese tribes use hippopotamus hide, either sewn together with iron-wire or shaped and roughly ornamented. One in my collection takes the shape of a long face, of which the nose is formed out of the knee of the animal, and the eyes and mouth are indicated by rough indentations. They are strong enough to resist any sword cut, and are very light. Another, of a pure Arab type, is of transparent leather, boiled, and moulded into a dome shape, covered with inscriptions in Arab letters enriched with flowers, intertwined in duplicate patterns so as, probably, to be read both ways, and enriched with pure floral arabesque gilt on the inner rim, probably from the early part of the seventeenth century.

In the Soudan both iron and silver are manufactured largely, and silver seems to enter into their ornament rather than gold. Burckhardt, in his "Travels" (p. 285), mentions that the common currency of Kordofan is said to be small pieces of iron, which are collected and made into axes and spear-heads.

The Arab guns and pistols which one meets with in the bazaars at Cairo resemble European shapes more than those of India; they are generally with flint and steel locks, and the butt is more in the shape of a Turkish stirrup, broad at the base and gradually narrowing. The ornament on the stock and butt is usually inlaid with floral arabesques in silver wire, and the barrels appear to differ in character, according as they are made in Persia, Bagdad, or Damascus, and they are often inlaid with silver patterns and inscriptions. The pistols are mounted, as the guns, with heavy, rounded butts, often in silver; the barrels terminating in dragon-heads, and are richly inlaid with arabesque patterns in solid silver, hammered in, others have butts like an old English blunderbuss, with open-mouthed barrels.

In the Khedivial Library at Cairo the earliest of the fine manuscripts of the Koran is about the tenth or eleventh century, but it is not until the fifteenth or sixteenth century that in their illuminations Sultans of Turkey and their warriors are depicted. The swords are generally of the Persian scimitar type, while the daggers are of the short, broad-bladed type, and they are probably mostly Turkish or Persian, and not pure Egyptian or Arab.

The shape of the weapons worn by the Arabs may, I think, be traced to a great antiquity. The crescent-shaped termination to the hilt, now used at Dongola, found its exact prototype in the sword and dagger of the twelfth dynasty in the museum at Ghizeh. There the crescent is of lapis lazuli and the hilt a diaper of gold mosaic; then follows the setting of gold from which the bronze blade starts. Another peculiar shape in Arab swords, of the

PLATE III

200

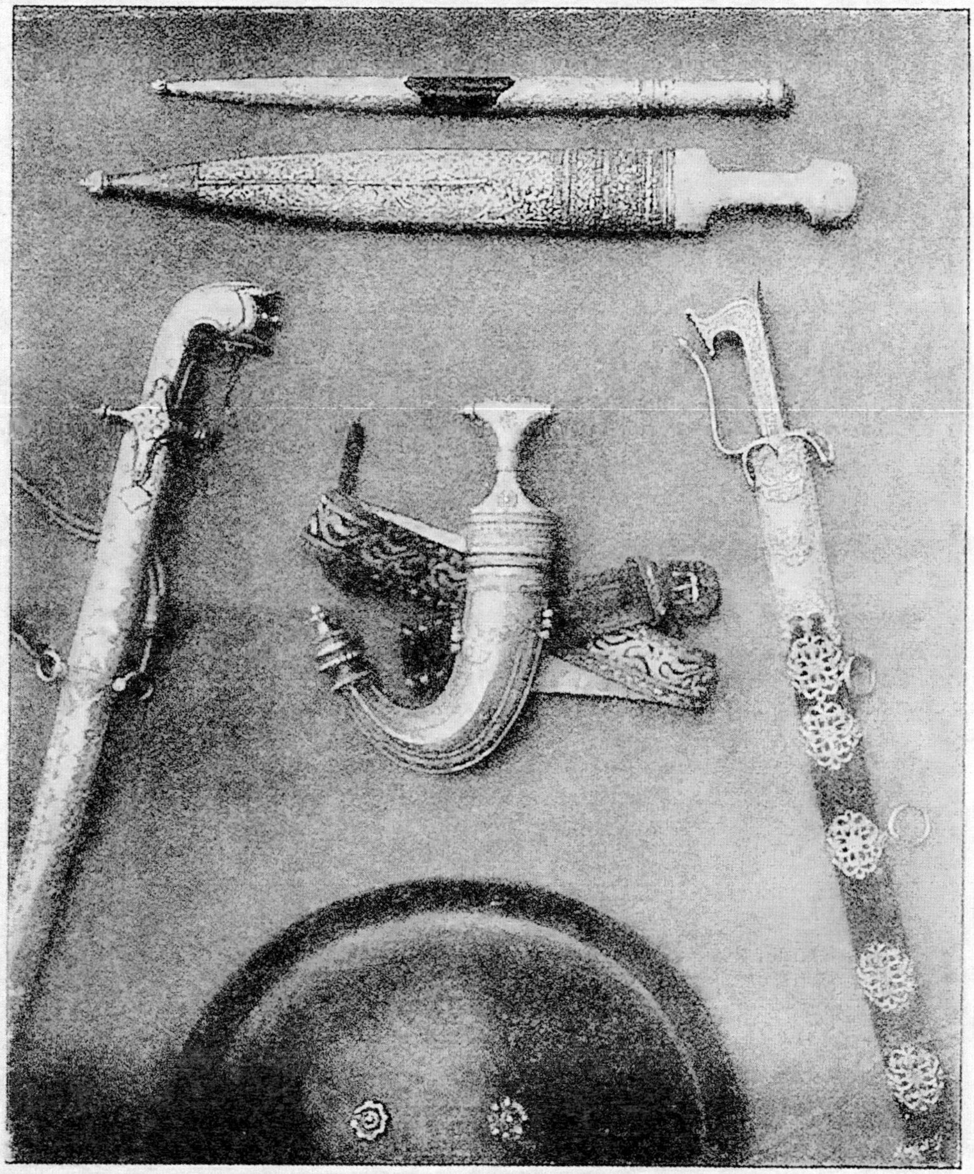

192

196

194

206
209

ARAB DAGGERS AND SWORDS, ETC.

recurved quillons, can again be traced to the ornament of an ancient Egyptian blade in the same Museum, which is a bull's head[1] forming the base of the hilt, and the two recurved horns forming the curved quillon drooping on each side of the blade; and the ancient Egyptian dagger has the blade broad at the base and gradually tapering till it widens to a tongue-shaped point. This shape is also followed in the Abyssinian dagger.

In the collection of Zubeir Pasha there are swords which have been handed down in the Soudan for several centuries. The oldest was a long fluted flexible blade without any mark, but his own name engraved on it. The handle was of arabesque raised silver work ending in a pear-shaped pommel. The other was like it in shape, but much more flexible, as it could almost be bent double; it had inscribed on the blade "Lisboa, 1609," and on the other side a Portuguese inscription in capital letters. They came from the Portuguese Settlements either in Abyssinia or India.

In the collection of Major Wingate, formed of arms taken in action during the Soudan war, besides the straight Soudan swords and those incurved, he had some sickle-shaped swords from the Gallas in West Abyssinia, and others with handles of rhinoceros-horn without guards from Abyssinia. There were also shirts of mail still used in the Soudan, with helmets, some round, some slightly conical, with their mail guards. The mail was usually formed of rings, each riveted like the Stamboul suits of the fifteenth century. The guns were mostly of the flint and steel old Arabian type, as before described, the barrels inlaid with silver-raised Soudan work; one only had the broad native butt shaped like a Turkish stirrup.

The most ancient trophy in the collection was a kettledrum, or noggara,[2] taken in action near Souakim, about two and a half feet in diameter, and covered with various raised inscriptions in Arabic, the oldest about 800 years old. The flags captured at Toski were sacred banners from some of the mosques. The shields, of hippopotamus hide, were of various shapes.

There is no public collection of Arab arms at Cairo, and the Armourers' Bazaar no longer contains anything of antiquity, so that it will be more difficult to collect any when the arms which were used in the Soudan war are dispersed from the bric-à-brac dealers in Cairo and Assouan. It is with the object of calling attention to this want, which might now be supplied, that these notes, collected during two winters spent in Egypt, are added to the description of the other branches of Oriental arms.

[1] The god Apis. Notice des principaux Monuments Exposes au Musée de Ghizeh Mariette, p. 212, 1892. Cf. "Egyptian Archæology," p. 318, fig. 294, Maspero, 1889.

[2] The Mahdi had war drums made of brass, called naba, while the ordinary drums made of wood were called noggara.—Ohrwalder.

COLLECTION OF ORIENTAL ARMOUR AND WEAPONS

FORMED BY LORD EGERTON OF TATTON, AND NOW HUNG IN THE ARMOURY, TATTON PARK.

ABBREVIATIONS.—(Ham. Coll.), formed by Colonel Hamilton after the siege of Delhi. The place where the arms were acquired is mentioned, except in the case of London or Paris, and the name of the Donor.

PART I.

ARMOUR, MATCHLOCKS, &c.

1. SUIT OF SIKH MAIL; consisting of hood, shirt, and trousers, steel and brass links, forming diaper pattern. (*Lahore*, 1855.)

2. PLATE HELMET; with coarse chain mail neck screen, of which each link is riveted. Persian inscription on helmet. (*Ham. Coll.*)

3. SIKH HELMET; richly inlaid with gold, and fine chain mail neck screen. (*Lahore*, 1855.)

4. SIKH HELMET; with inscription, finely damascened steel, with fine chain mail neck screen. (*Ham. Coll.*)

5. SIKH HELMET; formed of alternate links of plate and chain mail. (*Ham. Coll.*)

6. PLATE ARMOUR; four pieces with raised steel pattern, the front and back pieces have been jewelled. (*Ham. Coll.*)

7. PLATE ARMOUR; four pieces, damascened steel, borders richly inlaid with gold. (*Ham. Coll.*)

8. GAUNTLETS; plain steel. (*Ham. Coll.*)

9. GAUNTLETS (belonging to Khurruck Singh); finely damascened steel, rich gold borders, with gloves of fine chain mail, lined with velvet. (*Lahore*, 1855.)

10. GAUNTLETS; larger pair. (*Ham Coll.*)

11. SHIELD (1 ft. 9½ in. diameter); rhinoceros hide, black, with four engraved silver and parcel gilt bosses. (*Delhi*, 1855.)

12. SHIELD (1 ft. 2½ in. diameter); boiled rhinoceros skin, transparent, with four gilt bosses, and gilt patterns painted on it. (*Indian Museum*) *Bombay.*

13. SMALL SHIELD; with two daggers from the handle. Four bosses, 8 in. in diameter, pattern engraved in brass on steel. (*Delhi*, 1855.)

14. SHIELD; probably from Rajpootana, fine damascened steel. Four gilt bosses and patterns inlaid with gold, the external rim of raised work, lined with velvet, embroidered with gold (1 ft. 8½ in. diameter). (*Delhi.*)

15. SHIELD (SIKH) (1 ft. 6 in. diameter); finely damascened steel, with richly inlaid gold border and animals. The four centre bosses are gilt lizards with ruby eyes. The centre is a disc representing the sun, with human face. (*Ham. Coll.*)

16. STEEL DISK; worn by the Akalees in their head-dress on the pointed roll of their turban. (*Ham. Coll.*)

17. STEEL DISK; both sides richly inlaid with floriated patterns on one side, and with the arms of Col. Hamilton on the other side, and his name inscribed in Persian. (*Ham. Coll.*)

18. MATCHLOCKS; pair of them, from Bundelcund. Barrels 3 ft. 8 in. and 4 ft. each long, lotus-shaped muzzle. (*Ham. Coll.*)

19. MATCHLOCK; from the Punjaub. Barrel 4 ft. 1 in. (*Ham. Coll.*)

20. MATCHLOCK; from the Punjaub. Fine Damascus barrel, 3 ft 8 in. long, with engraved silver mounts and partly inlaid with gold and silver gilt butt. (*Ham. Coll.*)

21. MATCHLOCK; Afghan. Fine barrel inlaid with gold. 3 ft. 8 in. long. (*Ham. Coll.*)

22. MATCHLOCK; with engraved silver butt and silver mounts, fine steel barrel from Afghanistan. 3 ft. 2 in. long. (*Ham. Coll.*)

22a. LONG GUN. Barrel 5 ft. 4 in. long, with short stock, 11 in., with Malay, Indian, and Chinese ornaments, made probably at Bali, with Javanese inscription on brass spring of the trigger. (*Guthrie Coll.*)

23. MATCHLOCK. Fine steel barrel, 3 ft. 4 in. long, gilt mounts, dragon-headed muzzle. Stock inlaid with geometrical patterns in ivory. (*R. Cholmondeley.*)

24. MATCHLOCK. Square barrel circular bore, 3ft. 7 in. long, the breech and muzzle richly inlaid with geometrical patterns in gold. The butt carved and lacquered and richly painted with flowers, fruit, and figures of men and animals. Probably from Central India. Old. (*R. Cholmondeley.*)

25. BLUNDERBUSS; bell-mouthed, fine steel barrel, 1 ft. long, flint and steel lock, and butt, imitation of European work. Made in Cashmere. (*Ham. Coll.*)

PERSIAN SWORDS.

26. SCIMITAR; Persian dress, sword, with waved edges, gilt and inlaid with silver and gold patterns, with inscription and date 18th century. The blade 2 ft. 11 in., long. Pistol-shaped handle, 6 in. long, The scabbard of green velvet with wavy pattern of gold and silver, inlaid work running along it. (*Beyrout.*)

27. SCIMITAR (Khorassan); blade of finely damascened steel 2 ft. 8 in. long. The hilt is without a guard, with flat circular pommel. The whole richly inlaid in gold with flowers. The scabbard

15

14

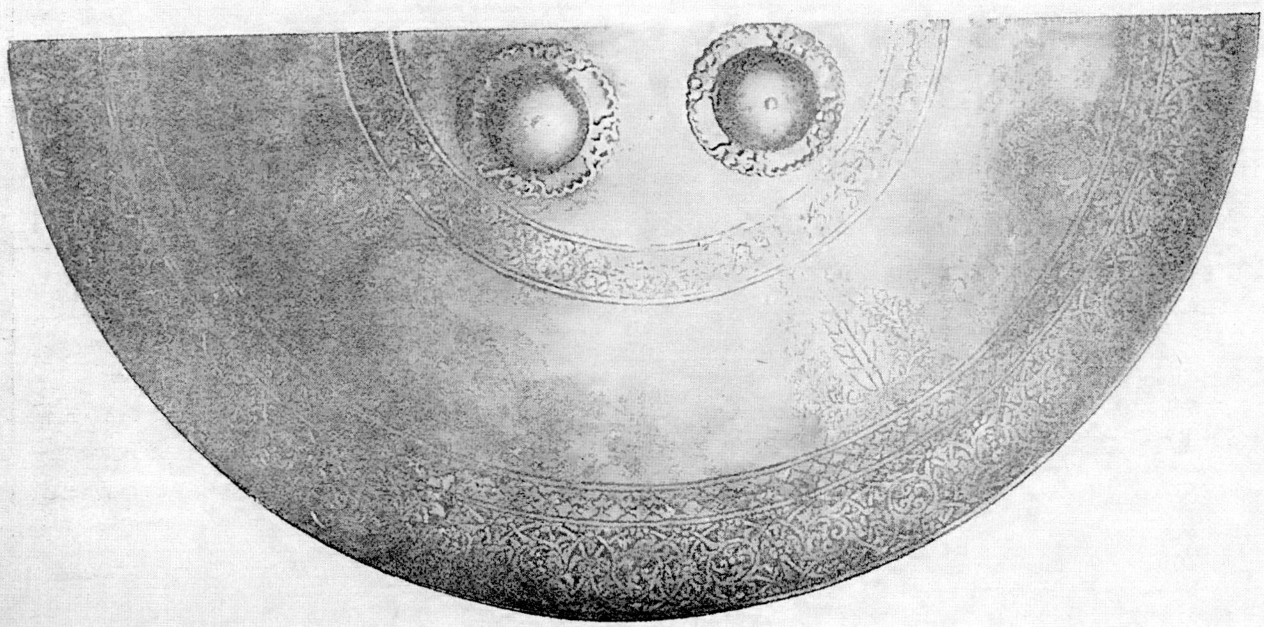

SHIELDS.

of red velvet with the end richly inlaid with gold similar to the hilt, on the blade a Persian inscription. (*Bought.*)

28. Sword; from Afghanistan with Khorassan blade, and long Persian inscription :—"Shah Abbas, Shah Taherasp, Shah Ismail; made in Egypt by Muallein."

29. Sword; hilt of ivory with silver niello mounts, terminating in acorn-shaped boss, inlaid with patterns of birds and flowers. Blade, 2 ft. 5⅛ in. long. Curved and channelled. (*Bought.*)

30. Dress Sword; curved scimitar shaped, 3 ft. 1 in. long; blade, 2 ft. 8 in. Blade covered with panels of arabesque work, with quotation from the Koran, between a narrow border of silver damascened work running down the edge. (*Bought; modern work.*)

31. Sword; 2 ft. 11½ in. long; blade, 2 ft. 5½ in. Processional sword with blunt end. Waving serpent runs down the centre of the blade; near the hilt is the usual Persian badge of the rising sun and lion across it, rising from scrolls of arabesque foliage. The hilt is of steel, inlaid with fine lines of arabesque in gold. The quillons terminate in two scrolls curved downwards. (*Bought; modern work.*)

Indian Swords, Daggers, Knives, &c.

32. Tulwar; blade, 2 ft. 6 in. long; from Cashmere. Hilt without knuckle-guard. Raised geometrical patterns chiselled in six compartments on each side of blade, containing representations of Hindoo deities, "Hanuman, Krishnah, and Ganesh." On reverse side are elephants and tigers fighting and pursuing a man on horseback. (*Bought, modern.*)

33. Curved Sword; hilt without guard; blade, 2 ft. 2 in. long, with two-edged point, 1⅞ in. wide. Blade finely damascened on one side and polished on the other, with inscription on the blade and on the back in gold. Handle ornamented with raised flowers in Bidree work. Scabbard of green shagrin leather with silver mounts used by Mahrattas. (*Delhi.*)

34. Straight Sword; 2 ft. 3 in. long, triangular point, double-edged. Made of finely damascened steel, strengthened both sides with scolloped pattern of raised work in steel inlaid with gold. Hilt has a heavy guard and curved pommel. The whole richly inlaid with flowers in gold. Scabbard terminates in a crescent-shaped ornament, inlaid with flowers in gold, probably used by Rajpoots. (*Delhi.*)

35. Tulwar; blade, 2 ft. 7½ in. long, fluted and two-edged at the point. Hilt, richly inlaid with patterns in gold. Pommel, flat and circular. Guard terminates in the head of a monster. (*Presented by Futtenarain Singh at Benares*)

36. Sword (from Bundelcund). Polished steel blade, 2 ft. 7½ in. Inscription on back of blade. Hilt, with raised floral pattern on it, gilt all over; with light guard. Scabbard of velvet, with silver gilt mounts. (*Ham. Coll.*)

37. Sword (from Bundelcund); blade, 2 ft. 8½ in.; two-edged at point; fluted down the centre. The hilt, richly ornamented with embossed silver patterns in a diaper of chevron and quatrefoils. Guard, similar to the one previously described. (*Ham. Coll.*)

38. Sword (from Bundelcund); blade, 2 ft. 8¾ in.; two-edged at the point, double grooved down the centre. Hilt, without guard, terminating in a parrot's head, and covered with coarse pattern of flowers, cut out in steel and gilt. (*Ham. Coll.*)

39. Sword; nearly straight. Blade, 2 ft. 7¾ in. long, slightly curved at the point, and double-edged, two grooves down the centre. Inscription in Roman characters. The hilt, bronze, which appears to have been partly gilt. Broad guard, of a half-basket shape, of pierced work. The quillons of the hilt are formed of two monsters, whose tails curl over and strengthen the tang of the sword. The pommel ends in a point 4 in. long. (*Codrington Coll.*)

40. Curved Sword (probably from Sind). Two-edged at the point. Blade, 2 ft. 10½ in. long, and finely damascened with a pattern called Mahomet's ladder. The hilt, rudely ornamented and gilt; and short curved pommel. (*Lewis Coll.*)

41. Sword; blade, 2 ft. 5½ in. long, 1½ in. wide, covered on both sides with Arabic inscription from the Koran, in raised letters on polished steel. The hilt, nearly plain, with twisted guard and saucer-like shield to pommel. The Arabic inscription is, "In everything there is speedy victory from God;" "God is the best of Protectors;" "O, God, have mercy. O, Defender. O, Protector;" &c. (*Lewis Coll.*)

42. Sword; fine Damascus blade, 2 ft. 6½ in. long, nearly straight. Hilt, without guard, and covered with diaper of raised silver quatrefoils, and chevron pattern at the side. (*Ham. Coll.*)

43. Scimitar; with heavy blade of finely damascened steel. 2 ft. 9¼ in. long. The quillons of the hilt, 5 in. across, terminating in floriated points inlaid with gold. Pommel, composed of tiger's head carved in ivory. Persian inscription on blade. Probably comes from Seringapatam at the time of Tippoo Sahib. End of the scabbard of metal gilt, with raised figures of tigers, antelopes, &c. (*Bought at Davis'.*)

44. Sword; blade, 2 ft. 9½ in. long. Heavy two-edged, from Scinde. Broad groove running up centre. Gold inscription in Persian. Hilt, plain, and gilt. Silver tag at end of pommel. Scabbard, richly embroidered in leather, the ends encased in silver, richly carved in rel[illegible]n flower patterns. A small damascened knife and silver sheath fit into upper part of scabbard. Belt of embroidered leather, with silver clasps and buckles. Translation of Persian inscription shows it belonged to an Ameer of Sind, "Sakar Mir Mahomet Ali Murad Khan Talpur Sahib, 'Bahadur,'" who lived 1848. (*Lewis Coll.*)

45. Sword; gold mounted hilt; blade 2 ft. 9 in. long, with double points 9 in. long. Serrated edges; on both sides inscription, probably name of Rajpoot chief on the blade, from Rajpootana.

Scabbard of green velvet with fine mounts of pure embossed gold. (*Guthrie Coll.*)

46. SWORD; two-handed with European flexible blade, 3 ft. 3. in. long. Handle 21½ in. with brass knobs. (*Ham. Coll.*)

47. SWORD; nearly similar blade, 3 ft. 2 in. long. Handle, 21½ in. with fluted brass knobs. (*Ham. Coll.*)

48. SWORD; blade 37½ in. long. Gauntlet 12 in., with brass mounts and bells. (*Ham. Coll.*)

49. SWORD; similar to the last. Blade 36½ in. long. Gauntlet 11½ in. long. (*Ham. Coll.*)

50. SWORD; "Raven's Beak," from siege of Delhi. Steel handle 17 in. long. Broad blade, and curved, 21½ in. long, 2¾ in. wide, gradually tapering at the end. (*Ham. Coll.*)

51. SWORD STICK; blade 33 in. long. Three stars marked on blade. Handle and sheath of teak. Tho whole 39½ in. long. (*Ham. Coll.*)

52. BROAD SWORD; blade slightly curved 30 in. long. Two deep grooves and inscription. Handle of silver without guard, with finely traced floral pattern. Hilt terminates in a nearly flat circular shield. Scabbard of green shagrin, with richly engraved silver mounts. (*Ham. Coll.*)

53. BROAD SWORD; curved, and two-edged at point, 30 in. long. Hilt of steel with raised floral pattern. Guard terminates in a raised tiger's head. The shield of the hilt is nearly flat. (*Ham. Coll.*)

54. STRAIGHT SWORD; blade 29 in. long. Handle of steel, a continuation of blade with square edges and plain steel knuckleguard. (*Ham. Coll.*)

55. STRAIGHT SWORD; European blade, 39 in. long. Star and two half-circles on each side of blade. Hilt of brass with raised work. Broad finger-guard, with figures of elephants, tigers, antelopes and bulls in combat. The rhinoceros is charged by a tiger, and two disks on his body signify that his hide is used for shields. Quillons terminate in lotos flowers, also the pommel, which is slightly curved. (*Delhi*, 1855.)

56. GAUNTLET SWORD; blade 39 in. long. Gauntlet 13 in. European blade with part of inscription remaining. Gauntlet is of iron, plated with silver. It is partly pierced like basket work, and partly with embossed floral pattern. Probably from South India. (*Lewis Coll.*)

57. GAUNTLET SWORD; broad blade 38 in. long. Very flexible; European. Gauntlet 12½ in. plated with silver. In handle are figures of Hanuman kneeling on one knee, and in gauntlet are figures of dragons and birds intermingled with foliage in high relief. Armguard of gauntlet is jointed in three pieces with a raised rose in each. Probably Mahratta. (*Lewis Coll.*)

58. SWORD; short straight blade 16 in. long, hilt 5¼ in. long. Terminates in a crutch shape, from which proceeds a narrow guard of silver. The scabbard is of shagrin leather with silver mounts. The tip terminating in a square tassel of silver.

Called the "Cushion of Victory," used after a battle when long sword is taken off, and the short sword is used to lean on when seated cross-legged. (*Ham. Coll.*)

59. BROAD SWORD; two-edged; blade 33 in. long. The point increases in size towards the end to 2½ in., and gradually tapers off in an ogee shape. A richly engraved band runs 14 in. up blade, the centre of which is diapered with a band of flowers on each side, on a ground of red lacquer. Hilt richly inlaid with patterns in gold. The quillons terminate in flowers inlaid with diamonds and rubies. Thumb-guard contains representations of various animals and landscapes with buildings. The guard is inlaid with rubies and diamonds. The pommel is curved, and projects 3 in. The scabbard is on one side of red and the other of green velvet, embroidered with gold. Cf. p. 70, fig. 14. (*Lewis Coll.*)

60. STRAIGHT SWORD; 38 in. long. Probably Spanish or Portuguese blade. On one side a part of an inscription remains, "Iro," with a cross on a globe. On the other side a date, 1634, with a helmet and plume above it. On back of blade an inscription in Nagari, translated by Captain Eastwick to be the names of a ruler of Nagpore in 1755, of the Bhonslee family, "Shrimat Janagi Bhonsle sena Sahib." The hilt is covered all over with a floral diaper in gold. The guard and thumb-guard are 2 in. broad. The spike of the pommel is 4 in. long. The shield of the pommel is saucer-shaped. The blade is strengthened by a portion of the hilt projecting 4 in. beyond the tang of the blade. (*Lewis Coll.*)

61. LONG SWORD; straight blade, 42½ in. long of elastic steel; European workmanship. Handle like that of a claymore, with broad guard. Pommel rises 1½ in., and terminates in a ball. The whole is of iron, which has been plated with silver. Cf. p. 65, fig. 11. (*Codrington Coll.*)

62. GAUNTLET SWORD; with open guard going up to the elbow; 46 in. long; blade, 32 in., of flexible steel; European workmanship. Stars and crosses on the blade. The hilt is formed of steel, plated with brass, and enriched with tigers, elephants, and heads of monsters, and raised floral decorations in the centre. Cf. p. 55, fig. 9. (*Lewis Coll.*)

63. LONG SWORD; rapier blade, 44 in. long, of elastic steel; European workmanship. The handle is : wrought iron, and runs 8 in. down the blade, riveted in tongue-shape. The hilt is 9 in. long, and is composed of a succession of iron plates, with wrought iron ornaments, which protect the hand, without guarding the knuckles. The inside of the hilt is covered with raised patterns in iron. The quillons of the side terminate in points. Probably an old Indian weapon from Seringapatam (*Codrington Coll.*)

64. SHORT SWORD; straight blade, 28 in. in length, of finest Indian steel, 2½ in. broad at the hilt, gradually tapering to the point. Handle of wrought-iron, 6½ in. long without guard. Crescent shaped quillons, and riveted on to the blade with a tongue-shaped ornament. The hilt is grooved with a series of rings, and the pommel

PLATE V.

148 51 140 144 111 65 154 152 153 151 155 113 137 136 55 149

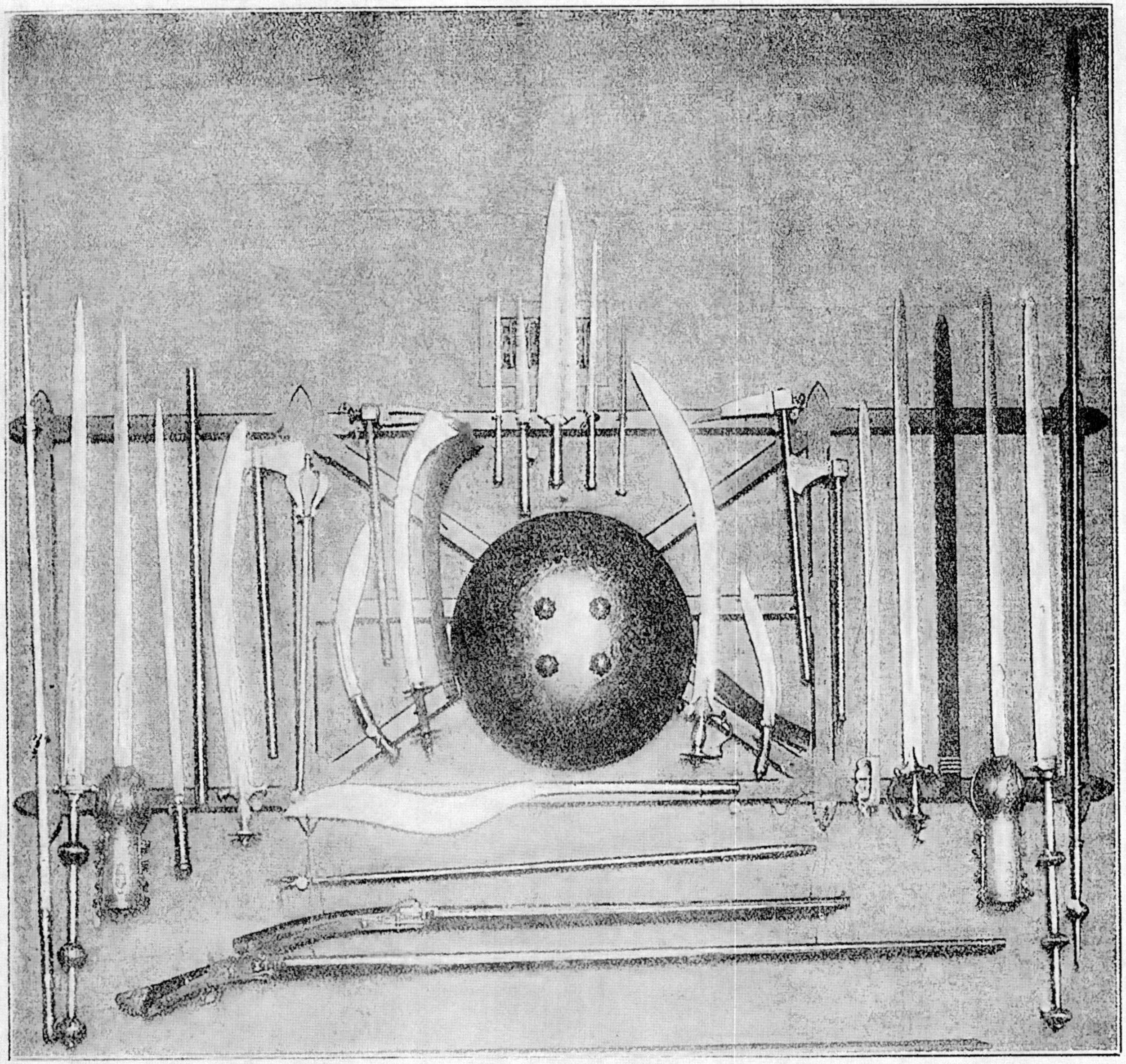

46 48 22*a* 52 147 175 138 50 11 53 54 49 47

INDIAN SWORDS,
SPEARS AND AXES.

is short with four wrought-iron ear-shaped projections. Cf. p. 65, fig. 12. (*Lewis Coll.*)

65. NEPAULESE SWORD; blade $22\frac{1}{2}$ in., curved at the end; the handle, 6 in. long, with gilt pattern on steel. (*Delhi*, 1855.)

66. CINGALESE SWORD; blade $17\frac{1}{2}$ in. Handle and scabbard of tortoise-shell. Hilt terminates in monster's head, from which a smaller dragon's head forms the guard, holding a tassel in his mouth. Below this a small seated figure of Buddha. Serpent heads from quillons. A raised floral pattern runs down scabbard, proceeding out of a monster's mouth.
(*Sir Emerson Tennant's Sale, to whom it is said to have been presented by a native chief.*)

67. SWORD; probably from the Malabar Coast; 34 in. long including the hilt; blade $26\frac{1}{2}$ in. long. Sharpened on curved inner edge; strengthened near the hilt with raised and engraved steel work of an architectural character. The guard of the hilt is movable, and composed of steel and a square cushion of wood. The pommel is encircled by two loose rings of twisted steel. A Nair sword, described in Catalogue, p. 80, fig. 18.
(*Meyrick Coll., No.* 1136.)

68. SWORD; 2 ft. long; hilt $5\frac{3}{4}$ in. long. Blade curved upwards, and chased with elaborate floral pattern on both sides. Hilt in raised brass work. Scabbard with rich floriated brass work in relief.
(*Colonial Exhibition; from Sind.*)

69. SWORD; with plain blade.

69a. SHORT SWORD; with wooden hilt, bound with bands of fine silver wire. Sword let in to wooden sheath, which covers only one side. Two silver bands (ornamented) encircle it showing the blade on one side. End of scabbard enriched with fine silver filigree work inlaid with turquoises, stretching about 2 in. beyond end of blade, and terminating in a segment of a circle, 1 ft. 11 in. long; blade, 1 ft. $5\frac{1}{2}$ in. long.
(*From Bhotan or Nepalese Frontier.*)

69b. STRAIGHT SWORD; blade 2 ft. 4 in., common wrought-iron hilt. Circular guard. From Khatmandu, Nepal. (*A. Heber Percy.*)

70. AFGHAN KNIFE; blade, $16\frac{1}{2}$ in. long, of fine watered steel, and inlaid with gold floral pattern near the handle. The handle is partly of steel, inlaid with gold and walrus-horn, made at Jellallabad. (*Peshawur*, 1855.)

71. AFGHAN KNIFE; blade, $17\frac{1}{2}$ in. long, of polished steel, inlaid with gold and silver Arabesque ornament for 5 in. from the hilt on both sides. The handle is of brass and of horn. (*Ham. Coll.*)

72. AFGHAN KNIFE; blade, $23\frac{1}{2}$ in. long. Handle of brass and horn, $6\frac{1}{2}$ in. long. (*Ham. Coll.*)

73. AFGHAN KNIFE; blade $18\frac{1}{2}$ in. long. Handle of ivory and brass, $5\frac{1}{2}$ in. long. (*Ham. Coll.*)

74. KHYBER KNIFE; blade, $23\frac{1}{2}$ in. long. Handle, $5\frac{1}{2}$ in. long, of brass and horn. Sheath with brass mounts. (*Ham. Coll.*)

75. KHYBER KNIFE; blade 26 in. long; handle 6 in., of brass and horn. Sheath with brass mounts.
(*Peshawur*, 1855.)

76. ASSAMESE DAO; blade 23 in. long, square at the end, $2\frac{1}{2}$ in. broad, at the hilt $1\frac{1}{2}$ in. Handle is 6 in. long, made of brass and bamboo, bound with twisted cane. (*Bought.*)

76a. ASSAMESE DAO (from Angami Nagas); blade triangular, 10 in. long, 4 in. broad; tufts of red hair dyed, hanging from handle, 17 in. long, representing number of slain enemies. (*Bought.*)

77. COORG KNIFE; blade $13\frac{1}{2}$ in. long, $3\frac{3}{4}$ in. wide; back of blade inlaid with brass. Handle, $8\frac{1}{2}$ in. long, of ebony, with richly-engraved brass work inlaid on it, and some of the interstices filled up with red lacquer. (*Pritchett's Coll.*)

78. COORG KNIFE; blade $14\frac{1}{2}$ in long; back of blade inlaid with silver border. Handle $8\frac{1}{4}$ in. long, and made of ebony richly inlaid with bands of silver work. (*Pritchett's Coll.*)

79. COORG OR MOPLAH KNIFE; used as a bill for clearing jungle; blade curved, 15 in. long, and $3\frac{1}{2}$ in. in the widest part. Engraved pattern runs along back of blade, and where the blade runs into the hilt. There is an inscription on the blade. Handle 7 in. long, with square silver mounts where it is connected with the blade. Handle of ivory, with angles taken off at the grip. Base of handle is heart-shaped, let into engraved silver mounts. Hitched into brass or iron ring fixed in a belt at back of wearer. (*Lewis Coll.*)

80. COORG KNIFE; blade 7 in. long; pistol-shaped handle $4\frac{1}{4}$ in. long. Coarse steel. Sheath of teak wood mounted in silver in narrow strips showing wood between. It has a hook to attach it to the belt and a massive silver chain and tassel, from which two silver chains hang, terminating in a bunch of steel instruments.
(*Exhibited at Vienna*, 1873. *Bought.*)

81. SCYTHE-SHAPED WEAPON; rudely-engraved wooden handle, bound with iron. From Tinnevelli or Coorg. Blade 1 ft. 6 in., whole 2ft. 7 in.

82. CINGALESE KNIFE; carved wood and brass handle; length 1 ft., blade $7\frac{1}{2}$ in. Ancient work.

83. DHA, 2 ft. 5 in. long, blade 1 ft. 7 in.; fine brass; teak sheath and handle, bound with bands of brass; blade of metal, probably fine yellow bronze. Said to have belonged to Thebaw, King of Burmah. (*Bought. From Mandelay.*)

84. DAGGER; curved blade $8\frac{1}{2}$ in. long, grooved down the centre. Handle of green jade, pistol-shaped, inlaid with a star of mother-o'-pearl.
(*Ham. Coll.*)

85. DAGGER; blade $10\frac{1}{2}$ in. long, two-edged, grooved down the centre, curved upwards, mounted with brass. Pistol-shaped handle of ribbon jasper.
(*Ham. Coll.*)

86. KNIFE; blade $10\frac{1}{2}$ in. long, turning upwards. Steel handle $4\frac{1}{2}$ in. long, with curved end of green jade, inlaid with ivory and stars of mother-o'-pearl on red lacquer. (*Ham. Coll.*)

87. DAGGER; straight two-edged blade, 10 in. long, of fine laminated steel in large wavy pattern. Handle, with guard, $5\frac{1}{2}$ in. long, with pistol-shaped handle. (*Ham. Coll.*)

87a. **Knife**; incurved blade 13½ in. long; two grooves. Handle of horn, 5 in. From Khatmandu, Nepal.

88. **Knife**; straight blade 8 in. long, gradually tapering to point. Made in Cashmere, of finely-twisted steel, in imitation of the "Jowher" or Damascus watering. It was made to order for me to replace a blade broken in cutting up a bear. Handle of steel, coated with dark green jade; at the end is a silver ring, with short silver chain and tassels. Sheath tipped with silver. (*Presented; Benares*).

89. **Knife**; blade 9¼ in. long, tapering to point, of polished steel. Handle of steel, inlaid with green jade. (*Ham. Coll.*)

90. **Knife**; blade 9 in. long, of finely-watered steel, gradually curving to the point. Handle, 5 in. long, is octagonal, of brass inlaid with jade, ivory, and mother-o'-pearl, on red and black lacquer in stripes. Grip of handle gradually curves till it terminates in an animal's head of light green jade. (*Ham. Coll.*)

91. **Dagger** (Katár); blade 14 in. long, formed of end of European sword, handle terminating in animals richly carved in steel relief. Guard of pierced steelwork, richly ornamented. South Indian. (*Bought.*)

92. **Dagger** "Scorpion" (Bichwa); curved blade, 6 in. long, of finely-watered steel. Handle of steel, with knuckle-guard 4 in. long. (*Ham. Coll.*)

93. **Dagger**; with waving blade 8½ in. long. Handle curved, with knuckle-guard for left hand 3¾ in. long. (*Ham. Coll.*)

94. **Knife**; blade, 10¼ in. long, of finely-watered steel, inlaid with gold near hilt. Handle of ivory, coloured green, mounted with steel, inlaid with gold. Scabbard of black leather, with ornamental silver mounts. (*Ham. Coll.*)

95. **Delhi Knife**; blade 14¼ in. long, tapering finely to point, of the finest Damascus water, with the bars known as Mahomet's ladder running up it. Hilt of engraved silverwork. Handle, 5 in. long, of solid ivory. Scabbard of green shagrin leather, with silver mounts, richly engraved with floral patterns. (*Ham. Coll.*)

96. **Knife** (from South India); blade 6½ in. long; whole length 11¼ in. Cutting part of the blade 4½ in. long; slightly curved, with an inlaid gold pattern running down side nearest back; the rest encrusted with embossed silver, which is let into handle. This is of carved wood, pistol-shaped, and inlaid with silver. A griffin's head of chased brass, inlaid with silver, strengthens the junction of the blade and the hilt. The scabbard is of teak wood 9½ in. long; the point covered for 3 in. with embossed brasswork, and the upper end covered with a sheet of pure silver, bound round with silver wire in delicate filagree patterns, 4¼ in. long. (*Holt Coll.*)

97. **Knife** (from Burmah); blade, 7½ in. long; handle, 5¾ in. long, of bamboo, covered with a thin silver plate, and bound with silver wire. The usual lotos-shaped ornament terminates it. The scabbard is a piece of bamboo, cut off square at the end, and covered with silver like the handle. (*Bought.*)

98. **Dagger** (from Damascus); blade grooved down centre of fine damascened steel, 9 in. long, inlaid with gold near the hilt. Handle of fine steel inlaid with gold in Arabesque patterns, 4½ in. long. Scabbard 11¾ in. long, with steel mounts inlaid with gold. (*Bought at Beyrout*, 1856.)

99. **Delhi Knife**; 11½ in. long; handle of clear rock crystal 4½ in. long. The blade is of the finest damascened work. Green velvet sheath, with elaborate floral silver mounts. (*Bought.*)

100. **Persian Dagger**; 11 in. long. Hilt and scabbard of finest white and blue enamel, with raised flowers in gold and various colours. The blade is of very fine damascened work, with the Bedouh or talismanic square upon it; 6½ in. long. (See page 53.) Probably made in Persia or in Sind. (*Bought.*)

101. **Dagger** (from Damascus); curved blade, 10½ in. long, of finely-damascened steel, with Arabic inscription, inlaid in gold near hilt. Handle, 5 in. long, of steel inlaid with gold. Sheath, 13½ in. long, with steel mounts inlaid with gold. (*Bought at Beyrout*, 1856.)

101a. **Dagger**; curved blade, 12½ in. long, fine Damascus or Persian. Handle, 5 in. long, with Persian inscriptions .Sheath, 13½ in. long, covered with a rich floral diaper in gold, gradually tapering to the point. (*From the Sultan's Collection, Constantinople.*)

102. **Dagger** (Katár); blade, 9½ in. long; double groove down the centre of finely-watered steel. The handle is in the shape of an H, of silver, with an engraved floral pattern. The sheath is mounted with silver engraved to match. (*Ham. Coll.*)

103. **Dagger**; with short curved blade 7½ in. long. Handle 5 in. long, inlaid with Bidree work in floral patterns. Sheath of red velvet and Bidree work. (*Bought.*)

104. **Dagger**; with short curved blade, double-pointed, 9 in. long. Handle 5¼ in. long, of steel, with raised floral patterns and gilt. Sheath of velvet, with gilt mounts. (*Bought at Delhi*, 1855.)

105. **Dagger** (Katár); with broad blade, 5¼ in. long, grooved down the centre. It is of one piece, with handle 4¾ in. long, of finely-damascened steel inlaid with gold. Sheath is red velvet tipped with gold. (*Bought.*)

106. **Dagger** (larger Katár); blade, 7¾ in. long, of fine steel, with raised patterns on both sides inlaid with gold, representing a man followed by a horse on one side, and on the other a man running away from an elephant. Handle is 7¼ in. long, inlaid with gold. Sheath of velvet tipped with gold. (*Bought at Delhi*, 1855.)

107. **Dagger** (Katár); with double serrated blade, 7½ in. long, with raised floral pattern on steel gilt. Handle 7 in. long, ornamented to match the blade. Sheath is of red velvet with gilt tip. (*Bought at Delhi*, 1855.)

110a

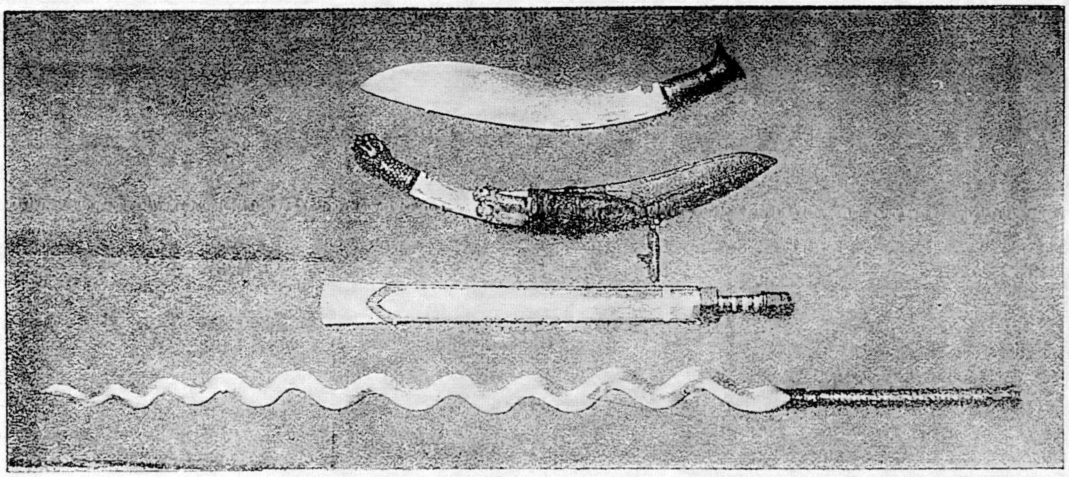

111a

69a

155a

NEPALESE AND BHUTANESE ARMS.

5

29

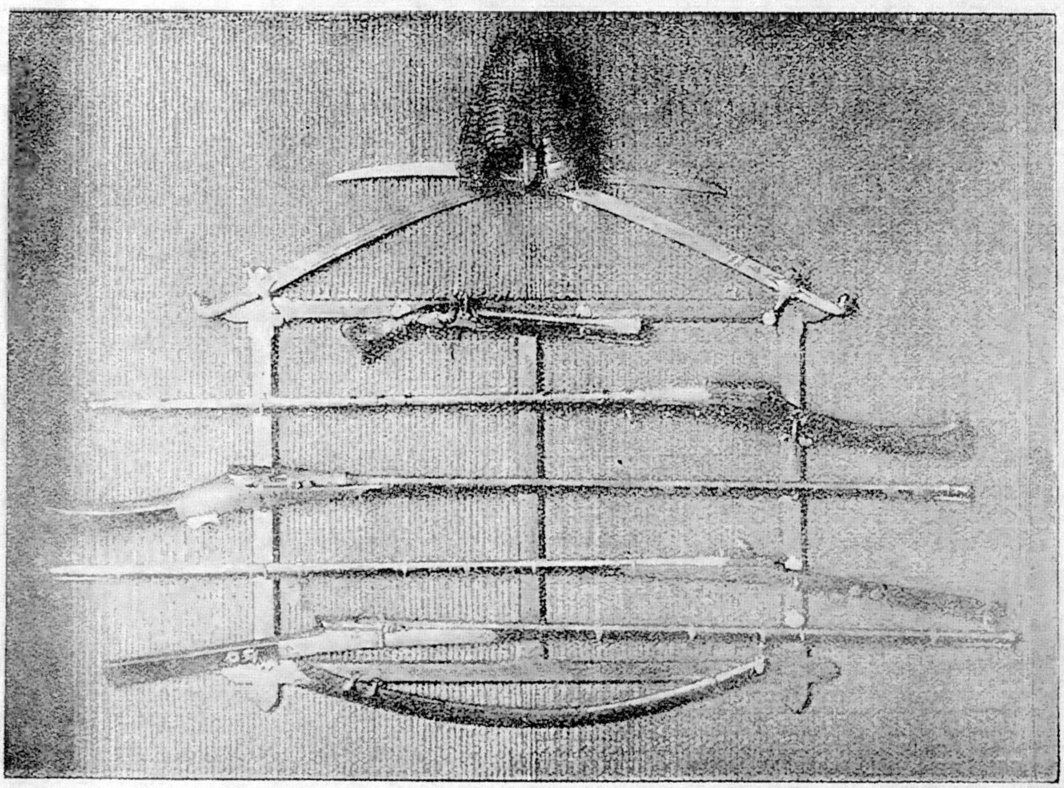

28

25

18

19

20

MATCHLOCKS AND PLATE MAIL HELMET.

108. **Dagger**; blade curved and deeply grooved down the centre, of finely-watered and polished steel, 8½ in. long. Where it joins the hilt it is richly inlaid with raised pattern in gold. The handle, formed of two pieces of ivory on each side of the guard, which is of steel richly inlaid with gold, and terminating in a tiger's head. The ivory is secured to the steel handle with gold studs. Handle is 4½ in. long and 4½ in. wide at the pommel, where it terminates in a crescent shape. The sheath is of red velvet, with pierced gilt floral mounts.

The dagger was made by Veernana of Koodooroo, Madras, and presented by H.H. Maharajah of Vizianagram, 1871, to the International Exhibition. (*Bought.*)

109. **Dagger** (Katár); used by Mahratta horsemen; blade 14½ in. long, with raised rib down the centre; handle has a hand-guard 6½ in. long, terminating in a monster's head. That and the rest of the handle are of steel, with basket pattern and raised floral decorations. The H-shaped handle is very narrow, being only 3 in. wide. (*Lewis Coll.*)

110. **Gorkha Knife** (Kukri); blade 1 ft. 5½ in. long, whole 1 ft. 9 in., used for executioner's axe. (*Bought from Khatmandu.*)

111. **Gorkha Knife** (Kukri). The blade is curved, 14 in. long; the handle is of dark wood, 6 in. long. (*Ham. Coll.*)

111a. **Gorkha Knife** (Kukri). 1 ft. 5½ in. long, blade 1 ft. 1¼ in. long, handle of black horn. Two small knives, 6½ in. long, blades 3½ in. long, with handles of bone inlaid with gold. (*Bought from Khatmandu.*)

112. **Gorkha Knife** (Kukri); 1 ft. 4 in. long, curved blade 1 ft. long, hilt of ivory bound with brass. Sheath with dagger, leather richly ornamented with raised work in silver, and fine silver twisted filigree chain attached to the hilt. Small knife, usually worn attached to the sheath, missing. (*Bought.*)

113. **Gorkha Knife** (Kukri); curved blade 12½ in. long, with raised gilt pattern near the hilt; handle 4½ in. long, with gilt raised pattern. Red velvet sheath, with steel mounts and floral decorations to match the handle. (*Bought 1855, Delhi.*)

114. **Dagger** (from Central India); old Indian; 16 in. long, worked out of a single piece of fine steel; blade 10½ in. long, curved and pointed, fluted in the centre of the blade; the hilt inlaid with floral design in gold, projecting in two leaf-shaped ornaments at each end of the hilt. (*Meyrick Coll.*)

115. **Malay Kris**; blade slightly waved, of laminated steel, 14½ in. long; handle of light coloured wood, 4½ in. long, pistol-shaped. Sheath of wood covered with pure gold richly embossed. It is divided into nine compartments, with beasts and flowers in each of them. (*Presented to Wilbraham Egerton, Esq., my Grandfather.*)

116. **Kris**; probably from Burmah or Assam. Wavy blade, 14 in. long, and two grooves running down the centre half way down the blade.

116a. **Kris**; 14¼ in. long, 3¾ in. wide, gradually tapering downwards, carved wooden hilt. Scabbard modern, of wood bound with brass. Given to me by General Hon. W. Feilding, to whom it was presented in 1874 by Prince Mankanegoro of Sacrokarta, Java. Said to be over 500 years old.

117. **Malay Kris**; blade, 1 ft. 7 in. long, with black wood handle curved upwards. Sheath 1 ft. 10½ in. long, of wood inlaid with ivory. Probably from Siam or Tonquin. (*Bought.*)

118. **Sword**; 2 ft. long. Blade 1 ft. 6 in.; pistol-shaped handle of light wood. Sheath ditto, with silver bands. Probably from Tonquin or Siam. (*Bought.*)

119. **Sword**; 2 ft. 4 in. long. Pistol-shaped handle. Straight blade, 1 ft. 9 in. long. Scabbard, wood bound with bamboo, traced with floriated pattern. Probably from Tonquin or Siam. (*Bought.*)

120. **Rude Knife**; point of old sword. Blade, 9½ in. long. Handle of wood carved with floriated trefoil, 3½ in. (*Bought, Ceylon.*)

121. **Arab Dagger** (Jambiya); broad blade, with groove down the centre. Blade 8½ in. long. Handle, 5½ in., ornamented in silver, terminating in architectural pattern of small silver domes. A Mohammedan weapon.

122. **Dagger** (from Cutch); crutch terminating in bird's head on either side. Shaft hollow, containing a pointed dagger 1 ft. 5 in. long. The whole inlaid with silver Arabesque. (*Colonial Exhibition.*)

123. **Dagger**; crutch of raised Arabesque work in brass gilt, terminating in horned heads. Dagger same length. (*Colonial Exhibition.*)

124. **Axe** (from Cutch); blade 6 in. long, springing from an elephant's and tiger's head. Handle, 13½ in. long. It carries a knife concealed in it of which the blade is 4¼ in. long. The whole is engraved with a silver and gilt raised pattern, and set with glass jewels. The sheath is gilt with a raised floral pattern and architectural forms. Exhibited at Vienna, 1873. (*Bought.*)

125. **Tiger's Claws**, "Bagh nakh," 4 in. long; with 5 cutting blades, 2 in. long. (*Presented by Futtenarain Singh.*)

126. **Chinese Knife**; blade 5 in. long. Handle of ivory, with brass mounts, held in black wooden sheath inlaid with ivory and mother-of-pearl, containing two ivory chopsticks, and small brass instruments. (*Bought.*)

Maces, Axes, Spears and Bows, &c.

127. **Mace**; with concealed dagger in handle; 15 in. long; screwed into a hilt 8 in. long; terminating in shield-like pommel. Handle of mace covered with fine floral pattern in gold upon steel; mace formed of two hemispheres, studded with waving points 1½ in. long, and terminates in a spike, 3 in. long. Cf. p. 108. Fig. 25.

128. **Persian Mace**; 2 ft. 9 in. long; terminating in human head with horns. With floriated arabesque in silver. 17th century.

129. Persian Mace; 2 ft. 7½ in. long; terminating in hollow, cow-shaped head, with twisted horns. Covered with Arabesque in silver. Inscription on the front, "Shah Abbas Wulayul." Abbas, King of the country. 17th Century.

29a. Two Crutch-Shaped Maces from Scinde.

130. Single Axe; 2 ft. 1 in. long; terminating in spear head. Blade covered with Arabesque in silver; handle of raised brass-work, containing dagger 7½ in. long, terminating in tiger's head. *(South Kensington Museum, Indian Department.)*

131. Single Axe; the head covered with floriated brass-work. The solid shaft is inlaid with Arabesque in silver. *(Col. Exhibition.)*

132. Processional Axe; two headed; half-moon shaped; with floriated Arabesques in raised work and gold. Probably worn by a guard on State occasions. Handle wanting. *(Brought from Central India by Octavius Brooke, Esq.)*

133. Processional Axe; terminating in spear-shaped point; length, 2 ft. 1½ in. Shaft of arabesque work in silver; contains small dagger, 7½ in. in length. A tiger's head forms the handle of the dagger. *(Colonial Exhibition.)*

134. Processional Axe; with sheath to the spear-shaped head; 2 ft. 4 in. long. Handle solid. *(Colonial Exhibition.)*

135. Processional Axe. Similar, except that the head of axe forms two tigers' heads, and two birds, with wings outstretched. *(Colonial Exhibition.)*

136. Axe; 19½ in. long; embossed with raised silver and gilt patterns on brass. The head has floral patterns in raised work gilt; the head is 5 in. long. *(Delhi, 1855.)*

137. Pickaxe; handle, 21¼ in. long, of brass, with spiral raised pattern running up it; head, 10 in. long, terminating in a point which has a cutting edge on each side. *(Delhi, 1855.)*

138. Pickaxe; handle, 19 in. long, of brass, with raised pattern, in silver, running up it. The head is 9 in. long, of steel, terminating in two forked points, with raised gilt patterns of flowers and serrated edges till within 1¾ in of the point. *(Delhi, 1855.)*

139. Kole Axe. The handle is of wood, quite plain, 21 in. long. The head is triangular, 9½ in. long, tapering gradually at each end. *(Ham. Coll.)*

140. Axe; wooden handle 24½ in. long. The head heavy, and furnished with a hammer on one side, and riveted to the top with a circular plate. The blade is very thick, 3½ in. by 3 in., of fine steel, which is engraved with simple floral patterns. *(Ham. Coll)*

141. Axe; used by the Khonds for human sacrifice. The wooden handle is 3½ in. long, tipped with brass at both ends, and with a small steel spike at the head—of rude workmanship. The blade is 8½ in. long, with a curved cutting edge.

142. Axe; handle 23½ in. long, of lacquered wood, bound with 4 fillets of gold; base terminates in a gold knob shaped like a fir cone; head terminates in similar ornament let into the steel, which is inlaid with gold. Steel blade is of the finest water, and has a cutting edge 5 in. long by 1 in. broad. This axe was used at State ceremonials. The sheath is of red velvet bound with plates of pure gold. *(Ham. Coll.)*

143. Sacrificial Axe, "Kargas," used by Hindoos for their sacrifices. Probably from the borders of Nepaul; 36 in. long. The blade 28½ in. long, 3½ in. wide, with curved end gradually widening to 6 in. The blade is inlaid with brass at the outer edge. It has an inscription engraved in red letters, according to Dr. Roost, in an old Hindee character which was obsolete 200 years ago. The handle is of teak bound with brass. It was used with both hands. *(Meyrick Collection, No. 1,147.)*

144. Mace (Shashpar); handle of steel, 21½ in. long; six-bladed. Cf. p. 71. *(Ham. Coll.)*

144a. Fakir's Crutch, forming also a mace; carved out of solid steel, the handle 21 in. long, ending in an antelope's horn coming out of a human hand on one side, and emerging on the other as a serpent with a tiger's head. Cf. p. 47, Fig. 4.

145. Flail; steel handle, 19 in. long, from which hang two chains 16 in. long, carrying two heavy balls. *(Ham. Coll.)*

146. Elephant Goad (Aukus); the handle is 17 in. long, of steel inlaid with gold and silver; and hollow containing seven bells. The point is 3½ in. long, and the hook projects 3 in. from the handle. Both are likewise inlaid with gold. *(Lewis Coll.)*

147. Elephant Goad; Processional; from South India. Used on foot in State processions; 4 ft. long, head 7 in.; shaft lacquered in red, black, and yellow patterns; head terminates in a dragon-shaped hook inlaid with silver. *(Guthrie Coll.)*

148. Spear (from Bikanir); 6 ft. long, of bamboo, bound with brass at the handle, and cased with steel gradually tapering to the point, which is four-sided. *(Ham. Coll.)*

149. Light Spear; 6 ft. 6 in. long. Shaft of bamboo, lacquered. There is a steel spike at the end, and a small tongue-shaped blade. *(Ham. Coll.)*

150 Spear Head; socket engraved with a chevron pattern. Blade is broad, and engraved with figures of a tiger and an antelope, and is 8½ in. long. *(Ham. Coll.)*

151. Lance Head; 16 in. long; quadrangular point. *(Ham. Coll.)*

152. Lance Head; 18 in. long; tongue-shaped point. *(Ham. Coll.)*

153. Spear Head; broad blade, 3 in. across, 18 in. long. *(Ham. Coll)*

154. Spear Head; 18 in. long, terminating in four-leaved point. *(Ham. Coll.)*

108 66 103 181

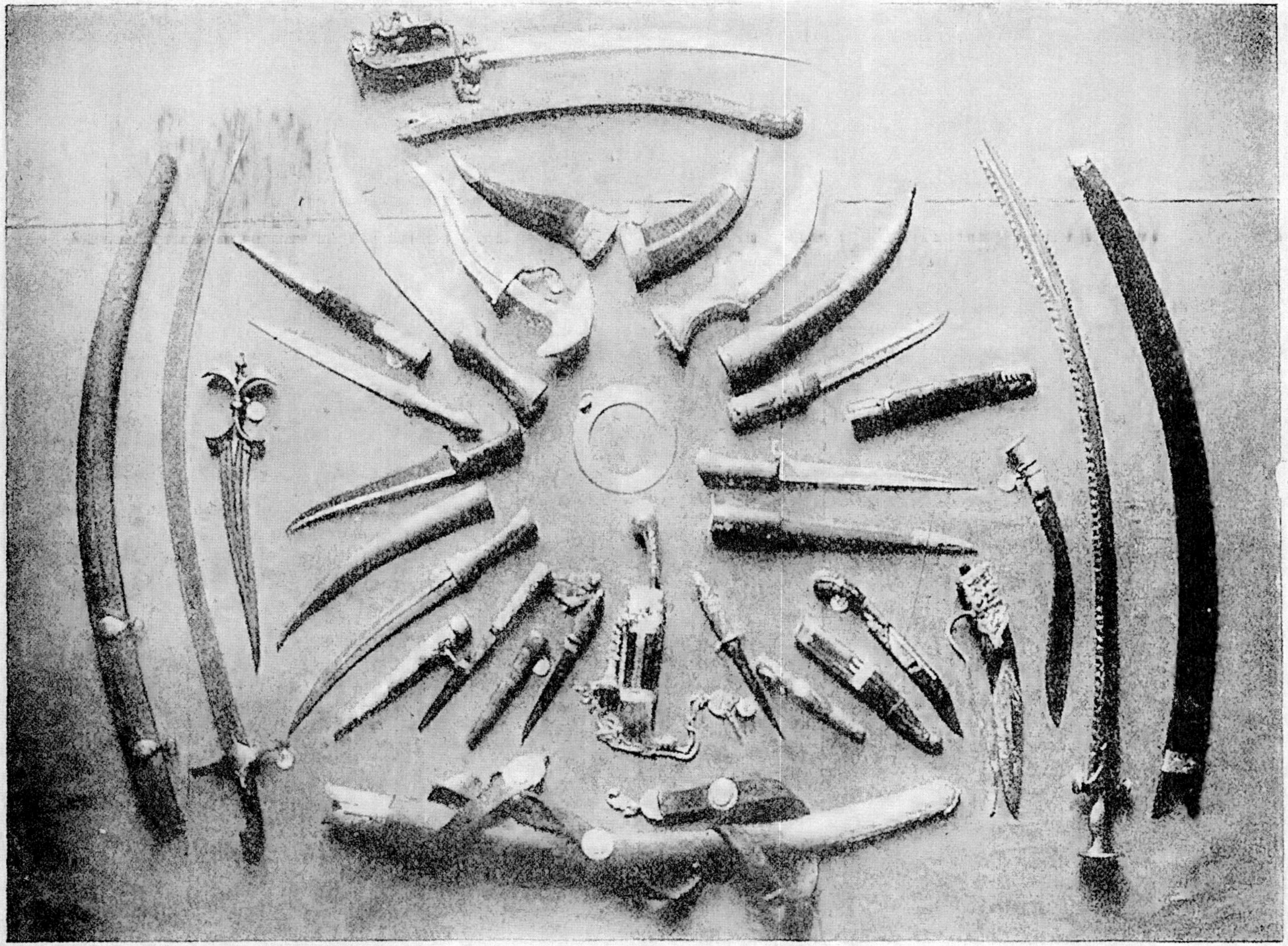

183 44 182 96 112

PERSIAN, INDIAN, CINGALESE SWORDS, DAGGERS, AND KNIVES.
TURKISH AND JAPANESE DAGGERS.

155. Spear Head; 15 in. long, terminating in triangular point. (*Ham. Coll.*)

155a. Flaming Processional Spear; 3 ft. 7 in. long in blade. Handle, 12½ in. long, inlaid with diaper floral pattern. Brought from Khatmandu.

156. Persian Bow; 4 ft. 9 in. long; of painted bamboo. (*Lewis Coll.*)

157. Pellet Bow; 4 ft. 9 in. long; of bamboo, bound with strips of split bamboo. (*Ham. Coll.*)

158. Indian Curved Bow; of horn, lacquered and painted. (*Indian Museum.*)

159. Arrows; with different heads. Each 2 ft. 4 in. long. (*Ham. Coll.*)

159a. Arrow; for killing birds, with crescent-shaped point 4½ in. wide.

Accoutrements.

160. Powder Flask; shape of ram's horn; covered with velvet, and richly embroidered in gold arabesque pattern.

161. Bullet Pouch; with belt. (*Ham. Coll.*)

162. Bullet Pouch; containing bullet-mould and knife.

163. Bullet Pouch; long box, embroidered in green velvet, containing cotton match cord.

164. Priming Horn; formed of curved horn, tipped with brass, with ivory mount, 1 ft. 3 in. long.

165. Priming Horn. Mouthpiece representing winged female figure coming from mouth of monster; 1 ft. 3 in. long. Cf. p. 47, fig. 5.

166. Priming Horn; Persian work of six'eenth or seventeenth century. Body of horn contains figures of antelope and tiger, in relief; at other end heads of animals devouring each other.

PART II.

Japanese Armour, &c.

167. Helmet and Breastplate of papier mâché.

168. Helmet; with crest and dragon in fore part. Mask of papier mâché. Moustache of cut hair.

168a. Helmet with white metal mounts and studs.

169. Breastplate of steel, with figure of deity on a dragon riding on a cloud, waves of the sea below. Gold and silver gilt.

170. Shirt of Plate Mail made of papier mâché, lined with silk brocade.

171. Arm-piece and Skirts of Shirt (front and behind). Gauntlets of plate and chain mail.

172. Circular Cap; 11 in. across when folded, of strips of bamboo, gilt inside. (*Brought from Japan by Reginald Cholmondeley, Esq.*)

173. Matchlock; 3 ft. 7 in. long; barrel 2 ft. 4 in. in length; diameter of little finger. A heavy gun to be fired from a rest. Barrel engraved with dragons and gilt clouds running up it. Silver engraved work at breech. (*Brought from Japan by Reginald Cholmondeley, Esq.*)

174. Matchlock; with pistol-shaped butt, 3 ft. 6½ in. long, barrel 2 ft. 9 in. long, diameter, size of forefinger. Name and crest of Daimio, to whose retainer it belonged. Figure of human-faced deity engraved in gold and silver upon the barrel together with floral decorations. Butt of light-coloured wood. (*Brought from Japan by Reginald Cholmondeley, Esq.*)

175. Matchlock; 4 ft. 5 in. long, barrel 3 ft. 3 in., diameter of little finger. Silver-gilt pattern of dragon, floral decorations engraved on it. Name and crest of Daimio, to whose retainer it belonged, also engraved on it. Butt of light-coloured wood. (*Brought from Japan by Reginald Cholmondeley, Esq.*)

176. Pair of Stirrups; 11 in. long; inlaid with silver (mostly perished). Floral decorations in silver (mostly perished) on steel, lined with lacquer. (*Brought from Japan by Egerton Leigh, Esq.*)

177. Sword; 3 ft. 1½ in. long; blade, 2 ft. 3½ in.; leather handle and gilt mounts. Sheath of lacquer, with foliage and birds and gilt mounts.

178. Sword; 2 ft. 3½ in. long; blade, 1 ft. 9 in.; metal handle, with gilt mounts. Shark-skin hilt. Pommel with two figures of silver gilt. Hilt of plain leather and lacquer, which contains a small knife. Handle enriched with dragon clasping sword; 8 in. long. Blade inscribed with Japanese characters.

179. Japanese Sword Stick, of bamboo, with bronze and silver mounts, 2 ft. 11 in. long. By pressing serpent's head which encircles it, spring releases short sword, 9in. long. (*Paris Exhibition*, 1878.)

180. Dagger (Hari Kari); 1 ft. 11 in. long; blade, 9⅓ in. long, with gilt band (with inscription) at the hilt. Handle of shark-skin, intertwined with fretted gilt. Bosses ornamented with a grass-hopper on barley. Sheath of avanturine lacquer, with cocks and hens in silver, and sheaves of barley in silver and gilt. Scabbard contains knife 8½ in. long; blade, 4½ in.; with raised work in gold and silver of a rat amongst barley. On reverse side is another instrument, on the handle of which the moon is rising behind the clouds. With inscriptions, the name of the maker. (*Brought from Japan by Reginald Cholmondeley, Esq.*)

181. Dagger (Hari Kari); 1 ft. 2 in. long, blade 8¼ in., hilt 5 in., hilt covered with lacquer, imitating the bark of a tree, on which a prawn is enamelled on raised silver work. Scabbard contains small blunt dagger, 4¾ in. long, the handle of

silver representing on one side waves of the sea. Hilt ornamented with prawns in relief in silver, and figures of gilt fish on silver sea, bound round with silk cord over shark-skin. (*Colonial Exhibition.*)

182. DAGGER; 10½ in. long, blade, 6 in. Engraved with dragon and flowers incised. Hilt of silver with a centre of ivory, upon which is carved in relief a moon, with rushes waving in the wind. Signed. Handle and hilt alike carved with silver and silver gilt storks, ducks, and geese in relief. Handle contains a stork, in relief, amongst the lotus-reeds in flower and seed; on reverse, a number of small birds flying across the sky.

183. DAGGER; 9½ in. long, blade, 6 in. Plain work. Hilt and sheath plain brass work with geometrical and floral patterns.

184* A STRAIGHT SWORD; in wooden sheath lacquered with dragons on gold ground, the blade is 25 in. long, with signature, and probably of great age and of excellent workmanship; it is welded to the wrought-iron hilt with curved quillons, to which the sword-knot of red silk cord is attached, and the pommel of the sword is triangular, and pierced to receive it.

185* A SUIT of LATE XVI. CENTURY ARMOUR OF THE IMPERIAL BODYGUARD; bearing the dragon and sun crests, on the breastplate is a figure in high relief.

(*Bought at Hon. L. Wingfield's Sale.*)

* These were in the armoury of Osaka Castle, and at its destruction were bought by Sango, of Nara, the descendant of the family of the Mikado's armourers, and were purchased from him by the late owner.

PART III.

ARAB ARMS,

USED IN EGYPT AND SOUDAN.

186. SHIELD; with spear 2 ft. 4 in. long.; composed of shell of land tortoise. The spear is tied with strips of leather, and bound with wire and crocodile-skin. Leaf-shaped head, 10½ in. long, 3¾ in. wide.

187. SHIELD; 2 ft. in diameter, composed of hippopotamus hide, laced together with wire.

188. SHIELD; 2 ft. 6 in. long, formed of the knee or hock of hippopotamus, so that it forms the nose of a face, the eyes and mouth being roughly indicated by indentations, and a rude pattern worked round the edge in like way.

189. TWO-BLADED DAGGER; with handle of ivory in the centre. Blades curved outwards in opposite directions; one blade 8 in. long, the other 8¾ in.; width 1½ in.; engraved with a sentence from the Koran. The sheaths bound with a diaper of wire and deer-skin. Scabbards joined together with loose twisted leather strap.

190. DAGGER; in shape of spear-head, serrated. Handle covered with snake-skin, with loop of leather attached; rude triangle and cross worked on face of it. Probably old Abyssinian weapon. It has five double sets of points, terminating in three points like a trident. Length 17 in.; width at top 3¾ in.

191. SWORD; large; probably originally two-handed. Three deep channels down blade; flexible. Probably old European. Plain cross hilt, covered with snake-skin. Handle probably modern. Used in Soudan. Blade, 38¼ in. long; hilt, 5½ in. Engraved with quotations from the Koran. Scabbard of snake-skin, sewn up at back; 3 ft. 3 in. long, 2½ in. wide.

192. PERSIAN SHORT SWORD; made on Circassian frontier. Handle of walrus horn, engraved with floral pattern. Blade, 16¾ in. long, gradually tapering from 2½ in. Deep channel down centre of blade. Diaper pattern near hilt, and stamp on each side of blade. Scabbard of delicate raised silver-work in floral pattern, and diaper different both sides. Bound with silver wire at the base, terminating in ornamental knob. Old Persian work. (*Bought at Cairo,* 1894.)

193. AXE; shaped with crescent and point; inlaid with silver-work of floral patterns. Handle of steel, bound with snake-skin, and leopard-skin in centre; bound round with leather, so as to hang loosely round wrist; 24 in. Breadth of blade, 7 in. Probably made in Soudan by Persian or Arab workmen.

194. ARAB SWORD; scabbard enriched with geometrical patterns, with silver-gilt mounts. Blade slightly curved, 36 in. in length, with "Jesu Maria" on it. Hilt, 5¼ in., with recurved quillons. Probably a presentation sword in the eighteenth century. (*Bought at the "Fountain" Sale.*)

195. ARAB SWORD; used in the Soudan. Blade, 3 ft. long, of flexible steel. European. Probably from Solingen. It has been engraved roughly by native workmen, in imitation of other European blades, near the handle with six-pointed stars and the sun and moon, with human faces introduced into them on both sides; but the artist could not draw the outline of a face accurately. Hilt, 5¼ in. long, covered with snake-skin, and bound with narrow strips of leather. Scabbard, 3 ft. 1½ in. long, of plain leather, tapering to a leaf-shaped point, with a short leather strap; probably worn over the shoulder, and used with both hands.

(*Bought at Assouan.*)

196. ARAB SWORD (from Yemen, in Arabia), said to have belonged to Arabi Pasha. Blade is slightly curved, 2 ft. 4½ in. long, of finely-grained Damascus watering. Probably European without any inscription. The hilt, including the crosspiece, which descends above the blade, is 7½ in. long, of silver, bound with wire, and carved, a large indentation for the little finger, terminating in a curved boss which rises at the centre into a dome, and with wings, the whole beautifully carved with floral ornaments, and connected by three silver chains with the crossguard. The scabbard is of wood covered with silver, 2 ft. 5¼ in. long, and bands across it with two rings, to which are

PLATE VIII.

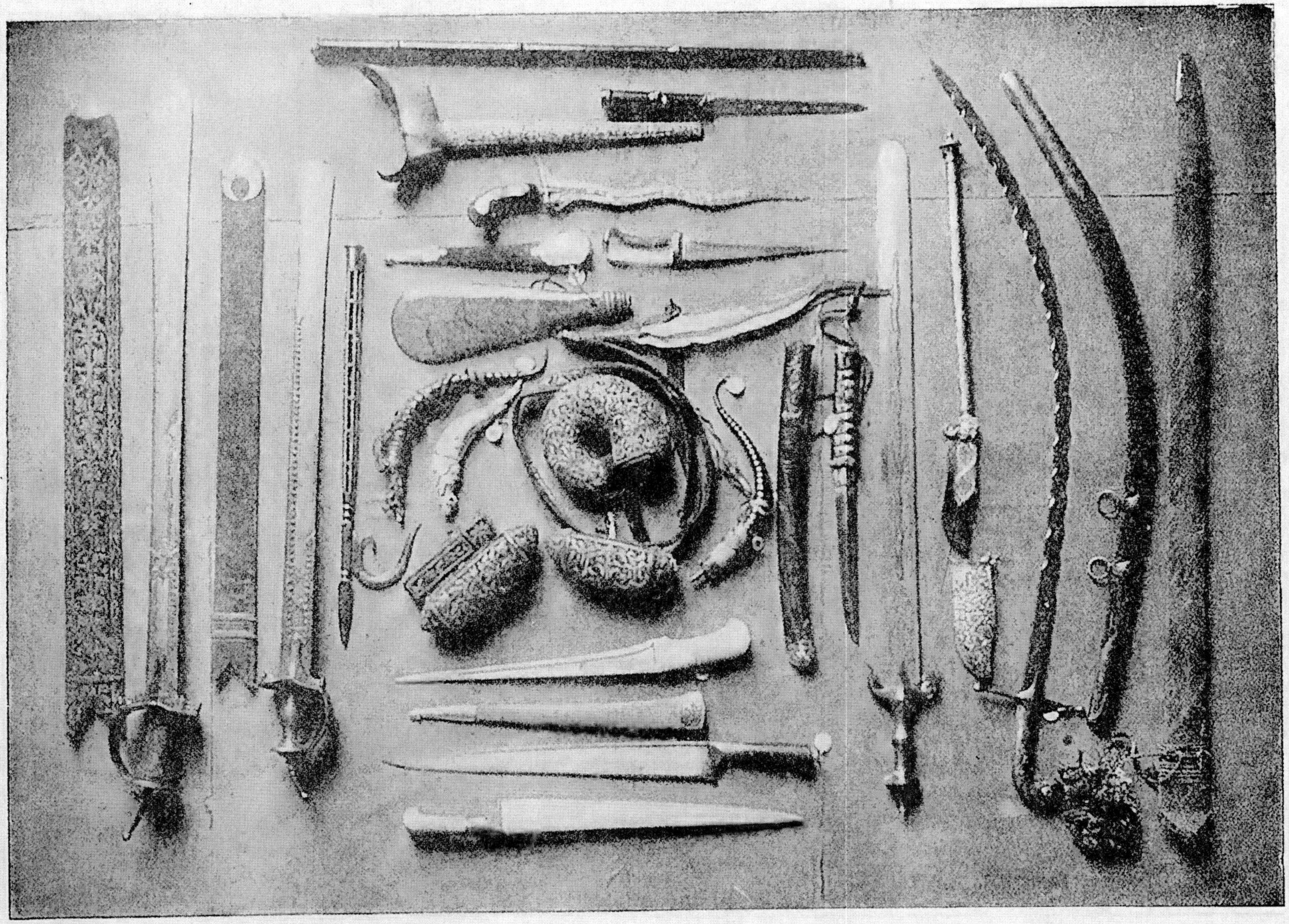

SWORDS—MALAY, JAPANESE,
PERSIAN, INDIAN—AND ACCOUTREMENTS.

attached copper swivels and gold cords which have been worn from the waist; the latter are of modern cavalry pattern, more recent than the sword; a raised pattern runs down the scabbard of architectural character, terminating in a curved end cut out in relief. (*Bought at Cairo.*)

197. Arab Sword; blade of plain steel roughly engraved; a crocodile is rudely traced and cut out of the solid; 2 ft. 1¼ in. long. The hilt is made of ebony and ivory, crescent-shaped at pommel, with a crosspiece and guard of horn, terminating in a silver point, 6½ in. long. Made in Dongola, and used in the Soudan. Scabbard of crocodile-skin, 2 ft. 2 in. long.

198. Sword; used in the Soudan; 2 ft. 1¼ in. long, slightly curved and terminating in a point with three deep channels round the lower end of the blade. Probably German of the seventeenth century. Has two stars on either side, with the sun and moon and faces inserted, and arabesque work near the hilt in floral patterns about 4 in. long. The hilt, 6 in. long without guard, is of wood covered with snake-skin, terminating in two curved wings as a guard, and of the usual Albanian type. The scabbard is of snake-skin on one side, and crocodile-skin on other side, length 2 ft. 3 in. (*Bought at Assouan.*)

199. Blade; used in Soudan; probably made in Abyssinia, 2 ft. 2½ in. long; rudely engraved with diagonal patterns in squares gradually tapering to a point. The hilt is made of ebony for 2 in. near the blade, and the remainder in ivory 6½ in. long, without any guard. It is turned in geometrical patterns and lines and small circles in succession, terminating in a silver stud. (*Bought at Assouan.*)

200. Long Dagger (ornamental); belonging to the Janissaries. The blade is 12⅞ in. long, ¾ in. wide, of finely damascened steel, with a pattern running round at the back of blade. The handle is of silver, 5⅝ in. long, terminating in a dome-shaped fluted pommel with ornamental bands. A Government stamp is raised in the silver in the hilt where it runs into the scabbard. The scabbard is 15¼ in. long; the sheath is in silver, richly ornamented with floral patterns of European character terminating in a pierced ornament, with the exception of about 3 in., which is bound with black leather. This was worn by the officers of the Janissaries, while the privates had a similar one with brass mounts. (*Bought at Cairo.*)

201. Short Sword; blade, 17¼ in. long, with circular and diagonal ornaments rudely engraved on it, and a conventional crocodile running down centre of tapering blade incised on it. The hilt is 6 in. long, rudely formed of rhinoceros horn, terminating in a crescent-shaped guard, used in Kordofan. The scabbard is 17 in. long, of yellow crocodile-skin and brown leather stamped in patterns. (*Bought at Assouan.*)

202. Dagger; used in the Soudan; leaf-shaped blade gradually tapering, 6½ in. long. Hilt of turned ivory, 3½ in. long; geometrical patterns, terminating in a flat boss. Probably made in Abyssinia. Scabbard of brown leather, 7½ in long. (*Bought at Cairo.*)

203. Curved Dagger; terminating in sickle shape; made in the Soudan. Handle of ebony, rudely shaped with projections at either end, 3¾ in. long. (*Bought at Cairo.*)

204. Rude Incurved Dagger; blade widening towards the point, 6¼ in. long; three deep channels round the straight part of blade. The handle, 4 in. long, made of ebony, bound round with silver filigree wire, and incrusted at either end with silver filigree work. A band of filigree work at the base of the handle terminating in a silver stud in the centre, from which the pattern springs. Probably made at Khartoum or in the Soudan. Scabbard is of snake-skin, 6¼ in. long, and with belt worn round the waist. (*Bought at Assouan.*

205. Knife; for ordinary purposes (from Zanzibar). Blade terminating in point tapering outwards. The handle, partly of square-cut steel, and partly of ebony, 3½ in. long, and terminating in rudely-carved horn. Scabbard, of plain leather, 10½ inches long, stamped and fluted, and bound with snake-skin, with twisted leather, to hang round neck probably. (*Bought at Cairo.*)

206. Arab Dagger; "Jambiya," with broad curved blade, strong rib running down the centre, width of top, 2 in., gradually curved outwards. Handle, silver gilt, with raised floral patterns, and filigree work encrusted on it. Handle, 4½ in. long. Scabbard, richly mounted in silver gilt, curved like a ram's horn, terminating in pointed and dome-shaped ornament, the principal part with silver roses and filigree work, and architectural ornaments running down the base, 18 in. long, on either side of the curve, attached round the waist by a richly-embroidered leather belt, in gold and coloured velvet. (*Bought at Cairo.*)

207. Rude Cutting Axe; with double points, made at Khartoum, a rude ornament down the centre. Intended probably to cut the bridles of horses, or cut or tear anything opposed to it. Round outside of curve 2 ft. 5½ in. long. Rude handle, bound with leather, forming the base of it, 4½ in. long. (*Bought at Assouan.*)

208. Long Spear Javelin; used in the Soudan, 5 ft. 2 in. long, of flexible wood; a socket at one end of the blade of twisted steel, 12⅞ in. long, terminating in a leaf-shaped blade 6 in. long. (*Bought at Assouan.*)

209. Arab Shield; made of transparent hide (boiled rhinoceros), a bright yellow, on which are letters of the Koran. They form an interlacing pattern, on which are gilt flowers, in continuous series; the letters are probably to be read both ways, Allah. The outer rim, as well as the inner one, has rich floral patterns alternately in gold, and in the self colour of the ground on gold back. It is domed, and has four silver bosses to hold the chains inside for its support, about 18 in. in diameter. There is one in British Museum of similar shape, but not same material or colour. (*Bought at Cairo.*)

INDEX.

N.B.—The Numbers in brackets are Catalogue numbers; those not in brackets, page numbers.

A.

B.

C.

L.

M.

Q.

R.

S.